REFUGIO A. ATILANO

The **LATINO** LEADERSHIP PLAYBOOK

A TOOLKIT OF INSIGHTS TO ACCELERATE YOUR IMPACT IN THE WORKPLACE

Foreword by YAI VARGAS

The
LATINO
LEADERSHIP PLAYBOOK

© Copyright 2023, Refugio A. Atilano.
All rights reserved.

No portion of this book may be reproduced by mechanical, photographic or electronic process, nor may it be stored in a retrieval system, transmitted in any form or otherwise be copied for public use or private use without written permission of the copyright owner.

This book shares personal insights from numerous people who have contributed their opinions throughout the chapters. It is intended to provide inspiration and added viewpoints to our readers. These views are solely their own.

It is sold with the understanding that the publisher and the authors are not engaged in the rendering of psychological, legal, accounting or other professional advice. The content and views in each chapter are the sole expression and opinion of its authors and not necessarily the views of Fig Factor Media, LLC.

For more information, contact:
Fig Factor Media, LLC | www.figfactormedia.com
Refugio A. Atilano | www.refugioatilano.com

Cover Design by Marco Alvarez
Layout by LDG Juan Manuel Serna Rosales

Printed in the United States of America

ISBN: 978-1-959989-68-4
Library of Congress Control Number: 2023918345

DEDICATION

This book is dedicated to my late father, Refugio Atilano, who passed away earlier this year. He was the patriarch of my family and led life as a pillar of absolute strength. From an early age to his final days, he was revered as a fierce protector and ultimate supporter of his family and friends—he was our leader, loved by many, and respected by all.

After his passing, I used his spirit and strength to push through every tough moment to deliver this book for you. It is because of my father that I was able to give you my best. I now present *The Latino Leadership Playbook*, brought to you by Refugio Atilano Sr. and Refugio A. Atilano.

TABLE OF CONTENTS

Acknowledgments 6
Foreword by Yai Vargas 9
Introduction 13
The Latino Leadership Model 21
How to Read this Book for Maximum Development 24

Part 1: Latino Population and Impact Data Awareness 27

Part 2: Latino Cultural Navigation 37
    How to Work Smart 41
    How to Advocate for Yourself 56
    How to Effectively Challenge Authority 72
    When to Use a Family-First vs. Me-First Approach 86
    How to Be Bold and Go After What You Want 99
    How to Be Vocal with Your Perspectives 116
    How to Earn the Trust and Respect of Your Teams 132
    How to Proactively and Strategically Chart Your Path 147
    How to Use Your Latino Culture to Your Advantage 164

Part 3: Introduction to Leadership Focus and Capability 181
    How to Become a Strong Communicator 185
    How to Identify and Leverage Mentors and Sponsors 209
    How to Build a Network to Advance Your Career 230
    How to Create and Leverage Your Unique Brand and Value ...249
    How to Build Your Executive Presence 273
    How to Lead with an Impact and Extreme Ownership Focus ...294
    How to Be an Effective Change Leader 310

How to Be Politically Savvy 327
How to Be a Strong Collaborator 342
How to Ask for a Promotion 356
How to Prepare for and Negotiate Your Salary 374

Part 4: Bringing it All Together: Leveraging Our Natural Passion and Grit 391

Bonus Chapter: A Practical Guide for Non-Latinos on How to Support Latinos 403

Latina and Latino Spotlights 408
Bibliography 412
About the Author 419
About *The Latino Leadership Playbook* Contributors 421

ACKNOWLEDGMENTS

Looking back, writing *The Latino Leadership Playbook* over this past year was a herculean effort. It was a success because of so many people committed to the same vision—to accelerate the collective leadership development of the Latino community. Here are all the people that made this vision a reality.

MY FAMILY

First, I want to thank my beautiful, and very patient, wife—Beti Atilano. She was on board from the beginning, sacrificing nine months (and counting) of our lives to ensure we provided a quality book for the world to use. She was also an incredible sounding board and pushed me hard to provide the best possible product for all of you!

Second, I would like to thank my kids, Sara and Ref Jr., for their support, patience, and encouragement throughout this journey. They always made me smile when I had to find the inspiration to push through.

Also, I want to provide a special thank you to my mother, Delia Atilano, for her strength and support during an extremely difficult year for our family due to my father's passing. God and my father are watching over all of us.

MY INSPIRATION

There are two people that inspired me to write the book and helped me to believe in my passion to get it done—Greg Macias and Jamie Walters. Greg has been my sounding board and encouragement from Day 1. It's because of him that you are reading this book today. Separately, I still remember Jamie telling me late last year, "You caught fire!" when I was explaining my passion and vision for potentially helping the Latino professional community. Her comment sparked a flame and I never looked back!

ACKNOWLEDGMENTS

I also want to thank my manager, Jeff Mohr, who is an ERG leader, DEI advocate, and just a great guy. He has supported me during this tough journey and am extremely grateful to have him in my corner.

BRINGING IT ALL TO LIFE

Next, I cannot say enough about the amazing Yai Vargas! We are so aligned in our passion and philosophy in developing Latino leaders. She's an incredible wealth of knowledge, a great cheerleader, and one of the best connectors in the world today!

I also want to say a special thanks to my superstar publisher, marketer, strategic advisor, and connector—Jackie Ruiz, CEO of Fig Factor Media. Jackie is a special breed. She's highly skilled and talented and would highly recommend her for your publishing and/or marketing needs.

And finally, to my brother Michael Atilano, who was a cheerleader and sounding board throughout this process. Also, as a corporate HR professional, he helped me strategize on several approaches so the content and approach would resonate with all of you.

MY SUPERSTAR NETWORK

In order to make *The Latino Leadership Playbook* and its concepts a top-tier product, I needed strong, successful Latino/a connections and contributors. Carlos Orta and Maryanne Pina Frodsham led the way and were always there to support me, offer ideas, and make high-profile connections without expecting anything in return. They were in it to add impact for all of you and this is the type of selfless leadership that's a tremendous example for all of us to follow.

I also want to give a special shout out to Frank Carbajal. We just met this year and I already feel like we're brothers. He's a one-of-a-kind genuine soul who loves our community and is always ready to help. He's been an inspiration and a great supporter; I am so glad to he's part of this experience!

I also want to thank Dr. Robert Rodiguez for his accomplishments in creating the strong foundation for Latino leadership, as well as for the guidance and support he has provided me on my journey thus far.

CONTRIBUTORS AND PEER REVIEWERS

Everyone who contributed to this book was all-in from the start. They believed in the vision and wanted to do their part to help all of you and everyone still to come behind us. In this book, you will see the quality of leaders that have provided insights that are going to change the Latino leadership landscape for the current and future generations. I know you will enjoy and apply the lessons they will share in this book.

Finally, the chapters in this playbook were carefully vetted by Latino peer reviewers. My goal was to ensure I provided relatable and relevant content that you can apply to your development and career. The following people were the quiet force behind the scenes to help bring you a quality product: Jen Silfa, Greg Macias, Lenny de la Rosa, Evelyn Aranda, Jeff Martinez, Priscilla Martinez and my sister, Jennifer Atilano.

FOREWORD

Yai Vargas, Vice President, Learning and Development at the Hispanic Association for Corporate Responsibility (HACR).

MY BACKGROUND

My journey began like many of you reading this book, navigating a life where your roots, culture and traditions don't naturally blend well with the colleagues who surround you. I immigrated to this country when I was just three years old, which gave me the privilege of growing up and feeling "American" while also keeping my Dominican identity. My first language was Spanish, since that's the only language my family spoke around me growing up in Washington Heights, NYC, and I very quickly was able to pick up English as my second thanks to all the cartoons you can imagine.

Fast forward to my professional life where I spent almost 15 years in corporate America leveraging my Latina-ness to help companies develop products, programs, and services for the Hispanic market in both Spanish and Portuguese. I have worked in the automotive, public relations, sports, and financial services industries, as well as launching my own consulting business as an entrepreneur. I am now a Vice President leading Learning and Development at The Hispanic Association on Corporate Responsibility, a national non-profit organization that focuses on Hispanic representation in corporate America and on boards.

THE IMPORTANCE OF *THE LATINO LEADERSHIP PLAYBOOK*

This playbook is like having a number of different counselors, guides, and mentors in the palm of your hand—giving you diverse perspectives and expert advice that will get you at least where they have gotten and more importantly, further than you could ever imagine for yourself. This book that you're about to dive into can be a catalyst for your career, at any point in your development journey, but I am so glad it came now, at a time where our Latino influence and representation is not just accepted but celebrated and encouraged.

Having someone like Refugio, a Latino leader in corporate America who has achieved significant success share a playbook that prepares you for your next level is a game changer. By reading these stories and insights, learning about new resources and gathering the tools necessary, you'll be career mapping your way to a role with impact, influence, and access.

My career has always been guided by people who've walked the walk and led me in the direction that they knew would get me ahead. Whether it was my high school counselor that pushed me to apply for college or my college counselor that helped me apply for scholarships and internships that would set me on a path to success—I was grateful. If it hadn't been for these individuals that passed on their wisdom, I may not be where I am today.

I have worked with many successful leaders across industries and noticed one thing in common: their focus on professional development is intentional and to some extent more important than the current role they hold. Their obsession with upskilling, earning degrees, and seeking sponsors is what helped them internally mobilize.

The significance of the Latino leader in the workplace is more important than ever and it all begins with leaders like Refugio who have dedicated their lives and careers to making sure we have the insights and tools to become high-performing leaders with a grand purpose.

THE IMPORTANCE OF A STRONG NETWORK TO ADVANCE YOUR CAREER

Personally, I had never experienced anyone, not even in my family or immediate circle, spend so much time and energy on their professional development until I started to expand my circle. These leaders and mentors showed me that the skills they would invest in would outlast any job or role they currently held. They could take these skills and networks with them and continue to build upon them for their benefit, and I was taking notes. Those mentors told me to take risks, invest my own money in learning and how to also ask a lot of questions about authentic and purposeful leadership.

For me, I knew that I wanted to continue learning about integrated and multicultural marketing, so I picked up a certification at NYU and went deep into this subject matter expertise. I began to realize that the roles and spaces I found myself in were full of highly successful professionals and I had a gift of being able to connect and develop personal relationships with them. I knew then that my network was my net worth, as they say, and that developing a strategic network would be my superpower (among many others).

I have spent the majority of my career intentionally seeking out professionals that had the career trajectory I was hoping to carve for myself. Not only did I seek out people who had similar interests, but I was also purposefully looking for diverse perspectives that could teach me new ways of thinking in various industries.

It has been said before that a good majority of roles are filled via referrals and it clearly shows how one can leverage these relationships after they have been cultivated for some time. It's imperative that these allies, mentors, or sponsors know you personally, your career goals and want to see you succeed—this all takes time. I am beyond excited and proud that you're here at this very moment, looking to learn, grow, and accelerate your career!

IT'S TIME FOR LATINOS TO LEVEL UP

As you will learn in this book, Latinos are one of the most overlooked and underestimated groups in corporate America and when it comes to Latinas, there's an enormous opportunity. Research shows us that Latinas hold only 1% of Fortune 500 board seats—that's with a possible 5,000 seats and we know that only

59 Latinas are sitting at those tables. As you'll hear from Refugio, Latinas have been an incredible source of support, strength, and growth for his career and it's our collective responsibility to make sure more Latinas are promotion-ready, as well as board-ready. This book will equip you with the data needed to propel you and your community forward. At the end of the day, it's data that tells the truth and encourages us to seek more.

Here's another datapoint you may not have known, currently, there are about 21 Hispanic CEO's in the Fortune 100 who are leading some of the world's most admired companies. Seeing how these leaders have skyrocketed in their careers to lead and inspire hundreds of thousands of employees, this gives us enormous confidence in ensuring even more of us make it.

By purchasing and sharing this book with your community, I know and believe that you will accomplish your next level of success and that you'll continue to share the resources within this book with those that need some guidance.

This book makes it possible for anyone interested in investing in themselves professionally to create a roadmap to their success. At the end of the day, we're here to make sure that the sacrifices our parents and grandparents made to get us here do not go unrecognized. As you begin this journey, I leave you with this: You have everything you need to level-up and achieve what's next for you by leveraging your unique and diverse perspective for collective progress. I hope that you take the time to reflect on your leadership journey and see how you can be an inspiration for the advancement of other Latino leaders.

This journey of becoming a confident promotion-ready Latino leader begins now—get excited!

INTRODUCTION

> *"If you want to be an impact player; then you need to develop impact behaviors."*
>
> **- Refugio A. Atilano**

Developing confident, informed, high-impact, and promotion-ready Latino Leaders is my sole purpose in writing this book. I am so incredibly passionate about this topic because I experienced and fully understand the struggle, frustration, and ambiguity of having to navigate an academic and professional career with limited/no guidance. Like most Latinos, I thought that as long as I worked hard and perfected my craft, the promotions would come rolling in. That did not happen; I stood by as it felt like everyone else around me got tapped on the shoulder for special assignments and promotions.

Through pure grit, and a lot of luck, I was able to finally shift my narrative and become a senior leader at a world-class top-10 pharma company that supports the recruitment, development, and advancement of the Latino professional community. The only reason I was able finally make the leap is because a few years ago a Latina senior leader took time and gave me the guidance and leadership lens I needed to use if I wanted to move up in my career—it's as if someone gave me a pair of glasses and I was able to see the unseen for the first time! It changed everything for me and now I am going to share those insights, as well as some other important focus areas I've discovered along my leadership development journey: I will provide you with targeted direction to be more effective and to develop yourself into an impact player and strong Latino Leader in the workplace!

THE IMPORTANCE OF LATINO LEADERSHIP IN THE WORKPLACE

As captured in the Latinx Business Success, Jesus Mantas, Senior Managing Partner at IBM states, "Hispanics represent about 19 percent of the U.S. population, yet only 4 percent of the executive ranks. Hispanics are the fastest growing and youngest minority in the United States. And yet despite the advantages of size, power, and youth there is still a huge lack of Hispanic leaders" (Carbajal, 23). In the same book, Esther Aguilera, Former CEO of Latino Corporate Directors Association (LCDA), states that she "continues to hear the excuse that companies can't find qualified Latinos" (Carbajal, 18). These insights reflect a significant Latino leadership gap (also known as the 4% shame, coined by Dr. Robert Rodriguez) that requires immediate attention, a game plan, and collective action. It's time to take action and change the narrative—it starts now... and starts here!

There is attention and focus on the gap described above. In working with various Latino Employee Resource Groups (ERGs), Latino Professional Organizations, and fellow Latino leaders, there is agreement that we need to continue to work towards closing the gap, from both the corporate and Latino community perspectives. The focus of this book is on what we, as Latinos, can do collectively to improve our impact and leadership capability and make ourselves more promotion-ready. There are a lot of great organizations providing leadership development opportunities for Latinos. For example, there are superb Latino leadership development programs, such as Hispanic Alliance for Career Enhancement's Emerging Latino Leadership Program (ELLP) and Angel Gomez's and Dr. Robert Rodriquez's Latino Leadership Intensive (LLI) training course—of which I both attended and highly recommend for every Latino. As great as these courses are, however, there is currently limited penetration into the greater U.S. Latino market, which is 62-million strong today according to current U.S. Census data. That's why this book, *The Latino Leadership Playbook,* is so important. Although it will not provide detailed training (like the programs referenced above), this book will give all Latinos a targeted roadmap on where you need to focus your development, as well as be your pocket mentor that will provide specific cultural effectiveness and leadership insights and strategies so you can work towards becoming an impact player in your career path!

We are at a significant and exciting point in our journey as Latinos and one where we need to take control of our story and begin to show up differently in the workplace. Claudia Romo Edelman, Founder of We Are All Human, said it best at the 2022 Hispanic Leadership Summit, "We need to unite as a community to drive progress; Hispanic progress is American progress." In that spirit, advancing Latino leadership is all of our responsibility and I look forward to partnering with you as we begin to collectively shift the narrative of Latino leadership in corporate America.

MY UPBRINGING

I am a second-generation Mexican-American born and raised in Chicago. My grandparents left Mexico in the 1960s with the goal of driving to and making a life in New York; as they made their journey through the U.S., they eventually got tired of driving, settled in Chicago and the rest is history. Now 60 years later, we are four generations strong with many college graduates and business professionals contributing to the American workforce.

Like so many of us, I was the first to graduate college and am a first-generation professional. I grew up with limited guidance, exposure, and mentorship on how to approach an academic or professional career. Even though I came from a large family, I didn't have that one person who could help me clearly navigate what I needed to do to drive my career and leadership capabilities; looking back at my high school years, I remember my bar was low as the minimum expectation of me was to get Cs. I was definitely short-sighted and remember doing just enough so that my parents were content with my grades.

Although good grades weren't a priority, the things I always had going for me was that I was very sociable, naturally curious, and above all, highly ambitious. I also loved playing team sports and was always the one who organized the team, created our playbooks, and drove my teams to strive to be the best—I never believed in losing and always led and held us to a high standard on the field. I would have never guessed that these traits would re-present themselves later in my career!

After high school, it was a total crap shoot and I made it up as I went along. I didn't plan on or want to go to college—my mother essentially forced me to apply, and I was accepted at the University of Illinois at Chicago. I blindly decided to pursue a psychology major because that's what sounded most appealing to me at the time. My college experience was the tale of two experiences. During my first two years, I remember continuing to just do enough to get Cs; my priority was definitely not education and was more about having fun. After two years of mediocre academic performance, I found myself uninspired and decided to drop out. This was the period that changed my life forever.

I LEARNED TO APPLY MYSELF

When I dropped out, I began doing electrical work full-time with my uncle's small company. It was a good way to earn money, but it was definitely hard labor—for context, when doing electrical work, there is typically no power where you are working. This means you are often times working in extreme heat or extreme cold and something that I knew I could not do for the long term.

The silver lining in the experience is that I learned some great life lessons from Uncle Victor (and best friend) and quickly discovered that it was time to go back to school and give it my all. I had made up my mind to put ultimate focus on my future—I committed to give the final two years of college everything I had and shot to get straights As and to get involved in school programs/internships. I was all-in and wanted to prove to myself that academic success was something I could achieve. My GPA over my last two years was 3.89; my performance and the recognitions I obtained gave me the confidence I needed when entering the workforce.

INTRODUCTION

EARLY CAREER: A TORN ACHILLES TENDON CHANGED THE COURSE OF MY LIFE

After graduating from college, I took an entry level job at Rush Medical Center in Chicago as a research assistant in the Department of Cognitive Neuroscience. After learning limited career path options in this space, I redirected my career and bet on myself to work myself into a professional position in the booming telecom industry at the time. One of my good friends worked at a major telecommunications company and convinced me to join as a cable installer (given my electrical background) and somehow work my way into a management role. At the time, it paid much better than my current job and I made the decision to take the leap of faith. I quickly found myself going nowhere as a cable installer. I remember regretting the decision and started looking for alternatives. This is when the course of my life changed forever, I tore my Achilles tendon outside of work and could no longer install cable.

To this day, I give my supervisor a lot of credit as he saw my ambition and potential. He didn't have to, but he recommended that I be offered a staff role in the central management office supporting all the field teams as I was immobile and on crutches. My responsibility was doing paperwork for all the supervisors and was perfect as it put me in a position to get exposure. While in the office, I noticed an unused room full of telecom training materials and computers stacked against the wall. I remember being incredibly bored, so I started going through the trainings and learning the telecom business. I then set up the room with all the computers—next thing you know I pitched a training program to the office supervisors and I started training our Illinois field teams on telecom. This accomplishment put me on the map and my office supervisors recommended me for a professional position at company headquarters as a junior project manager. The outcome of this experience was the catalyst for my corporate career—it was a combination of luck, ambition, and a whole lot of support from others!

MY PROFESSIONAL JOURNEY: LESSONS LEARNED THAT I WANT TO SHARE WITH YOU

For the first half of my career, I worked hard on perfecting my craft as a project manager and was laser-focused on leading large teams to deliver solutions for many large companies in various industries—telecom, retail, healthcare, aviation. My thinking was that as long as I was a strong performer and delivered results, the promotions would follow. I learned quickly that this was not the case and that landing higher level positions required strong leadership capabilities, maturity, and a whole lot of support from others to guide and advocate for me.

Once I finally began to understand the rules of the game, how to effectively weave in my Latino culture values into my work, intentionally applying valuable lessons learned, and aligning myself with great mentors, my career started projecting upward to where I am today—and I'm still on my journey! The lessons and insights I have gained over the years are invaluable and ones that I feel a great responsibility to share, so that you can begin to operate with quicker effectiveness and efficiency as you reach your full leadership potential. I will be covering all of them in this book.

Success	Success
what people think it looks like	what it really looks like

INTRODUCTION

LATINO LEADERSHIP: WE NEED TO UNITE AND COLLECTIVELY CHANGE THE NARRATIVE

The Latino Leadership Playbook will position you to be a force in the workplace; it will help you begin to operate with confidence and provide the needed clarity on what it means to be an impact player. It will help carve out and spotlight the Latino leader within you and position you to take control of and drive your career narrative. Your mindset will be shifted. Not only will you improve your capabilities, but you will begin to impact all Latinos you touch—the impact mindset is contagious, and you will notice that your peer discussions will start to change from being frustrated on why you didn't get a certain position to which position are you going to get next!

Your success is the success for all Latinos. It is critical that we unite in developing ourselves; it will take a collective and focused effort to make an impact on the four percent representation (Latino Leadership Gap) covered earlier. I have organized this book so that you can take advantage of the experiences and insights of those that have paved the road ahead of you. I will introduce what I refer to as the Latino Leadership Success Model where we will focus on four key elements, which will be covered in more detail in the next chapter:

1) Latino Population Data Awareness - Understanding the data around the Latino community.

2) Latino Values Navigation - Better understanding how and when to use our values in the workplace.

3) Leadership Capability Development - Understanding the skills needed to add impact.

4) Latino Passion, Inspiration, and Grit - Using our natural strength to help elevate our workplace impact and careers, individually and collectively.

You will be provided with many personal stories and insights in each of these areas. In addition to my experiences, this book covers the perspectives from various influential Latina leaders, as well as thoughts from many other top senior leaders from corporate America. Regardless of where you are in your development, my goal is to arm you with as much targeted knowledge, references, and *practical guidance* as possible in order to position you to becoming a strong Latino impact player that is promotion-ready!

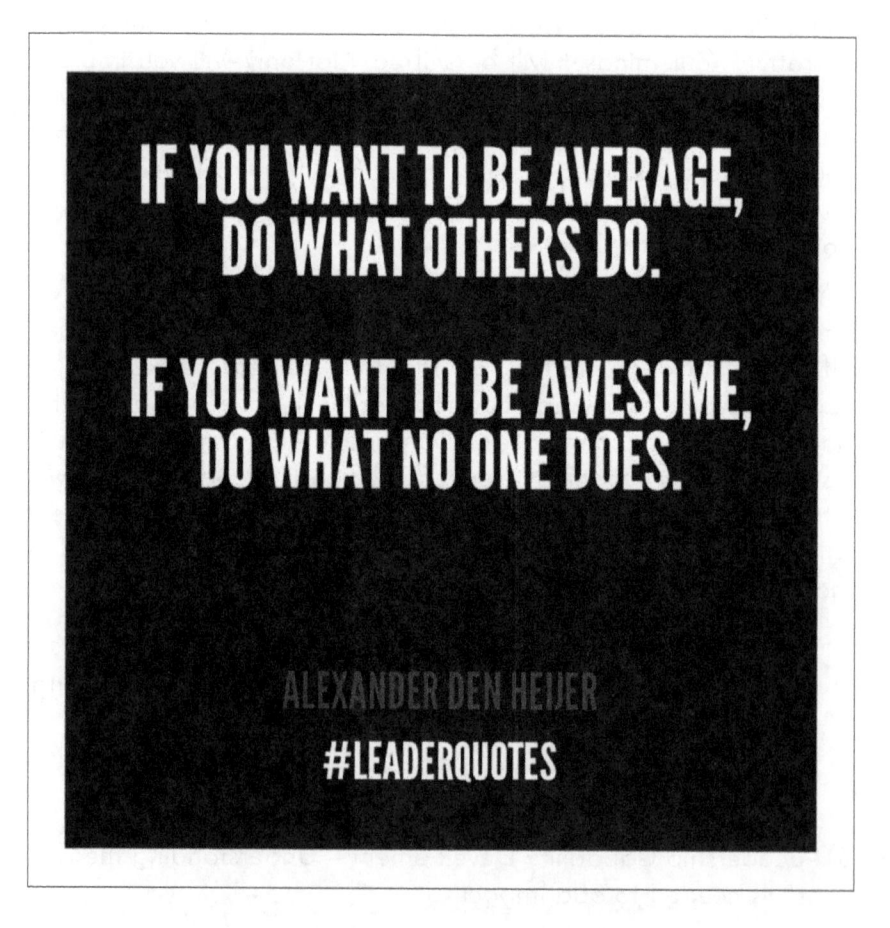

> **IF YOU WANT TO BE AVERAGE, DO WHAT OTHERS DO.**
>
> **IF YOU WANT TO BE AWESOME, DO WHAT NO ONE DOES.**
>
> ALEXANDER DEN HEIJER
> #LEADERQUOTES

THE LATINO LEADERSHIP SUCCESS MODEL

> "High achievement always takes place in the framework of high expectation."
> - Charles Kettering

As discussed in the Introduction, Latinos are represented in only four percent of senior leadership corporate positions although we represent about 20 percent of the population—this is the Latino Leadership Gap. There are two major factors that are needed to address this gap. First, corporations must make a commitment to the recruitment, development, and advancement of Latino talent. Second, Latinos must provide the leadership-ready talent to compete with non-Latinos for management and senior level roles. The focus of this book is on number two—as Latinos we need to take total ownership of our leadership and impact development and work together to improve our representation numbers at the top.

In order to begin working towards closing this gap and get more Latinos into management and senior leadership positions, we have to shift our mindset and approach if we want to a realize a strong and sustainable Latino Leadership talent pipeline. Traditionally, we have been brought up to think that if we just work hard and do our jobs well that we will be rewarded with promotions and higher pay. Unfortunately, this is not the case—working hard is only one piece of the puzzle and this approach is hindering our growth potential. Instead, we need to update our mindset and begin to collectively "work smarter" to begin to realize the true potential of our great community.

To begin tackling how to work smart, I have broken it down to what I call the **Latino Leadership Success Model**—a new leadership development framework that we can align to and game plan around. I have created this four-pillar model as a result of talking to many influential Latino leaders, non-Latino corporate leaders, attending various Latino leadership courses, my own personal experiences, and through conducting research on what corporate America is seeking in promotion-ready professionals.

Note: A key assumption of this model is that Latinos have achieved the required education and have competency in their respective professional field.

The Latino Leadership Success Model: Focus on Working Smart

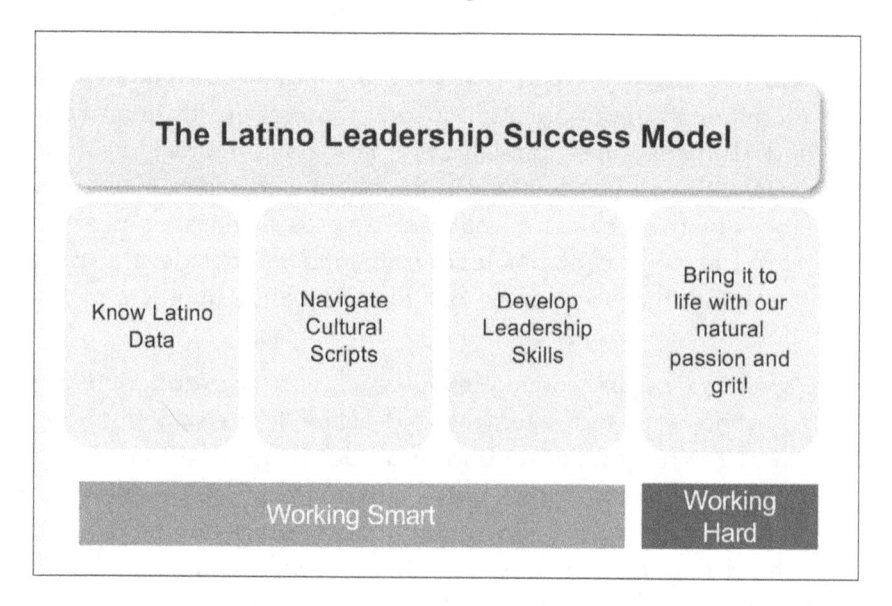

The Latino Leadership Success Model

- Know Latino Data
- Navigate Cultural Scripts
- Develop Leadership Skills
- Bring it to life with our natural passion and grit!

Working Smart | Working Hard

SUMMARY OF EACH OF THE FOUR PILLARS:

1. **Latino Population Impact Data Awareness:** In order understand our current and potential impact and how we fit into the future of this country, Latinos need to understand the facts and figures of our population growth trajectory, buying power, challenges, and the growing influence we will continue have in the future of the U.S.

2. **Cultural Values Navigation:** We were raised with cultural values that are often in conflict with what the traditional corporate culture looks for in senior leaders. It's critical that we examine these values and determine how to best apply them or navigate around them in order to become a confident, promotion-ready impact player in the workplace.

3. **Leadership Focus and Capability:** Latinos need to be very thoughtful, intentional, and focused on developing specific leadership capabilities and soft skills that will help us become promotion-ready. We need to be targeted and very efficient on where we spend our time and how we develop in the workplace.

4. **Passion, Inspiration, and Grit:** This is our natural strength—we are known as loyal and hard-working. Utilizing this approach along with the first three pillars is what is going to change the game for Latino leadership in corporate America for the current and future generations!

To recap, Latino leadership success will require a solid understanding and the effective application of each of the four pillars—this model is designed to put you in a position to begin *working smart* while maintaining our natural disposition to work hard. Making this approach our new normal will position us to show up as confident, informed, high-impact, and promotion-ready Latino leaders. Now let's get started!

HOW TO READ THIS BOOK FOR MAXIMUM DEVELOPMENT

My priority is to strengthen and optimize your leadership and impact potential as efficiently as possible. You will learn that my style is very direct and results-focused—I cut out the fat and give it to you straight. I don't believe in wasting time and I promise the elements I have captured in this playbook are "must-haves" for your career; when you read this book and apply the expert knowledge provided, you WILL position yourself to be set up for success. The practical guidance and instructions with examples from many of the top Latino (and some non-Latino) voices in the world today are going to change how you show up and operate in the workplace!

WHAT THIS BOOK IS... AND IS NOT

What it is.	What it is NOT.
• Most powerful group of mentors in the palm of your hand	• A training program
• A book of proven action-oriented leadership development insights	• A novel, story, or anthology
• A reference guide to keep by your side; it is meant to be consistently referred to throughout your career	• Something you put on the shelf to sit – this book should be an active part of your professional development and career journey. Keep it at your desk for maximum impact.

HOW TO READ THIS BOOK

First, I acknowledge this is a larger-size book. I had to decide on whether to give you a comprehensive "one-stop-shop" resource or to settle and just give you some information with a smaller book. I decided to go with the larger book and give you everything you will/might need to support your long-term carer development.

HOW TO READ THIS BOOK FOR MAXIMUM DEVELOPMENT

I have also taken steps to organize the book and provide a framework that makes it consumable, so you can optimize your learning experience. The following is a view of the book structure and options on how to read it based on your learning style.

***The Latino Leadership Playbook* Reading Guidance**—you don't need to read it all at once!

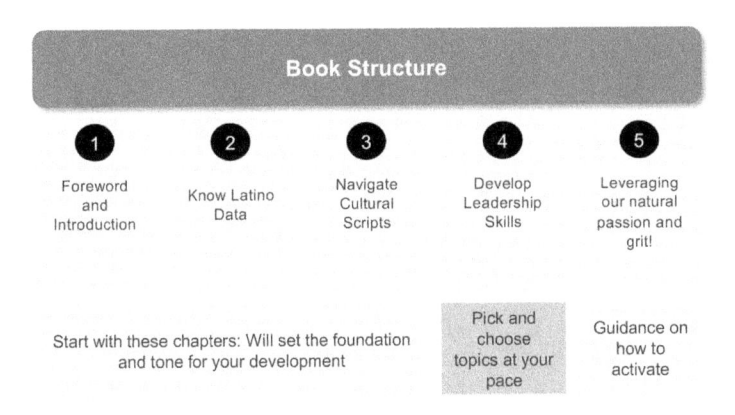

Book Structure

1	2	3	4	5
Foreword and Introduction	Know Latino Data	Navigate Cultural Scripts	Develop Leadership Skills	Leveraging our natural passion and grit!
Start with these chapters: Will set the foundation and tone for your development			Pick and choose topics at your pace	Guidance on how to activate

Step 1: Establish your learning experience foundation and mindset in Parts 1-3.

- Read these chapters first and in order; they will set the tone for the book and get you excited about the following section.

Step 2: Begin your leadership skills development in Part 4.

- There is much more reading flexibility in this section. Focus and go deep on topics based on your development needs and/or interests—you do not need to read these topics in order or all at once. Feel free to jump around as needed.

Step 3: Bring your development plan to life in Part 5.

- Guidance is provided on how to activate your development plan, individually and collectively.

Note: After reading each chapter, reflect on the key insights and start to build a draft action plan. Use the Latino Leadership Workbook, it's a free resource that can be downloaded at: RefugioAtilano.com.

PART 1:

Latino Population and Impact Data Awareness

"In God we trust; all others must bring data."
- W. Edwards Deming

Note: The data sets and key insights captured in this section were provided by Weareallhuman.org, the 2020 census data, and through an interview with Claudia Romo Edelman, Founder of We Are all Human. Her organization's mission is to advocate for every human to be respected and empowered by focusing on our common humanity. I want to extend a special thanks to her and her team.

As Claudia always states, "we must be factivists" (not just activists) and take time to understand and internalize the current state of Latino data in this country. This is a great perspective, and I could not agree more. In fact, in order to begin moving the needle and get more Latinos into senior level positions, we need to first educate ourselves and level-set on the facts of where we are today so that we can accurately set goals on where we want to be tomorrow.

Understanding there is an abundance of Latino population and market analytics, the goal of this section of the book is to provide general Latino stats as well as zoom in on the data sets that will help directly shape the story around Latinos in the workplace and what we need to do to increase our senior level representation. For your reference, there are several resources out there for broader Latino data. For example, you can go to Weareallhuman.org and there is a great new book out by Isaac Mizrahi, *Hispanic Market Power: America's Business Growth Engine*. Trust me, there is no shortage of Latino data.

LATINOS ARE THE FUTURE: POPULATION AND INFLUENCE

The data covered below clearly shows that Latinos are the fastest-growing demographic in the U.S. Here are some key figures provided to me by We Are All Human:

Population

- Latinos make up almost 20% of the current population at 63 million and we are expected to grow to 33% of the population by 2060.
- 58% of Latinos are younger than 33 years of age; our community will be increasingly important due to the youthfulness of our demographic.
- Mode age of Latinos is 19; mode age of non-Latinos is 61.

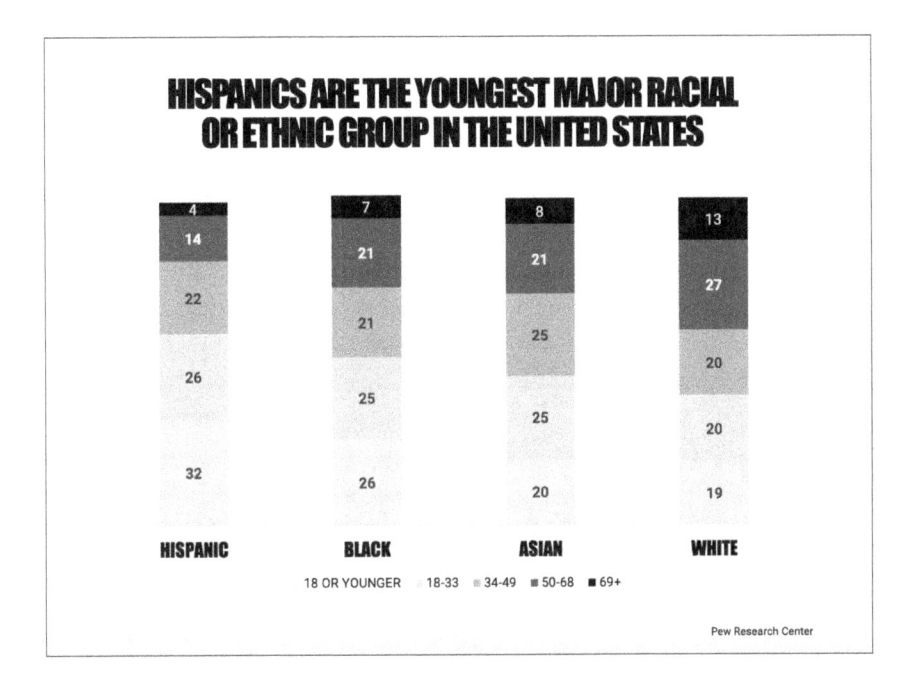

HISPANICS ARE THE YOUNGEST MAJOR RACIAL OR ETHNIC GROUP IN THE UNITED STATES

Age group	HISPANIC	BLACK	ASIAN	WHITE
69+	4	7	8	13
50-68	14	21	21	27
34-49	22	21	25	20
18-33	26	25	25	20
18 or younger	32	26	20	19

Pew Research Center

Buying/Purchasing Power
- Latinos account for 2.7 trillion in buying power, which makes us the fifth largest GDP in the world. This data point makes it critical for companies to rethink their business strategies and how to best tap into this emerging market.

Latino Data Awareness
- 77% of Latinos are unaware of the Latino data around influence and buying power. It is critical that books like this help level set all Latinos on our significant current and future impact in this country.

As you can see, Latinos are the future of our country and it's critical that we all understand our current and potential impact, and, just as important, how we will position ourselves to play a key role in driving that impact. Companies will be positioning themselves to target and connect with the Latino market; this is why your leadership development is so critical. Better than anyone, we understand our community, culture, and challenges.

We are in the best position to help drive business in this segment (as well as others), and it's critical that we set ourselves up as the go-to leaders in this space!

LATINOS DATA: COMMON STEREOTYPES

We Are All Human conducted the Hispanic Perception Study in 2018, where they performed approximately 2,500 interviews—half with Hispanics and half with the general population. Here were some key takeaways as they relate to this book:

The Good

It was broadly shared among respondents that Hispanics are not seen as destroyers of the American way of life by bringing their own culture. White Americans and Hispanics are the most likely to believe Latino culture to be a contribution rather than a threat to the American way of life. Hispanics are:

- Liked, trusted, smart contributors to American society, culture, and economy.
- Hold strong potential for upward mobility.
- Proficient in English.

The Challenge and Perceptions We Need to Overcome

As a community, the perception of Hispanics is overshadowed by the dominant public opinion issue of immigration, which leads to an apparent underestimation of their collective power, impact, and true potential.

- Overall, the sentiment regarding Hispanics is they are viewed for great cooking, dancing, hard-working, family-oriented, happy, responsible, smart, and proud.
- Within the general respondents, Latinas are recognized for their physical characteristics (beautiful, sexy, loud) vs. the Latino respondents which sees them for their strength of character, intelligence, and entrepreneurship.

PART 1: LATINO POPULATION AND IMPACT DATA AWARENESS

- General respondents view 70% of the Hispanic population as illegal—the actual number is 13%.
- Respondents reported that 50-60% of Hispanics are eligible to vote—the reality is 84% are eligible.

As you can see, there is a mixed bag of perceptions regarding the Latino community. This is why it's critical that we Latinos understand and know our data well—this will position us to have a clear view of the real story and educate the broader community. We can then begin to align the Latino narrative with reality and begin to remove the unwanted stereotypes.

LATINO DATA AND THE WORKFORCE

The target metric for this book is that Latinos currently make up almost 20% of the population and only have 4% representation in senior level roles. As stated earlier, this gap is known as the "4% shame," as coined by Dr. Robert Rodriguez. The goal of *The Latino Leadership Playbook* is to directly address this representation gap.

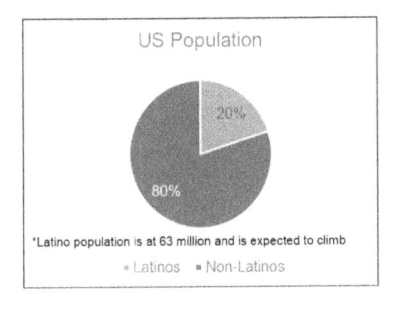

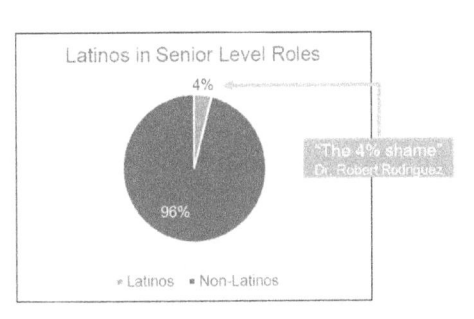

There are also other notable workforce metrics that we should all be aware of as we begin tackling the challenge of adding impact in the workplace:

All Latinos

- Latinos are 41% more likely to earn lower wages than non-Latinos.
- The median household income for Latinos is $60.5k vs. $75.5k for White Americans.
- 76% of Latinos do not feel they can be their authentic selves at work.

Latinas Breakout

- Latinas get paid 54 cents for every dollar a white male makes; Latinas also feel that they must work twice as hard to take home the same paycheck.
- 25.8% is the expected Latina labor force growth, which outpaces all other demographics.
- Afro-Latinas make up 3.8 million of the Latino population; Asian-Latinas account for 1.1 million.

As you can see from the data, we have work to do on many fronts. Not only do we need to upskill and position ourselves to be informed and more impactful leaders, but we need to also begin working smarter and demonstrating our strength at the negotiating table when it comes to compensation. The good news is that these are the topics that we will directly address throughout this book. I will provide strategies on how to immediately and effectively improve in these areas so that we can change the narrative for all Latinos!

USING DATA TO ADVANCE THE LATINO PROFESSIONAL

As covered earlier, Latinos are the future of America. As Claudia states, "Hispanic progress is American progress." Therefore, we need to be hyper-focused on our impact and position ourselves to advance the strategic goals of our organizations, particularly from a Latino perspective. For example, your advancement to senior level roles is a win for us, your influence and ability to connect your business with the Latino market is a win for us, mentoring/

coaching other Latinos is a win for us, and your ability to attract and grow Latino talent in your organization is also a win for our community. Adding impact in any one of these ways is all of our responsibility and I am confident with the guidance outlined in this book, that we are well on our way to changing the Latino leadership narrative!

INTERVIEW WITH AN EXECUTIVE LEADER:
Claudia Romo Edelman / Founder, We Are all Human

Favorite quote: "Never, never, never give up. Persistence is part of the deal." - Inspired by Winston Churchill

In closing this section, I was able to collect several great insights from Claudia in our interview that she'd like for me to share with you as you continue your leadership journey toward being an impact player in the workplace:

- **Be aware of and overcome our cultural barriers** - fight our natural tendency to not rock the boat or just focus on working hard, as these are things that can stunt your development.
- **Work to drive unity and reduce fragmentation** - for us to improve as a community, it is critical that we support each other, buy from each other, and cheer each other on every step of the way. Without unity, we will always be fighting an uphill battle to compete with non-Latinos.
- **Flip the script" and elevate your game** - identify what you are good at and drive it; own your voice and your destiny; stay committed to dismantling barriers.
  - For example, Claudia has leveraged her natural superpower as a visionary who can paint a picture and can influence through developing and delivering compelling stories.

- **Know and embrace the Latino data** - be an advocate and educator of the Latino power, influence, and impact in the U.S.
- **We have a responsibility and obligation to advance Latinos** - we are a transition generation, and it is critical that we provide our future generations with the roadmap to success based on the map we carved out.
- **Network and open doors for each other** - be an advocate, champion, connector, sponsor, facilitator for all Latinos, particularly for those who go above and beyond!

LEVERAGING THE DATA: OUR PATH FORWARD TOWARDS COLLECTIVE ACTIVATION

Now that you have been made aware of the data and have some great insights, it's time to get to work on improving yourself, which in turn, will improve the overall Latino community. You are now informed and can start to operate from an advantage position. *The Latino Leadership Playbook* will address many cultural and traditional leadership topics that will focus on your development to make you a confident, high-impact, and promotion-ready Latino. Once you learn and eventually master the concepts of this book, my thought is that the workforce metrics presented in this section will begin to shift to our advantage.

My expectation for our community after reading and applying the concept of this book is that we will begin to see an upward movement of Latinos. With your engagement, ambition, and commitment, I see three primary areas that we can begin to focus on moving the needle as a community:

- **Area #1:** Within ten years, Latino representation in companies (at all levels) will mirror the U.S. population representation.
- **Area #2:** Within ten years, Latino/a pay will be equal to non-Latinos.

PART 1: LATINO POPULATION AND IMPACT DATA AWARENESS

- **Area #3:** Within five years, all Latinos should feel comfortable being their authentic selves at work; I will cover strategies in this book on how to do this effectively.

Now let's get started...

PART 2:

Latino Cultural Navigation

An Introduction to Latino Cultural Values

"Preservation of one's own culture does not require contempt or disrespect for other cultures."
- Cesar Chavez

Survivors. Resilient. Loyal. Hard Working. Family-oriented. Passionate. Sound familiar? We are raised to always think of the family first (immediate and extended), to do your part in the household, to be humble, and to be respectful—especially to our elders. We celebrate *everything* and enjoy our large family gatherings (a.k.a. parties)! Our families are very matriarchal or patriarchal—there is always that one head of the family that we all will align around and behind.

As Dr. Robert Rodriguez captures in his book *Auténtico: The Definitive Guide to Latino Career Success,* "Many Latinos grow up in strong matriarchies or patriarchies—given the deeply held value of family and its inherently hierarchical structures, they tend to be more deferential to authority" (174). As such, we all know our role and our place in the family dynamic. Additionally, from an early age we are taught to work hard, keep our head down and good things will come. Our faith is strong, and we often use it to help us navigate key aspects of our lives. These elements embody a lot of what being Latino means and we are extremely proud of our culture!

> It's interesting when I think about how big family celebrations continue to be for me and my family. As I am writing this book, I had to make sure to create writing time around the hectic family celebrations scheduled this winter! Of course, like most Latinos, we do the big Christmas Eve and New Years celebrations, as well as my family/friends seven birthdays in January! We live for this!

THE NATURAL CONFLICT BETWEEN OUR CULTURE AND TRADITIONAL CORPORATE CULTURE

Mastering this section will be critical for your development. There is a significant gap between our cultural values and what traditional corporate environments expect from us in the workplace. For example, we are brought up to be humble and not to brag; however, if you want to be noticed, tapped for special assignments, and promoted in the workplace, you must learn how to effectively advocate for yourself—this goes against everything we know and is very uncomfortable for Latinos. This is one of many examples that we will need to solve for and will be covering in this part of the book.

THE LATINO MINDSET SHIFT: EFFECTIVELY NAVIGATING THE LATINO AND CORPORATE CULTURES

Although I will not be doing a deep dive into Latino culture in this book, what I will focus on is how to begin building towards making you a stronger leader who can *confidently and effectively* navigate our Latino and corporate cultures. As Dr. Rodriguez captured in *Auténtico,* "Latino executives featured in book view biculturism as a celebration—their key to not being lost in a cultural identity maze is to embrace a bicultural identity" (152). One executive explained that experiences stemming from both American and Latino cultures can help shape you into being a more well-rounded individual; it will position you to be more curious, more flexible, and can give you the confidence needed for the corporate world (153).

This mindset shift will be critical towards your growth and effectiveness as a leader. We must be open to and learn to master how to navigate and excel meeting corporate environment expectations while finding ways to effectively leverage our Latino cultural values and natural superpowers (i.e., team players, problem solvers) to add unique value to our organizations. *(Note: I will introduce strategies on how to use your culture to your advantage later in this book. The Latino professionals who become proficient in this area will be better positioned for success and increase their chances of landing those coveted higher level roles to elevate our careers.)*

My goal in this section is to, create awareness of the cultural gaps we need to address and provide you with targeted strategies on how to leverage and/or navigate our culture to your advantage in order to close the gaps quickly. At the end of this section, I want you to be operating from a new, informed advantage position and turn your Latinidad and your mindset into a superpower!

AN OVERVIEW: LATINO CULTURAL SCRIPTS VS. TRADITIONAL CORPORATE VALUES

As discussed, we as Latinos have been raised by our families with cultural scripts that often don't match with what's expected in traditional corporate environments. This gap is a blind spot for most professional Latinos and it's an area we need to focus on and master in order to be able to take our leadership capability to the next level. We must be aware of this gap and develop strategies on how to navigate our cultural values and when/how to apply or overcome them in the workplace. I will be covering various scenarios in this book to help you significantly improve your leadership capability.

Here is a summary of some Latinos Cultural Scripts and how they match up to traditional workplace expectations:

LATINO-WORKPLACE IMPACT FRAMEWORK

CORE LATINO SCRIPTS	WORKPLACE EXPECTATIONS
Always Be Respectful (i.e., defer to authority)	• Be comfortable with effectively challenging senior leaders • Be bold and go after what you want • Be vocal with your perspectives and ideas • Work to gain the trust and respect of your senior leaders and colleagues
Work Hard (Do a good job and you will be rewarded)	• Know how to work smart and drive broad impact for your organization, in addition to working hard • "Don't be defined by your role" – Marissa Solis
Family-oriented (Group comes first: Don't call attention to yourself)	• Know how and when to self-advocate, along with knowing when to lead with a team-oriented approach
Trust in God (What's meant to happen, will happen)	• Proactively and strategically drive your career, while also using your faith to support your journey

As you can see, the deck is stacked against us from how we were raised versus where we need to be in the corporate environment. The purpose of this book is to help create awareness of these gaps, and just as importantly, be the catalyst to closing them by providing strategies on how we can begin changing the narrative to becoming more impactful leaders in the workplace.

We will now go into detail on each of these elements, so you are better positioned to navigate and leverage them effectively in your career. Let's get started.

PART 2: HOW TO WORK SMART

How to Work Smart

> "Hard work is surely the key to success, but smart work is the key to being successful."
>
> **- Masood Ahmad**

To me, this section of the book is one of the most important for your development into becoming a strong, impactful leader. As Latinos, most of us are raised to focus on working hard, keep our head down, and good things will come. Unfortunately, this approach will be a very limiting factor in your career as *working hard* is only a small piece of the puzzle to advance in your career. You must start to think about how to "work smart" and add value above and beyond your hard skills and raw passion—working hard is table stakes and must be expanded upon if you are serious about advancing your career. According to an article by Northwest Executive Education, "Companies are continuously searching for individuals with refined leadership skills to join their organization as the economy is becoming more complex and unpredictable" (10 Leadership, 2023). You will need a combination of management and leadership traits for senior management if you aspire to be an effective senior leader.

> You must start to think about how "work smart" and add value above and beyond your hard skills and raw passion—working hard is table stakes and must be expanded upon if you are serious about advancing your career.

In a separate article by Harvard Business Review, their research shows that although technical and hard skills remain relevant for senior leadership roles (table stakes), they attribute less importance to those capabilities than they used to and instead prioritize one qualification above all others: strong social skills. These include certain specific capabilities, including a high level of self-awareness, the ability to listen and communicate well, and a facility for working with different types of people and groups—the capacity to infer how others are thinking and feeling (Sadun, 2022).

It took me over 15 years to discover this hard truth. Once I learned these insights, I put maximum focus on finding ways to create value and effectively develop my soft skills and leadership skills. As mentioned in the book introduction, if it were not for another senior leader sharing her insights on what I needed to do to get the next level (i.e., strong communicator, executive presence), I would have never known to apply this lens to my career journey and would most likely still be in the same position.

In this section, I will be covering various stories and insights to help you begin to add value beyond your hard skills and passion. Although it will be impossible to go into depth on all items, it will provide you with the awareness on where you need to focus your development. With this intelligence, you will be well-informed on where to spend your time to make a stronger workplace impact.

Here are some personal stories and insights I'd like to share as you begin to create your own narrative on how to work smarter for your career:

Personal Insight 1: Refugio A. Atilano, Business Leader at a Top-10 Pharma Company, ERG/DEI Leader, Author, *The Latino Leadership Playbook*

BUILDING A LEADERSHIP IMAGE

Before I made the leap into senior levels positions, I had not put any focus into how I presented myself. My mindset was to perform well and everything else would take care of itself. I always performed well as a standard project manager and always was asked to lead the best projects; however, I noticed that I was never invited to high level meetings nor was I asked for my opinion about the business aspects of a project. In short, I often felt overlooked by senior leaders.

After sharing my frustrations with trusted advisors, they said that I was lacking executive presence and that if I wanted a seat at the table, then I needed to take the steps to look and act the part. I remember feeling embarrassed and enlightened at the same time! After reflection, I took care of improving my image immediately as this was low-hanging fruit. I had a new wardrobe, new shoes, and fresh haircut within a couple of days—this was a game-changer! Without question, people immediately looked at me differently, approached me differently, and started engaging with me differently. Overall, I felt better about myself in the workplace, and it helped develop my confidence as a leader.

> Without question, people immediately looked at me differently, approached me differently, and started engaging with me differently. Overall, I felt better about myself in the workplace, and it helped develop my confidence as a leader.

Next, I put ultra focus into the area of executive presence (which I cover in more detail later in this book). I quickly identified and started plugging my previously unrealized blind spots: body language, poise, connection to audience, pace of communication, confidence, and consistency—to name a few. This was a total game-changer for how I was perceived and how more effectively I communicated my brand and my business acumen.

Fast-forward five years, I have mastered the art of executive presence, have been formally recognized for it in my annual reviews, and am often asked to mentor/coach others in this space. These are examples of career-impacting elements that will help bring the great work you do to life—you will be able to better deliver your message and imprint your brand in ways that will get you noticed!

Personal Insight 2: Refugio A. Atilano, Business Leader at a Top-10 Pharma Company, ERG/DEI Leader, Author, *The Latino Leadership Playbook*

IDENTIFYING STRETCH ASSIGNMENTS–HELP OTHERS ACHIEVE THEIR GOALS

I made it a habit to lead with a growth mindset. I am constantly on the lookout to learn as much about my company's business as possible, add impact to as many areas of the organization as possible, and create meaningful connections throughout the organization along the way. Creating value in unique ways and helping other leaders across the organization meet their business goals is always a great way to stand out and showcase your brand to new audiences. As an example, I make time to introduce myself to leaders throughout the organization, especially those in which I am thinking about potentially driving my career.

When meeting with them, I listen carefully to learn about their business goals, pain points, priorities, and determine if there's a way I can help them in moving their business forward by engaging in voluntary smaller efforts. *Note: This assumes you are already a good performer in your current position, and you have your leader's blessing to lean in on other parts of the business. The relationship and alignment you have with your immediate manager is critical for success of this approach.*

> Creating value in unique ways and helping other leaders across the organization meet their business goals is always a great way to stand out and showcase your brand to new audiences.

Assuming everything is in place, I typically identify opportunities to collaborate with the other leader and agree to develop a game plan that I will bring back for review. Walking out of the meeting, I develop a proposed short-term engagement plan and align with my boss to ensure we are on the same page before going back to the collaborating leader. Once I align with the new leader, I make sure to execute flawlessly while also showcasing my leadership brand (i.e., executive presence). I also put in extra prep time, talk to their team, learn more about the business, and learn from the new leader.

These types of experiences allow me to grow and make impact in different ways across the organization, continue to develop my leadership brand, as well as to develop my company business acumen in new ways. This type of approach is what will help you get recognized as adding unique impact and delivering results for the organization and something that can be part of your end of year story for during annual reviews!

Personal Insight 3: Refugio A. Atilano, Business Leader at a Top-10 Pharma Company, ERG/DEI Leader, Author, *The Latino Leadership Playbook*

PROTECTING YOUR BRAND AND MAKING FEEDBACK YOUR SUPERPOWER

I almost ruined everything I worked so hard to build—my professional brand. This is a story I want everyone to take to heart as I want to ensure that all the work you are going to put into yourself always remains protected.

A few years ago, I was going through some serious health issues for the first time that I decided to keep to myself (as I thought it would just pass) and I decided to work through it. The health issues persisted for three months and it was very difficult to work through. I was very distracted, and I was not my normal positive self as the only thing on my mind was the uncertainty of my health and the constant physical and mental stress I was going through. I never had to deal with anything like this and found myself just trying to battle through it alone one day at a time.

This period greatly affected my performance, my ability to connect with others, and put my overall professional reputation at risk. I was a different person and it showed up in the workplace.

Everything was put at risk, others noticed, and I received feedback about it. I had to work hard to recover from this period and it could have been avoided if I had been honest and open about my condition.

Looking back and a lesson I want you to take away from this experience is that you should always be honest with yourself and your immediate manager (to the extend where you are comfortable) when you are not able to perform due to illness— this is critical towards protecting your business and your brand. It took me years to build my reputation and it only took a few short weeks to put it at risk and create a brand I did not want. Note: *You will find that today's leaders are very supportive and compassionate and will help you whatever the situation is in your life.*

> Always be honest with yourself and your immediate manager when you are not able to perform due to illness – this is critical for protecting your business and your brand.

The other lesson I want to share during this process is that I found myself defending my behaviors during this period. Again, not being my normal self, it was hard for me to prioritize the feedback of others' given my focus on my condition. I started getting a reputation for not taking feedback well, and as a result, people were not comfortable with providing it any longer. This was a problem. I knew something had to change... and change quickly.

Once I got my health back and reflected on that period of my professional journey, I made it a priority to begin accepting feedback with open arms and start using it as my superpower. Although hearing constructive feedback can be uncomfortable, the insights and knowledge gained from those discussions are priceless. It quickly positions you with the information needed to grow, change your narrative, and can fast-track closing a blind spot.

I now view feedback as a means to becoming a stronger leader. For example, recently a colleague shared some concerns about a term I was using and offered her thoughts on how it looked and how it can be taken the wrong way. *I immediately thanked her*, and we jointly came up with alternate messaging to communicate my point. I now also see every constructive feedback moment as an opportunity to connect with others and jointly collaborate on new outcomes! This is what making feedback your superpower looks like; it will help you develop a reputation for someone who is always willing to listen, learn, and apply. This is a great way to add to your brand and is a good example of working smart!

> Although hearing constructive feedback can be uncomfortable, the insights and knowledge gained from those discussions are priceless. It quickly positions you with the information needed to grow, change your narrative, and can fast-track closing a blind spot.

Personal Insight 4: Enrique Acosta Gonzalez, CEO, Triad Leadership Solutions, LLC

HOW TO WORK SMART: A SEAT AT THE TABLE

As a young Sailor my mindset was to outdo everyone in the performance of my duties. I got in early, stayed late, and wasn't done until the work was finished. I believed that what others were not doing was my ticket up the ladder. What my superiors saw was a young man that couldn't manage his time and needed extra assistance that no one else was asking for. My hard work became a liability. It wasn't until a senior Sailor pointed this out to me that I realized that I was going about it all wrong.

After a recalibration, I started adding variety to my so-called services. I started strategizing my time to the mission, scheduled work, volunteering, education, and adding value to those around me. Within a year, I became the go-to person for mentorship and leading other Sailors on how to implement strategic workflow and planning in their careers. To get a seat at the table you must know there is a table and how to work the room to ensure a seat has your name on it.

The following tours of duty greeted me with kindness because my reputation preceded me. This totally changed my trajectory in the Navy and allowed me to share my work smart tactics and lessons learned. Not only was I succeeding, but my Sailors were flourishing under my charge.

Fast-forward 30 years, I have taken those moments and lessons and have incorporated them into my own business. I teach, mentor, and coach professionals around the world to consider working smart versus just working hard and lives are being changed in every interaction. You can also experience the benefits of working smart and finding your seat at the table.

Personal Insight 5: Enrique Acosta Gonzalez, CEO, Triad Leadership Solutions, LLC

HOW TO WORK SMART: THE FINISH LINE MAY NOT BE FOR YOU

Early in my career, I worked for a leader that wanted me to fail. Well, that never stopped during my whole career and every three years another clone would take his place. This is when working hard and working smart comes in handy. When you work hard people notice and when you add working smart people remember.

I was nearing my final years in service and was coming into my next duty station. It was a dream come true because it was in Hawaii and at the site of my first duty station. One day a senior leader of mine asked me to visit him because he needed to speak with me before I took off to paradise. In that conversation he lauded me for the hard work and encouraged me to continue in my smart work. However, at the same time, he told me that I had reached my limit and I was being sent to a considerably smaller command with the intention that I ride off into the sunset and die professionally.

PART 2: HOW TO WORK SMART

I was speechless, and he noticed. I am sure they thought I had been strategically outsmarted, but I used this as an opportunity to turn it around on them. Immediately I went into planning mode and used the advice I gave you in the previous sections. I started calling Hawaii and making connections, I planned in-person meetings for when I arrived. I met every key player on the island and made myself an asset to those leaders. I became the source of action and was determined not to be outsmarted. I ensured that my Sailors were reaping the rewards of my efforts and they thrived. That small command of less than 50 Sailors became the envy of the community, and they deserved every accolade they received. I, unfortunately, did not make the finish line of my final promotion.

Sometimes all the hard work and smart work will only get you but so far. My Sailors, on the other hand, reaped the rewards and what a way to go out. Seeing your people shine and surpass you is the greatest compliment a leader can receive. Always remember that there is honor in working hard and there is legacy in working smart. The combination of the two are powerful but powerless the more you use it just for yourself. As you continue your leadership journey, focus on building a reputation for being the leader that doesn't just go places, but takes their people with them. That's when all your hard work and smart work combine to benefit all!

Personal Insight 6: Delia Gutierrez McLaughlin, President/CEO | AzTech Innovation

WORKING SMART: STRATEGIES TO ACCELERATE YOUR IMPACT

In our fast-paced world of today's professional landscape, the mantra "work hard(er)" was ingrained in us from our culture, our parents, etc., and often touted as the key to success. However, the relentless pursuit of hard work can lead to burnout, diminished creativity, and reduced, productive outcomes. A more sustainable and effective approach is to "work smarter, not harder." This strategy involves evaluating your approach, optimizing your efforts, leveraging resources, and prioritizing tasks to achieve maximum productivity without overexerting yourself.

What is the point of working smarter not harder? Why embark down this road at any point in your career? It is the perfect combination of hard work and smart work evolution that helps us realize our full potential as a valued resource to any organization.

What are the outcomes of working smarter? Here are just a few:

- Higher valuable productivity at work
- Greater job satisfaction
- Become a more valuable resource to your organization
- Job confidence—enhanced possibility for promotion or raise

SELF-AWARENESS AND OUTCOMES MINDSET

The first step in working smarter is to understand your strengths and weaknesses. Self-awareness is a powerful tool that allows you to identify areas where you excel and areas that require improvement. Early in my career, my idea of working smarter was to develop my ability to multi-task. My perspective was that the ability to demonstrate this skill meant I was performing at a high-level. What I found is I stacked the deck on myself. Not only was I working to achieve my deliverables, but my focus also to develop superior multi-tasking skills diverted energy away from delivering outcomes that were impactful.

In retrospect, what impact did my ability to multi-task have on the outcomes of my performance? Did I impact my organization's goals, business outcomes in a meaningful way? Did our customers realize more value? To all of the above the answer is: No! Thus, I invested in myself by becoming more self-aware and embracing a significantly beneficial mindset to both myself as a professional and to every organization I have ever worked for—an outcome-based mindset. Every task, every deliverable I began to view from an outcome-based lens; everything I did as a team member, a leader, and as a member of an organization should lead to a value-driven outcome of impact to either our organization, our customers or both.

Commit to cultivating an outcome-based mindset. View challenges as opportunities for learning rather than as insurmountable obstacles. This mindset encourages continuous learning and adaptation, both of which are essential for working smarter. By viewing setbacks as opportunities for growth, you can continually evolve your strategies and approaches, leading to long-term improvement and success.

Working smarter also involves maintaining a healthy work-life balance. Overworking can lead to stress, decreased productivity, and burnout. Ensure you take regular breaks, engage in physical activity, and pursue hobbies outside of work. These activities can help clear your mind, boost creativity, and improve overall productivity.

LEVERAGING RELATIONSHIPS TO WORK SMART

Finally, it's important to foster strong relationships and networks. Collaboration and knowledge sharing are key to working smarter. By leveraging the collective intelligence and skills of your team or network, you can achieve more than you could alone.

Most recently, the organization I worked for established an escalation framework for our professional practice. On paper the framework looked flawless; a well laid out process created to bring business unit executive visibility and action to customer engagements in need of help, review or otherwise. Prior to any escalation's review by a business unit executive, each region's leadership within the U.S. took a first pass at aiding the customer engagement team. However, the framework did not lay out the process that each region should employ. Thus, inefficiencies and inconsistencies arose; one region had one process for escalations that took a week, another region had come up with their own that took two days. At a team leaders meeting, a few of my colleagues brought up their frustration with the escalation framework. Colleagues cited inconsistencies with the level of detail the region required as compared to what the business unit executive requested.

Rather than one of us trying to solve these issues, we harnessed our collective intelligence and created a tiger team of three colleagues from three different regions to streamline the escalation framework and bring stability to our customer engagements. Our value-driven outcomes were to remove inefficiencies in the escalation framework and to reduce time to resolution and keep the trust of our customers. The impact to our organization across the enterprise: an optimization of the escalation framework. Our professional practice gained back precious time to focus on their customer engagements, and a rebuilt escalation framework that truly impacted our ability to address customer escalations expeditiously. Furthermore, strong relationships can provide support during challenging times like this and open up opportunities for growth and development.

Key Takeaways:

- In conclusion, working smarter, not harder, is about optimizing your efforts to achieve value-driven outcomes and impactful benefits to our customers and our organizations. Your foundational landscape of skills and talent are fortified with substance not symbolism.

- It involves understanding your strengths and weaknesses, leveraging technology, managing your time effectively, cultivating a growth mindset, maintaining a healthy work-life balance, and fostering strong relationships.

- By adopting these strategies, you can enhance your productivity, avoid burnout, and pave the way for a successful and fulfilling professional career all while transforming our organizations and customers in an impactful way.

DOS AND DON'TS

Now that we have covered the background, stories, and insights into how to work smart, here are some additional Dos and Don'ts to further support your development in this area.

Dos	Don'ts
Do: Over prepare and be a thought leader Do your homework and always show up ready to contribute ideas, plans, perspectives to move the business forward—applies to any/all interactions. It shows you are always ready, thoughtful, and a strong contributor. Always make time to think through an approach, ideas, and goals before going into any meeting. Being a strong leader requires strong thought leadership. Making time to "do your homework" will position you to add impact in any discussion you are a part of!	**Don't: Stay solely focused on perfecting your craft** This is the kiss of death if you want to move into senior leadership roles; it increases the probability of hindering you from growth, exposure, and new opportunities. Learn to add value/impact in different ways in your organization. This will help you stand out and help build your leadership brand. We will cover more on this topic in later chapters. Note: If you are comfortable with your current role and it fits your personal situation and is what works for you and your company, then this can also be a good spot to be.
Do: Learn to carry yourself with confidence This comes with implementing behaviors covered in this book; confident people immediately stand out, will get opportunities, and will attract those around them. Confidence comes with experience, practice, and knowledge—commit to making this one of your superpowers.	**Don't: Navigate your career in a silo** There are no senior leaders who have not had the help of someone to get where they are today; be smart and be sure to use your network of trusted advisors and your manager to pressure-test ideas and help you progress as you drive your career.
Do: Operate with an ownership mindset This is critical. If you want to be a leader, then you need to lead. Take extreme ownership of everything you do; don't wait for others around you to lead. Take the leadership role whenever the opportunity presents itself. This will build your brand as someone who is not afraid to take charge and lead an effort to drive an outcome.	**Don't: Get involved with office gossip** Just don't—doing so will take down your reputation and brand in an instant. Stay focused on your goals, your development, your impact, and connecting with those around you.

Do: Tie your work to company goals Being able to tie your work to the goals of your company, business unit, and team goals clearly demonstrates your value to driving the business forward. It puts you in a great position to showcase your work and your worth to the organization. Effectively implementing these behaviors will position you to operate with impact—we will cover this topic in more detail in a separate chapter.	**Don't: Operate without a big picture** Thinking big picture is a great way to add value to your business and can provide perspectives nobody else has thought of yet. Do your homework—what is the global landscape, what is the competitor landscape, what are the external/internal business risks and best practices that need to be considered? What are the immediate, short-term, and long-term impacts of solutions? This mindset automatically puts you in a position to add unique value and perspectives and will help your brand.
Do: Prioritize work/time effectively Being a strong leader involves knowing how to allocate your time. Demonstrate that you are aware of work that needs attention and that you are thoughtful and pragmatic on where you put focus. To be a senior leader, focusing on busy work doesn't cut it; you will need to make sure you are laser-focused, able to articulate, and are delivering on company-impacting objectives.	**Don't: Stop pushing your growth** Operating with a growth mindset is an important approach as you develop yourself and explore new opportunities. Remember to be intentional with your growth. For example, know where you want to grow, what parts of your brand you'd like to develop, which areas of the business you'd like to learn about, which skills you are trying to master.
Do: Know and leverage your brand Being self-aware and how you are perceived by others is extremely important as you prepare to work smart. It's important to know where you stand with others versus how you want to be perceived as a leader. Once you know your brand, keep refining it and use it as your superpower in everything you do. Make sure that when people see you in action or talk about you behind closed doors, that your brand is always front and center. *We cover this topic in depth later in the book.	**Don't: Be late** Always be on time, if not early—never be late. This shows that you have control of your calendar, you know how to prioritize, are organized, you are ready to contribute/lead, and that you respect the time of those whom with you interact. This is one of the easier items to master and one that can immediately improve your brand. Showing up early also can help you establish great relationships with other leaders who also show up early; this is a great way to create advocates.

PART 2: HOW TO WORK SMART

RECAP

As Latinos, we already know how to work hard; it's a given—now we are learning what it means to work smart. It is critical that we take these lessons and insights and thoughtfully begin applying them in our current roles and careers. Remember, your career development is a marathon and it's going to require thoughtful planning as you to chip away one piece at a time. The good thing is that you now have the start of a roadmap towards success. Going back to your job, and now armed with this information, it's going to change how you approach adding impact in the workplace. It's going to start to change your mindset and how you want to be perceived. It's going to change how you collaborate, how you support, and how you interact with trusted advisors and leaders across your organization. It's going to help improve your image, as well as how you prepare for and show up in meetings. The working smart leadership foundation is now laid for you to begin to show up at work differently and there is no going back!

PLANNING AND ACTIVATING YOUR DEVELOPMENT

To support your development and to help you organize and activate the concepts in this chapter, please go to my website (www.refugioatilano.com) and download the free templates for **The Latino Leadership Workbook**—this is a great set of tools to help organize your target areas and map a plan on where to focus your growth. It also includes a notes page and a development roadmap template so you can begin to think through and draft your personalized improvement plan that will set you up for maximum growth and success.

HOW TO ADVOCATE FOR YOURSELF

> "You are responsible to yourself, to love yourself, to care for yourself, and to help yourself."
>
> **- Akiroq Brost**

By far, this is one of the most talked about topics in the Latino professional community—advocating for ourselves continues to be a major barrier for Latinos in the workplace. We are raised to be humble and not draw attention to ourselves as individuals. As captured in a Latinas Uprising article, "Being humble is often held up as a positive attribute among Latino families" (Willman, 2014). This can be a great quality and looked at with great respect within our community. However, along with being humble comes the perception of being submissive and one that accepts limitations. This can be a career limiting trait in the workplace if you are trying to advance your career and one we must address head on.

For me, being humble in the home environment is still a big part of my DNA. For example, I rarely discuss my career or what I am achieving professionally with my extended family when I visit, including talking about this book. When I see them, it's always about family and we focus on enjoying each other through food, music, laughter, and stories—discussions are never about work or personal accomplishments. Doing so just feels unnatural and very uncomfortable as we, as Latinos, are not raised to draw the spotlight to ourselves. On the other hand, in the workplace, I flip the script and go total beast mode! This is part of the art of being an effective bicultural leader.

PART 2: HOW TO ADVOCATE FOR YOURSELF

WHAT IS SELF-ADVOCACY AND WHY IS IT IMPORTANT

According to an article by Everhour, "Self-advocacy is best described as the professional approach towards speaking about yourself and communicating your worth. Essentially, self-advocacy is the process of speaking up for yourself and your needs. Self-advocacy helps you present yourself in a way that will make for a positive and lasting impression" (Guilani, 2022).

This is a critical skill for promotions, building a meaningful network, obtaining mentors and sponsors, showcasing your talents in front of the organization, building/reinforcing your brand, being able to lead others, etc. Bottom line, in order to move up the leadership ranks, you are going to need to learn how to effectively advocate for yourself, as well as advocate for others.

> In order to move up the leadership ranks, you are going to need to learn how to effectively advocate for yourself, as well as advocate for others.

Until later in my career, I didn't realize the importance of advocating for yourself. As mentioned earlier in this book, I was regarded as a strong project manager—and that was it! I was not looked at as a leader, my opinion was not solicited on non-project matters, and it just seemed like I was being ignored overall. It was a very uncomfortable place and I remember feeling confused and frustrated about why I was not viewed as a leader. I knew something had to change and I built this into my development plan.

STRATEGIES ON HOW TO ADVOCATE FOR YOURSELF

As part of my focus to develop in this area, I quickly realized that there was no guide or training on how to develop this capability. I have worked very hard over the past several years on how to master the art of advocating for yourself. I started my growth in this area by learning from those who were successful, so I started paying close attention to senior leaders and how they articulated their brand, their accomplishments, and their story in a very impactful, but in a very discreet and respectful way. I remember feeling how graceful they were in their delivery, and I knew that this was a skill I needed to master if I wanted to be viewed differently as a leader in the workplace.

During this period, I was able to capture and incorporate many new strategies into my toolkit and will now be sharing those with you. I am going to share stories and insights (from myself and others) that will immediately help you take your game to the next level. Knowing how critical this topic is for your development, my goal is for you to walk away from this chapter with the intelligence and knowledge needed to continue your journey of showing up differently in the workplace.

Advocating for yourself can take on many forms and can vary depending on the situation. It can be a one-time event, or it can occur over a series of moments. Anytime you are interacting with others is an opportunity to advocate for yourself—take advantage of every one of them! I will be covering many different examples so that you can parse through and determine which ones work best for your career needs. Now let's get started!

> Advocating for yourself can take on many forms and can vary depending on the situation. It can be a one-time event, or it can occur over a series of moments. Anytime you are interacting with others is an opportunity to advocate for yourself—take advantage of every one of them!

Personal Insights 1: Refugio A. Atilano, Business Leader at a Top-10 Pharma Company, ERG/DEI Leader, Author, *The Latino Leadership Playbook*

ADVOCATING FOR YOURSELF THROUGH EXECUTIVE COLLABORATION

This story is near and dear to my heart as it helped me obtain a sponsor and a trusted advisor for my career.

One of our business teams was recently going through major transformation and I saw a need for a Change Management initiative to support the rollout of their new business model. Having experience in Change Management, I was able to then develop and convince the senior management decision-makers that this was a critical business need toward meeting our goals and I would be able to lead it. This was me advocating for myself through strategic vision: I created and sold the proposal, put myself in an ownership position, as I knew it was an opportunity to *impact* the organization in a big way.

Once I started leading the initiative, I partnered closely with the VP and his leadership team. The first step is to always build the connections (our natural Latino ability) through taking time to understand their needs, wants, pain points, etc. I also took time to get to know each leadership team member personally and share some of my personal story as well. Making the time for these connections is critical toward developing trust and building the relationships needed to create a great collaborative foundation.

The goal was to develop strong relationships and understand their business needs so we can operate as smoothly as possible on this program. Doing so allowed me to advocate for myself through showing that I am a strategic, collaborative, and caring business partner who is laser-focused on helping the team meet its goals. I see and use every opportunity as one where I can advocate for myself and drive my brand. Who you are is always radiating - be aware of and take advantage of it!

> I see and use every opportunity as one where I can advocate for myself and drive my brand. Who you are is always radiating - be aware of and take advantage of it!

Partnering closely with the business group VP allowed me to showcase my talents, passion, and grit day-in and day-out. I essentially had the opportunity to advocate for myself everyday with an influential person in the organization. I knew this was his baby and there was no way I was going to let us not be successful. I did my homework, studied the organization on how we can be most effective, took time to understand and adapt to his style, brought my own ideas to the table, and always took time to develop proposed strategies for our business.

My VP was super-busy, and I knew he appreciated the thought leadership and coming to the table with proposed ideas and frameworks was important to him. This was a great opportunity for me to show my value and leadership ability. Although my ideas and work output were not always used, it always served as a great starting point to get us to our final end state. In short, our styles, our rapport, and our ability to collaborate effectively made us a great team. He is now one of my sponsors and is one of my biggest advocates at the executive management level.

> My VP was super-busy, and I knew he appreciated the thought leadership and coming to the table with proposed ideas and frameworks was important to him. This was a great opportunity for me to show my value and leadership ability.

Personal Insight 2: Refugio A. Atilano, Business Leader at a Top-10 Pharma Company, ERG/DEI Leader, Author, *The Latino Leadership Playbook*

ADVOCATING FOR YOURSELF THROUGH EMPLOYEE RESOURCE GROUPS (ERG)

Until a few years ago, I didn't realize the importance of being involved in an ERG, let alone a Latino ERG. Let me tell you, it's magical! You get to bond with those who understand exactly how you were raised, our culture, our challenges, and what's important to us (like family). We support each other to no end and root for the success of each other. If you haven't already done so, get involved—there's nothing but upside in doing so!

I was recently given the opportunity to co-chair the Latino ERG for a top global pharma company. Unexpectedly, this opportunity and experience took my Latinidad to a whole new stratosphere! I remember when I took on the role that I was concerned about having the time to focus on my regular job and that I would do my best to contribute. That concern didn't last long. Now I can't get enough of it—it's fuel for me!

I have fallen into a passion for developing Latino leaders and have absolutely no quit in me! It has led to me fighting for opportunities for our ERG Latino leaders, advocating to get more dollars into our ERG, and leveraging our talent to impact our organization in new ways! It has led to me writing this book, to fighting for your leadership development, and doing everything I can to tee up the new and next generation of Latino leaders! This passion and focus has spilled into everything I do and is now a big part of my brand. This is an example of advocating for yourself on your brand, passion, and vision.

> It has led to me writing this book, to fighting for your leadership development, and doing everything I can to tee up the new and next generation of Latino leaders! This passion and focus has spilled into everything I do and is now a big part of my brand.

I have leveraged our ERG to also develop my leadership capability, and you should as well by working with your direct manager and building in learning goals into your annual development plan. For example, one of my focus areas was to develop my strategic toolkit, so I took on the task of taking the lead in developing our overall ERG strategy and strategy deck. I was able to pull together an integrated plan and when we presented it to our executive sponsor, he said it was the best strategy he's ever seen from our ERG. I shared this great feedback with our ERG leadership, other executive sponsors, as well as my manager. This is an example of me advocating for myself (and our ERG) through sharing the feedback received about the output of our approach and work in an objective fashion.

Finally, I use communications like social media platforms to promote my brand, accomplishments, and my ERG work. Given most of the professional community is on this platform, it's a great opportunity to reinforce the message you want the world to know about you—your brand. I would encourage you to do the same about topics that are important to you and that you'd like for others to know. I can't tell you how many times I get asked about my posts.

For example, I had the opportunity to attend the We Are All Human Hispanic Leadership Summit recently and have had numerous people at work (Latinos and non-Latinos) ask about my experience and comment about the work I am doing in the Latino leadership space. Because of these posts, I have seen the narrative and discussions shift about me. This is another example of how I advocate for myself and drive my brand in the ERG and Latino leadership space.

> I use communications like social media platforms to promote my brand, accomplishments, and my ERG work.

Personal Insight 3: Jacqueline Ruiz, CEO of JJR Marketing, Inc. and Fig Factor Media Publishing

HOW TO ADVOCATE FOR YOURSELF

One thing that I know for sure is that our core values are the guiding lights that create our reputation, our path, and the opportunities that present themselves. It is through our core values demonstrated through our actions that we are able to tell the world who we really are.

PART 2: HOW TO ADVOCATE FOR YOURSELF

When it comes to advocating for oneself, there is no better way than the alignment of our beliefs and actions. The "pattern" of our consistent actions form what is known as those core values. I always tell my children, imagine that you live in a transparent, glass house where your actions were exposed to the world. Imagine that anyone can see you. Would you act differently? Would your actions be the same? Ultimately, it is the transparency of our actions that aligned in a congruent with our words that builds our reputation to the outside world. Most of the crimes happen in dark spaces when people think no one is watching. Do good when no one is watching.

So, based on what I covered thus far, what are the next steps in advocating for yourself? What deliverables can you start implementing to bring them to life? Here are some simple ways to start:

Share Your Core Values

Let your network know what your core values are through your actions. There are many ways to be intentional about this. For example, create an email signature line, a short blog that you share with others, get involved in your ERG and express your point of view, and make initiatives happen around that with your team.

Get Involved in Organizations that Align with Your Vision

Find out about organizations in your area that you can support. For example, if you like rescuing animals or supporting the elderly, then find organizations that help with those. Many leaders are eager to give back to the community. There are many ways to give back, including mentorship, donations, volunteering your time, etc. If you cannot find an organization that aligns with your vision right away, you can begin by getting people together for a common goal, even if it is not structured at the beginning. This is how you can begin giving back to the causes that matter to you the most.

Elevate Others

There is no better way to show how you value others than to honor them. Create a way to highlight people in the company or community. You will be known for taking the time to genuinely recognize others and they will totally appreciate it. There is nothing more beautiful than to serve others and be known as someone that truly cares. I have known many leaders that created blogs, books, awards programs, special annual lists, mentions that showcase the expertise and accomplishments of others, and there is always a positive response to that.

Become a Thought Leader

There are so many mediums to express your thoughts nowadays. Use your time wisely and intentionally to comment on industry news, relevant news, and accomplishments of others. Dedicate 10 minutes daily to this activity so that you can be known for your thoughts and ideas and start to get recognized for your contributions. Reach out to industry trade publications to pitch your point of view in the form subject matter articles that express your opinions.

Start Mentoring Others

Someone needs your advice, experience, and knowledge today. Look around you. People in the same department, industry, or community are seeking a mentor that cares. You can be that person that others need. Share your expertise with others and help them reach new heights. When you make time to intentionally help, others notice and the fabric of your reputation continues to grow and expand. Your opinion truly matters.

Start Writing

My German teacher once told me, "Writing is an extension of your soul." I was only 16 years old and perhaps I did not understand the true meaning of this profound quote. It wasn't until I went through a near-death experience at the age of 23 that I started living to write and writing to live in every medium I can think of, from journals to blogs to 32 books! There is something magical about writing and expressing what is inside of you—one of the most powerful ways to create legacy.

Advocating for yourself is an ongoing process. There are many ways to do it and the most important thing to remember is to stay authentic to yourself. There are so many ways to spread your legacy and to share what you stand for. The best time to start is today!

Personal Insight 4: Anthony López, Founder L&L Advisors, Senior Executive, CEO, Board Member, Leadership Expert and Author, Leadership & Management Consultant and Executive Coach.

ADVOCATING FOR YOUSELF

As I considered what the first paragraph of this short chapter should be, I found myself struggling to come up with the words. For days and even weeks, I thought about it, and even now as I pen these words, I am not exactly sure what my fingers would type next. Then it dawned on me that this is precisely the point or, perhaps better stated, the problem! Sometimes, especially for Latinos, we don't know how to self-advocate. So, when I was asked to write a few pages on how we should advocate for ourselves, I thought, I wish someone had given me the answer to that mystery early in my professional career!

Advocating for oneself is not comfortable for most people. As part of our Latino culture, most of us are thought to be humble thus making this idea of "promoting ourselves" rather a foreign concept. I suppose those of us who struggle with self-advocating likely feel it may be perceived as arrogant or narcissistic to speak about our own abilities, skills, accomplishments, and goals. I can speak from personal experience that, depending on how and when you go about self-advocating, it can either be a smart career move or a derailing one. Regrettably, other factors may come into play as well, including the culture of the organization you are in, perhaps dimensions of diversity become a consideration, and certainly our own style and how we come across, among others.

Here's what I have learned over my thirty-five-year career: first, self-advocating is not easy, may not be comfortable, but we must learn to do it and do it well. Second, there is a right way and a wrong way to self-advocate. The right way includes, making sure the timing of it is appropriate, that we have planned the discussion with the person or persons we are intending to self-advocate with, and that we are prepared to hear (and act on) feedback that we may receive. Third and most importantly, I believe we must be ready! By that I mean, if we are going to self-advocate, we must prioritize our efforts effectively. This means that we must have prepared ourselves well through our education, experiences, and track record of success to be credible in our move to self-advocate.

From my experience, I think there are some key actions that we can take throughout our career to always be in a strong position to be able to advocate for ourselves. They are:

- **Always be learning.** You should educate yourself—both formally and informally—constantly. Stay informed by reading, paying attention to global news, stay current on global social and economic trends, and become an expert in your field.
- **Always deliver results.** Results matter! They are our track-record and something that is undeniable. Thus, we should focus on doing a great job in all that we do so that we gain a reputation for delivering great results.
- **Become an effective communicator.** Seems almost trivial to have to list this as a criterion for success, however it really is that important. Being an effective communicator is directly related to our ability to influence outcomes, and that is what leaders must be able to do extremely well. Additionally, if you speak with an accent or struggle with speaking English (for those in the USA), remember that

you know at least two languages! Most people in the world speak only one, so that makes you a rather smart person. Additionally, practice drives improvement, so work at it, and never let that become a barrier to you leaning into the conversations.

- **Be a connector.** Most people focus on networking to get to know other people and be known by other people; and that is not a bad thing. However, what you should try to become is a "connector" enabling other people to network with each other. Gain a reputation for being someone who helps bring other influential people together. That makes you a part of a more powerful triangle of key people.

- **Evolve yourself to develop a high level of emotional intelligence (EQ) and a high level of cultural intelligence (CQ).** As leaders our ability to connect across emotional barriers and be empathetic, as well as be effective across all dimensions of difference (not just cultural ones), will determine how good we are as leaders. Thus, we should work hard to become high EQ and CQ leaders.

- **Pace yourself.** Your career is a marathon and not a sprint. Thus plan your moves carefully and over a longer period. Don't be in a "career rush," but also don't sit on the sidelines too long. Like most things in life, it's about balance.

- **Ask to be mentored and sponsored.** Some people have asked me, what is the difference between a mentor and a sponsor? The answer is rather simple: a mentor shows you the way, a sponsor clears the way! Anyone can be a mentor to you if they have experience and wisdom that they can share with you and help you to think through things in your life. They may or may not be in a position to enable you or open doors to help accelerate your career, but their advice may certainly be key to your success. This is especially important as a mentor's advice can keep you from making silly mistakes.

Sponsors on the other hand, may be good mentors as well, but the difference is that they are indeed in a position of influence or power, and can—through their direct action or through the influence of others—enable your next promotion or career move. The next question I hear often is, do I need a mentor or sponsor? The answer is yes! You need both. Seek them out and ask them to take you on as your mentor or sponsor. This is not a time to be shy. If you have done all that you needed to be prepared, ready, and able, then you have as much right as anyone else to be mentored and sponsored. One last thought on mentors and sponsors: be one yourself! Always look to be helpful to others in their journey. I find it not only educational for myself when I have done that, but quite rewarding.

If you are like most of us, and struggle with the idea of self-advocating, I trust you will be encouraged by this: believe in yourself and remember that you have worked very hard to achieve all that you have. Continue to learn, evolve, and grow personally and professionally. Ask for help! Ask to be mentored and sponsored! Certainly, you should ask for stretch assignments. Most certainly, when appropriate and earned, absolutely ask for that promotion you have worked for.

Being a self-advocate is not being arrogant or narcissistic. If you are a life-long learner, action and results oriented, a great communicator, focused on the long-term, a student of EQ and CQ, and you pace your career, you have every right to advocate for yourself. In the end, your success is your own doing.

One last thought: when you achieve your inevitable success, reach down, and offer a hand-up to as many people as you can and enjoy the journey with them.

DOS AND DON'TS

Now that we have covered the background, stories, and insights into how to advocate for yourself, here are some additional Dos and Don'ts to further support your development in this area.

PART 2: HOW TO ADVOCATE FOR YOURSELF

Dos	Don'ts
Do: Take on Opportunities Nobody Else Will This is a great way to set yourself apart from the rest as a leader. Being a fearless problem-solver is a brand attribute that is desired in the workplace. It shows your agility, your confidence, and your commitment to driving value in the organization—regardless if in your comfort zone or not. Taking on these opportunities will set you up for the next steps of your career.	**Don't: Forget to Share Your Career Aspirations** Think through where you want to take your career and communicate it. Utilize research and the support of your manager, trusted advisors, mentors, and sponsors to develop a career plan. Once developed, be able to concisely communicate it and make it part of your story; don't forget to revisit it at least twice a year and refine as needed.
Do: Define Your Brand and Narrative Think through your brand, what you want your story to be, what your growth plan is, and how you plan to communicate it. Knowing these elements will set the stage for how you will communicate to your direct manager and everyone else in your organization. It will show you have direction, confidence, and purpose in your career journey.	**Don't: Forget to Advocate for Others** It's just as important to advocate for others as it is for ourselves. Doing so for others shows maturity and leadership—part of your leadership journey is to develop other leaders. Advocating for great talent (Latino and non-Latino) shows the organization you are non-biased and supportive in helping elevate those that can help the organization reach its goals.
Do: Embrace Your Culture Leverage the Latino culture and values to your advantage. Leverage our natural passion and pride, our hard work ethic, our ability to connect with others, our ability to collaborate, and our respect for others to drive value in your teams and across the organization. These are trademark traits that differentiate us and will be even more important as we begin to master the leadership concepts in this book.	**Don't: Forget to Have a Plan to Address Limitations** Take time to understand your skill gaps and develop a plan for how you will/are addressing them. Work closely with your manager on this task so you are aligned on where and how you are going to develop. Once this is in place, you will be able to talk about this plan as you communicate. Senior leaders will be interested to know what you are doing to improve yourself; having a well-thought-out plan shows personal leadership and confidence in where you are going.

Do: Operate with a Focus on the Business One of the best ways to advocate for yourself is tying everything you do to business goals, priorities, and objectives. It shows you are in tune to what's important for the company, your business unit, and your team. Be able to clearly articulate how your work supports specific goals and use your passion to show how important it is to you to drive value for the organization. This will help you stand out.	**Don't: Forget to Use Thoughtful, Crisp Communications** When speaking to and communicating to senior leaders, you want to make sure you prepare and practice how to communicate. Whether it be verbal or written, make sure you get the point quickly and concise—be sure to cover what they need to hear, say, do. They will be interested most in how the business is impacted, any risks they need to be aware of, and any decisions they need to make.
Do: Use Every Moment to Advocate for Yourself In my opinion, ALL interactions matter—business updates, meetings, social events, water cooler discussions, etc. If you are serious about showcasing your brand and advocating for yourself, then you need to prepare well and show up at all times. Your image, leadership behaviors, messaging, attitude, and communication style *always need to be on point*. You will find that consistently showing up with your A-game and executing against your plan will shift the narrative to where you want it to be!	**Don't: Forget to Get Personal** Take advantage of our natural ability to connect with others and get personal. Develop a plan for those in your organization who you need to connect with to advance your career—see the Networking Chapter later in this book. Take time to learn about your colleagues' worlds and share parts of yours. Work hard to develop rapport with those in your organization and on your teams; using your natural Latino ability to connect with others is an asset that can open doors for your career as well as helping the careers of others.

In addition to the insights captured in this chapter, I developed this framework to help you think through target areas to incorporate into your plan as you improve upon how to advocate for yourself. As you can see, it's much more than talking about yourself; it's showcasing your brand and how you operate.

PART 2: HOW TO ADVOCATE FOR YOURSELF

THE LATINO LEADERSHIP ADVOCATING FOR YOURSELF MODEL

Lead with Confidence, Passion, and Conviction

Lead with vision/ideas	Always be well-prepared	Take extreme ownership
Be a confident communicator	On-point image / presence	Go above and beyond
Be impact- and results-focused	Be an effective collaborator	Be able to articulate your brand

RECAP

As you can see, advocating for yourself can be done in many different ways and it's all in the spirit of promoting your brand and the value you bring to the organization. The stories and insights shared are to help differentiate you in your respective organization. Keep in mind that you don't have to do everything in this section to be an impact player—pick and choose the elements that best fit the needs for your situation and develop a plan to build your capabilities one-by-one and in the timeframe that works best for you. I cannot tell you how important the relationship you have with your direct manager is in planning for and executing on your development plan—this collaboration will be critical and, if done effectively, you will find that your manager will also advocate for you!

PLANNING AND ACTIVATING YOUR DEVELOPMENT

To support your development and to help you organize and activate the concepts in this chapter, please go to my website (www.refugioatilano.com) and download the free templates for **The Latino Leadership Workbook**—this is a great set of tools to help organize your target areas and map a plan on where to focus your growth. It also includes a notes page and a development roadmap template so you can begin to think through and draft your personalized improvement plan that will set you up for maximum growth and success.

How to Effectively Challenge Authority

> "It is not enough these days to simply QUESTION AUTHORITY. You have to speak with it, too."
>
> – Taylor Mali

Like many of us, I was raised to NEVER challenge or disrespect my parents and elders within my (or anyone else's) family. It was a no-go, a non-negotiable, a non-starter—that's the way it was growing up and continues for me today for me as an adult. As Kim Keller wrote in a Fox News opinion article, "Respect for parents and elders is important to Latinos. It's not oppression or a dominance issue; it's just the way things are" (2013). This mindset applies to parents, grandparents, and other relatives.

> "Respect for parents and elders is important to Latinos. It's not oppression or a dominance issue; it's just the way things are." - Kim Keller

MY FATHER: THE PATRIACH

I come from a very large family where my father is the patriarch. He is The One everyone in our family has gone to for advice and blessings. He has always been a natural leader, a great friend, a great husband, and a great father. He always took time to help others in need; no matter if they were family or not. He was always there—just a great human being. Even with his recent major stroke that took a lot of his physical and cognitive abilities away, he is still regarded as our family leader and remains strongly influential within our family. His inner strength and the way he has handled himself post-stroke has given me the determination and inspiration to give you all of me and write this book.

PART 2: HOW TO EFFECTIVELY CHALLENGE AUTHORITY

I still remember the one and ONLY day I ever challenged an elder and it was in front of my father. I was in 6th grade and my parents were called into school with me and my teacher to discuss my conduct. Admittedly, I was not the best when it came to behaving in the classroom and, although I definitely was at fault for some of the issues, it was a group of us that were causing problems. So, the teacher tells my parents about my behavior and how I was disrupting class (which I was), and I remember voicing my opinion back to her that I was not the only one. That was a mistake. Let's just say my father took that moment to show he was not pleased and made sure I never did anything like that ever again. I definitely touched a hot stove in that moment and quickly learned about the lesson of respect at all times. My father used to tell me, "Even when I'm wrong, I'm right." It sounds a little funny later in life but going through it definitely kept us in line.

I use this story to illustrate how we, as Latinos (generally speaking), are raised with this absolute respect of authority. So, when we arrive in the workplace, many of us don't make the mindset shift that we can actually speak up, provide our perspectives, and respectfully challenge our manager and/or senior leadership. This lack of an effective bicultural shift around this topic is a limiting barrier for us and something we need to be aware of and develop strategies on how to overcome in the workplace. As Dr. Robert Rodriguez wrote in *Auténtico*, "Given the deeply held value of family and its inherently hierarchical structures, they tend to be more deferential to authority. This leads to the passivity more prevalent among Latino talent" (174).

When we arrive in the workplace, many of us don't make the mindset shift that we can actually speak up, provide our perspectives, and respectfully challenge our manager and/or senior leadership.

MAKING THE SHIFT: CREATING THE CAPABILITY TO RESPECTFULLY CHALLENGE AUTHORITY

"Biting our tongues when the boss is around is a natural instinct for most of us, but employment experts say regularly challenging your superiors could be a good thing for your career—provided you are smart about it. Choosing your words carefully and finding the right forum to express your challenge could boost your career prospects, rather than damaging them, but it's important to get to know your boss well before speaking your mind" (Clark, 2017).

As Latinos trying to improve our impact in the workplace, we must now add this capability to our impact toolkit. Understanding, appreciating, and respecting how we obey authority is something we will always have in our culture - in the workplace, we must be able to make the leap to challenge authority *respectfully and effectively* when needed. This is an example of the bicultural mindset shift we need to make towards changing the game. We must be aware of and overcome our natural tendency to not challenge authority and begin to develop and implement strategies that showcase our great ideas and perspectives that can add value in new ways for the companies who employ us.

> Understanding, appreciating, and respecting how we obey authority is something we will always have in our culture - in the workplace, we must be able to make the leap to challenge authority respectfully and effectively when needed.

You will find that balancing both your Latino culture and corporate culture effectively is a skill that will take time to develop—with practice and support, you will become a pro in no time. The key thing for you is to realize there are two cultures at play and it will be critical that you effectively navigate both, especially if you want to position yourself to drive your career forward. Here are some stories and insights that helped shape my career that I will pass on to you as you continue your leadership development journey.

SPECIAL NOTE: *I am not advocating for you to begin to go out and challenge your manager or other senior leaders for the sake of doing it; instead, this chapter is focused on strategies to help you present ideas thoughtfully and effectively for times when you have to present a new idea and/or proposals that might go against the grain in your company.*

Personal Insight 1: Refugio A. Atilano, Business Leader at a Top-10 Pharma Company, ERG/DEI Leader, Author, *The Latino Leadership Playbook*

SCANNING AND UNDERSTANDING YOUR ENVIRONMENT

Before thinking about challenging authority in any situation, it will be critical you first understand the environment and culture of your company and immediate team. I have seen environments that are very supportive of collaboration and ideas; I have also experienced environments that are very hierarchical and stay-in-your lane focused.

For example, in one of my previous companies as a senior program manager, it was made very clear that my job and the expectation of me was to only focus on my responsibilities—nothing else outside. It was a chain-of-command culture and we were instructed not to deviate. I remember that cross-functional senior level communication was not advised and there was a lot of scrutiny on how we operated across the organization. It was clear that our "order" was to deliver on projects using stringent PM methodology, period. That is exactly what I did and did it as well as I could to help our business meet its goals.

Based on the team culture vs. the way I lead (very collaborative and relationship-oriented), it definitely led to a constant struggle in philosophy. However, I had to abide by the rules of the road and do my job... if I wanted to continue working there. In this scenario, I did not challenge authority and/or offer my ideas for improvement because they were not wanted or appreciated. This led to a bigger question for me about making sure my style and cultural beliefs are aligned with the company's values and beliefs. I am sharing this as you navigate your career—working for companies aligned with your values will improve your happiness, engagement, and opportunity for overall growth and success. The lesson of this story is to always make sure to scan the environment of your organization and immediate team and confirm that you have the support and a culture that allows for the respectful challenging of authority.

Before thinking about challenging authority in any situation—it will be critical you first understand the environment and culture of your company and immediate team.

Personal Insight 2: Refugio A. Atilano, Business Leader at a Top-10 Pharma Company, ERG/DEI Leader, Author, *The Latino Leadership Playbook*

WHAT EFFECTIVELY CHALLENGING AUTHORITY LOOKS LIKE

Although I can't get into company names, there are many great ones out there that are very supportive of sharing ideas and perspectives of all its employees to help achieve its goals. One of the best examples is around one of my ERGs taking the lead in a company-wide integrated strategy initiative to drive Latino talent into the organization. The norm in these situations is for the Talent Acquisition team to take lead in recruiting all talent for the organization. However, our company culture in this case is for everyone to take a leadership role, regardless of where you are within the organization.

That's exactly what me and my team did—we developed a vision, strategy, and game plan for how to leverage our Latino professional organization partnerships to drive talent into the organization. We had access to this great talent source and quickly aligned with Talent Acquisition and other teams to help refine and get behind our plan to drive value for the organization. They also helped us articulate its value across the organization, helped us obtain additional resources, and it ended up being a good win for our company. This was definitely outside the norm, and that was okay. We were all focused on the same goal and we had an on-ramp to attract more talent in new ways. It was an easy sell, and we were able to secure the resources, alignment, and recognition for our work. This was a great example of taking a leadership role to effectively challenge authority/norms for the benefit of our company. We had a great strategy, plan, and the people needed to execute.

> This was a great example of taking a leadership role to effectively challenge authority/norms for the benefit of our company.

Personal Insight 3: Refugio A. Atilano, Business Leader at a Top-10 Pharma Company, ERG/DEI Leader, Author, *The Latino Leadership Playbook*

CHALLENGING AND COLLABORATING WITH YOUR BOSS

I have another useful story to share about how to effectively challenge your boss and have it become more of a collaboration session. I had a recent discussion with my direct manager on how to approach assessing the resource impact of a project on our organization. The output of this work was a big deal for our executives and we had to make sure to get it right so we can make sound business decisions. Although he had his thoughts and I had mine, we were able to have a healthy debate and come up with a joint plan based on both of our perspectives.

First, my boss and I have a good relationship and trust that we can have professional debates and discussions on any topic. Second, we had the discussion privately in our one-on-one. This ensured we had a safe space to share our perspectives without judgement or with the dynamic of others around. Third, I did my homework—I was ready for the discussion. I thought through all scenarios, impacts, and the plan to get us to the end state. I was able to state my case concisely and confidently so that my manager knew I was prepared for the discussion and to execute the plan.

This is an example of what effective challenging looks like. As stated earlier, it's also an opportunity to showcase your preparation, your confidence, and your ability to navigate solutioning discussions. When done right, challenging authority is an opportunity to showcase your preparation, your confidence, and your ability to innovate to drive the business forward.

> When done right, challenging authority is an opportunity to showcase your preparation, your confidence, and your ability to innovate to drive the business forward.

Personal Insight 4: Miguel A. de Jesús, Adjunct Faculty, Director of Business Development | College of Business Administration, California State University San Marcos

HOW TO DISAGREE WITHOUT BEING DISAGREEABLE: NAVIGATING DIFFERENCES WITH GRACE AND RESPECT

In today's interconnected world, differences of opinion are

bound to arise. Recommendations may not be accepted or approved. Ideas must be adequately discussed or elevated for more available group discussion. Whether in the workplace, within your social circles, or even in family discussions, the ability to disagree without being disagreeable is an invaluable skill that fosters healthy communication, maintains relationships, and leads to productive outcomes.

UNDERSTANDING THE IMPORTANCE OF CONSTRUCTIVE DISAGREEMENT

Constructive disagreement catalyzes growth and innovation. By exchanging diverse perspectives, new ideas emerge, and existing ones are refined. However, the key lies in how these disagreements are approached and communicated. Instead of fostering hostility, a well-managed difference of opinion can lead to enhanced understanding and collaboration.

THE ROLE OF EMOTIONAL INTELLIGENCE IN DISAGREEMENTS

Emotional intelligence (EI) plays a crucial role in navigating disagreements effectively. It involves recognizing and managing your own emotions, as well as understanding and empathizing with the emotions of others. You can create a more empathetic and conducive environment for reaching agreements by harnessing EI. While we will not be discussing this topic at any great length, please note that there are four areas of Emotional Intelligence which are:

- Self-Awareness
- Self-Management
- Social Awareness
- Relationship Management

STRATEGIES FOR REACHING AGREEMENT AND FOSTERING CHANGE

1. *Active Listening with Empathy*

   Practice active listening by genuinely focusing on the speaker without interrupting or formulating your response. Combine this with empathy, where you try to understand not only the words being said but also the underlying emotions and motivations.

2. *Framing the Discussion Positively*

   Frame the conversation positively by highlighting shared goals and common interests. This approach shifts the focus from differences to collaborative problem-solving.

3. *Acknowledging Valid Points*

   Acknowledge the valid points made by the other party. This demonstrates respect for their perspective and encourages reciprocity, making them more likely to consider your viewpoint.

4. *Finding Middle Ground*

   Identify areas of compromise where both parties can make concessions. This helps bridge the gap between differing viewpoints and facilitates agreement.

5. *Exploring Alternatives*

   Encourage creative thinking by exploring alternative solutions that address the concerns of both parties. This approach widens the range of possibilities and can lead to innovative outcomes.

6. *Utilizing Nonverbal Communication*

   Pay attention to nonverbal cues such as body language and facial expressions. These cues can provide insights into the emotions behind the words and guide your responses.

7. *Continual Learning and Improvement*

   View each disagreement as an opportunity to learn and improve your communication skills. Embrace a growth mindset that values ongoing development in your ability to reach agreements.

PART 2: HOW TO EFFECTIVELY CHALLENGE AUTHORITY

FOSTERING POSITIVE CHANGE IN THE WORKPLACE THROUGH CONSTRUCTIVE DISAGREEMENT

By combining emotional intelligence with effective communication strategies, you can drive meaningful change in the following ways:

1. *Cultivating a Culture of Respect*

   Promote a workplace culture that values respectful communication and encourages employees to express diverse viewpoints. When individuals feel heard and respected, they are more likely to contribute to positive change.

2. *Encouraging Employee Involvement*

   Invite employees to participate in decision-making processes. Their unique insights and perspectives can lead to well-rounded solutions that drive positive change.

3. *Promoting Learning and Development*

   Offer training programs focusing on emotional intelligence, active listening, and effective communication. These skills empower employees to engage in constructive disagreements that drive positive change.

EMBRACING A CULTURE OF CONSTRUCTIVE DISAGREEMENT

In conclusion, mastering the art of disagreeing without being disagreeable is a multifaceted skill with the potential for positive change in various aspects of life, particularly in the workplace.

Here is an example of the biggest and boldest issue I have overcome in a corporate environment:

The corporation, in my opinion, desperately needed additional automation. I had expert skills and knowledge in this area to support and personally present a business case for an investment of $5M to the CEO. I discussed it with my boss, who discussed the proposal with the CEO. My proposal to "pilot" a sales force automation project for an investment of $5M was not supported by the CEO upon the presentation by my boss.

So, the CEO setup up an appointment with me in headquarters to make a presentation. I was well prepared for what turned out to be a 3-hour 1:1 presentation, the longest one in my career of more than 40+ years.

KEY TAKEAWAYS:

- Be very, very, very prepared.
- Refrain from attempting to change too much of the culture too fast.
- Understand the impacts on all the company's stakeholders and take personal responsibility for the flawless implementation of program concepts.
- Surround yourself with a competent team of people who believe what you believe.

The outcome of that discussion: I did not get approval for the $5M I requested, but I did get permission to proceed with the "Pilot Project" with $2.5M.

DOS AND DON'TS

Now that we have covered the background, stories, and insights around how to effectively challenge authority, here are some additional Dos and Don'ts to further support your development in this area.

PART 2: HOW TO EFFECTIVELY CHALLENGE AUTHORITY

Dos	Don'ts
Do: Do Your Homework—Know Your Stuff One of the most important elements of challenging others and making a case is to have a great grasp on your proposed solution. You must be able to think big picture, tie your proposal to corporate goals, have a vision, have a plan, and how you will own the execution. Show the common ground between other's solutions and yours and how you want to collaborate to make the best solution possible.	**Don't: Challenge in an Open Forum** This is where emotions and embarrassment can come into play and can be a detriment to your career. Instead, take the time you need to organize your thoughts/ideas and get in the right headspace to present your ideas thoughtfully and confidently in a safe space. Use scheduled 1:1s, ask for dedicated time, and always give a heads-up about what you'd like to discuss. A brief exec summary might even help the other person mentally prep for the discussion so that both parties are prepared to work through solutions.
Do: Always Operate from a Respectful Position Challenging effectively comes with the ability to approach the situation respectfully, positively, and with sincerity. It requires you to have an open mind and to check any (emotional) luggage at the door. Come in ready to respect their position, partner, collaborate, and articulate that you want to find joint solutions to help achieve business goals. This mindset and approach will take you a long way.	**Don't: Get Defensive; Know When to Walk Away** Although your manager or other senior leaders will appreciate a well-thought-through proposal, you must be prepared to accept that they will not always get approved. Approach these discussions with the mindset that you are both making a good-faith effort and at the end of the day, the leader needs to make a final call based on their understanding of the situation and needs of the business.
Do: Speak with Confidence When going in to challenge your boss or anyone else, in addition to being well-prepared, practice your delivery and anticipated questions/answers. Make sure to know the body language (upcoming chapter) that you want to use and practice it before the meeting. Putting all these pieces together shows that you are ready for the discussion, any questions, and you can deliver your message with precision. This is a great place to be!	**Don't: Forget to Ask if You Can Challenge** This is key in making sure the person is open and ready for a discussion on alternative solutions. Ask: "Do you mind if I challenge your thoughts on that? Or can I share an idea I had for us to consider?" This helps set up a safe space for an open discussion. *Make sure to ask these questions in private so that they don't feel attacked in a public setting.

Do: Present Your Proposal Thoughtfully	**Don't: Challenge Unless You Know You Can**
Know your data, facts, and figures. This is part of doing your homework—the more vetted your idea is, the more credible you will be and the more likely your proposal/challenge will have a positive outcome. Depending on the audience, put your proposal in an executive summary, short presentation, or other communication. This will help organize your thoughts and communicate your message.	Having a relationship with the person you are going to challenge is critical. You must know the person and make sure it is safe to challenge (per above). I want to make sure you are set up for success—that means a successful proposal, an opportunity to showcase your leadership, and finding new ways to collaborate with new senior level contacts.
Do: Ask Powerful Questions	**Don't: Forget to Test the Waters**
Instead of leading with conclusions, learn to generate and ask questions that will reveal a gap in the current thought processing. Delivered in a sincere, positive tone, this can lead to a new line of discussion and solutioning and can help reveal new outcomes. This will help build your brand as an innovative, solution-oriented thought leader who adds value.	Pressure test new ideas, facts, and hypotheses with subject matter experts. Make sure your story and pitch are air-tight, and that you have accounted for key scenarios. Also, test the receptiveness of your audience for the challenge—make sure they are ready to discuss your ideas. If you pick up any hesitation, be mindful of it and I would recommend to hold back until they are fully ready. Sometimes for business or personal reasons, they may never get there. Be sure to read these signs carefully before progressing.

RECAP

As a leader, you are and will be expected to add value, ideas, and perspectives to help drive your business forward—your company is counting on it and it's why they hired you. With the information presented in this chapter, you are now armed with the strategies and insights you need to respectfully and effectively challenge and bring new ideas to your manager and other senior leaders in your organization. You have also learned about when you might need to hold back. You are now prepared to walk into these situations with confidence, strong proposals, a positive and sincere attitude, and knowing that you are now ready to take your leadership game to the next level.

I still remember when I was first told that my ideas and perspectives were needed and expected—I felt like, "Wait. What! I can do that?" After that time, it was GAME ON! And from this point forward, I want it to be GAME ON for you too!

PLANNING AND ACTIVATING YOUR DEVELOPMENT

To support your development and to help you organize and activate the concepts in this chapter, please go to my website (www.refugioatilano.com) and download the free templates for **The Latino Leadership Workbook**—this is a great set of tools to help organize your target areas and map a plan on where to focus your growth. It also includes a notes page and a development roadmap template so you can begin to think through and draft your personalized improvement plan that will set you up for maximum growth and success.

When to Use a Family-First vs Me-First Approach

> *"Your individuality is important, but so is belonging. Recognize the parts of your culture that have shaped your past, and the parts you want to carry with you into the future."*
>
> **- Sol Peralta**

Our family-first mentality is a Latino superpower and one that can add a ton of value for your company performance and overall career. We are natural collaborators, supporters, and relationship builders... all attributes that are great for team settings. At the same time, we also must know when to put on the breaks and shift to a "me-first" approach. There will be times when we have to be *"front and center"* and talk about and present ourselves, our plans, and our accomplishments. To be a truly effective bi-cultural leader, mastering both sides of this topic will be critical for your leadership development and advancement.

> Our family-first mentality is a Latino superpower and one that can add a ton of value for your company performance and overall career. We are natural collaborators, supporters, and relationship builders... all attributes that are great for team settings.

THE FAMILY-FIRST DYNAMIC

"The family unit is the single most important unit in the Latino culture. It influences the perception and behavior of its members as to how they see the outside world. Latinas/os see themselves as representing their family in outside contacts" (Nicoletti, 2010).

PART 2: HOW TO EFFECTIVELY CHALLENGE AUTHORITY

Similarly, in an article from Dimensions of Culture, Marcia Carteret writes that, "Latinos tend to be highly group oriented. A strong emphasis is placed on family as the major source of one's identity and protection against the hardships of life. This sense of family belonging is intense and includes immediate/extended family and close friends" (2011).

When I think back all the way to my childhood and through today, my family and close friends remain at the top of the list of importance for me. In my mind, we come as ONE unit and there's nothing that separates us. We are like a strong chain-linked fence and everyone has a role to play. I still remember when growing up that I looked forward to every weekend and spending time with all my cousins—those bonds were made back then and haven't changed 40 years later. I also have the same core group of friends from when I was a kid—for us, we are family and I consider them all my brothers. I even carry that spirit into my company's Latino Employee Resource Group (ERG). As Latinos, we will go the extra mile to support each other and make sure everyone is taken care of—nobody is left behind. Family/team first, that's the way we are built!

BALANCING FAMILY-FIRST AND ME-FIRST APPOACHES IN THE WORKPLACE

"Family-First"

Our family (team) first approach is definitely something we should bring to the table in the workplace to drive value—one of the immediate impacts that we can make with this capability is to bring a stronger sense of community, collaboration, and support to our teams. If we can bring this natural ability to our professions and incorporate these powerful Latino scripts into how our teams operate, it can create greater unity, synergy, engagement, and business results! This is where the magic is. If you can do this effectively, you will begin to add being a great *collaborator* and *team leader* to your brand. This is a great position to be in.

I think we all know that Latinos love our parties and get-togethers—this is very important in our community and for the bonds we create. However, as Dr. Rodriguez writes in *Auténtico*, "The high value of community is not just about work-related get-togethers. It shows up in how many Latinos would prefer that workplace performance would be more about group results than individual results. There is a high sense of importance in achieving group goals, a desire to have equal distribution of regard within a group, and a strong sense of loyalty to the group" (178). I think Dr. Rodriguez hits the nail on the head, in short, for us Latinos, it's all about the team—period.

> Our family first approach is definitely something we should bring to the table in the workplace to drive value— one of the immediate impacts that we can make with this capability is to bring a stronger sense of community, collaboration, and support to our teams.

"Me-First"

Now let's talk about the need for the "me-first" approach

in the workplace. Yes, this is VERY UNNATURAL and UNCOMFORTABLE for many of us and one of the areas where I get the most feedback from Latinos. As such, we will take our time walking through this topic in this chapter.

As you know, my singular focus is to help develop you into a confident, informed, promotion-ready leader. In order to get there, it's critical that you are in the best position to compete with non-Latinos for the coveted positions you are seeking. Part of that readiness is being able to lead with a me-first approach (also known as advocating for yourself) when the time requires it—this is critical. Developing this skill will require a commitment to the process, the courage to know you can make this leap, and the practice required so you hit the mark when you need to effectively deliver your message.

The following will cover several stories and insights from various professionals that you can use for your personal development. Don't forget, your development is a life-long journey. I highly encourage you to use your mentor/sponsor network, trusted advisors, and connect with all the great Latino/non-Latino leader talent in this book (via LinkedIn). We are all here to support your growth and help you make the leap on this challenging topic. We got your back!

Personal Insight 1: Refugio A. Atilano, Business Leader at a Top-10 Pharma Company, ERG/DEI Leader, Author, *The Latino Leadership Playbook*

USING MY FAMILY-FIRST APPROACH TO DRIVE MY CAREER

I lead with an abundance mentality and am a strong believer in that, "If we all don't make it; none of us makes it." Throughout my career, I have had the reputation of being the connector that brings everything and everyone together. This has served me well, especially as a program manager and ERG leader who is responsible for leading large global teams. I am even using the same approach in writing this book. I have connected with some of the most influential Latino and Latina leaders today and have brought everyone together to create an exceptional leadership toolkit for all of you!

For me, genuine relationships and connections are the foundation to all work. I go above and beyond to getting to know the person first before any work is done. This has been my super-power and one that I put an extreme amount of focus and energy into. I developed this skill easily because of how I was raised as a Latino; I learned it early in life from my father who seemed to always be surrounded by great friends and a large family. I saw the power, and love, in numbers and how the quality of each relationship was important to him. I have now implemented those same lessons into my career and it's one of the things that sets me apart.

> For me, genuine relationships and connections are the foundation to all work. I go above and beyond to getting to know the person first before any work is done. This has been my super-power and one that I put an extreme amount of focus and energy into.

If there's one thing I want you to take away from this section, it's to use your natural ability to connect with and help others. Focus and work hard to establish a reputation as someone who connects well with others, someone who is a great team player/collaborator, someone who supports their team (servant leadership), someone who is relatable and personable, and someone who will go above and beyond for a team member. This approach will begin to shift your brand in new ways. People will start asking to work with you, people will be more open to advocating for you, and you will start to open new doors for yourself as you drive your career forward!

Personal Insight 2: Refugio A. Atilano, Business Leader at a Top-10 Pharma Company, ERG/DEI Leader, Author, The Latino Leadership Playbook

PART 2: HOW TO EFFECTIVELY CHALLENGE AUTHORITY

LEARNING TO MAKE THE SHIFT TO A ME-FIRST APPROACH

I lost a great job opportunity with a great company earlier in my career because I didn't know about the importance of advocating for myself in the job interview. I remember going and being so excited about interviewing for the job, which was a promotion, and feeling great about how the interviews went. I was so pumped about talking about all the great accomplishments of "my team" and everything "we" have done to meet business targets. Unknowingly, this was the kiss of death for my candidacy.

> I was so pumped about talking about all the great accomplishments of "my team" and everything "we" have done to meet business targets. Unknowingly, this was the kiss of death for my candidacy.

When I was told I didn't get the position, I remember being in disbelief! How could they pass up on a rock star like me who has led several teams to bring new solutions to market? It didn't make sense, that's until I was given interview feedback by my manager. The theme from all the interviewers was that they understood what the team did, but did not understand the "value I brought to the table as an individual." I quickly discovered that I undersold myself and was not effective in showcasing my capabilities, my passions, my talents, and my potential impact for the role. Yeah, I NEVER made this mistake again.

The lesson here is to make sure you learn how to effectively sell yourself and how to advocate for yourself in the right situations, i.e., 1:1s with your manager, meet and greets with senior leaders, job interviews, etc. We will cover more elements of this topic in the "How to Build and Leverage Your Brand" chapter later. Make sure to always scan the environment and identify when you have to pivot to a "me-first" approach, so you are delivering powerful messages to the right audiences at the right time. Developing this capability will be key to help showcase your brand and value, help you land opportunities, open new doors, as well as better position you in front of senior leaders who might be interested in potentially mentoring or sponsoring you.

Always scan the environment and quickly identify when you have to lead with a "me-first" approach so you are delivering powerful messages to the right audiences that can influence your career growth.

Personal Insight 3: Mimi Garcia, Senior Manager, Growth Strategy & Innovation, Accenture Song

ADVOCATING FOR YOURSELF

One of the most pivotal points in my career happened while I was aiming for an early promotion.

My mentor encouraged me to go for the new role after realizing I was already performing at a managerial level. At the time, I was overseeing coworkers who were also up for promotion and working alongside a peer pushing to become a manager, too. All year long, I was not only focused on delivering quality work, but helping develop my team members and advocating for them. I regularly shared details about the contributions, growth, and value they were providing, helping leadership keep a pulse on their accomplishments.

At the same time, I never vocalized my own ambitions to get promoted, instead believing my work would speak for itself. While preparing for my performance review, I asked leadership to support me in my efforts to get promoted. Instead of support, I was met with shock. They had no idea I was seeking a promotion. I was heartbroken, embarrassed, and frustrated by their reaction. It was a tough pill to swallow knowing I had advocated for those around me but failed to be direct about what I wanted and, frankly, deserved.

Vocalizing my accomplishments was an uncomfortable space for me, but I quickly learned I needed to deal with discomfort if I ever expected to progress in my career. I recognize that I'm in the driver seat, no one else is going to speak to MY story as well as I will because it's mine. Since then, I've been promoted twice, currently serving as a Senior Manager within my firm.

Now, I put intentional effort towards making my ambitions for career progression clear to leadership. I seek actionable feedback to ensure I'm clear on my role's expectations and bring leadership along on my journey. My advice to anyone looking to advance in their career is to be comfortable with being uncomfortable. Don't let anyone, not even yourself, get in the way of reaching the heights you're working towards.

Key Takeaways:
- Don't assume leadership knows your ambitions or goals simply because you're delivering high quality work.
- It's important to pull others up with you, but don't lose sight of pushing for yourself.
- You are in the driver seat of your career—it's your job to advocate for yourself and seek your path for growth.

Personal Insight 4: Angel Gomez, President, AG Gomez Consulting, LLC

THOUGHTS ON COLLECTIVISM

In November of 2017, Facebook invited me and my colleague, Dr. Robert Rodriguez, to run a workshop for their Latino and Latina employees at their annual Latino Leadership Day near their headquarters in Menlo Park, California. It was an inspirational day filled with phenomenal speakers, both internal and external to the company. The day was broken up into plenary sessions, motivational speeches, fireside chats, and hands-on workshops, like the one we were asked to deliver. I was so excited to take part in that day.

Dr. Rodriguez and I ran our workshop for about 100 people focused on understanding the needs of others as a way of practicing inclusive collaboration. Those needs included the desire for achievement at work, the necessity for control of how the work gets done, and the need to work collaboratively with others. We delivered the workshop in the context of the Latino Cultural Script, which is a set of deeply rooted cultural norms that impact how Latino and Latina talent choose to inclusively collaborate with others at work. After running this particular session, it became clear to all of us in the hall that those participating over-indexed on the need to work collaboratively with others—that they were operating under the Latino cultural script of "Collectivism."

Collectivism is a script that values the interdependence among people and is deeply engrained in many Latin American cultures. Collectivists see themselves as connected to others and often define their identity in relationship to others, like membership in a group, a community, or family. As a result, maintaining harmony among members of the collective becomes a high priority.

For Latinos and Latinas there are tremendous benefits to playing the role of a collectivist at work. Our culture teaches us to be good team players, which is essential in any organization. It also promotes the needs of the many over the needs of the few (or the one), which perpetuates inclusion. We know how to get along with others and avoid social conflict which can often fester in team environments.

But playing a collectivist role at work can also have its drawbacks. As we ended our breakout session at Facebook, we were invited to the great hall to attend a fireside chat with none other than Sheryl Sandberg, then COO of Facebook. Sheryl shared her story of growing up in Miami, FL, the influence of Cuban American culture on her and how she tends to view the world. Not surprisingly, she was informative, charming, inspirational, and quick to act from the learnings of the day.

During her Q&A session, a young Latina in recruiting stepped up to the microphone to recant a story of a panel interview she had with a fellow Latina candidate for a key position at Facebook.

PART 2: HOW TO EFFECTIVELY CHALLENGE AUTHORITY

She told Sheryl that every time the interviewers asked the Latina candidate for examples of prior experiences, she answered with "We did..." and only responded with "I did..." when pressed by the recruiter and the panel to speak to her actual accomplishments. The Latina candidate was playing the role of a collectivist, downplaying her individual contributions in service of others—and this is how collectivism can hurt advancement—by over-focusing on the "we" and not the "I," which is critical in American corporate culture.

The recruiter continued with her story and how the rest of the panel did not look upon the Latina candidate favorably because of her responses. But the recruiter stood her ground, explained the cultural influences that were at play and convinced the group to extend an offer to the Latina candidate, despite the initial impact of her answers. Sheryl was shocked, yet grateful that the young recruiter had the wherewithal to educate others and advocate for her fellow Latina. She commended the recruiter and pledged to do more to educate hiring managers on the nuances of interviewing people of color.

Dr. Rodriguez and I cover these issues in our Latino Leadership Intensive seminars that we host on the campus of Harvard, Stanford, and the University of Chicago for upwardly mobile Latino and Latina talent every year. While companies, like Facebook, have a responsibility to improve the interviewing capabilities of their hiring managers, we teach our participants that they too must be hyper-aware of their cultural influences and on how they show up in work situations. It is only through a heightened level of awareness that they can strategically use or modify their behaviors to accelerate their advancement.

Key Takeaways:
- Collectivism is a Latino cultural superpower that drives teamwork, collaboration, and sets up those who identify and lean into the cultural norm for future leadership success.
- Collectivism, left un-checked, will not be useful in many corporate American business ritual like interviews or performance reviews where the focus is primarily on your individual performance and not on others.

DOS AND DON'TS

Now that we have covered the background, stories, and insights around when to use a family-first vs me-first approach, here are some additional Dos and Don'ts to further support your development in this area.

Special Note: *Because of the bi-cultural nature of this section, I am going to restructure the following insights between the Family-first vs. Me-first approaches to summarize when to use each one for maximum impact.*

Family First	Me First
Team and Group Settings Be sure to leverage your natural family-first approach in team/group settings, either as the leader or an active participant. Use this natural super-power to take care of your team's needs, listen to them, help them, be a sounding board for team members, and be a great partner and promote strong collaboration by leading through example. Approach each team situation as you would at home—*think through* and find ways to contribute and "bring something to the table" that will add impact for your team and your business.	**Don't: Challenge in an Open Forum** Make sure to shift to the "me-first" mindset whenever in interviews. The interviewers will want to know what you bring to the table, not your team. Be ready to articulate your unique value, skills, accomplishments, and passion when interviewing—remember to talk in terms of "I..." This single shift will be very impactful for your ability to showcase your brand and value... and better position you to land that great job!
Network and Relationship Development Leveraging your natural ability to connect with others at *all levels* of the organization will be critical towards your success as you move into senior roles. Be yourself, be vulnerable, be passionate, and be real. Also, make a focused effort on building relationships with those around the organization that can help influence your career, your development, as well as connect with those where you can help others do the same.	**Don't: Get Defensive; Know When to Walk Away** These are natural settings to discuss yourself with other leaders. Whether it's talking to your manager or other senior leaders about your goals, accomplishments, thought processes, or career aspirations, you are in a position to advocate for yourself. Make sure to optimize these opportunities to showcase your brand and talk about how you are helping to advance the goals of your business and your team. This will leave no doubt about your focus on the company impact and how you are contributing. This is a great way to help others understand your value.

Working Relationships and Collaboration

Use this ability to be the ultimate team player. Do things like you would at home; offer to help when needed, offer to listen and understand what your team needs, make time for personal time/connection (i.e., go out to lunch, group outings), understand what's important to them and find ways to help or find help.

Collaboration is a natural strength for us Latinos and one that companies need more than ever before—use it to help your team drive business value as well as to help refine your brand as a strong influential leader.

Formal Reviews

It is very important to document your accomplishments—do not hold back on what you achieved throughout the year. Be specific, thoughtful, and ensure your accomplishments always tie to the organization and team goals. This is a big part of how your impact will be measured.

*Note: Be sure to stay aligned with your direct manager throughout the year on your accomplishments. This is part of the ongoing practice of advocating for yourself. The end of year review should never be a surprise; it should be a summary of the all great discussions you've had throughout the year.

RECAP

Knowing when to use our natural family-first ability vs. when to your our unnatural me-first approach will be critical toward your success as a professional. Being able to effectively navigate these waters will continue to build your bi-cultural mindset and capabilities. It will be important to quickly assess and understand how to approach various team-first and me-first situations so that you can deliver the right messages to the right people, at the right times. This is a skill that will take time to develop. Once developed and eventually mastered, it will begin to open doors you didn't know existed. You will begin to find yourself talking to more senior leaders who are willing to help you, and you will continue to develop a reputation as an impact player—someone who is a strong team player/leader, a great collaborator, and someone who knows how to articulate the impact they are ultimately making to the business and their team.

PLANNING AND ACTIVATING YOUR DEVELOPMENT

To support your development and to help you organize and

activate the concepts in this chapter, please go to my website (www.refugioatilano.com) and download the free templates for **The Latino Leadership Workbook**—this is a great set of tools to help organize your target areas and map a plan on where to focus your growth. It also includes a notes page and a development roadmap template so you can begin to think through and draft your personalized improvement plan that will set you up for maximum growth and success.

PART 2: HOW TO BE BOLD AND GO AFTER WHAT YOU WANT

How to Be Bold and Go After What You Want

> *"You miss 100% of the shots you don't take."*
> **- Wayne Gretzky**

The quote above by Wayne Gretzy is one of my favorites—it's one that I ran into a few years ago and use it as a guiding principle to this day. In fact, it's another key reason I am writing this book; I didn't want to look back in life and ask myself "What if...?" I am taking this shot and letting the chips fall where they may!

As Latinos, we are generally raised to appreciate what we have as many of our immigrant and first-generation families did not have much in terms of possessions. We come from large families and often had to share and make do with what we had. We sacrifice, we have a strong faith in God, we find ways to survive, we respect and take care of what we have, we work together, we don't ask for much, and we often accept and settle on the way things are for us.

> *I still remember my mother sacrificing the last of her change in her purse to make sure we had enough lunch money for school—each of us was given 40 cents for our school lunch meals. I just remember her giving us that money with pure love. It was all the money she had; and to be honest, it was all we needed. I learned not to ask for much because I knew we didn't have the money—and that was okay with me. I came from humble beginnings where my father was a truck driver making $17 per hour and my mother was a secretary. They worked hard and gave everything they had to make sure that me and my three*

siblings had what we needed to get through life. Although there weren't many vacations or family dinner outings because of our financial position, we were rich with love, support, and a tremendous family. That was our measure of success and our purpose in life.

> Although there weren't many vacations or family dinner outings because of our financial position, we were rich with love, support, and a tremendous family. That was our measure of success and our purpose in life.

LATINOS APPRECIATING "WHAT WE HAVE" MINDSET IN THE CORPORATE ENVIRONMENT

As powerful as this mindset is in our Latino culture, it can be self-limiting in the business world. I have experienced, as well as heard, so many stories on how we hold ourselves back because of this cultural script. Some Latinos use our family accomplishments as the baseline for our success. For example, when I was a young man, my goal was to land a job that paid more than my parents made—that was success for me as it showed that our family was making progress across generations. Looking back, this was definitely a short-sighted approach and one that we, as Latinos, need to shift away from as we gear up to compete stronger in the workplace.

When I think of the opportunity in front of us, I go directly to compensation, skill development, and new roles. As we strive to master bi-cultural leadership, we must **GET BOLD** and begin to go after what we want in each of these spaces. It's no longer good enough to hang back and hope these things come our way—it's not going to happen. We must immediately shift our approach and begin dreaming big—and just as importantly—to start swinging big! There is opportunity in front of us, we just need to go after it!

Dreaming big "brings positivity in yourself thus you deal with every challenge successfully both in your personal and professional life" (Marsh, 2018). It's the first step towards achieving your goals. It also gets you mentally strong and will help you tackle any situation as you drive your career forward. You will begin to overcome limiting beliefs, you will find yourself able to deal with challenges differently, and you will start to develop new habits and networks that are focused on your progression. Developing and striving to reach new ambitious goals will create opportunities; it will open new doors for you, add to your leadership brand, as well as help attract potential mentors and sponsors to you.

Dreaming big "brings positivity in yourself thus you deal with every challenge successfully both in your personal and professional life." It's the first step towards achieving your goals.

Personal Insight 1: Refugio A. Atilano, Business Leader at a Top-10 Pharma Company, ERG/DEI Leader, Author, *The Latino Leadership Playbook*

MAKING THE SHIFT FROM A JOB FOCUS TO A LEADERSHIP CAREER FOCUS

It feels like forever ago when I started my career as a junior project manager; I still remember feeling so fortunate, excited, and grateful about the chance to work for a corporation in any capacity. My sights were set on being the best project manager I could be—work hard, keep my head down, and call it a day! At that time, I didn't even know what leadership and driving your career meant. I thought that was only for the senior management team who went to great schools and were extremely smart… definitely not in my league.

It took me a long time to finally realize and understand that I had a career to drive and not just a job. It wasn't until my first executive mentor started pushing for my development, awareness, and promotion into new areas of the business (which made me initially very uncomfortable, by the way) that I finally realized I could accelerate my growth and opportunities. He spoke about me in ways that I didn't even think about myself; he advocated for me, he pushed my brand, he inspired me to work hard on developing my relationships across and outside of the organization. Working with my mentor was the start of my leadership development journey. I no longer looked at work as a job, it was a career that I needed to own. This mindset shift was critical to where I am today as a senior leader for a world-class company.

Because of my experience, I now do the same for other talented Latino professionals who just need a little vision/push to see the possibilities and opportunities in front of them. For example, I am personally mentoring my new hand-picked Chief of Staff for my current Employee Resource Group. She is highly talented, hungry, and a quick learner. I am making her a business agility machine, exposing her to various senior leaders across the organization, advocating for her to her immediate senior leadership team, as well as helping develop her leadership capabilities. I fully expect that she will be a successful senior leader someday and I can't wait to see it happen!

My key takeaway is for you to make sure you Dream Big, Show Up Big, and Swing Big in your career and for every opportunity in front of you. Do not hold back and make sure to drive your career hard. These are the attributes that will position you to start taking those shots you would not have taken in the past! You will begin to create new opportunities and develop your professional network in ways that will advance your career!

> My key takeaway is for you to make sure you *Dream Big, Show Up Big, and Swing Big* in your career and for every opportunity in front of you. Do not hold back and make sure to drive your career hard.

Personal Insight 2: Refugio A. Atilano, Business Leader at a Top-10 Pharma Company, ERG/DEI Leader, Author, *The Latino Leadership Playbook*

NOT FIGHTING FOR MY WORTH DURING SALARY NEGOTIATIONS

I had the unfortunate experience of not asking for what I was worth during salary negotiations for a position I landed with a great company. Because of the company's reputation and the fact that I wanted to be a part of it so badly, I accepted the first offer they gave me, which was lower than market value for the position. I did not know I could/should negotiate and felt grateful that they gave me an offer at all, because of the way I was raised, the last thing I wanted to do was be perceived as greedy for asking for more money. I was appreciative of what I was given and took the job.

Fast-forward, I found out that less-experienced (non-Latino) team members were making more than me and I still remember my old boss telling me years later that I did not do myself any favors by not negotiating for a better package. I couldn't help but think why/how nobody opened my eyes to the salary negotiation process and that it was something I could have used to help my financial position. After that experience, I vowed to be an informed and tough salary negotiator, as well as help others with their compensation negotiations. From my point of view, there would be no more short-changing ourselves and accepting the bare minimum on what was offered to us. Latinos are one of the worst-paid demographic groups and a lot of it has to do with us not understanding and fighting for what we are worth.

Later in this book, I will cover "How to Negotiate Your Salary" and "How to Ask for a Promotion" so you too will be a well-informed, tough negotiator, who is positioned to get compensated at or above market value. It is critical that you know your worth, go after what you deserve, and do not settle for anything less. The days of us Latinos being grateful and appreciative for sub-market compensation packages is over. It's now time for us to do our homework, practice negotiating, and to start fighting for what we want—and deserve!

It is critical that you know your worth, go after what you deserve, and do not settle for anything less.

Personal Insight 3: Melissa Sanchez, Student, University of Chicago

HOW TO BE BOLD

Growing up as a first-generation Latina and the oldest daughter, I was taught that if I worked hard, got amazing grades at school, and followed the rules, I would be successful. I knew that I wanted to make my mom proud and repay her for all her hard work and sacrifices, so I did just that. I excelled in school, worked a part-time job while taking care of my siblings, and was accepted into one of the best universities in the nation. But when I arrived at college, I learned that wasn't enough. I soon discovered that beyond getting a job that pays the bills and helps me achieve upward mobility, I didn't know what else I could bring into the world.

I was scared to dream bigger because I felt like I didn't have the skills or resources to achieve them. My dream of building my own business or making a change to help my community prosper started to feel hopeless. But everything changed after I did something bold that changed my perspective and path forever. In my second year of college, when I first got my internship at a nonprofit called We Are All Human, I learned that there was a whole organization dedicated to advancing the narrative of Latinos. I was inspired to know that there are people out there dedicating their lives to helping people like me find their power.

I was told that networking was an important skill to equip yourself for your career. I was always anxious about reaching out to people and asking them about their story, but I knew that I had to get out of my comfort zone to grow. One day, I decided to schedule a call with the CEO of the foundation, Claudia Romo Edelman, and ask her about her story and how she came to build such a wonderful organization. When I met with her, I was prepared to learn about her. However, I was surprised when she asked me questions about my background instead. At the end of the call, she told me she was impressed by my courage to schedule a call with her since many interns did not do that. She ended up inviting me to her Gala and the Hispanic Leadership Summit at the United Nations to give a speech about my story in front of hundreds of Latino leaders and corporations and demonstrate how I am an example of a Hispanic Star. I was shocked in disbelief but full of excitement when she asked me this. I had never done such a thing, but I knew opportunities like this come once in a lifetime, so I accepted.

After this experience, I was introduced to the Hispanic Star network and learned about the inspiring leaders who have similar backgrounds as mine and who are fighting for change in our world. I am now working with different professionals on initiatives that strive to create progress for diversity and inclusion within the Latino community. I am also now leading my own podcast where we engage with young first-gen Latinos and talk about our experiences in facing adversity. I am now empowered to believe that my dream of helping my community and becoming a Latina entrepreneur can come true. I learned that sometimes being bold and going for what you want, even in the face of uncertainty or fear, can lead to amazing opportunities.

Key Takeaways:
- Be open to trying new experiences even if you feel unprepared or afraid of failure.
- Dream big and chase them because you can be surprised how far you can go when you conquer limiting beliefs.

Personal Insight 4: Frank Carbajal, Founder @EsTiempo, LLC, Founder of Silicon Valley Latino Leadership Summit

HOW TO BE BOLD IN YOUR CAREER

My Early Years

I was born in El Centro, California, on June 19, 1969. Being the youngest of five taught me early on how to be bold and resilient. My mother shared with me that she worked so hard up until her third trimester, spending 10-12 hours a day in the fields. Sometimes she worked in the blistering heat of 110 degrees, often feeling like she wasn't going to make it. Pure determination pushed my mother through these conditions.

My dad also worked these long hours; however, he was treated with more fairness as a male migrant worker, at the time. My father knew how to communicate his thoughts and express his frustration, which was the result of my mother working very long hours and having to begin work again only a few days after I was born. My dad at this point began to realize the importance of being a father, a man of the household.

After I was two years old, my father had the ambition and boldness to move us to the Santa Clara Valley, today known as the Silicon Valley. In 1973 my parents were fortunate to find work in canneries, which was an industry considered better than working in the fields. However, my parents could only afford to live in Meadow Fair, which was based in East San Jose, California, known as a barrio (Spanish-speaking neighborhood).

This was a great success for my father because we moved into a one-bedroom home. Everything my parents needed was within a two-mile radius.

Learning to Be Bold

I learned how to be bold in my early childhood, which would transpire into my adulthood as an entrepreneur. During those early years, my life centered around staying out of trouble and my father instilled in me the need to keep busy. I remember during the summer when I was twelve years old, I helped my father clean offices, which was his part-time job on top of his full-time job at a

PART 2: HOW TO BE BOLD AND GO AFTER WHAT YOU WANT

cannery. My father's focus was always to keep me busy, especially on weekends and summers. He wanted to do everything he could to keep me out of joining a gang in the barrio and ensure I had a bright future.

I believe his motive was to make me realize the significance of working hard and making time to focus on education. My dad didn't want me to work as hard as he had to; he wanted me to be BOLDER and work smarter. I remember when I worked with him cleaning buildings in Silicon Vally that I spent many hours reflecting on how I just cleaned the office of the CEO of a successful tortilla company. I would slowly push the vacuum cleaner as I admired everything in the office from the rich smell of mahogany to the awards of recognition he received as an outstanding executive leader. I also enjoyed looking at his recreational ticket stubs from my favorite team, San Francisco 49ers!

Using a Bold Mindset to Drive My Entrepreneurial Journey

On my journey, and in my profession as an entrepreneur, I used my bold mentality to create my business plan—just as a head coach and all the team coordinators would do for the San Francisco 49ers. The process takes due diligence, insight, strategy, and execution.

My ability to be bold and drive my own business has led to publishing my own books, Building the Latino Future (Wiley, 2008) and Latinx Business Success (Wiley and Sons, 2021). Being a Founder of my own company @EsTiempo, LLC, ultimately encouraged me to create a platform known as the Silicon Valley Latino Leadership Summit, an inclusive platform that encourages Latinos and Latinas to be bold from the Silicon Valley and all regions throughout the United States. I want you to also follow your dreams and boldly make them come to life!

KEY TAKEAWAYS:

- Never forget the sacrifices those before us made to help provide opportunity for you.

- Take advantage of the roads others have paved for us—be smart and use these lessons and insights to your advantage
- Remember, regardless of where you come from, being bold is an asset. Put yourself and your dreams out there, and then execute! You will reach places you never thought possible!

Personal Insight 5: Xavier Cano, President, Xavier Cano Coaching

HOW TO BE BOLD AND GO AFTER WHAT YOU WANT

Being bold means having the courage to become the person you were meant to be and do the things you were meant to do. However, many do not understand the concept of self-limiting beliefs. These are negative thought patterns, that if not managed properly, can prevent you from making bold moves. These beliefs can be so deeply ingrained that it can be challenging to identify them, but, once you do, you can manage them accordingly.

For example, if you catch yourself thinking "I can't because..." or "I don't deserve because..." then it is likely you have a self-limiting belief. To overcome this, challenge it by saying the opposite. "I can because..." or "I deserve to be (or to do, or to have) because..." By doing so, you will find yourself taking the necessary steps to achieve your goals.

There was a time when people thought humans could not fly. But now, airplanes take us all over the world. Someone was bold enough to challenge that belief and find a way to make it possible.

Unblocking My Power

Being bold is all about challenging yourself to achieve the impossible and leaving an impact. In 2022, I left my full-time job to grow my coaching and speaking business. It took courage to leave my steady income, but I knew it was my destiny. The

PART 2: HOW TO BE BOLD AND GO AFTER WHAT YOU WANT

universe confirmed it the same day when a non-profit organization asked me to speak in front of 20,000 people in India!

At first, I heard the little voice in my head saying, "I can't because…" However, I knew that if I wanted this coaching practice to succeed, I would need to do great things. I would need to be bold. So, I challenged the little voice and said, "Yes, I can because my goal is to be an international speaker!" And, in February 2023, I traveled across the globe and spoke in front of 20,00 people in India. (Talk about impact!)

It was one of the best experiences of my life. I was greeted with open arms and many of the people in attendance swarmed around me to take pictures. They treated me like a movie star! The speech was about the concept of unblocking your power.

Whether your dreams are to run your own business, or become the CEO of a Fortune 500 company, or something else, you have the freedom to be bold. The only person that can get in your way is YOU. Challenge your self-limiting beliefs and make your impact.

Impact on Others

Being bold does not just benefit you, it can inspire others too. By pursuing your dreams, you can help others overcome their self-limiting beliefs and achieve their own aspirations.

However, the opposite is also true. Not pursuing your dreams can perpetuate self-limiting beliefs in others, and even deter those closest to you from making bold moves.

Cultural Influences

As Latinos, it is important also to recognize cultural influences that may prevent us from being bold. While the Hispanic/Latino population is diverse and not meant to be generalized, there are limiting beliefs that can hold us back. As a coach, I have personally encountered a few of these limiting beliefs with my Latino clients.

Limiting Belief 1: "You should be grateful for what you have and not ask for more."

While it is important to appreciate all the blessings that have come your way, sometimes being bold also means not settling. You might have a well-paying job, a nice house, and a beautiful family. Others may see you as a model of perfection. If we aspire to reach a level of success greater than our present situation, we cannot deter our wishes by feeling guilty for aspiring for more. We have a calling to do something more spectacular, so we must be grateful for what we have, but then reach for the sky and accomplish the goals we were meant to achieve.

Limiting Belief 2: "Women are supposed to raise children. Let your husband provide."

Unfortunately, several of my Latina clients have heard this before. Their immigrant parents were raised with a specific family structure that no longer serves the present-day situation. This belief perpetuates stereotypes about women working in corporate settings. But times have changed, and it is essential to listen to our hearts and determine what our path looks like. We must be bold and go for our dreams, even if it is completely different from what our parents did.

Limiting Belief 3: "Do not challenge your elders."

While we should show respect to those who have come before us, we all play a bigger role in someone else's life. If we choose not to challenge our elders, we are getting in the way of potentially sharing important insights. We must challenge the status quo, including people who are older than us, if we want to make bold moves. So yes, show respect, but politely be you as well.

Limiting Belief 4: "Do not boast about your accomplishments. Be humble."

If we want to make bold moves, we must share with others why

PART 2: HOW TO BE BOLD AND GO AFTER WHAT YOU WANT

we are the best at what we do. It is about recognizing our value and taking credit for the things that will take us to the next level. It is about showing up and taking space so that we can be seen and heard. Otherwise, why would anyone else take a chance on us?

KEY TAKEAWAYS:

- Identify and challenge your self-limiting beliefs.
- Write down your goals and structure them as achievable objectives with specific time frames.
- Create a plan by breaking down the necessary steps to achieve each goal. Assign dates for each step to keep yourself on track.
- Follow your plan and adjust as needed.
- Celebrate small wins along the way.
- Surround yourself with a positive support system of people who believe in your dreams and can provide guidance when needed.
- Communicate and share your goals with your manager, leaders who have influence on your performance, and trusted advisors.

DOS AND DON'TS

Now that we have covered the background, stories, and insights into how to be bold and go after what you want, here are some additional Dos and Don'ts to further support your development in this area.

Dos	Don'ts
Do: Identify Opportunities to Reach Your Goals Part of being a leader is to always be scanning the environment for opportunities to add value and impact. As you develop your goals, look across the organization for opportunities that will help you reach them—these could be existing opportunities (i.e., new job posting) or you can create the opportunity (i.e., proposed a new program that you can drive, engage in an ERG). You also have the option to find opportunities outside of your organization to develop yourself and reach your goals—for example, being a board member, getting involved with Latino professional development organizations, etc.	**Don't: Forget to Use Your Passion** We are naturally passionate, ambitious, and innovative. Use these traits as you develop your goals—determine how to add value in new ways for yourself and the organization. Be passionate about what you want to achieve and how you are going to go about achieving them. This passion will inspire you, others, and show how serious you are about where you are going as a leader!
Do: Develop and Share Bold Goals Now that Dreaming Big, Showing Up Big, and Swinging Big are part of your mindset, you will need to think through what are those new bold goals that you want to target for the short-, mid-, and long-term. I challenge you to think beyond your current role; think in terms of leadership, skill development, and other opportunities to showcase your brand. Be sure to discuss and align with your immediate manager on a game plan—their support, insight, and total alignment will be critical to your development.	**Do: Develop and Share Bold Goals** Now that Dreaming Big, Showing Up Big, and Swinging Big are part of your mindset, you will need to think through what are those new bold goals that you want to target for the short-, mid-, and long-term. I challenge you to think beyond your current role; think in terms of leadership, skill development, and other opportunities to showcase your brand. Be sure to discuss and align with your immediate manager on a game plan—their support, insight, and total alignment will be critical to your development.

PART 2: HOW TO BE BOLD AND GO AFTER WHAT YOU WANT

Do: Be a Tough Salary Negotiator	Don't: Forget to Elevate Other's Dreams
Latinos, and specifically Latinas, are among the worst-paid demographics in the US today. It's time to change that narrative and not to accept job offers given to us that are less than market value as compared to some of our non-Latino counterparts. Note: We will cover compensation negotiation strategies later in this book and will be looking for you to exercise them so that we can begin to close the current pay gap	Latinos supporting Latinos is how we win. We don't succeed until everyone succeeds—it's that simple. Uniting and helping each other grow, holding each other accountable for strong leadership, and advocating for one another is how we will change the game. Now that you are armed with critical leadership information, we are counting on you to continue to share these messages, mentor, and do everything you can to elevate all other Latinos you touch.

OPERATING WITH A "GROWTH MINDSET"

Looking back at how I was raised, I was told to get a job and hopefully I was lucky enough to stay with the same company until I retired. That is how my father managed his working years as a truck driver. He was at the same company for 30 years before retiring and he/our family enjoyed the stability it provided. I thought that was the ideal scenario and it's how I approached my early career—working for the same company approach was all I knew and it sounded reasonable to me at the time. That's until I got into the corporate world and saw right away how much people moved around; what I found more interesting is that *they expected to move around.* This went against everything I was taught, and it confused me greatly.

After finally getting a mentor, the first thing I asked is why do so many people move around and should I be doing that too? He said that I needed to operate with a "growth mindset;" begin thinking through what the key skills, capabilities, and network are needed to land new desired opportunities and to keep progressing in my career—inside or outside the company. I remember at first feeling like that approach would get my fired as I thought it would show that I am not content with my current job. I found out quickly that this was quite the opposite.

My mentor said that I needed to operate with a "growth mindset;" begin thinking through what the key skills, capabilities, and network are needed to land new desired opportunities and to keep progressing in my career—inside or outside the company.

After that time, I have always put focus into growth. I am always pushing myself to develop myself—and now, others (like you)! Whether it's growing my strategic network, pushing myself in different ways in my core responsibilities, developing/refining a leadership skill, volunteering my time for another area in my company to learn another part of the business, getting involved with professional organizations, leading an ERG to get more strategy/leadership experience, mentoring/coaching others to help them develop, or doing self-reflection based on feedback from my peers. I am always working to improve myself so that I can set myself up for that next great role!

I want you to always think about what your next role is going to be and become maniacal about landing it; partner closely with your direct manager and have discussions about your career and come up with a game plan on how to get there—then execute on that plan. A good manager will want you to succeed and will help you along your journey to help you prepare for that next great opportunity!

Key Insight: In talking to various VPs, I have heard that their journey has often taken them through various geographical locations. As daunting as moving to another location might sound, they recommend to always take the opportunity if you/your family can do it. Doing so will provide the development, network, and leadership experience that you will be able to leverage as you progress throughout your career.

RECAP

The time for Latinos to start dreaming BIG and driving our careers hard to achieve those bold goals is here. The days of accepting the way things are, being short-sighted, and not fighting for what we want and what we are worth will be a thing of the past. You are now armed with the key elements and insights to begin shifting your mindset towards a Going After What You Want approach. There is nobody stopping your path to leadership success, your path to great pay, and your path to new opportunities—it's there if you want it. My call to action for you is to begin to dream big, develop solid plans, drive hard to reach your goals, be vocal with your plans, and always remember to elevate all Latinos around you!

PLANNING AND ACTIVATING YOUR DEVELOPMENT

To support your development and to help you organize and activate the concepts in this chapter, please go to my website (www.refugioatilano.com) and download the free templates for **The Latino Leadership Workbook**—this is a great set of tools to help organize your target areas and map a plan on where to focus your growth. It also includes a notes page and a development roadmap template so you can begin to think through and draft your personalized improvement plan that will set you up for maximum growth and success.

How to Be Vocal with Your Perspectives

> *"It's not about finding your voice, it's about giving yourself permission to use your voice."*
> **— Kris Carr**

When I found out that I could and should be voicing my opinions and perspectives to senior and executive leaders (authority figures) in the workplace, I felt as though a whole new world opened up. I remember feeling like, "I can do what? Really? Say that again?" Why didn't someone tell me this sooner? I felt as if I had been missing out all these years and it's what everyone else knew—and probably a reason why they were getting promoted and was not. Similar to advocating for ourselves, voicing our opinions and perspectives to authority figures does not come naturally for the general Latino community. Fortunately, there are many Latinos that have broken this barrier and a couple of them will be providing great insights for you later in this chapter.

LATINOS DEFERING TO AUTHORITY

If you are Latino, respeto is a core tenet of our culture and often times drives how we show up in the workplace. "Latinos place a high value on demonstrating respeto in interactions with others, which literally translates into respect. Respeto means that each person is expected to defer to those who are in a position of authority because of age, gender, social position, title, economic status, etc." (Carteret, 2011).

Similarly, Susan G. Komen reports that, "In general, Hispanic/Latino populations place a strong emphasis on showing respect to authority figures. Many families and communities believe that the father or oldest male relative holds the most authority. This respect often extends to other authority figures, as well" (2022).

When I look back throughout my life, respecting my elders was engrained in my head—from parents, grandparents, uncles, aunts, friend's parents, teachers, sports coaches, advisors, etc. Anyone who was in an authority position was automatically given respect and without question. I still hold these same values today—I am especially formal with family and friends' elders and am always sure to address them appropriately to show the utmost respect. For example, earlier this year, we went to New Orleans for my wife's close friend's 50th birthday celebration. The birthday girl's parents and aunt also joined us for the trip. Regardless of how informal the environment was, I always addressed them as senora and senor and they were very appreciative. Respect in our community is king and we are proud of this cultural script.

While this approach works well in our traditional cultural environments, we must recognize that we often need to show up differently in the workplace. In our journey to become strong, confident, and effective bi-cultural leaders, we must make the shift and learn to be ready and to deliver our perspectives in the face of all audiences—executives, senior leaders, and colleagues. Deferring to leadership for their thoughts and direction is okay in some situations; however, now more than ever, organizations are counting on the ideas, thoughts, and leadership from all employees. This is where we Latinos can differentiate and compete at a different level than we have in the past. It's time for us to show up bigger than ever before and begin to push the envelope and help shape our businesses for now and into the future!

WHY BUSINESSES NEED LATINOS TO BE VOCAL IN THE WORKPLACE

"The Latino community is the 5th largest economy in the world; if businesses want to thrive for now and into the future, they must effectively connect with us and tap into our market."

– Refugio A. Atilano

From a Business Perspective

This is one area where we can add immediate value and why it's so important for Latinos to have more influence, land senior roles, and be impact players in the workplace. We need to help lead the way for companies and organizations to connect with the Latino community and to organize products and services that solve for our needs. We are in a unique position to be the link between traditional business strategy and the opportunity to effectively grow market share and influence with the Latino community.

> We are in a unique position to be the link between traditional business strategy and the opportunity to effectively grow market share and influence with the Latino community.

As an example, Toyota ran a successful Latino-focused Camry campaign in 2017 by partnering with Conill, a Hispanic-focused agency. They focused their commercial on the family values scripts were able to connect with the Latino audience in new ways to sell more cars (Kennedy, 2018).

As an ERG leader, I am always challenging myself, and all of you, to find new ways to add organizational impact through identifying opportunities to better tie our products and ways we work to the Latino market. This can take on several looks; for example, helping sales teams understand the Latino market numbers and opportunity, being as sounding board for marketing and brand teams trying to connect with the Latino community, educating people leaders on Latino cultural scripts to help facilitate their recruitment and advancement of Latinos, and educate ERG members on Latino scripts and how to effectively navigate them in the corporate environment. These are all impactful strategies and a great way that we Latinos can continue to add value for our organizations.

From an Employee Engagement Perspective

Another reason why Latinos need to be more vocal in the workplace is because it can lead to increased engagement, which can lead to great impact, prolonged and sustainable company growth. Will Murray, CEO of Oak Engage, says, "Encouraging an open, honest, and transparent environment within your business is a prerequisite to creating a more positive and productive workplace. Champion your team and they will champion you" (Southern, 2023).

We Latinos are loyal, committed, and hard-working. We are also ambitious and ready to provide innovative and creative ideas to advance our business strategies; we want to be at the table, heard, and to help shape new solutions. As Dr. Robert Rodriguez states in *Auténtico*, "Latinos lead with *ganas*, a hard-to-translate Latino term that alludes to driving forward with total heart, body, mind, and soul" (251). Companies can always count on Latinos to being all-in. Given the opportunity and space to share our thoughts, ideas, passion, and opinions that add value to our organizations are a great opportunity to achieve a win-win for both companies and our professional Latino community!

> We Latinos are loyal, committed, and hard-working. We are also ambitious and ready to provide innovative and creative ideas to advance our business strategies; we want to be at the table, heard, and to help shape new solutions.

In the following section, we will cover some personal stories with some really great insights and lessons on how to navigate and drive your career forward through being vocal with your perspectives in front of any audience.

Personal Insight 1: Refugio A. Atilano, Business Leader at a Top-10 Pharma Company, ERG/DEI Leader, Author, *The Latino Leadership Playbook*

USING MY LATINO ERG TO DEVELOP MY LEADERSHIP BRAND

Generally speaking, making the jump into a senior leader role was a new world for me as I quickly discovered there were different expectations than from previous roles. It was critical that I began showing up with my own vision, perspectives, opinions, strategies, and to be able to articulate the supporting rationale, story, data, and plan to execute upon them. It was about assuming and taking complete ownership for driving our business forward rather than deferring to other authority figures to do so for me.

Being able to help lead a Latino ERG at a global company has been an absolutely wonderful experience! It allowed me to develop and refine my leadership muscles while developing new ways to provide value to our members and our business overall. For example, in partnership with my ERG leadership team, I was able to create our annual strategy, host our first all-member call with our Chief Diversity Officer, and lead an organization-wide initiative to get more Latino talent into our company. In order to bring these great initiatives to life, it was critical that I was vocal with my perspectives, had an air-tight story/rationale to pitch them, developed a great communication package, and put myself in a position to align key stakeholders at all levels (including executive officers) across the organization.

The output of great work and an effective approach can have a positive impact on your leadership brand. Being able to make your pitch and sell your position (vision) is a critical piece of your leadership development. Once you master this skill, this will help develop your leadership brand as someone who brings vision, know-how, as well as someone who is a strong communicator and collaborator who effectively works with stakeholders across the organization.

In our case, my ERG received feedback from our Executive Leadership Team sponsor that our annual strategy was the best he's ever seen from our group, and we were also recognized for taking the initiative to make a company impact through leading and driving efforts to get more Latino professionals into the organization. None of this would have been possible had I not vocalized my perspectives and had a supporting strategy and plan to drive the business forward. I am hopeful you can take this example to pitch, gain alignment, and drive bringing new ideas to life for your role as well as to help develop your brand as a strong leader who consistently impacts the organization!

> It takes nothing to join the crowd.
> It takes everything to stand alone.
> - Hans F Hansen

Personal Insight 2: Refugio A. Atilano, Business Leader at a Top-10 Pharma Company, ERG/DEI Leader, Author, *The Latino Leadership Playbook*

GOING AGAINST THE GRAIN TO DRIVE IMPACT

There will be moments in your career where you need to be bold and take a stand—and there will be times when these situations will be in direct conflict with your manager and/or other executive leader(s) positions. You might find yourself having the knowledge, perspective, and pressure-tested ideas that nobody else possesses that can solve problems and drive business results in more innovative, effective, and efficient ways. So, what do you do? I am calling on you to **BE BOLD**—put yourself, your ideas, and your leadership brand out there for the world to see. Of course, this assumes that you have done the homework, have a nicely packaged story, pressure-tested your ideas and the supporting data with trusted subject matter experts, and you have confirmed that everything checks out. Given all those elements, you are in a great position to influence and help shape business decisions, as well as develop your leadership brand.

For example, I was in one of these situations where I had to seriously go against the grain to convince an entire project team including four VPs on why my idea should be considered and supported. For context, I was leading a high-intensity project and large cross-functional team where we needed to meet a target date in a few months, so we didn't disrupt operations. The stakes were high, and the pressure was even higher!

We spent the first three weeks collecting data and team input to identify potential solutions. I remember coming up with seven options, which we paired down to two options for executive review, discussion, and approval. I quickly discovered that several members had default positions they were defending (people preferred different options), and I was in the middle attempting to help the team navigate these treacherous waters—not a fun place to be to say the least. Fast-forward after numerous "healthy debates," we finally landed on one of the solutions that took us right up to the target date; it was aggressive, but doable. We were good, until— by pure chance after we landed on a path forward—I stumbled upon a new alternate solution that would save us about three weeks and put us in a great position to meet the target date way more easily.

Before taking it up to our executive team, I organized my thoughts, examined the pros and cons, put them in a decision-making framework, pressure-tested the ideas with several trusted team members (although some were questioning why I would even bring it up at this point), before finally taking it to leadership for consideration. Long-story-short, my recommendation was championed and supported, even after we aligned on a previous approach, and we met our target in plenty of time which led to the project sponsor recognizing my efforts as the best project he's seen run.

As stated earlier, there will be moments in your career where you will have the opportunity to take a stand and go against the grain. As Latinos, we must seize those moments and share our innovative thoughts, leverage our relationships to tease them out, and be vocal with our ideas and share them with key decision-makers across the organization. This is another example of what will make you stand out, develop your confidence, and continue to develop your brand as a strong impact player in the workplace!

Personal Insight 3: Illianna Acosta, Leader at Major Tech Firm and Global Speaker

HOW TO BE VOCAL WITH YOUR PERSPECTIVES

The power of finding your superpower is transformational and can make all the difference in your career trajectory and the legacy you will leave behind. Once I realized my voice was my superpower, I went from fearing what could happen if I said something to fearing what could happen if I didn't say something.

MY EARLY CAREER STRUGGLES

You don't have enough "executive presence." That message came loud and clear from my manager at a time where she wanted to consider me for a leadership role on our team. She wanted to prepare me for what was working against me and what senior leadership thought of me, should I decide to go through the interview process. I felt defeated before even starting. I thought, "Why should I even try? I'm just going to hit a brick wall and there's no point. Their mind is made up!"

Funny how much power we give negative voices in our heads. After speaking to my mentors and respected Latina leaders, they helped reframe my mindset and essentially smacked some sense into me. They encouraged me to push past these limiting beliefs and work to shift that perception and go through the process. At the very least, it'll signal I was ready for more responsibility and was prepared to do what I needed to succeed.

I thought, "What am I doing (or not doing) to have given them that perception of me?" Was I leveraging every opportunity I had with executive leadership to demonstrate curiosity, to vocalize my viewpoints on any given topic? Was I fully present in conversations? Was I being a seat-warmer this whole time? Was I taking advantage of the seat I was given to demonstrate my commitment to driving the business forward in a meaningful way? I wasn't. Period. Point blank. This whole time I was allowing my imposter syndrome to show up and silence what I was fully capable of doing.

It was a scary realization and a wake-up call when I realized I was two different people living in the same body—one who had all the confidence outside of the office, spoke her mind on all topics, and whose voice was valued and listened to. The other, silenced by the belief that she wasn't as smart (or smarter) or valued as others around the table.

I think back to a phrase I heard often growing up and as a young professional: "*Callaita te vez más bonita.*" A phrase many Latinas are likely familiar with. It was often shared with us as we navigated opportunities offered to us and the notion that we should just be compliant and complacent with the opportunity and not dare speak up, even if we felt strongly about something, or negotiate for more not to ruffle any feathers or affect any chances we had for growth.

MY CAREER CHANGED

This was a pivotal moment in my career. I hadn't realized that not speaking up was costing me so much more than I could have imagined. It was derailing my growth and the opportunity I had for upward mobility in the organization. How much further could I have been in my career, had I realized this much earlier in my career?

At first, it was uncomfortable to speak up. It wasn't easy breaking out of these learned limitations and out of the stories I had made up in my head. But I did it. People listened and they gave their perspective to what I had shared. Often times, people would thank me for saying what they wanted to share but

didn't have the courage to. I started realizing the power of my voice and the power of my influence on

others. I started seeing/feeling perceptions and my personal brand becoming stronger with my colleagues, senior leaders, and professional community. My confidence grew. I started owning my Latinidad like never before.

I wanted to be seen as a thought leader and a thoughtful leader in my approach to driving the business forward. I started being a lot more intentional with my words and actions, when I contributed, how I worked with my team on scalable ways to grow our business, and how and when to vocalize feedback/questions/opinion. The key was understanding a few key rules:

- A growth mindset will allow you to see and do things differently to help you grow and thrive.
- Lead by example. You never know who is watching and who you can influence.
- Build your tribe. Mentors, coaches, sponsors, allies—you need them all, even if you think you can do it all on your own… you can't. No one ever got that far alone.
- Learn how to play "chess" not checkers in the workplace. You need to know how and when to make your move.
- Not every mountain is yours to climb; strategically choose the goals you want to achieve.

Needless to say, I was no longer a "seat-warmer," my seat stayed hot and ready! Afterall, as a Latina I have a responsibility to not only represent for myself, but for my Latino community at large.

MY VOICE IS MY SUPERPOWER

This experience led me to identify my superpower: My voice. I went from fearing what could happen if I said something to fearing what could happen if I didn't say something. It's moved people to tears, it's helped others find comfort in their own voice, it's led me to speak around the world on the power of your own voice and the impact it has on your personal brand, it's what has allowed me to be in rooms I had never imagined being in, sitting with CEOs who want to hear from me on everything from creating a more diverse and equitable workforce to discovering new ways to scale a business.

Reframing my mindset and finding my superpower has allowed me to use my voice to speak up on ways senior leaders across organizations must start and/or continue to support our Latino community, identifying new opportunities, opening new doors, elevating this community to new heights. Heights we helped others build. It's what led me to launching my newsletter, *Lost in Translation*, to shine a light on the challenges and limitations that historically excluded groups experiences everyday and life nuances that impact us deeply as people, professionals, and peers.

As creating more diverse and equitable spaces becomes more crucial to the growth of any organization, it's important that companies and leaders are aware of the vast differences that exist based on your cultural upbringing and how that impacts us at work and in life. Sometimes our actions, reactions, or what we say may get lost in translation.

While I am not responsible for a whole entire Latino community, I am responsible for playing my part in what the future could look like for other people who look like me. As you navigate your own career, whether you are just starting out or a seasoned professional, what is the legacy you want to leave behind? How can you, too, break past your own learned limitations or generational trauma to build a life and legacy you are proud of.

PART 2: HOW TO BE BOLD AND GO AFTER WHAT YOU WANT

KEY TAKEAWAYS:

- Active listening is critical. Listening to comprehend vs. listening to respond are two different things. The former is your friend.
- Curiosity is a superpower. Asking the right questions can help drive a conversation forward and uncover new ways of thinking.
- Know when to contribute. Think: "Does this need to be said? Does this need to be said now? Does it need to be said by me?"

Personal Insight 4: Gabino Martinez, Regional Operations Manager, World Electric, President & Founder, Hispanos Unidos ERG, Sonepar USA.

HOW TO BE VOCAL WITH YOUR PERSPECTIVES

I was blessed by the great parents I had that raised me with family values, including honesty and integrity, and taught me to always work hard, be the best I could be, and never be shy to express myself to others. This allowed me at an early age to join high school and college clubs or organizations and reach leadership positions within them. After I joined corporate America, one of the areas where I saw that I could be vocal was on the work-life balance that companies often preach, but few follow.

I was fortunate through the early stages of my life to learn leadership lessons that helped shape me; I was in situations where I was able to learn from other leaders and show my talent and desire to go above and beyond. As a result, I was given the opportunity to manage a group of people at the early age of 23! This was a different experience for me than my college or high school years, because I was dealing with a different group of people, a different environment, and how I needed to use a different mindset.

During this experience, I learned quickly how different things were in the business world; it was interesting to experience how other managers would treat their direct reports. During my first managerial position leading a small team of three, we were all Hispanics, so we all felt like *familia* and treated each other with great respect and eventually became very good friends outside of work. I thought this was normal.

It wasn't until later on in life that I worked with other managers and saw that they were not really following the work-life balance that our company promoted. These managers were mainly focused on getting work done at all costs, rather than taking the time to understand and support their employees' family commitments. This was hard for me to experience, especially seeing a father or mother not being able to be there for their children.

At this moment, I knew I had to step up and had to be vocal with my perspective rather than defer to authority. I took it upon myself to go to a higher-level manager, including the Human Resources Department, so that we could address the situation. Oftentimes, as managers, I understand we have a lot more flexibility with our schedule than an hourly associate, but that doesn't mean that we'll treat people in different ways. We need to treat each one the same and give them the same level of respect that one would expect from anyone. Because of my actions, I was able to change our culture around work-life balance, and employees were very grateful to me because I had stood up for them. I really take pride in helping others to the best of my abilities—not only Hispanics, but everyone. I saw it at a young age with my family always helping others and even to this day I continue to do so without asking for anything in return.

KEY TAKEAWAYS:

- Don't allow anyone to dictate what you need to do about an important family life event or an emergency. Take charge of your actions regarding important family life events or emergencies, refusing to let others dictate your choices.
- Have empathy towards others by understanding their life events and looking at them as if they were yours.

PART 2: HOW TO BE BOLD AND GO AFTER WHAT YOU WANT

- If you are in a leadership position, speak up for those who are not being treated fairly.

DOS AND DON'TS

Now that we have covered the background, stories, and insights around how to be vocal with your perspectives, here are some additional Dos and Don'ts to further support your development in this area.

Dos	Don'ts
Do: Be Bold—Seize the Opportunity to Impact It is critical that we bring our perspectives, innovation, creativity, ideas to the table. Unlike how we sometimes operate within our culture, we need to effectively make the shift and speak up whenever we see the opportunity to add value to our business and team goals. Showcase what you have; make sure your ideas are well-structured, well-vetted, well-planned, and that you are ready to communicate them with confidence and passion.	**Don't: Act Like You Don't Belong** I remember one of my (white male) mentors taught me early-on when we went to an executive meeting to "Act like you've been here before." In other words, make the commitment to show up with confidence and give it everything you've got. Once he said that to me, I relaxed and did exactly that. He told me that I was hired for a reason and that they believed in me. He said that I need to also believe in me! So, ever since then, I have. Now I am asking the same of you—go in with a game plan, with ultra confidence, locked and loaded—no exceptions.
Do: Lead with Great Presence Now that you will be more confident in engaging with senior and executive leaders, it will be key for you to develop your executive presence. It will add to your credibility and will help you deliver your message so that you can command the room (virtual or in-person), so that you can get the support you are seeking. You want to show that you are ready to be a strong leader and executive presence is essential in doing so—**we will cover this topic in more detail in a later chapter.**	**Don't: Act Like You Don't Belong** As discussed previously, be careful about challenging authority figures in an open forum. It's great to be bold with your ideas, but also remember to challenge senior leader ideas *effectively and at the right time*. You want to make sure you come across as someone who has maturity and good situational awareness. When in doubt, regroup and work offline when challenging ideas of senior leaders. Be sure to read the chapter on Challenging Authority.

Do: Always Be Extra Prepared	Don't: Forget to Bring Your Unique Perspective
Do your homework! Make sure that any new idea you bring to the table is well-researched, well-positioned to meet the need, and that it has been pressured tested with people who know the subject and the business problem. When you present your idea, you want to be locked in. Make sure you practice your delivery, identify any/all questions that might be asked, and have backup information at your fingertips. You want to come across as an expert and someone who is extremely well prepared. This will make you stand out in front of anyone!	You are Latino—use it! **It's an asset.** You are creative, innovative, a great team-player, empathetic, passionate, loyal, a connector, know the Latino culture/market, etc. And now you are adding all the skills from this book that will compound your potential impact! These are things our non-Latino counterparts might be lacking so make sure you bring those things to the table all day, every day!

RECAP

Being vocal with your perspectives is an effective way to develop yourself into a strong, confident, bi-cultural leader. As you begin to incorporate these elements into your leadership game, you will continue to see your brand take shape and **you will be noticed.** Unlike our natural disposition in our culture to defer to authority figures (i.e., our father calls the shots), you are expected to be vocal with your perspectives in the workplace. As Latinos, we are innovative and have many ideas to offer. We need to be able to communicate with them effectively and confidently with a sound plan as we present them to senior leaders for approval. It is critical you make this shift so that you establish a reputation as an effective leader who knows how to identify and sell ideas that will impact the business. You will quickly position yourself for those great assignments, stretch opportunities, as well as begin to attract those highly coveted mentors and sponsors who would love to support a rock star!

PLANNING AND ACTIVATING YOUR DEVELOPMENT

To support your development and to help you organize and activate the concepts in this chapter, please go to my website (www.refugioatilano.com) and download the free templates for **The Latino Leadership Workbook**—this is a great set of tools to help organize your target areas and map a plan on where to focus your growth. It also includes a notes page and a development roadmap template so you can begin to think through and draft your personalized improvement plan that will set you up for maximum growth and success.

How to Earn the Trust and Respect of Your Teams

"Trust is not a request, trust is earned."
- Jeffrey Gitomer

As covered earlier in this book, respect is one of the key attributes of our Latino culture. As Latinos, we are raised to love and respect our family, close friends, and elders. "There's a deep connection between family members that cannot be broken even in the worst of economic or health situations" (HopGroup, 2023). Our culture is characterized by loving and respectful gestures, such as welcoming guests into our homes with open arms—as we say, mi casa es su casa.

> I have had the same core group of friends since my high school years. Back then, my family didn't have much materially and our home was not large; however, it seemed like our house was the hub for all gatherings—formal and informal. For example, my friends would come over all the time and always addressed my mother as Mrs. A. and my father Mr. A.—there was always ultimate respect. My mother always made sure our house was welcoming to all—our home was their home. I still remember my mother buying extra ice cream because that's the first thing the guys would go for in our freezer when visiting our house!

Because of the way I was raised, I automatically brought this approach into the workplace. I always lead with respect and connection—respect is always given up-front. For me, if we can learn about each other, develop a good relationship, or at least find common ground, then the work becomes easy.

What's interesting, is that I have found non-Latinos to question this approach, claiming that, "He just wants to get along with everyone," without understanding the context of why I do it. It's because I'm Latino and it's the way I was raised! Providing respect, showing love for each other, and helping each other is what we do. This is definitely a Latino superpower and one that we should all be using to propel our careers and teams forward.

LATINO RESPECT AND CONNECTION IN THE WORKPLACE

Dr. Robert Rodriguez states in *Auténtico*, "The Latino employee feels as if he or she is working with colleagues who could be considered friends and extended family members" (177). Similarly, as reported by Diversity Jobs, Hispanics prefer a certain degree of intimacy and interaction. "Hispanics innately want to establish a personal connection, including a close relationship with co-workers... Latinos want to get to know others as complete human beings. They are aware that their co-workers have a life after work and are interested in knowing more about it. Small talk is our way of learning about the wants, needs, and feelings of others" (Hispanic Culture, 2022). Furthermore, personal contact is also important to us—hugs, kisses on the cheek, and pats on the back are a normal part of our interaction.

> *When I look at the Latino Employee Resource Groups I have been involved in, we bring the same respect and family-oriented approach to the table. When I see my fellow Latino and Latina ERG members, I don't see them as co-workers, I see them and treat them as family from the start. I have their backs and I expect that they have mine. It's the same with professional Latino organizations, I treat everyone as family.*
>
> *As Latinos, we have a special bond—a very unique connection—and it's in our nature to engage at a deeper level from the start. To take it a step*

> *further, I also show a great deal of respect for my elders and those with earned titles. For example, I always address Dr. Robert Rodriguez as "Dr. Robert." Regardless of how comfortable I feel with others, I always lead with respect as it's one of the things that has stuck with me since my early days.*

> When I see my fellow Latino and Latina ERG members, I don't see them as co-workers, I see them and treat them as family from the start. I have their backs and I expect that they have mine.

YOU HAVE TO EARN YOUR RESPECT AS A PROFESSIONAL IN CORPORATE AMERICA

Unlike the automatic respect given in our culture, we must earn our respect and trust in the workplace—it is not automatically given and something we need to work very hard on until it's achieved. As reported on Indeed.com, respect is important because "if you have the respect of your co-workers, they are more likely to cooperate with you. Communications between you and your co-workers will more often be friendly, helpful, and supportive." Similarly, when your management respects you, "they are more likely to notice your performance. They are also more likely to remember you when considering important projects, and when recommending people for special recognition or promotions" (How to Gain Respect, 2022).

A key component of building your respect in the workplace is to ensure your partner, support, and align with your direct leader (your boss). At work, this is the most important relationship you must focus on and develop—your manager is the person that knows you best, can help you develop, can be your biggest cheerleaders, and who can be in the best position to advocate for you to advance your career. In addition, your manager is a trusted leader in the organization to whom key decision-makers will listen when it comes to your performance, your potential, and

PART 2: HOW TO EARN THE TRUST AND RESPECT OF YOUR TEAMS

future assignments. As a result, it is critical that you work hard (and smart) to obtain the respect and trust of your manager. If you do not have the respect and trust of your manager, career advancement at your current company will be extremely difficult.

> It is critical that you work hard (and smart) to obtain the respect and trust of your manager. If you do not have the respect and trust of your manager, career advancement at your current company will be extremely difficult.

Now it's time to build your capability in this area. We will review specific insights and strategies on how you can earn respect and trust in your organization. Using the following experiential stories, you will be armed with battle-tested, valuable information that will further your development as a bi-cultural, confident, and impactful leader it the workplace!

Personal Insight 1: Refugio A. Atilano, Business Leader at a Top-10 Pharma Company, ERG/DEI Leader, Author, *The Latino Leadership Playbook*

HOW NOT SUPPORTING MY BOSS ALMOST GOT ME FIRED

I am sharing this story as I almost self-sabotaged myself out of a job earlier in my career; I am covering this so that you don't repeat the mistakes I made in this space. There was a situation where I was not happy with the appointment of my new manager, and I pushed back on their credentials and capability every step of the way. This was the wrong approach; it was an immature approach, and something I would never do again.

This change was very difficult for me as I loved my previous manager and we connected extremely well; he supported me to the hilt and I was very happy with our reporting structure. To me, there was no need for a change. When I was assigned a new manager (for business reasons that I didn't understand), I was very upset about it. I pushed back, gossiped, and was not a good team member. Fast forward, my annual review was not a good one, my bonus was horrible, and I had to fix the reputational damage I created during that year. It took a while, but I got there.

In the end, my immature response was all for nothing as my new manager turned out to be one of my greatest advocates, a good friend, and someone who I highly respect. The lesson here is to always lead with maturity and understand that the relationship you have with your manager is critical, regardless of who it is or how you both got paired up. Knowing what I know now, I make sure to always prioritize my relationship with my manager. I make time to connect, learn their style, find out how I can help them meet their goals, and show them my commitment and excitement around personal growth. Remember, you are going to have several managers during your career—they are all temporary, so use each opportunity as a way to develop a group of advocates as you progress through your professional journey!

> Remember, you are going to have several managers during your career—they are all temporary, so use each opportunity as a way to develop a group of advocates as you progress through your professional journey!

Personal Insight 2: Refugio A. Atilano, Business Leader at a Top-10 Pharma Company, ERG/DEI Leader, Author, *The Latino Leadership Playbook*

HOW TO ACCEPT RESPONSIBILITY LIKE A CHAMP!

Being able to accept responsibility for and own your mistakes (and their resolutions) is the sign of a strong leader and maturity; it will put you on a path towards gaining respect and trust of those impacted. I want to share some of my favorite examples of this based on an experience with someone in my ERG.

PART 2: HOW TO EARN THE TRUST AND RESPECT OF YOUR TEAMS

There was an ERG communication that went out to our entire membership and executive sponsors where one of our leadership team's member's names was misspelled. Once we noticed it, we quickly engaged the leader of the communications team and her attention to the matter and associated response could not have been better! Here is a **great example** of what owning a mistake looks like:

> Hi Leadership Team,
>
> Ref flagged the errors in the latest newsletter including the misspelling of your last name, (leader A), and the edits to your piece, (leader B). These should have been addressed and confirmed before the communication went out—I apologize for our miss in not catching these. It was certainly not our intention and though it wasn't our intention, I understand this still went out with errors which is not reflective of the quality we aim to have in each communication. We would like to issue an updated version with the corrections—are you both aligned with this plan? In addition, our communication leadership team will ensure this does not happen again. Thank you.

This is the type of ownership, solutioning, and leadership that helps set you apart from the rest. I have been part of activities where leaders did not take ownership and tried to deflect/shift responsibility to someone or something else. This approach is not helpful for development and can often harm your leadership brand. On the other hand, the experience with our communications lead deeply impressed me and our leadership team; her character shined through and took my respect and trust to another level!

Personal Insight 3: Refugio A. Atilano, Business Leader at a Top-10 Pharma Company, ERG/DEI Leader, Author, *The Latino Leadership Playbook*

THE TRANSFORMATION OF AN AFRO-LATINA

This is a short new story that I'd like to share with you. I recently had the pleasure of mentoring a strong Dominicana, and her development is accelerating faster than anyone I have ever seen! Fortunately, I was able to secure her as our ERG Chief of Staff. I recall her approaching me last year and sharing her story, as well as some of her frustrations and challenges in navigating new opportunities in our organization.

I could tell she was talented and innovative right away because she was always looking at things through a broad lens and coming up with new proposed solutions for our ERG. I remember two things from our initial conversations: she thought her accent was a disadvantage and she wasn't using a virtual background during her meetings, not realizing that a neat professional background makes a strong statement and helps to make a great first impression. To me, a strong leader was already present; it just needed to be carved out!

Fast-forward to only one year later after some light mentoring, she has been promoted two levels, is getting outstanding reviews, is embracing her accent, and now has an immaculate leadership image! I mean—wow! Although I am confident she would have landed additional opportunities without my coaching, sometimes it's small behavioral and mindset micro-adjustments that can help you refine your leadership brand and have an immediate and significant impact that can lead to increased respect, trust, and opportunities in the workplace!

Personal Insight 4: Carlos Garcia, Vice President, Finance, Global Food Company

HOW TO EARN THE TRUST AND RESPECT OF YOUR TEAMS

Self-confidence: While you can't control other people's opinion of you, you can control your own actions and self-confidence to earn respect in the workplace. In my experience this is the key to establishing your credibility no matter your cultural, educational, or professional experiences. Remember, if you believe in your own power, others will as well.

When I first started my career as an accountant, I was eager to prove myself. I believed that if I worked hard and produced quality work, respect would naturally follow. However, I quickly learned that earning respect was not that simple. My colleagues were polite, but I was not taken seriously for leadership roles. I often found myself being overlooked or dismissed for open positions I thought I deserved. I knew I had the skills to lead, but I couldn't seem to break through and achieve a leadership role.

I decided to take action and learn more about how to earn respect. I read books and articles on leadership, communication, and workplace dynamics. I also sought feedback from my colleagues and mentors with clear intentions to listen and improve. One thing I learned was that respect is not just about competence. It's also about how you treat others and how you present yourself. I realized that I needed to show more confidence and assertiveness in my interactions with others. I also needed to listen more actively and show more empathy.

I started implementing these changes in my daily work. I spoke up more during meetings and shared my ideas with confidence. I scheduled regular feedback sessions with managers and mentors, displaying greater ownership with my career. I also tried to understand my colleagues' perspectives and show appreciation for their contributions. Over time, I noticed a shift in how my colleagues treated me. They started to listen to my ideas and give more responsibilities. I also noticed that my confidence had grown, and I felt more fulfilled in my work.

Earning respect has been crucial to my career success. It has helped me build strong relationships with my colleagues and gain opportunities for growth.

In conclusion, earning respect takes effort and time. It's not just about being competent, but also about how you treat others and present yourself. By taking steps to show confidence, empathy, and respect to others, you can build strong relationships and achieve career success.

KEY TAKEAWAYS:

- Begin with self-assessment—taking time to understand yourself, your style, and your biases is one of the best investments you can make.
- Commit to a plan to establish your credibility—do what you say.
- Understand this is a life-long journey that will transcend the workplace.

Personal Insight 5: Ruby Garcia, Founder of Ruby Garcia Coaching, LLC., Leadership Coach & Hypnotherapist

HOW TO EARN RESPECT IN THE WORKPLACE

My mother always taught me to respect everyone I encountered at home, school, and at work. She would tell me it didn't matter what they did for a living, but that every person was deserving of respect. When I started working, she would remind me, "Treat the janitors and kitchen staff the exact same way you would treat the CEO." Respect was so engrained in me that I never thought anything of it, but navigating professional spaces as a first-generation Latina was an eye opener for me, especially when I began to see how my interpretation of respect was different than my non-Latino peers.

The first time this came up was when I was having a monthly one-on-one meeting with my manager. I was several months into a new role and was working remotely when my manager asked me how I felt about my transition into the role. I was eager to share with him what I had been learning and working on, but before I even got a chance, he interjected by saying that he thought I was aloof and disengaged.

My jaw dropped. I was flabbergasted and asked what led him to this conclusion. He responded that I never called him or updated him on my work. I assumed the quality of my work would speak for itself through metrics and KPI's, all of which he had direct access to through monthly reporting. I was exceeding expectations according to my revenue goals and was confused to why we seemed to be having this disconnect.

This is when it hit me. He perceived the lack of communication as being disengaged. I perceived it as being respectful to his time and energy as a senior leader with many ongoing priorities. This was a cultural difference in our communication and expectations.

BEING AWARE OF MY CULTURAL SCRIPT AND ADJUSTING

Thankfully, we were able to have an honest conversation about our varying perspectives. From that point on, I made it a priority to send him weekly updates and schedule brief meetings in between our monthly one-on-one deep dives. Initially, calling my manager was uncomfortable, but because I respected him, I knew this was one way I could build rapport and regain his trust. Because he respected me, he wanted to understand more about my communication style and listened before making assumptions. In the end, we were able to hear each other and move on from what could have been a sticky situation. When we genuinely listen to each other's perspectives, we can bridge communication gaps, clear up misunderstandings, and develop stronger relationships.

USING RESPETO AS A SUPERPOWER

There are many traits that can make you an influential leader including your skills, expertise, and experience, but one virtue that we naturally possess and is ingrained into our cultural makeup is that of respect. For us respect isn't something that needs to be earned or developed over time, but we give it freely from the very beginning. It is important to realize that cultural scripts like "respeto" can influence the way that we show up at work and how we relate to others. By developing a strong sense of self-awareness and understanding of how we can use this virtue as to our advantage, we can begin to use "respeto" as a superpower to drive impact, make positive changes, and transform the workplace into a more inclusive environment. By embracing our natural inclination to freely give respect, we can challenge and reshape the corporate landscape and fast-track our way to success!

As an example, in my past corporate role, I was assigned to lead a change management initiative within a large and complex university system that impacted about 400,000 people. My role was to onboard this new university system, implement a contract within their organization, and generate 10% new revenue within the first 90 days of the contract. The challenge was that my organization's sales framework, including its solutions and offerings, were built around the private sector. Because of state governed regulations, the onboarding process was reduced to selling the contract and not the outcomes. The impact was slow sales growth and missed opportunities. My vision was to create a new and more robust way of doing business that would result in stronger partnerships, higher quality engagements, and increased revenue and growth opportunities. It also meant being respectful of the previous work done and gaining a deeper understanding of how things were done, both within my organization and within the university system.

Respect is the foundation upon which trust is built. I knew the fastest way to create change would be to gain endorsement from Senior Leadership. I leveraged the relationships in which I had developed trust and ultimately approached the Regional Vice-President because he was influential, forward-thinking, and passionate. Change requires a "one bite at a time" approach, so I began by enrolling him in the possibility of using an upcoming project as a pilot program. With his buy-in, I formed an additional sponsorship team which included stakeholders with a diverse set of knowledge, skillset, and expertise. I was intentional about cultivating an environment where every team member felt seen, heard, and valued. This motivated the team to share ideas, collaborate, and work towards a common goal.

We exceeded the goals within 90 days as expected, and we continued to have exceptional results for the remainder of the year. The client's contract grew revenue 46% over the previous year, customer interactions doubled, and we grew our contact list by 18%. The customers increased their productivity, reduced costs, and perceived our team as a valuable business partner that was irreplaceable. Due to the phenomenal results, the company decided to implement this process nationwide for our public sector customers since it was proven to have significant impact. I was nominated to present the launch of this new process at our annual sales conference and further gained the respect of my leaders, clients, and colleagues.

Respect can change an entire culture. When it's woven into the culture, it creates a culture of risk-taking, innovation, and collaboration. As Latinos, we can leave an impact on the corporate world by utilizing our superpower of respeto to drive meaningful impact and create a lasting legacy.

KEY TAKEAWAYS:

- **Treat everyone with the same level of respect.** Lead with kindness and empathy. Make personal connections with individuals, ask questions, actively listen, and acknowledge their perspective.
- **Tap into your leadership potential.** Take calculated risks and communicate your ideas to leaders and key influencers within your organization. Be strategic, provide context, problem solve, and consider how, when, and with whom you will communicate.
- **Value diversity and inclusion.** Embrace the differences on your team or within your organization. Valuing the wisdom, experiences, and expertise of others will foster creativity, innovation, and productivity.

DOS AND DON'TS

Now that we have covered the background, stories, and insights around how to earn the trust and respect of your teams, here are some additional Dos and Don'ts to further support your development in this area.

Dos	Don'ts
Do: Understand Your Boss As stated earlier, the relationship you have with your direct manager is critical for your development and career success. Take time to get to know them personally, their ambitions, their goals, and determine how you can help them to drive impact for the organization. Let them know you have their back and partner with them on your development and business goals. Find out what's important to them and be a solution that adds value for what they are trying to achieve. This is a great way to partner with your leader and will put you in a position to get a great advocate.	**Don't: Forget to Provide Solutions** A great way to earn respect and trust is to take advantage of our natural ability to innovate—make sure to come to the table with new ideas and proposed solutions to drive the business forward. Putting those great ideas together with a well-thought strategy and plan will get you noticed as a thought leader, innovator, and driver/owner. These are the types of leaders organizations crave as these are the people who will put the business in the best position to compete and succeed.
Do: Be Professional Developing a professional image and brand will show others in the organization that you take yourself seriously. Make sure you are on point with your attire, your communication, and your workspace. Coupling that with acting professional and respectful at all times can go a long way; this is just as important for work hours and after-work events.	**Don't: Forget to Be Respectful to Others** This is another one of our natural Latino abilities—make sure to leverage it in the workplace to connect with others and develop those great relationships. The relationships you develop will be the building blocks and foundation for your job and career success. More times than not, if people like you, they will help you. Make sure to put time into this space and lead with your natural respect for others.
Do: Add Value / Help Others Succeed One of the best ways to earn respect and trust is to deliver for the organization. This can take on many forms—deliver on your immediate responsibilities, help your manager achieve their goals, help other leaders in the organization achieve their goals, lean into an ERG to drive their strategy, etc. Actively work to identify opportunities to deliver on goals that impact the company on many different levels. *Note: Of course, your primary responsibilities come first; assuming you are doing those well, then work closely with your manager to engage in other parts of the organization.*	**Don't: Forget to Meet Your Commitments** Being a person of your word is critical toward earning the trust and respect of your manager and those in your organization—your credibility counts on it. When putting yourself on the line, make sure to properly assess what you are committing to so that you can ensure you deliver on what you set out to achieve. Developing a reputation for someone who comes through on their commitments is great for your leadership brand.

PART 2: HOW TO EARN THE TRUST AND RESPECT OF YOUR TEAMS

Do: Be Positive and Level-headed	Don't: Forget to Be a Team Player
This is another effective way to gain the respect and trust of your team. Tackling business problems and conflicts with a positive and level-headed approach is critical. It will show that you are committed to the bigger picture, can stay cool under pressure, and help lead teams to desired outcomes. This will help teams believe in your leadership style and get them to follow you towards resolution, through both good and bad times.	Collaboration and teamwork are another one of our natural Latino strengths. Make sure to use it effectively in everything you do as this will show the organization that you are amazing in working with different teams and they can trust you with different assignments across the organization. This will be critical as new assignments/roles are considered for your development; being a strong collaborator will strengthen your leadership brand.

Sources: Indeed.com, "How to Gain Respect in the Workplace"; Cleverism.com, "How to Gain Respect from Your Boss or Manager"

RECAP

Now that you have these additional insights on how to earn respect in the workplace as well as use your natural ability to give respect, you are now positioned to continue your development as a high-impact, bi-cultural, and confident leader. These are the building blocks that will create your new leadership foundation as you start to drive your career forward. Effectively using these strategies as well as the ones from previous chapters WILL get you noticed in the workplace; you will be viewed differently and will see doors start to open for new opportunities, assignments, and potentially attracting new mentors and sponsors who want to champion a rock star!

PLANNING AND ACTIVATING YOUR DEVELOPMENT

To support your development and to help you organize and activate the concepts in this chapter, please go to my website (www.refugioatilano.com) and download the free templates for **The Latino Leadership Workbook**—this is a great set of tools to help organize your target areas and map a plan on where to focus your growth. It also includes a notes page and a development roadmap template so you can begin to think through and draft your personalized improvement plan that will set you up for maximum growth and success.

HOW TO PROACTIVELY AND STRATEGICALLY CHART YOUR PATH

> *"The beauty of a career plan is that it will help you explore opportunities and various career paths so you can confidently determine a long-term career goal for yourself and then take steps to achieve it."*
>
> **– Amanda Augustine**

FAITH IN THE LATINO COMMUNITY

As Dr. Robert Rodriguez writes in Auténtico, "The belief that a person's destiny, their path of life, is determined by God is the mindset of fatalism" (167). Similarly, the Stanford Encyclopedia of Philosophy Archive writes that faith in God is strong in the Latino community and they are strong believers in fatalismo (fatalism), which follows the belief that every event and circumstance is predetermined; an attitude of resignation in the face of future events which are thought to be inevitable (Rice, 2023).

> As Latinos, we are taught to work hard and great rewards will come. Earlier in my career, I led with that approach and trusted my faith would take care of the rest with promotions and assignments. I learned quickly that more was needed and I had to update my approach and after a lot of trial and error. Eventually I was able to elevate my career and there is no doubt my faith has taken care of me and has helped me to push, learn, and realize all the things I needed to do in order to elevate my career—and now the careers of you and others.

I have no doubt that my belief in God put me here today to write this book and to share my knowledge and my network of industry professionals to elevate all Latinos. Additionally, I am convinced He put me in various situations throughout the years to collect knowledge, to meet the right people, and to develop the right skillsets (including writing) to create something special for you. The work I am doing is way bigger than me — it's about all of us! And I am happy to do it.

> I have no doubt that He put me here today to write this book and to share my knowledge and my network of industry professionals to elevate all Latinos.

TURNING FATALISM INTO OUR SUPERPOWER IN THE WORKPLACE

Although this mindset is a strength in our personal lives, it does not always translate into being an effective leader in the corporate environment. Of course, there are varying degrees of how much fatalism is applied across individuals. For the sake of this book, I am addressing this topic in more general terms as it relates to the broader Latino community. According to a Pew Research study cited by Dr. Rodriguez, 53 percent of Latinos in the U.S. agreed that it doesn't do any good to plan for the future because one has no control over it (167). This is a cultural script that we must be aware of and navigate effectively; we have to be careful because this script can be a self-limiting factor. We must be aware of it, and more importantly, determine how to turn it into an asset that will make us a strong bicultural leader.

In order to position ourselves to become impact, competitive players in the workplace, I would like to propose that we update our mindset and approach in this area; start to begin to leverage our fatalism/faith-based approach and add it to the leadership elements discussed in previous chapters. Rather than taking a passive approach and leaving the promotions and opportunities solely up to God, I would ask for us to take an active role and to use our faith to inspire, focus, and drive our development for the leadership areas discussed in this book. For example, I use my strong faith in God as fuel for my development. It's one of my superpowers and He provides me with the guidance and energy I need to keep pushing my career and impact to the next level using the strategies outlined in this book.

PROACTIVELY AND STRATEGICALLY CHARTING YOUR CAREER PATH

In order to be a strong bi-cultural leader in the workplace, it's critical to be very intentional and thoughtful about where you want to take your career, as well as how you want to get there. This effort is always a work in progress as your career options and perspectives will always be evolving. Take the time to chart your career path options, pressure test them with trusted advisors, and then execute on what you need to do to get there is an important aspect of your development and ultimate success. Don't wait back for others to come to you to tell you where to take your career— you must assume complete ownership and be the one driving your career. This activity is constant throughout your career journey; it takes discipline, ambition, a growth mindset, commitment, and the right relationships and support network to help you optimally execute your development plan and land that next role(s)!

In order to be a strong bi-cultural leader in the workplace, it's critical to be very intentional and thoughtful about where you want to take your career, as well as how you want to get there. This effort is always a work in progress as career your options and perspectives will always be evolving.

Personal Insight 1: Refugio A. Atilano, Business Leader at a Top-10 Pharma Company, ERG/DEI Leader, Author, *The Latino Leadership Playbook*

USING MY NETWORK TO ACCELERATE MY DEVELOPMENT

One of the questions I get the most is around how to obtain and leverage mentors and sponsors. Although I have an entire section later in this book dedicated to the topic, I am going to give you a small dip into how I use my network to drive my career.

Having a strong network of advisors, mentors, and sponsors is critical for your development and success. They can provide insights, introductions, referrals, and be a great sounding board for your career planning, in addition to any other topic where you are seeking a different perspective.

First and foremost, I work hard to keep my relationships active with those key people in my network. Whether it's a monthly, quarterly, or semi-annual touch base, I am always in contact to let them know I am there and what I am working on. In addition, I am always asking what I can do for them in return as our relationship is a two-way street.

Second, I activate discussions based on the specific topic. For example, I asked for the perspective of five advisors (trusted colleagues, mentors, and sponsors; inside and outside of my organization) in my network about me writing this book. After creating and sharing my draft vision for writing the book, I made sure to get the perspective of Latinos, non-Latinos, Latinas, and my manager as I wanted to get a great cross-section of thoughts as I made the decision to take on this significant effort.

Third, harness and contextualize the feedback to help you chart a path forward and make key decisions. You will find that you will get lots of different views on potential paths. In my case, I had many supporters with a lot of great ideas. I used some of them to help round out my approach and game plan (for example, incorporating more stories like this one as part of the book). You will find that regardless of the topic, you are going to get a ton of different perspectives and it will be important to assess and leverage the ones that will advance your vision in a way that works best for you.

Unfortunately, you will also sometime come across guidance

that you don't necessarily agree with. For example, I had one very trusted advisor strongly recommended that I should not write this book at this time as there are probably others already out there... and it gave me a moment of pause. However, after getting different and positive feedback from my entire target network on this topic, I made the decision to pull the trigger and move forward. That is the beauty of a great network—they can help bring clarity so that you can make great decisions.

The lesson here is to leverage your trusted network to strategically and proactively chart your path forward for your career or any critical business topics where you need to make key decisions. It will show senior leaders and your manager that you are thoughtful, engaging, and serious about how you prepare for and drive key decisions for yourself and your organization.

> Having a strong network of advisors, mentors, and sponsors is critical for your development and success. They can provide insights, introductions, referrals, and be a great sounding board for your career planning.

Personal Insight 2: Refugio A. Atilano, Business Leader at a Top-10 Pharma Company, ERG/DEI Leader, Author, *The Latino Leadership Playbook*

LEVERAGING YOUR MANAGER AND PERSONAL DEVELOPMENT PLAN

One of the best and most effective ways to chart your path forward is to work with your direct manager to define where you want to go next and create a development plan to help get you there. I know this might differ by company and by manager, but for the sake of this book, let's assume that you have a manager and company that supports your growth and development.

To start, your development will be a career-long journey. You must always be improving in some way to keep raising the bar of your performance and potential. Even in my current role, I continue to work closely with my direct leader on the skills I need to focus on to land my next target role within the company; these are the capabilities that I need to refine and/or develop in order to move up the in the organization.

Each year, your manager will have target improvement areas for you; it's also important that you identify areas where you want to grow (hopefully targeting some of the leadership areas in this book). Take complete ownership of your development and make sure you are driving with the support of your boss and trusted advisors. Amanda Augustine, a career advice expert at TopResume, says, "If you're not managing your career path, someone might do it for you—and you might not like where it leads" (Vemparala, 2023).

> "If you're not managing your career path, someone might do it for you—and you might not like where it leads."
> **- Amanda Augustine**

As you jointly define development opportunities with your manager, it's critical to make them part of your individual development plan so you can both track progress against them. This is a great opportunity for you to perform, shine, and create a strong narrative and reputation for yourself. Being able to address and clearly articulate how you developed over the year against outline goals is an effective way to help others see your work and start to advocate for you! Internalizing and applying these insights is another example of how you can proactively and strategically chart your path forward. You will continue to build your leadership brand and will be known as someone who takes ownership of their career and is hyper-focused on taking their performance and capabilities to the next level. In short, you will continue to position yourself as an impact player.

PART 2: HOW TO PROACTIVELY AND STRATEGICALLY CHART YOUR PATH

Personal Insight 3: Michael Atilano, HR Operational Excellence Lead, Google

HOW TO PROACTIVELY AND STRATEGICALLY CHART YOUR CAREER PATH

Breathe... release your grip... breathe.

Navigating your career is a complex ongoing exercise that requires decisiveness, innovation, and focus. It is highly unlikely that you will be able to manifest sound career plans by forcing or rushing the process, so give yourself the patience you need to make the right decisions. The planning and actions you are going to take from this book will affect you, your familia, and your future, so it's important to release the grip of frustration, fear, and pressure during this time. Breathe... release your grip... breathe.

During my HR career, I have worked across several industries, company sizes, and coached their leadership teams. With the lens of a Latino professional, there are unspoken learnings on career advancement that are commonplace and NEED to be shared with our community. While the focus of these learnings is at the mid-level professional, it is never too early or late to apply them to your career as you prepare for or strengthen your seat at the executive table.

As Latino professionals, the first-generation college graduate experience is very familiar to us and there is a lot of struggle and new learnings that come with that process. Similarly, once we move past graduation and advance our career, we realize that we once again don't have the answers that we need; how do we advance to senior leadership?

While our performance ratings are positive and we are not receiving negative feedback, we are still not advancing to the next level. It is at this moment when we really experience the struggles of being a first-generation professional and, just like in college, there are new learnings that need to be absorbed to reach success. I'll just say one of the key learnings very plainly, YOU need to make an impact! Regardless of the effort, your contributions and how you elevate others needs to make an impact for your team, department, and company.

A FRUSTRATING STORY MANY OF US EXPERIENCE: THE OTHER PERSON GETS PROMOTED

Here is a familiar story on impact that I have seen across companies from the perspectives of three different people. It's Monday morning and they have just announced Carmen as the new U.S. Director of Operations. While the VP, Global Operations, Arun, acknowledges this is Carmen's first role in operations, he is very confident that Carmen's new perspective will result in more growth. Elena, the current Senior Manager of Operations, is frustrated beyond words for being skipped over and now she is being asked to train the new leader on how to do her job!

Elena POV (passed up for promotion): Elena has been in operations since her first day of her 12-year tenure with the company. She has been promoted three times and has held the positions of Coordinator, Lead Coordinator, Manager, and Senior Manager. Her last five years of reviews reflect the highest rating category and she has been given feedback as being extremely reliable and the strongest subject matter expert in operations. Based on her previous strong performance, Elena feels she is the best person to run operations most efficiently and effectively.

Carmen POV (promoted): Carmen has not been at the company as long as Elena, but her nine-year tenure is still significant time. During Carmen's first year with the company, she met with her external mentor who advised her that it would be best for her to diversify her experience in the company if she wanted to reach her aspirations of becoming COO one day. As a result, Carmen has taken roles in finance, customer service, and sales; while Carmen was always evaluated as above average in these roles, she did not always receive the top performance rating. In addition, Carmen received positive feedback that she was a forward thinker and excelled in bringing teams together to work on a common goal.

Last year in her role as a Sales Manager, Carmen proposed an idea for creating a new line of service and cited some changes in customer service and operations that would be needed to deliver this service offering. Arun, the VP, Global Operations really liked the idea and afforded a lot of credibility to Carmen after seeing her other successes in finance and customer service. Arun met with Carmen again to learn more and the executive team soon moved forward with the proposal based on Arun's endorsement. Three months later, Carmen was promoted to the U.S. Director of Operations.

Arun POV: Like most executives, Arun is constantly looking to grow the business. While company performance has been relatively stable over the last three years, Arun knows that the company needs to evolve more aggressively if they are going to grow. At a recent Executive Team meeting, Arun listened to Carmen's proposal to expand into a new service offering but he felt there was a real challenge with operations. While operations is a very efficient team and they have been recognized for their strong execution, they do not handle change very well. They are very accustomed to following their Standard Operating Procedures and this becomes a big obstacle during times of change, especially when they have to work with other teams.

Arun has informally been following Carmen's career and knows that she is very good at influencing and bringing teams together. To make the new service offering work, Arun needs an operations leader that knows how to navigate the company to make an impact and sees Camen as a natural choice. With Elena at Carmen's side as a subject matter expert, Arun believes this can be the first of many new offerings and he promotes Carmen to the U.S. Director of Operations role.

CONCLUSION: WHAT IT WILL TAKE TO CHANGE YOUR PROMOTABILITY

In this familiar narrative, we see that one's ability to create change and make an impact is what is most valued for long-term career growth. Based on what she felt was best, Elena focused on what was assigned to her and the success of her personal goals even if it meant mediocre partnerships and success for other teams. If she had a mentor(s), they may have asked, "While you may have strong performance and are constantly 'doing it all yourself,' are you uncovering and solving new company problems? Are you elevating the performance of those around you?" While strong performance will bring you success to the manager level, senior leadership is measured by impact.

Conversely, as Carmen worked on her development with her team of mentors/sponsors, she learned that advancing her career would require clear goals, applying mentor feedback, identifying needed experiences, and bringing your new ideas forward. As first-generation professionals aspiring to senior leadership, we must not accept "it was not meant to be" and instead author our own story of success with the help of our professional community.

Breathe... release your grip... breathe.

KEY TAKEAWAYS:

- Identify clear career goals and milestones; these should evolve over time as you gain experience.
- Mentors and sponsors are required, not optional; they will provide guidance and opportunities through the eyes of decision makers, so it's strongly recommended you apply their feedback.
- Don't be afraid to fail: This book is filled with Latino professionals who learned from their mistakes so don't be afraid to scrape your knees as you learn to "walk and run."

Personal Insight 4: Kristin Coleman, DEI Director, Advancing Hispanics & Latinos with Top 100 Financial Services Firm

OWNING YOUR CAREER AND LEANING INTO AUTHENTICITY

Own your story, but also be careful with gratitude.

PART 2: HOW TO PROACTIVELY AND STRATEGICALLY CHART YOUR PATH

As I reflect on my career journey, I am deeply grateful and do attribute opportunities I've had to my Latina privilege—the generosity from the people and organizations that serve the Hispanic and Latino community that were contributors to academic or professional success. Looking back through a new lens, these moments were also drivers for a lack of professional tenacity caused by the fog of gratitude.

As a Latina who has spent a majority of a two-decade career in human resources, I have been fortunate to be a trusted advisor, to consult with individuals around career tips and advice to grow their careers, yet I wasn't always heeding my own advice of being bold and taking risks or building a roadmap for my career.

I recognize that like others in our community that are "the firsts," I put others' needs ahead of myself. I set my own glass ceiling and often forfeited my own self-efficacy and self-advocacy. I was grateful to have met the threshold of success that others defined for me, appreciative and humble. I soon realized that leadership and further organizational success and impact requires constant and intentional steps to be in the driver's seat of your own career and truly owning it. You can't let gratitude get to a point of stunting your potential or growth, that's a recipe to fuel self-limiting beliefs, complacency, and a stalled career.

INVENTORY YOUR STRENGTHS AND WEAKNESSES EARLY

Owning your career often requires a very intentional, strategic shift in perspective that forces an individual to practice self-awareness around their technical skills, while also understanding the neuroscience of leadership and where there might be gaps in knowledge, skills, and tools. There are programs, assessments, books, and many other ways to assess areas to develop in order to become a transformational leader, be intellectually curious, and explore multiple approaches. Like many things in life, diversify. Regardless, the time is now that performance excellence, strategic networking/exposure, and leading with authenticity is a requirement and formula for success among c-suite leaders.

Strong performance are table stakes and spending equal time on developing your weaker skill areas and growth mindset is key, versus simply trying to compensate by over indexing on your strengths.

BUSINESS IMPACT AND FINDING THAT "IT" FACTOR

My "It" factor has always been around building trust, community, and relationships. Before I led DEI as a career, like many diverse leaders, I was a diversity champion on the side—apart from my daily responsibilities and career of building diverse teams, as a Talent Acquisition/Recruiting Director. I supported DEI through volunteer roles like sponsoring ERGs or diversity initiatives/programs, mentoring others, etc. I was slightly naïve to think that these roles positioned me well to understand the history, challenges, and resiliency of all diverse communities. As I became an executive sponsor for some of these diversity programs I felt proud and purpose-driven. However, when I landed my first official DEI role in HR for one of our largest business units (over 100k employees), I was honored that my passion job became my full-time job. Little did I know that starting a DEI role in May 2020 would be the best and worst of times to transition from talent acquisition to DEI.

COVID, remote work, social justice issues/racial and religious tragedies across the country—these were not the circumstances or conditions I thought I'd be starting my DEI journey. I was expecting to lead diversity talent programs, a clean dotted line from talent acquisition. In the months that would follow I would test all areas of my HR and business acumen, deepen my level of understanding and expertise around things like psychological safety, empathy, and vulnerability.

While these are not uncommon concepts to an HR professional, these topics awakened me to the realization that leadership effectiveness skills would need to adapt and look very different going forward. I was charged with increasing representation, advancing inclusion and belonging strategies and programs, addressing employee sentiment, and inclusive business practices/

processes/policies, in a time that was arguably the most challenging, emotionally, mentally, and physically taxing. I truly felt the burden of leading through unprecedented times.

SEIZING THE OPPORTUNITY

During the next year of my career, I was essentially doing DEI consulting with colleagues and leaders who were in desperate need of tools, resources, and skills to get proximate to complex issues and build new inclusive leadership behaviors to support their people. This was real impact—taking HR development to the next level, affecting employees, but also communities and society in general outside the workplace. Creating content to support leaders on how to forge through difficult situations as active listeners, leading with authenticity, vulnerability, and creating trust with employees at all levels, leading boldly through uncomfortable conversations was a unique way to bridge an HR background with a leadership need, through the lens of a diverse individual, a Latina in my case.

As we explored these topics, the conversations deepened around allyship to wider diverse communities and advocacy—an opportunity to understand the history and complexity of global communities more deeply, especially for myself as a U.S. born Latina with so much to learn about my own Latino community, particularly outside the U.S. Supporting all communities beyond my own heritage created business relationships that provided credibility outside a typical HR-centric scope. The ability to innovate HR and learning topics while leaning into culture, understanding a global DEI landscape, the business imperative of multiple diverse segments gave me an edge. My Latinidad provided added value to the business leaders/clients I supported, which led to a new, larger global opportunity and scope. The lesson here is that within every unexpected career turn or risk you make take, there is often a silver lining you can capitalize on if you seize the opportunity.

KEY TAKEAWAYS:

- It's not only okay, but necessary to be human at work. Finding common ground and being vulnerable is key to building trust and a strong team so take steps to intentionally invest in relationships (existing and new). Remember, leaders don't promote people they don't know, and people don't follow leaders they don't trust, so do the work.

- Embrace being the first. Your identity and your culture, particularly your Latinidad, needs to be nourished, for yourself/family and for those around you at all levels in the workplace.

- Always be learning and make time for development. Take the time to understand your strengths and weaknesses and spend equal time developing those areas; underdeveloped skills are more difficult to conceal in the c-suite.

- The future is Latino!! The sooner you can incorporate your industry knowledge and skillset with the business imperative and economic impact of Latinos, the sooner it will catapult your career.

DOS AND DON'TS

Now that we have covered the background, stories, and insights around how to proactively and strategically chart your path, here are some additional Dos and Don'ts to further support your development in this area.

PART 2: HOW TO PROACTIVELY AND STRATEGICALLY CHART YOUR PATH

Dos	Don'ts
Do: Determine Skills and Experience Required As you begin to research what roles interest you, determine the skills and experience required for those positions—review job description requirements, talk to your manager about their thoughts on your fit, talk to people in your network with similar roles, talk to your trusted advisors about their insights. Once you determine the skills and experience needed, align them to your current skillset; if there are gaps, use the strategies outlined in the book to find opportunities to develop (ERGs, volunteer assignments, personal projects for your manager, etc.). It will be critical that you develop these capabilities so you can prepare yourself to compete for that next role. Note: You do not need to meet 100% of the job requirements to apply; a good rule of thumb is to meet 75% of the requirements to show up competitively.	**Don't: Forget to Partner with Your Manger** As stated throughout this book, the relationship you have with your direct manager is the most critical one that you have in your current role. Keep in mind that this will only be temporary as he/she will also be looking to elevate their career. Use this opportunity to partner closely, help address their business needs, and leverage them as much as possible to support your development through providing guidance, resources, and/or opportunities. In the end, you want to make your boss an advocate for you—this can also come into play later in your career when references or an introduction are needed. Also, this is an opportunity for you to be an advocate for them as well! This is a two-way street, and we all need to support each other. Note: I admit that not all managers are going to be the best—use your best judgement based on your environment to navigate these waters.
Do: Set and Communicate Your Plan Once you align on your career plan, communicate it to those who can help you—specifically, your mentors, sponsors, and those who are in a position to advocate for you. Once you communicate your career goals and timeline, it puts structure and accountability on you to execute—and it positions you to provide structure and a level of focus for those who will support your career journey.	**Don't: Forget to Stay Confident and Committed** Leading with confidence and commitment to your plan is critical. Of course, things can change, and, in fact, they will change. However, show confidence in your capabilities, where you are going, and your ability to pivot with business changes. Regardless of what the business environment puts in front of you, show that you are more than capable of taking on any challenges, even at the risk of needing time to learn. Put yourself out there as a strong, bold leader who is committed to growth and will take risks to succeed.

Do: Refine Your Plan Periodically	Don't: To Use Your Faith as Fuel
Your career plan will always be fluid. As you develop skills and gain experience, the question will always be "what's next?" Your development never ends, and you must be disciplined as you review and update your plan. You will find that things change quickly—a sponsor might provide an opportunity, your business changes and needs you to step into a new role unexpectedly, you discover a passion you didn't know you had, etc. A good cadence to review your career plan is at least twice per year; think through and pressure test any updates with your manager and trusted advisors. This will help ensure you are considering key perspectives and options.	A big part of being Latino is our deep faith. As stated earlier in this chapter, rather than relying on it solely to drive your career, take ownership using the strategies and insights provided in this chapter. Use your faith as fuel and inspiration. It's a superpower that we naturally have and one that can be a game-changing catalyst to quickly accelerate your development!

RECAP

This chapter was another great example of the importance of being strong, bi-cultural leaders in the corporate environment. As Latinos, our faith is core to our culture and it's a natural superpower that we can leverage to accelerate our development. The combination of our faith-based approach along with the career path strategies outlined in this section is a recipe for long-term success. Effectively executing on the concepts covered in this chapter will help you stand out as a thoughtful, engaging, and future-focused leader in your organization. It will position you as a notable impact player who others in the organization will want to support, provide opportunities, and rally around!

PLANNING AND ACTIVATING YOUR DEVELOPMENT

To support your development and to help you organize and activate the concepts in this chapter, please go to my website (www.refugioatilano.com) and download the free templates for

PART 2: HOW TO PROACTIVELY AND STRATEGICALLY
CHART YOUR PATH

The Latino Leadership Workbook—this is a great set of tools to help organize your target areas and map a plan on where to focus your growth. It also includes a notes page and a development roadmap template so you can begin to think through and draft your personalized improvement plan that will set you up for maximum growth and success.

How to Use Your Latino Culture to Your Advantage

> *"I come from a neighborhood where they say, 'Don't talk about it; be about it.'"*
>
> **- Pitbull**

I could not say it better than Pitbull said it in his quote above—as mentioned in the Latino Data chapter, 76% of Latinos don't feel they can be their authentic selves at work. This perception continues to be a problem for us in corporate America and it's now finally time to flip the script! It's time to turn our cultural superpowers and the Latino scripts awareness and actionable insights covered in this section into a strength. This will help build your bi-cultural leadership capability, as well as accelerate your confidence, impact, and promotability in the workplace.

As Latinos and when it comes to our career and leadership preparedness, many of us grew up with different starting points than some of our Caucasian counterparts. As covered earlier, a lot of us have had limited resources, had parents who were not professionals, and often had to figure it out ourselves; we hoped to be lucky enough to get the guidance and support needed to advance in our careers. Unfortunately for most Latinos, advancing through the ranks has been a struggle and it's clearly reflected in our numbers in senior management roles (as coined by Dr. Rodriguez as the 4% shame).

The time for change is now! *The Latino Leadership Playbook* concepts and insights are set up to directly close the gap on those different starting points—this book is meant to raise awareness on and to start removing the traditional roadblocks by arming you with very targeted actionable insights on how to turn culture into an asset for your career acceleration.

This book is meant to raise awareness on and to start removing the traditional roadblocks by arming you with very targeted actionable insights on how to turn culture into an asset for your career acceleration.

A SUMMARY OF OUR LATINO SUPERPOWERS

I want to begin with this great quote by Mariela Dabbah in an article from Mamiverse.com, "In this tough market you should use all of the advantages at your disposal. The secret is to embrace and leverage those traits that you may have taken for granted, but that can give you a competitive edge. The beauty is that there's little effort required of you because these characteristics are part of who you are" (2016).

This quote is right on; because of how most of us were raised, we have a common set of *natural superpowers* that we should absolutely be leveraging in our current roles and driving impact in unique ways. Here is a list of some of these traits that we should be using as natural superpowers:

- **Adaptive/Innovative** - We are natural survivors, and this trait can be very effective to adjust to situations and/or create new solutions, business ideas, and proposals to advance the organization.
- **Passionate** - Our natural passion can help us lead teams, sell our ideas, connect with and inspire others. The Latino passion is undeniable and should be used to drive excitement and teamwork.
- **Team Players/Collaborators** - This can help us lead teams, be great team players, support other parts of the business that need help, and support our manager, when needed.
- **Loyal** - When we are in, we are all-in; we love taking care of our family and it doesn't matter if it's our personal or work family. Leveraging this trait is a great way to add value, especially as you take on new assignments, projects, or driving strategic relationships with mentors and sponsors.

- **Global Perspective** - A lot of us have family connections and experiences outside of the United States—it gives us a unique perspective and one that you should leverage in the workplace to bring more value to business solutions.
- **Heritage/Gatherings** - We love our culture and we are brought together by food, music, and togetherness. Use this superpower in your teams and begin to develop a brand of bringing others together (in-person and virtually) in both business and outside-of-business settings.

NAVIGATING OUR CULTURAL EFFECTIVELY IN THE WORKPLACE

My career changed and accelerated once I began using my natural Latino traits to my advantage. For example, I lead large global projects and teams and my ability to quickly connect with others is one of my core strengths and critical to the success of my desired business outcomes. This strength was developed early in my life and it's one that most of us Latinos have in our toolbox. Separately, I also use my passion strategically to generate excitement and/or get people behind a new business idea I want to push forward. I love coming up with and driving new transformation ideas for my ERG and my business. At the same time, I am very thoughtful on how I use my passion as it can be a great business catalyst if used wisely. If used too much, however, that can have an undesired effect—so be mindful of where and how you apply it. And finally, I also bring my love for large in-person events to the table with my ERG. Last year, we had an outing for a Chicago Cubs baseball game and had the opportunity to connect with many of our members who we met for the first time, and we instantly created those strong Latino familial bonds!

My career changed and accelerated once I began using my natural Latino traits to my advantage.

Personal Insight 1: Refugio A. Atilano, Business Leader at a Top-10 Pharma Company, ERG/DEI Leader, Author, *The Latino Leadership Playbook*

FINDING, LEVERAGING, AND NAVIGATING AROUND MY LATINIDAD

It wasn't until the past few years that I really saw the power of and embraced my Latinidad. Before that, I thought I had to fully assimilate to the traditional white American culture in order to be viewed as worthy in the workplace. Often times, I thought it was an uphill battle and just deferred to the white leaders as I didn't think I was worthy and meant to be in any type of leadership position. Without knowing any better and having no guidance, I almost accepted that was my final professional fate.

However, things have now changed after getting involved with ERGs, taking several great Latino-centric leadership courses, and with the help of mentors and sponsors. In addition to knowing exactly how I need to use my culture; I also know when I need to pause and pull back. For example, I am very group-oriented and like to include everyone; however, there are times when business requires me to work with speed and urgency. In these cases, my natural tendency to include everyone can be a detriment to the business—and my brand. Therefore, I am always aware of my natural tendency and always pressure-test the level of urgency and business expectations around including team members.

There is a delicate balance on how to effectively use your culture to your advantage vs. when to pull back and leverage the insights outlined in the chapters above. Mastering the concepts of this section will help you become a strong bi-cultural leader that will be impactful and add unique value. This will position you to stand out and contribute to your leadership brand.

Personal Insight 2: Eduardo Arabu, Chief Executive Officer, National Hispanic Corporate Council

HOW TO LEVERAGE CULTURE TO YOUR ADVANTAGE

Latinos have been a part of this country since pre-United States. The population has expanded tremendously over the past several decades. With better knowledge and educational attainments, Latinos have made great strides in corporate America, but there are plenty of opportunities to increase representation and elevate them into more senior roles.

Studies and research show that Latinos excel at the entry-level and management positions; however, they face a "glass-ceiling" for further career advancement. Why is that? One of the leading factors may be how our culture is unconsciously displayed or shown in the workplace. While it is important to understand how you present yourself and how others perceive you at work, you ought to feel comfortable in presenting yourself in your "true authentic self." Therefore, in certain environments, it is a delicate balance between yourself and the corporate culture to excel.

The "Latino Cultural Script," as presented by Dr. Angel Gomez and Dr. Robert Rodriguez, is a critical component of executive leadership development that leads to career advancement. Some of the Latino cultural traits—such as collectivism, simpatía, respecto, paternalism, and others—are examples of cultural identity that Latinos must be aware and competent in the workplace. Some of the traits are being humble, working hard, keeping our head down, and hoping that our work paves the way for promotions. However, that is not the strategy; we must show our work, self-promote, and obtain acknowledgements from leadership that leads to visibility, sponsorship, and other advancement opportunities.

Another leading factor may be how we understand the written and unwritten "rules" of the workplace. We have to understand that career advancement in the workplace is considered "a game." And like all games, there are rules to accomplish the objectives or win. You may choose to participate in the "game" or not, but you must understand that there is a game being played in career advancement. One of these unwritten rules is that the pathway to the c-suite or CEO position when promoting from within, typically comes from certain business units or functions. By understanding this particular rule, you can position yourself for advancement by associating yourself with that specific group.

I have always leveraged my Latino traits for educational and career advantages. I sought after DEI-related initiatives that allowed access and provided resources to advance my learning and development. I believe that competency leads to achievements, which leads to confidence, and that, along with the "Latino Cultural Script" methodology, is how Latinos overcome barriers and challenges. There are other ways towards advancement by:

- Excelling in your work
- Understanding your audience
- Leveraging culture as a cultural competency
- Telling your story/achievements (or self-promote)

Lastly, at this moment in 2023 and beyond, the U.S. Latino segment is rapidly growing in terms of population, consumer base, small business growth, and workforce growth. It is imperative for Latino leaders to leverage their cultural identities and competency to lead corporations and organizations.

KEY TAKEAWAYS:

- Embrace your Latinidad as you define it but elevate your cultural competency (and others). Learn how your cultural traits can serve as superpowers!
- Understand the corporate landscape or the career advancement "game" being played at work. Choose to participate or not.
- Trailblaze by advocating for yourself and others. Show up and show out! Lead by example. Pay it forward. Elevate our community!

Personal Insight 3: Melanie Rodriquez, PdD, PCC, Elevate Latinas, LLC. Talent Management, Leadership Coach, Inclusion Advocate

HOW TO USE YOUR NATURAL VALUE OF COMMUNITY

I've always prided myself on being a person that builds relationships well. I love connecting with people and sharing experiences. I know that my cultural value of community is a huge part of that. My memories are filled with moments of spending time in building community. As kids we always found ways to entertain ourselves. Hanging out with cousins and tías and tíos, going to family parties, spending late nights playing lotería. As we grew older, we spent much of our time hanging out sharing stories and reminiscing on all the good times we've had over the years. The time spent with family-friends was no different. My parents' friends are known to me as tíos and tías—their children, as my cousins.

A huge part of these memories is knowing that we were always there for one another. As a family, we would go out of our way to help people. Whether it was to make ends meet, to house someone in need, to throw a party, or to do whatever we had to do to make life better, my parents were up to it.

When I started my career and early in my days as a leader, I used that ability to create relationships and be helpful to others as a mechanism to be liked. I was known for a friendly smile and could often be found chatting it up in the office kitchen. I was known as the person who is always willing to help on projects. I was the person who never said, "No," to a networking event. For a long time, I considered this ability to build relationships to automatically mean that I was good at networking and helped me to shape my brand as a leader. Little did I know that the network I built lacked the influence and impact I really wanted to have.

What I did not understand was how being so involved in everything shifted the perspective of who I was as a leader. I could not understand how being a likable person who is doing my best to support people and projects could be seen as a negative trait. One day a mentor asked me the question, "Do you consider yourself to be known as a strategic thinker?"

At first, I did not understand why they were asking me this question. Of course, I did. Many of our mentoring sessions were spent talking about work going on in various business units and sharing our thoughts on future projects and work. Then came the follow up question, "Are you included in strategic conversations, or do people only come to you when it's time to execute?"

That's when it hit me. I was known as a doer. I fully emulated the Latino cultural value of a hard work ethic. I was someone who took direction well and executed without complaint or pushback. I executed other people's plans without providing input. This was the case even when I often had thoughts on how to do things differently. I had ideas, but I never shared them because it was not my place.

It took some time, but I grew the courage to ask some of the people I trusted most for feedback. What I learned was that I was known as "the fun one," the socialite, the person to have a relaxing and personal conversation with. People valued the time they spent with me but did not look for value in the conversations we were having. I did not spend any time talking about my views of the business. I never shared what I knew about other work groups. That's when the memories came flooding back. Culturally, I was raised to build relationships, to build community in the environments that I wanted to be in. I realized I was networking from a personal and operational space, rather than being strategic and intentional. There was no influence or impact on my network.

I took that feedback and changed the dynamic. I began doing what I considered "connecting the dots." I started asking my friends in different work groups and on different projects about the work they were doing. I learned about their pain points and their successes. Over time, I began helping other people network and learn about one another. Because I knew about what people were working on, I could gently ask questions about how it related to other parts of the business. This simple shift in how I approached conversations helped me become seen in a different light. I was now a conduit of people and resources helping myself and others to connect the dots.

As I grew as a leader, I homed in on how to become more intentional in the relationships that I create and in the way that I provided support for people and projects. This is what truly shifted my personal brand. I learned to recognize the people that were associated with various parts of my network— operational, personal, and strategic. I pay attention to people and spaces where I can generate significant impact and add value. I recognize that relationship building is a two-way street and I still always grow my network with the intention of being helpful.

KEY TAKEAWAYS:

- Recognize your ability to create strategic impact. Move beyond being the doer by voicing ideas, sharing knowledge, and actively participating in business related discussions.
- Building relationships is a two-way street. Understand how you create impact and add value in various spaces.
- Be intentional about networking. Consider how people fit in to your operational, personal, and strategic networks.

Personal Insight 4: Alejandra Rodriguez Mielke, PhD, Solopreneur, Executive Coach, Speaker, and Intercultural Expert, Founder of Interculturalyst and Co-Founder of El Puente Institute

HOW TO USE YOUR CULTURE TO YOUR ADVANTAGE

Twenty-three years ago, I relocated from Monterrey, Mexico, to start a PhD program and a part-time job at the University of Texas at Austin. Despite my fluency in English and familiarity with Austin from previous visits—not to mention my ability to appreciate humor in shows, like *Seinfeld*—the transition from Mexico proved to be a substantial cultural shock. Interpersonal interactions, the formation of friendships, and behavioral norms were all starkly different from what I was accustomed to. For instance, I could never predict whether colleagues in the hallway would greet me—sometimes it happened, while other times it didn't. People were definitely less warm and more business oriented.

Workplace dynamics were markedly different as well. The way supervisors communicated with students and assistants, and the manner in which students and research assistants challenged and questioned project leaders during meetings was intriguing and, by my standards, slightly irreverent. Interactions were more egalitarian—individuals addressed each other by their first names, openly challenged and accepted ideas, and shared professional aspirations and future plans. The "respect to authority" or the hierarchical tendency that was so prevalent in the Mexican workplaces I knew was definitely not here.

The palpable cultural differences were quickly apparent. Many of my ingrained cultural values and norms seemed out of place in this new setting, leading to a sense of alienation. Regrettably, this sentiment of not fitting in at the workplace often manifests as feelings of unpreparedness or inadequacy among many Latinos. It's as though a lack of proficiency in the traditional U.S. work context's cultural norms is misinterpreted as a deficit in capability, strength, or resolve—which is not the case.

I started to carefully and intentionally explore my cultural values and ways of being and living. Self-reflection and self-awareness questions filled my work and personal life. What is important to us? Why do we do what we do? Why do we care about the things we care about? Through my research and work around the Latinx community, I found some answers to these questions that were exemplified through numerous stories of resilience, hard work ethic, and determination of the Latinx community that fostered my appreciation and validation of my own culture. I became cognizant and proud of many of the values and ways that were part of my cultural heritage. Through trial and error, but always very intentionally, I learned to use these skills to benefit the different projects I was leading as I advanced in my professional career. For example, I proudly recognized that my value of respect allowed me to engage cordially with colleagues at all levels of the organization while my value of collectivism allowed me to successfully engage in collaborative team efforts where I was able to support, guide, and inspire research assistants, students, and external stakeholders.

I was also able to put a name to a concept that was so familiar, yet nameless—the Latin value of personalism. Latinos place value on interacting with others with whom we have a warm, caring, and trusting personal relationship. It is clear that we are relationship-based. Although we might be respectful and more coy with people in positions of authority or senior levels, we are truly skilled at getting to know other people in meaningful ways, giving and putting enough time and interest into the relationship. I learned to leverage my relational skills to ask questions, to get to know people, to develop relationships, to make friendships, and to bring warmth to any situation. It took some time to develop the right balance between the way relationships are made and developed in my native country versus the U.S., but I realized that I could hone this skill in the workplace. It became a matter of recognizing this skill and learning how to use it in the workplace.

I now understand that my intentional efforts to learn more about my culture values were strategies to counter the deficit thinking views about the Latino community that are prevalent in our society. This became a way for me to harness the strength of my community, leave behind fear and doubt, and demand a seat at the table where we can share and leverage the richness and power of our culture and the tremendous potential we have as a community. Indeed, as I deepened my knowledge about the Latinx experience in this country and unearthed story after story about the resilience, hard work, and determination that Latinos have demonstrated in their quest for a better life, I realized that our culture holds extraordinarily valuable traits that cultivate exceptional leaders. Many leadership skills that others must be trained in, are inherent in Latinos, thanks to our cultural heritage. It's our job to act on them.

PART 2: HOW TO USE YOUR LATINO CULTURE TO YOUR ADVANTAGE

KEY TAKEAWAYS:

- Familiarize yourself with your culture and history—learn as much as you can about our struggles, triumphs, and heritage, so you can absorb the many ways we have shown powerfully throughout history and the richness of our beliefs, ways, and values.

- Challenge your assumptions—every time a thought crosses your mind that might provoke doubt or fear about your leadership skills, question that thought to see if it holds true. You are creating your truth as you act, and you have the power to write and rewrite your story.

- Practice one of our most valuable cultural assets: flexibility. We often find ourselves torn between two cultural identities, striving to determine which one is the "right one." Yet, our story isn't just about the struggle to define what's right or wrong. It's about the underappreciated but quintessential facet of Latino culture: flexibility. We have developed a flexibility in thought and unique mental agility that allows us to see and understand the world through two perspectives. This flexibility muscle product of our cultural experience should always be part of our repertoire of skills to be honed and leveraged.

Personal Insight 5: Elisa Charters, Founder, Juego.Juegos AI & Mobile App, Principal, EAC Business International LLC Consultancy, Co-founder & President; Latina Surge National Nonprofit

HOW TO USE YOUR CULTURE TO YOUR ADVANTAGE

Cultural advantages are defined at an individual level, and the success generated from such advantages can really depend on one major characteristic: resilience. An individual's level of resilience may involve many facets including coping skills, an attitude of positivity, self-care, social relationships and networks, and asserting one's cultural identity with confidence.

Sometimes resilience can be unconscious rather than conscious. I have learned that the ability to apply EQ (emotional intelligence) and CQ (cultural intelligence) when contemplating and/or developing strategies to navigate less inclusive organizational cultures, is a major asset. This was the core of achieving my career success and having an impact to help others. Building relationships, navigating tough conversations, championing others, and seeing projects to completion were often an unconscious result of EQ and CQ.

Exemplifying resilience can be deeply meaningful to partners, clients, and management of all levels. Cultural diversity has been at the forefront of institutional governance and strategic planning. One's resilience is valued as paramount to both navigate and promote inclusivity. It is integral to the business case of operations and services, retention, and even drives product design. Leveraging one's *cultura* does not necessarily have to be viewed in a context of adversity, but rather as a competitive advantage. The capacity to maintain and apply one's cultural identity and integrity and adapt these to the demands and opportunities of any workplace sector, will continue to foster considerable value in achieving institutional and corporate goals.

Cultura manifested as success, early in my career. Early on, educationally there was no one to guide me among my family members. I had to figure it out. I suppose having been raised in a perfect melting pot of immensely diverse multicultural low-income boot-strappers in Passaic, NJ, gave me exposure to hardships and unique challenges. To survive and thrive required me to be resilient, emotionally intelligent, and, most importantly, to have grit.

For example, at 14 years old, I wanted to learn about fashion illustration and interior design. I begged my mother to pay for Saturday classes in NYC. My parents could barely afford it. I took the bus alone, and either took the subways or walked to the Fashion Institute of Technology from the Port Authority Bus Terminal. One can imagine that this was no ordinary walk. In the early 80s, NYC was a challenging place for adults and even more so for teens.

Taking public transportation was the only option, and a major drain on time having to wait for buses and trains and connections.

I understood the value of time, and how it negatively impacted me when mass transit was slow. A decade later, I often thought about shuttle services when there weren't really any offered in the NYC region. I recalled my experiences visiting family in Peru. There were all kinds of shuttles there; lots of minivans and larger vans transporting people from more remote areas to places of employment within Lima. It was quite unsafe to take public buses. They were over-crowded, and there was great risk of being pick-pocketed, or worse, having a handbag sliced open with a razor blade to get to your goods.

Interning in Tech Services of Interstate Transportation at the beginning of my professional career at the Port Authority of NY & NJ while attending NJIT, I thought about transportation dilemmas and potential solves. Sandy, my first manager, recommended me for the agency's prestigious Management Fellows Program. This program rivaled the White House Fellows program, and every year there were 500 to 600 graduate students, many being Ivy grads, that competed for the 6-7 coveted positions of this two-year program. This was a platform with high-level exposure to powerful government officials, c-suite decision makers, policy analysts, economic development and major regional infrastructure projects involving the best firms in the world.

Sandy, a Cornell alumna and tremendous champion of feminism and the empowerment of women, was a devoted mentor. She coached me and prompted the Director of the Interstate Department to sponsor me. I was given the opportunity to compete among the 700 graduate applicants. I was the first candidate in the history of the agency to apply from within.

I was one of seven finalists accepted to the program! Turns out, I scored very high on the written exam, where I shared my transportation vision for the shuttle service in supplementing the over-taxed bussing system to better support underserved communities in the NY/NJ port district (a radius of 25 miles). My monetization schedule took into consideration a public perspective of all socio-economic classes of people. It was my cultural experiences that quite effectively set me apart from the country's highest performers in the candidate pool.

DOS AND DON'TS

Now that we have covered the background, stories, and insights around how to use your culture to your advantage, here are some additional Dos and Don'ts to further support your development in this area.

Dos	Don'ts
Do: Embrace and Optimize Your Superpowers Now that we have covered the common Latino superpowers, commit to finding ways to introducing them into your current role to add value in unique ways. Think through carefully about where and when to apply your Latinidad in your work, your teams, and your interactions. When done effectively, people will notice and it's a great way to continue adding to your brand and creating unique value outside of your core work responsibilities.	**Don't: Forget to Support other Cultures** One thing that I learned during this journey is that it opened my eyes to other cultures and the importance of supporting them, regardless of if they are Latino or not. We all have a deep responsibility to the diversity and inclusion of everyone and it's up to us to take ownership of making sure we make space for anyone needing it.
Do: Be a Latino Ambassador and Advocate It is great that you are now armed with these great insights and recommended actions; however, it's only the start of your leadership journey. It's critical that you advocate for all Latinos, our culture, and what we bring to the table that will help drive businesses forward. There is a lot of education that is needed in the corporate world on the Latino professional and data. Make sure you are front and center sharing what you have learned in this book—share nuggets with colleagues, leaders, friends, family, mentees, etc. It will take all of us to shift the narrative and it starts here with you!	**Don't: Forget to Stay Committed to Improvement** Your development and your advancement is a win for all Latinos. There will be setbacks and failures—this is normal with anyone who is going through growth and it's an important part of your career journey. Never be deterred and stay focused on your career goals. You are never alone; use your trusted advisors, mentors, sponsors, and manager to keep you grounded and moving forward. Also, keep referencing this book as it will also help keep you grounded and focused. Work hard and stay committed to how you will use your Latinidad in your workplace to accelerate your career.

A CALL TO ACTION: EFFECTIVELY LEVERAGE AND NAVIGATE THE LATINO CULTURE

In closing out the "Navigating Cultural Values" part of the book, I would like to challenge you to bring new value forward through driving hard toward turning your culture into your superpower. Learn how and when to use it based on the principles outlined in this book. My goal is to optimize your effectiveness, impact, and promotability—mastering the concepts covered thus far (such as working smart, how to advocate for yourself, how to earn respect, etc.) will automatically boost your confidence, your leadership brand, and put you in a position to compete differently—for jobs, for sponsors, and for special assignments.

As I stated earlier, *it's all of us or none of us*. We need everyone on board with the direction of the "next gen" of Latino leaders and I want to hold each other to a high standard and a new a culture of accountability, so that we succeed for now and generations to come! Let's roll!

PLANNING AND ACTIVATING YOUR DEVELOPMENT

To support your development and to help you organize and activate the concepts in this chapter, please go to my website (www.refugioatilano.com) and download the free templates for **The Latino Leadership Workbook**—this is a great set of tools to help organize your target areas and map a plan on where to focus your growth. It also includes a notes page and a development roadmap template so you can begin to think through and draft your personalized improvement plan that will set you up for maximum growth and success.

PART 3:
Introduction to Leadership Focus and Capability

"A leader is one who knows the way, goes the way, shows the way."

- John Maxwell

As we continue your leadership journey on becoming an impact player in the workplace, it's now time to focus on the third pillar of the Latino Leadership Success Model—**Leadership Skills Focus and Capability.** My goal in this section is to provide you with the key focus areas and insights to continue to build upon your leadership brand and accelerate your development towards becoming a confident, informed, promotion-ready professional.

THE IMPORTANCE OF LEADERSHIP IN THE WORKPLACE

Being a strong leader will be critical towards your development, confidence, and promotion-readiness. Leadership is not just a role title or a people manager; rather, leadership is the ability to influence others. It's an action that can be exhibited from wherever you sit in your organization. Per an article by Siena Heights University on why leadership is important in the workplace, they state that "any organization, whether a business, a school, or a government agency, needs leaders to help guide the way. Leaders provide direction and vision, motivate and inspire others to achieve the organization's goals, and help to create an environment conducive to success by promoting communication and collaboration among team members." In short, leadership and strong management are essential for any organization that wants to achieve its objectives.

Leadership is not just a role title or a people manager; rather, leadership is the ability to influence others. It's an action that can be exhibited from wherever you sit in your organization.

As stated earlier, Latinos represent only 4% of senior level roles in corporate America and a lot of us are getting stuck in middle management. One of the opportunities we have that will move the needle is to begin putting targeted focus and investment in our leadership and soft skill capabilities. In an article by Vanessa Gibbs in *Blinkist Magazine*, she referenced a study done by Harvard University, the Carnegie Foundation, and Stanford Research Center that found "85% of career success comes from having well-developed soft skills and people skills. Hard skills, including technical skills and knowledge, only make up 15% of career success" (2022). Similarly, in an article by Indeed.com, it states that "Successful leadership commonly encompasses strong soft skills that enable leaders to motivate and inspire their teams." (21 Soft Skills, 2023). Soft skills ultimately determine how you interact with and influence your teams, senior leaders, and colleagues; this applies to any job in any industry. As such, it is critical that we put continued focus and dedicated effort into building our leadership and soft skill capabilities, so that we can position ourselves to fiercely compete for those coveted high-level roles (Benstead, 2023).

PART 3: INTRODUCTION TO LEADERSHIP FOCUS AND CAPABILITY

"85% of career success comes from having well-developed soft skills and people skills. Hard skills, including technical skills and knowledge, only make up 15% of career success."
- Vanessa Gibbs

What is required

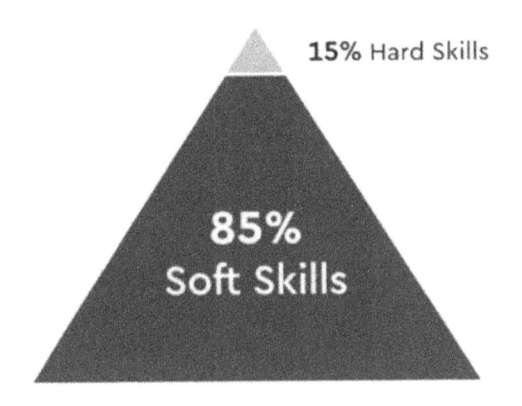

15% Hard Skills

85% Soft Skills

YOUR LEADERSHIP AND SOFT SKILL CAPABILITY DEVELOPMENT

In the spirit of accelerating your leadership development, one of the key objectives of this book is to continue to provide insights to help to you "work smart" rather than just "working hard." This section will tee you up to exhibit overwhelming, undeniable impact that will help you stand out from the pack and begin to land you those great opportunities! After reflecting on personal experience, performing research on what management looks for in promotion-ready candidates, as well as talking to various senior leaders and industry experts, we will be covering the following leadership and soft skill capabilities to facilitate your growth and impact:

- How to Become a Strong Communicator
- How to Identify and Leverage Mentors and Sponsors

- How to Build a Network to Advance Your Career
- How to Create and Leverage Your Unique Brand and Value
- How to Build Your Executive Presence
- How to Lead with an Impact and Extreme Ownership Focus
- How to Be an Effective Change Leader
- How to Be Politically Savvy
- How to Be a Strong Collaborator
- How to Ask for a Promotion
- How to Prepare for and Negotiate Your Salary

This part of the book will be fundamental to us changing the Latino leadership narrative and landscape together; it's another step in our journey towards chipping away at the 4% Latino representation in senior level roles. I want you to be deliberate as you read through each section. Spend the time needed to internalize the concepts and process the insights laid out by some of the most talented and influential Latino and non-Latino business professionals today. The insights and skills covered will apply to any role and industry; these transferrable skills will facilitate your development as a confident, promotion-ready impact player in the workplace—and for the rest of your career!

How to Become a Stronger Communicator

> "Good communication is the bridge between confusion and clarity."
>
> **- Nat Turner**

Being a great, confident, impactful communicator is the single most important skill you will need as you progress through your leadership journey. It's the one skill that will accelerate your development and success in the workplace. As reported by Corporatefinanceinstitute.com, "Having strong communication skills in also aspects of life - from professional life to personal life and everything that falls in between. From a business standpoint, all transactions are a result of communication. Good communication skills are essential to allow others and yourself to understand information more accurately and quickly (CFI Team, 2023)." Similarly, in a blog post by Emeritus.org, good communication is key for leaders to inspire and empower people around them; without these skills, a leader will not optimize being heard or understood by others (2023). Finally, according to an article by Harvard Business School, "If you want to be an effective leader, you need to excel in communication. In fact, the success of your business relies on it." (Landry, 2019).

"If you want to be an effective leader, you need to excel in communication. In fact, the success of your business relies on it." - Lauren Landry

> Earlier in my career, I was definitely short-sighted on what being a good communicator meant. I thought it was just being articulate in my peer interactions and project updates, so

that's where I put my focus. After seeing other great communicators in action, doing research on how to communicate with senior leadership, and testing and learning with what worked best for me, my mindset shifted. When I think of how I communicate today, it's completely different and it's a skill that I have put years of development into. Now, for example, it's about conciseness and structure, focused on business impact/vision, well-prepared messaging, listening intently to and understanding my audience, effectively reading the room/reading the person to I can assess if hitting the mark, knowing when to (and how much) emotion to share, being genuine and authentic, and sharing from the heart.

BENEFITS OF GOOD COMMUNICATION

Being a strong communicator has so many benefits that will accelerate the development of your confidence, impact, and opportunity in the workplace and for your career. For example, you will begin to build trust within your organization, you will be able to convey messages (i.e., advocate for yourself, your innovative ideas) much more clearly, you will develop better relationships and be able to connect with colleagues across all levels, it will help open new doors and networks for you, and will position you as someone who can lead teams and drive key strategic initiatives for the organization.

Being a strong communicator is at the forefront of everything I do professionally and personally. I don't believe in first impressions or taking moments off. I believe in every impression because at the end of the day, they all matter—every interaction is an opportunity to advocate for yourself, and trust me, word travels fast about how you communicate. I know that my image, by brand, and my communication style are always on display, and I work hard to make sure what I am communicating and how I am communicating it are always on point. Just as importantly, if I feel that I cannot live up to my brand (i.e., I am ill or going through a serious life/family event), I will intentionally reschedule to a time when I know I will be back at full strength. Although we will be talking about branding and protecting it in a future chapter, being a strong and consistent effective communicator will be key towards your leadership brand, your reputation, and overall workplace impact.

I don't believe in first impressions or taking moments off. I believe in every impression because at the end of the day, they all matter—every interaction is an opportunity to advocate for yourself.

KEY ELEMENTS OF COMMUNICATION

There are some misconceptions about what great communication looks like, as I had experienced earlier in my career. I am going to give you the four key areas of communication where you will need to put your development focus: Verbal, Non-verbal, Written, and Active Listening.

Note: As we get into the following concepts, my goal is to provide awareness for where you need to focus so that you can take them and work offline to practice and eventually master them. For the sake of this book, my goal is to provide direction and exposure so that you know where to focus as you accelerate your workplace impact.

Verbal Communication

Good verbal communication (using words to deliver your

message) is important for your leadership impact, especially with today's remote and hybrid environments. Your voice is part of what is going to help you give an update to leadership, align others to a new idea, share your personal story, interview, advocate for yourself, etc. After years of practice, here are some insights that have developed my confidence and accelerated my communication skills (I am taking a communication with senior leader approach to this section as this is what will help facilitate your impact with this audience):

- **Prepare, Prepare, Prepare** - This is, by far, the most important element of communication for me. I take time to build out what I want to say and how I want to say it. Then I practice, especially for leadership updates. After doing this hundreds of times, it becomes second nature; this is where you want to be.
- **Structure Your Content** - As a deeper dive on above, you always want take time to structure what you want to say. Your audience, especially senior leaders, will be looking for concise and structured messaging when communicating with them. If business-related, they will want to understand quickly what you need from them, a solid story, and any supporting data you need to make your case/recommendation.
- **Communicate in Terms of Impact** - When you communicate to business leaders, lead with the business impact and give just enough facts/process to help tee up your message. Senior leaders are focused on making decisions to drive the business forward, so ensure you are communicating in a way that facilitates their quick understanding of a topic, as well as sharing options with rationale that can drive the business forward.

Non-Verbal Communication

According to an article in Lifesize.com, "most experts agree that 70-93% of all communication is nonverbal" (Spence, 2020). Therefore, development and mastering this topic is critical to career development and success. This is a space that I have worked incredibly hard on over the past several years—it's a space where I have developed some mastery and my development journey continues today. Here are some key insights to raise awareness and to get your development going in the right direction:

- **Body Posture / Position** - Showing up with great body language can be a game-changer for you and your confidence. For example, I am always aware of my body posture and position when interacting with others. How you carry yourself and your body says a lot to the world—I even going as far as working out my back and shoulder muscles at the gym to support my focus on posture. I am also aware of the spacing I have with others, how I stand or sit, and where I point my feet. These small micro-elements are key to how you are perceived.

- **Gestures** - There are some great YouTube videos on how to use gestures effectively, such as "Make Body Language Your Superpower," which I highly recommend. While there is no one-size-fits all, knowing how to use your hands, your feet, and your eyes will help you become a more powerful communicator. Plus, watch how other leaders gesture and practice with different types. At the end of the day, make it your own and use what works best for you!

- **Tone and Pace** - Make sure (as part of your preparation) to practice the tone and pace at which you are going to deliver your message—tailor it to your audience and the venue. This is incredibly important so that you communicate your message in a way that resonates with the audience and is easily digestible. Take your time when delivering your message—rushing is not needed. You want to command your message and a great way to do it is to have control over your tone and pace.

- **Poise** - The key here is to deliver your message with confidence, with knowledge, and conciseness. Far too often, I see people who struggle in this area as they over-talk, don't know how to use their body, or are unsure of where they are going with the discussion. Don't be that person—prepare thoughtfully and practice exactly what message you want to deliver and how you want to deliver it. Over time, it will become a habit and will be a strong communicator that mentors others!

Written Communication

Written communication is key for your leadership journey. Whether it's an email, a presentation, or other, your written communication will be important to connect with your audience, and especially senior leaders. For the sake of accelerating your development, I will give you some insights that will help you stand out and become a stronger presenter of ideas:

- **Develop Your Story Telling** - As you share updates and ideas for senior leaders to consider, they will want to understand the business story and impact for what you are proposing. Make sure to provide an executive summary (one-pager with key messages), business background, why there is a need for change (define the business impact), and share options with recommendations for the change and how you plan to implement. Providing the story will increase your chances of gaining the support you seek, as well as develop your leadership brand.
- **Be Concise/Simple** - Ensure your messaging and your presentations are well-formatted and have just the right amount of information needed to tell the story. Do your homework on what leaders like to see in their presentations and how they like information presented. Every leader is different. Once you have the information, make sure to hit the mark—often times, less is more. Leverage your manager and trusted peers with experience to pressure-test your messaging so that you are positioned for communication success.

PART 3: HOW TO BECOME A STRONGER COMMUNICATOR

Active Listening

Active listening is another skill that will be critical for your leadership development and career growth. Per an article by Mindtools.com, "Listening is one of the most important skills you can have. How well you listen has a major impact on our job effectiveness and the quality of your relationships with other people" (2023). The article also references a report that we only retain 25-50% of what we hear. Therefore, "listening is a skill that we can all benefit from improving. By becoming a better listener, you can improve your productivity and your ability to influence, persuade, and negotiate. What's more, you'll avoid conflict and misunderstandings. All of these are necessary for workplace success!"

Here are some insights that will support your development in this area. I would also encourage you to do offline research and upskill yourself in these areas as there are a ton of great resources for your development and eventual mastery:

- **Pay Attention** - Face the speaker and use good eye contact, put aside distractions (i.e., cell phone, computer), watch for speaker body language cues.
- **Defer Judgement** - Don't interrupt and let the speaker share their message at their pace; be patient—seek to understand what they are asking and use clarifying questions along the way to help you capture the intended message.
- **Provide Feedback** - You want to ensure and show that you are tracking the intended message; continue to ask clarifying questions and summarize key points along the way to confirm understanding.
- **Respond Appropriately** - After listening, provide thoughtful, respectful responses. Show the speaker that you have listened (words and non-verbal communication) and are responding in a way that helps facilitate your understanding.

Now that we have covered the importance of good communication and how to incorporate it into your leadership capabilities, here are some additional insights and stories to show how they have impacted the career of other business leaders.

Personal Insight 1: Refugio A. Atilano, Business Leader at a Top-10 Pharma Company, ERG/DEI Leader, Author, *The Latino Leadership Playbook*

FAST-TRACKING MY COMMUNICATION SKILLS AND CONFIDENCE DEVELOPMENT

The single most impactful experience I had in developing my communication skills was participating in a company-wide speech derby for one of my previous companies. What's interesting is that I had no intention of developing my skills as I "thought" I was already a great communicator—not! When joining the derby, my sole intent was to be able to share my idea with the entire organization—how we can better collaborate across business units. I thought as long as I presented the idea that the organization would jump all of it. Yeah... that didn't happen, although I was a finalist. Instead, I achieved an entirely different outcome—a better outcome!

The speech derby forced me to present in front of others, taught me how to use the space in the room, how to use my body, how to use my hands and eye contact, how to use pace and tone, and how to craft a story and tell it with conviction. To be honest, I remember I was traveling during the practice rounds so I had to self-learn through YouTube videos as I didn't want to show up un-prepared or make a fool out of myself. This type of learning quickly accelerated my development; I just continued playing with different videos from different leaders in different industries. I was in awe about the content available to me and started to incorporate it into my development and made it my own. I still do this today; I'm always looking for that one nugget to add to my game.

PART 3: HOW TO BECOME A STRONGER COMMUNICATOR

The speech derby experience changed my outlook on how I communicate to audiences from a verbal and nonverbal perspective. I started to look at leaders' communication styles and began to take pieces that resonated so I can improve my communication delivery. The experience was transformational. I highly recommend you do the same or find opportunities to present in front of audiences. They don't have to be large audiences, they could be smaller business teams. This will give you a chance to work on your communication skills and delivery. This will develop your confidence and you will be ready once you begin presenting to senior leaders. Remember, practice is king, and the goal is to master this skill; it will accelerate your development into a confident impact player in the workplace!

Personal Insight 2: Monica Guzman, Executive Coach and Motivational Speaker, Excellence by Monica Guzman

HOW TO BECOME A STRONG COMMUNICATOR

I have always loved to talk. Even as a child, I enjoyed sharing my opinions and selling my ideas. I communicated every thought and never held back on telling others what was on my mind. It wasn't until I entered the workforce as an adult that I realized the true power of effective communication. I came to recognize that in order to sell my ideas and move my career forward, I would need to communicate with intention and strategy. It wasn't enough to just talk. I needed to relate my words to my goals and use them to move my brand forward.

I began to study the art of communication intensively and learned how to speak with confidence, eliminating language that would make me sound insecure. I learned how to focus my language so my audience could understand my ask and give me what I needed. I learned how to show others the impact of my ideas so they could invest in me and buy into the message. For example, in meetings, I began to use more assertive language and removed minimizers from my vocabulary. Instead of using phrases such as, "I sort of think that we could..." I began to begin my statements with, "I recommend that we..." or, "In my experience what would work here is..." This shift not only helped improve my executive presence but also sent a message of authority and expertise.

Imposter syndrome is a powerful force that tried to steer me in a different direction, but I rejected it and continued on a path to showcase my talents through my words, presentation, and delivery. I enjoyed my transformation and saw the results in the quality of my relationships and my ability to move up in business. My personal brand was exactly where I wanted it to be, and I have my evolving communication skills to thank. Now, as an Executive Coach and Speaker, I get the privilege of sharing the secrets to powerful communication to Latinos across the world who have big dreams and are ready to take their careers to the next level.

KEY TAKEAWAYS:

- Communication skills allow us to move our personal brand forward and achieve our professional goals.
- To be effective as a communicator, it is important to examine your words, behaviors, and all parts of yourself. Someone is always watching and you are also communicating something!
- Strong communicators understand that the role that confidence place in their development. Believe in yourself and the fact that you deserve to take up time and space.

Personal Insight 3: Lorraine K. Lee, Top-Rated Virtual Speaker, Consultant, LinkedIn Learning Instructor, President of RISE Learning Solutions, Previously LinkedIn, SlideShare, Prezi

HOW TO BECOME A STRONG COMMUNICATOR

I first learned about the power of public speaking in elementary school. I was a shy, quiet girl who did not like to be in the spotlight. One day, after I gave a presentation for a special student showcase, one of my friend's parents approached me and my parents. "Wow, Lorraine did a great job! I wouldn't have expected it because she's so shy." I wouldn't think about this moment again until I entered the working world.

In perhaps an ironic twist of fate, I ended up working at two of the biggest presentation companies— SlideShare (a LinkedIn company at the time) and Prezi. I learned everything that went into engaging, informative, and eye-catching presentations, as well as what it took to present them well. I worked with renowned keynote speakers and presentation experts, and soaked up what I could behind the scenes, from the importance of including visuals and movement to creating a clear structure and incorporating state changes for audience engagement.

It wasn't until a year into my role at Prezi that my mindset shifted. Each year we had to set goals for ourselves and I realized that as a more senior member of the team, I wanted to set a personal and professional goal to get more comfortable presenting. I was working at a presentation company, after all! And, after 10 years in the corporate world, I had seen just how impressive people were who could speak well. They appeared smarter, more articulate, confident, competent, and advanced the fastest because they were so visible—the list goes on. I wanted to stand out and continue growing, even if it scared me.

That was the start of a new direction for my career, one I couldn't have predicted.

I found a mentor at Prezi who agreed to watch my recordings, and I started learning by doing. I built my first talk around how to create a strong virtual presentation (it was particularly relevant since we were still in the midst of COVID). I was extremely nervous and had trouble sleeping the night before any presentation. Afterwards, I was exhausted from the adrenaline drop, but I was proud of myself and audience feedback kept improving.

I kept pushing forward. I reached out to people in my network who could bring me in to speak. As I got more comfortable with the material, I continued to improve and build out my talk. Eventually, people started reaching out to me! I began posting more on LinkedIn about my speaking engagements. Internally, people started seeing I was a thought leader outside the company's virtual walls. I got asked to represent the company by speaking at conferences like Zoomtopia and at Fortune 100 companies Prezi wanted to build relationships with.

Externally, I started receiving requests to interview me on podcasts and in articles. My public speaking became a side hustle for me that ultimately grew into a business after a layoff in November 2022. Now, I have the honor of helping others at all levels learn how to become strong public speakers.

Don't get me wrong, I still get nervous when I present. I think most presenters do, no matter how long they've done this for. However, instead of it feeling like something I have to manage, it's a source of energy and focus. I know that nerves and the discomfort exist because I'm pushing myself out of my comfort zone, which is where the most growth happens.

Most people don't ever learn how to become strong presenters because it's difficult and scary (there's even a term for this fear—glossophobia). If you can be one of the special few who push past that discomfort and leverage presentations and public speaking to your advantage, the world is your oyster. I'm excited for you to start your journey!

KEY TAKEAWAYS:

- The things that scare us the most are often what we need to do in order to grow.
- Being a strong presenter is one of the most significant ways to stand out in the workplace.

Personal Insight 4: Rafael Magaña, Founder & CEO of Latino Professionals, Latina Professionals, and Latinx Professionals

JOURNEY TO EXCEPTIONAL LEADERSHIP: SEVEN CRUCIAL COMMUNICATION TECHNIQUES FOR LEADERS

As I began my professional journey, I actively looked for experiences that pushed me out of my comfort zone. This led me to unexpected leadership roles in volunteer organizations, helping me grow both personally and professionally.

My love for volunteering began in high school and grew during my time at the University of California, Los Angeles. I joined several student clubs and organizations which gave me a platform to explore, practice, and improve my leadership and management skills. These experiences collectively shaped my career path.

I gained diverse experiences by working at multiple well-known organizations like the Emphysema Foundation, Breathe Southern California (previously known as the American Lung Association of Los Angeles County), and the United Cerebral Palsy of Los Angeles County (UCPLA). At UCPLA, I managed two important departments: Development and Communications.

At UCPLA, I had the privilege of working under an exceptional and insightful Vice President of Development and Operations. Under their guidance, we successfully expanded the budget from approximately $37.4 million in 2021 to over $50 million in 2022. Initially, we had a dedicated team of 664 staff members, including 508 full-time and 156 part-time employees, augmented by 208 committed volunteers. Remarkably, our workforce rapidly expanded to encompass well over 1,000 employees.

Each role I held added valuable insights and unique challenges to my leadership journey. They played a key role in shaping me into the leader I am today, providing me with a wide range of experiences and lessons.

Stepping into leadership positions early in my career was exciting, but also intimidating. There was a lot to learn quickly. The responsibility that came with these roles, such as supervising various tasks and conducting personal check-ins, was initially overwhelming. But I faced these challenges with determination, using the skills I had gained through years of volunteer work.

As I navigated these new responsibilities, I learned that effective communication is crucial for a productive work environment. Through trial and error, I found seven key strategies that helped me evolve from a new manager to an experienced leader. These strategies shape my leadership story and highlight the importance of effective leadership. They also show how crucial communication is for team dynamics and organizational success.

My journey allowed me to discover seven important strategies that transformed me from a beginner manager to a successful leader.

1. **The Magic of an Open Door Policy and Regular Staff Meetings**

   My first foray into effective leadership was the introduction of an open-door policy and regular staff meetings at the Emphysema Foundation. Despite the relentless pace of our workdays, driven by the pressing needs of those suffering from Emphysema, I committed to keeping my door metaphorically ajar. This availability ensured that my team had a constant open avenue for voicing their concerns, providing valuable insight that went beyond managing crises.

2. **Continuous Performance Evaluations**

   The implementation of continuous performance evaluations was another critical milestone. Traditionally, we had leaned on year-end evaluations, but I discovered that feedback given throughout the year delivered substantial benefits. It was a proactive way of staving off potential performance issues that team members might have been unaware of. By setting clear goals and monitoring progress either monthly or quarterly, our journey towards achieving our mission became smoother and more efficient.

3. **Timely, Straightforward Communication**

   Then there were those challenging conversations, some

related to funding, others to resource allocation, and even personal matters. Delaying these discussions, I realized, was similar to letting a time bomb tick away. To defuse potential problems, I learned to address sensitive issues promptly, providing team members the space and time to voice their concerns, while maintaining a diplomatic stance.

4. **Cultivating the Art of Listening**

   Interestingly, mastering the art of communication at the Foundation often meant speaking less and listening more. Previously, I had dominated meetings with updates and task assignments, stifling the voices of my team. Then, I learned to actively listen, understand body language, and validate key points. This not only ensured a shared understanding across the team, but also fostered a sense of ownership and camaraderie.

5. **Checking In with the Chain of Command**

   Connecting with the chain of command emerged as another integral aspect of my role. Whether liaising with the Board of Trustees, networking with potential donors, or collaborating with medical experts, I found myself advocating for my team at every level. I articulated their needs and aspirations, resulting in tangible changes that bolstered their trust and respect. In the process, I became their primary link for conveying workplace requirements and Foundation goals.

6. **Using Self-Assessments**

   The Foundation also embraced the 360 evaluations during my tenure. Providing a comprehensive understanding of the team's dynamics, this approach included self-assessments, peer reviews, and feedback from both superiors and subordinates. This wide-ranging perspective significantly contributed to the collective growth of the team, fostering a sense of unity and shared vision.

7. **Diverse Communication Techniques**

Last, but not least, I discovered that every member of my team processed information differently. Whether it was announcing a new outreach program or delegating tasks, I ensured to provide an overview at team meetings, followed by individual follow-ups. To ascertain understanding, I would ask them to summarize their understanding and supplement oral instructions with written emails for reference.

Summary

Over time, my relationship with the team deepened, and I became more attuned to underlying issues, which enabled me to address problems proactively. These robust communication strategies bolstered my team's effectiveness and resilience, allowing us to efficiently navigate our collective journey back to the safe harbor of productivity.

The transition from a novice manager to an experienced leader was akin to climbing a mountain; steep, demanding, and fraught with challenges. However, these seven strategies served as my climbing gear, aiding not only my ascent but also guiding my team alongside me. In the end, this narrative is not just my story but a testament to the transformative power of effective communication in leadership, especially within the rewarding realm of non-profit organizations, such as the Emphysema Foundation.

Personal Insights 5: Dr. Marisol Capellan, PCC - CEO at The Capellan Institute, LLC and Author of *Leadership is a Responsibility*

HOW TO BECOME A STRONG COMMUNICATOR

I have always been fascinated by human behavior, especially those that can contribute to great leadership skills. Great, responsible leaders motivate and engage people, set clear goals and objectives, and have a great sense of responsibility for everyone around them. One of the main ways leaders can accomplish these things is with great communication skills. Unfortunately, communication skills are commonly overlooked in leadership training and development.

A great communicator who effectively conveys information verbally and nonverbally can become a highly impactful leader in their organization. A great communicator can transform people's behavior and motivation regardless of the setting, whether at home, at work, or in a social setting. Throughout time, most of the leaders that have inspired us the most have been great communicators who can transmit power with their words.

As a young professional, I attended many panel discussions in my quest for knowledge. I would always raise my hand and ask all the panelists in attendance, "What do you think is one of the most important skills a leader must possess?" Almost all the time, without fail, the answer was "being a great communicator." Since English is my second language, the first thing that came to mind when I heard that answer was that I needed to work on my diction and grammar. I thought these two things would set me apart as a great communicator.

As time progressed, I noticed that it was not the grammar or diction, but the ability to engage in active listening and ask open-ended questions that made a massive impact on your ability to communicate effectively. It wasn't the ability to talk well, fast, and loud that makes a great communicator. Instead, it's your ability to become an active participant in the communication process and an active listener who asks excellent questions, which will set you apart as a great communicator and leader.

After completing my master's degree in management with a specialization in leadership, I decided to become a certified executive coach. To become a competent coach, you must invest hundreds of hours communicating with others. We are constantly training our active listening skills when we coach our clients. Imagine hiring a coach who does not know how to listen! The more I learned how to become a better communicator, the more my clients recommended me as a coach to their friends and family. Without a doubt, a skilled coach must possess highly active listening skills.

To become an active listener in a conversation, it is essential to fully listen to what the other person is saying, make sure you heard it correctly, and allow the person to elaborate on their stories. When we are in a conversation, we may fall into the trap of listening to someone speak and crafting a response before the other person is done talking, which hinders the communication process and is not active listening. Active listening requires us to fully understand the content, feelings, and intentions behind people's words.

One simple way to become a better listener is by asking open-ended questions during communication. Open-ended questions require a fully elaborated answer and usually start with how, why, or what. I used to teach Management and Organizational Behavior at the University of Miami, Miami Herbert Business School, and in my syllabus, I had to teach a chapter on communication. I witnessed a considerable improvement in my students' communication skills once I incorporated open-ended questions into our in-class communication. They seemed to become more engaged and felt confident in their skills.

I would incorporate active listening in my lessons by asking open-ended questions right after I delivered a lesson. I would ask them what they heard, what they thought I meant, and how they could apply the lesson they had just learned in their daily lives. Also, what would this lesson look like in a professional setting? What does it look like in the real world? The conversations we had in the classroom were very insightful. Not only did they learn the science of human behavior, but their reflection on the topic helped them put the lessons into practice.

In the corporate world, this active listening and open-ended questioning could be used right after you give a directive as a leader. Do not be afraid of asking open-ended questions such as: *What do your employees think about the new directive? How would this directive look like in their respective departments? Why should we move forward now with this initiative?* Using open-ended questions facilitates a participative leadership style, which is great for employee motivation and citizenship, and improves the employee's willingness to go above and beyond in the workplace.

Being an active listener has transformed my leadership and relationship skills. Undoubtedly, incorporating this technique of active listening and open-ended questions will be a game changer in your leadership development journey.

KEY TAKEAWAYS:

- Remember communication is usually a two-way process. Listen attentively to the other person, make sure you understand the information they are trying to convey.
- Practice not interrupting while the other person is speaking.
- When in doubt, opt for asking more open-ended questions than closed-ended questions.

Personal Insight 6: Marlene Gonzalez, President LCG Group, LLC, Doctor of Business Administration Candidate in Organizational Neuroscience

EMBRACING THE BRAIN-HEART CONNECTION: MY JOURNEY TOWARDS EMOTIONAL INTELLIGENCE

The Voyage to Self-Understanding

My upbringing in a traditional Latino family was a vibrant tableau of emotions. Passion, exhilaration, and the occasional fiery disagreement added color to our lives. Our hearts were etched on our sleeves, but deciphering those emotions, understanding the root of those feelings, was a voyage I had yet to undertake.

As I maneuvered through my professional journey, it was clear that this voyage was not just necessary but integral. I must confess that achieving this was not an easy journey for me, as my team at one point gave me the nick name of "Sargent Pepper," because of my short fuse and controlling and inpatient reactions. Emotional acumen, often called EQ, became a pivotal tool in advancing my career, having a positive impact on strengthening relationships, and enhancing self-understanding. The synergy between our mind and brain became palpable, and my plunge into affective neuroscience began.

I am now pursuing my Doctorate in Organizational Neuroscience with a concentration on affective neuroscience. My career journey unmasked a universe that was a nexus of feelings, behaviors, and neural connections. I realized that emotions weren't ethereal constructs that they have a real impact on us and on people; they were rooted in the neural networks of our brain. Understanding their impact helped me comprehend that dealing with emotions wasn't about suppressing them, but about conscious navigation. Emotions were not antagonists; they were tools for insight, signposts guiding our perception of the world around us.

Ascending to the role of global executive leader at McDonald's Corporation was the crucible where my emotional acumen was tested. Leading a globally diverse team, each with their unique backgrounds, cultural perspectives, and emotions was about managing hearts as much as tasks. Every day I practiced empathetic listening, striving to understand not just the words of my team members, but their underlying emotions. Empathy became my beacon, guiding me to understand their viewpoints, their drives, and their apprehensions. Recognizing and managing my own emotions was equally vital. Self-awareness became my north star, helping me regulate my feelings, leading by example.

I learned that emotional acumen wasn't about being swayed by emotions; it was about handling them with intelligence. It was about steering through the intricate maze of feelings that affective neuroscience had unveiled. It was about transforming their impact into concrete actions, forging deeper connections with my team.

PART 3: HOW TO BECOME A STRONGER COMMUNICATOR

Key Takeaways: Techniques for Cultivating Emotional Acumen

Here are some takeaways from my journey. While the understanding of affective neuroscience provided the academic groundwork, the real work has been in its practical application with clients and organizations. Emotions are seen. Here is a practical facet model I developed to help others create a positive impact on emotional intelligence:

1. **S**elf-awareness: Recognizing and understanding your own personality, preferences, and emotional blind spots empowers you to control them, rather than being controlled by them.
2. **E**mpathetic Listening: Listening with intent and understanding withhold judgement. All emotions are real, and words have meaning and an underlying emotion; connecting the two helps you foster a deeper emotional connection with everyone around you.
3. **E**valuate Understanding: By imagining yourself in others' shoes, you can comprehend their viewpoints, fears, and drives, enabling you to relate better with others. Show interest and curiosity, seek to understand with a sense of humility and ask questions. Emotions cannot be avoided; they are primal connections to our nervous system.
4. **N**avigate Emotional Regulation: The ability to maintain a calm demeanor in stressful situations by managing and regulating your emotions is crucial to keeping the team's morale high. If you are put on the spot, you can use the phrase: "I understand this is an important subject for you, why don't you think about it and let's talk later."

Again, my journey was not easy, nothing worth learning is but when I applied these techniques intentionally, I noticed a profound transformation in myself and people around me. There was a stronger bond between my team members and me that surpassed professional ties. We were able to communicate effectively, understand each other better, and work together harmoniously—and the business results exceeded my expectations. I was awarded the highest honor in the company given to only 1% of global corporate employees, the President Award. The benefits transcended my professional life, extending into my personal relationships. I was able to form stronger, deeper connections with my family and friends.

For all the Latinos maneuvering their professional journeys, remember, our emotions are integral to us and comprehending them is essential for our growth. By embracing our own emotional intelligence journey, we can evolve into not just better leaders, but better individuals. So, let's embark on this voyage of understanding, self-awareness, and growth, and let's undertake it together.

DOS AND DON'TS

Now that we have covered the background, stories, and insights around how to become a strong communicator, here are some additional Dos and Don'ts to further support your development in this area.

Dos	Don'ts
Do: Study I would highly recommend you go deep in this area—there are tons of great resources on all the elements covered in this section. Whether you use books, online videos, or training, prioritize the concepts that will make the most impact for you and work them into your game. Be thoughtful and strategic on where you focus. Share your plan with your manager and peers; this way, you can gauge your effectiveness as you develop. Bathe yourself in the art of being a strong communicator and you will get there before you know it.	**Don't: Forget that Simple and Concise are King** I am trying to tee you up to speak to any leader, especially senior leaders. Keep it short and simple. Whether verbal or written, your message must be structured and concise, with the key ask or update in mind. *Note: I used only two sentences in this section as an example of keeping it simple.

Do: Practice	Don't: Forget to Be Ready for Questions
I can't say this enough—to master this critical skill, you will need to make this part of your DNA and practice in both personal and professional settings. It will expedite your development and you will find that your communication game will move to a whole new level. Commit to working on two concepts a month to work into your life at home and at work. Ask for feedback, make adjustments, and keep playing with different elements. It took me 3-4 years to master my communication delivery (and I am still learning), so be patient, but keep developing!	Anytime you are communicating, especially to leaders, prepare yourself for any questions that might come your way. Proactively think through what might be asked and have a response prepared that you can succinctly deliver and keep business impact in mind. Your responses should be concise and meaningful; also, it's a great opportunity to show poise, pace, and confidence. All of these are key elements for demonstrating your communication capabilities!

RECAP AND LATINO CULTURAL SCRIPTS AND COMMUNICATIONS

As discussed in previous chapters, we need to continue to work through shifting to a bi-cultural mindset to be an effective and impactful leader. Because of how we were raised (i.e., respect or respeto), we naturally defer to authority figures and don't feel confident advocating for ourselves or communicating while putting ourselves first. This element traditionally has been intimidating for our community as a whole and the purpose of this book is to show the pathway on how to blast through those barriers! To quote Soudeh Mansourian, a good friend and an immigrant executive at a major airline, "Keep breaking the glass ceiling and believing in yourself!"

The intent with this section was to give you key impactful insights and strategies that increase your awareness on key develop areas so that you can begin to shift the narrative and elevate your communication game. As stated earlier, being a great communicator is the single-most important leadership soft skill you can have and now you are armed with the information you need to accelerate your development. Remember to study hard, practice even harder, and use your trusted network as you work toward mastering this great leadership capability and develop into that impact player inside of you!

PLANNING AND ACTIVATING YOUR DEVELOPMENT

To support your development and to help you organize and activate the concepts in this chapter, please go to my website (www.refugioatilano.com) and download the free templates for **The Latino Leadership Workbook**—this is a great set of tools to help organize your target areas and map a plan on where to focus your growth. It also includes a notes page and a development roadmap template so you can begin to think through and draft your personalized improvement plan that will set you up for maximum growth and success.

How to Identify and Leverage Mentors and Sponsors

> "A mentor advises. A sponsor advocates."
> - Steve Miller

Although we will cover some basics around mentors, the focus of this chapter is going to be around how to identify and leverage sponsors—the **real fire power** behind what can quickly catapult your career! As covered earlier, had it not been for a Latina executive at a previous company providing insights and guidance about where my focus should be, I would not be writing this book today—and that is no joke. That's the power the right mentors and sponsors have, with the proper guidance, you can change a career, an organization, or an entire Latino community!

WHY IS SPONSORSHIP IMPORTANT

I think one of my current sponsors said it best when describing one of his VP-level trainings. As soon as the group organized, he reported the training facilitator told the room that, "There is nobody who got here without the help of someone else." This was very insightful as I had no idea this was the case; I thought VPs moved up the ranks due solely to their exceptional performance. As I started studying this topic more, the theme was resounding— we need support from executive leaders if we are going to move up the corporate ladder to those coveted senior level roles. If you ask any successful person how they advanced in their career, they will often talk about a sponsor or someone who believed in them and helped them climb the ranks (Saperstein, 2022). This hit home for me because it made me realize that getting mentors, and especially sponsors, is serious business; I knew that if I wanted to accelerate my career, my development, and my overall impact that I would need to put serious focus in this area—and that is exactly what I did.

If you ask any successful person how they advanced in their career, they will often talk about a sponsor or someone who believed in them and helped climb the ranks.

Sponsors are the holy grail of relationships. They are the ones who are going to fight for you—promotions, reviews, special assignments, etc. They will put in all their chips on the table and lay their reputation on the line for you. A sponsor is a senior, influential leader who can open opportunities for you. They will advocate for getting you job opportunities and advancement within the organization to other senior leaders and key decision-makers within the company (Reeves, 2021).

> *It is interesting that I once had a sponsor earlier in my career before I ever knew about sponsorship. I was a project manager partnering with an influential executive on a highly visible project that was creating a whole new business arm for our organization. For me, I was content just to be working on such an important project and not even thinking about all the great career opportunity that was at my doorstep. While working with the executive, we spent a lot of time together and got a chance to hang out professionally and personally; we got to understand each other's styles and worked extremely well together as we delivered for the organization. Over the couple of years I worked with him, he was eager to open doors for me; he introduced me to other executives across the organization, he fought for ensuring I received the highest bonuses and recognition, and personally called a hiring manager to advocate for my eventual promotion. In my head, I thought that just what friends do, not knowing that this is the epitome of how sponsors can help you drive your career. We have total trust and confidence in each other, and it happened so organically. Looking*

PART 3: HOW TO IDENTIFY AND LEVERAGE MENTORS AND SPONSORS

back, this was a great experience to show the benefits of a great sponsorship relationship.

For awareness, here are some fascinating metrics on the impact of sponsorship on career:

- Americans who have a sponsor are paid 11.6% more than their peers[3]
- Professionals of color are nearly 40% less likely to report having a sponsor[1]
- 41% of Hispanic U.S. executives say they benefited from formal mentoring or training but only a quarter of junior managers report access to mentoring programs[1]
- Latina women with sponsorship earn 6.1% more than peers who lack sponsors[1]
- Latinos with sponsors are 42% more likely to be satisfied with their career progression than Latinos without sponsors[2]
- Only 5% of full-time, high-earning Latino professionals in large companies have a sponsor in their corner[2]

Sources: (1) Theglasshammer.com, "Why Creating Inclusion at Senior Levels Requires Formal Sponsorship"; (2) Hbr.org, "U.S. Latinos Feel They Can't be Themselves at Work"; (3) and CNBC, Report, "The Race and Gender of Your Office 'Sponsor' can Affect Your Salary"

LATINOS AND SPONSORSHIP

As you can see, if we are going to be impact players in the workplace, we need to step up our game around obtaining and leveraging sponsors. Seeking and/or positioning ourselves for sponsorship requires abilities like thoughtfulness, patience, and a willingness to advocate for ourselves. These are all elements that can be uncomfortable for Latinos, and we must commit to blasting through those barriers. In a study done by the IBM Institute for Business Value, "Untapped Potential: The Hispanic

Talent Advantage," in Collaboration with We Are All Human, the Hispanic leadership participants overwhelmingly agreed that mentorship and sponsorship were critical for senior-level career advancement. They noted that we need to also address our mindset limitations and begin to get comfortable advocating for ourselves and putting ourselves out front in order to get noticed by prospective sponsors and those in the organization. We must work past being labeled by fellow Hispanics as "being selfish" or "trying to be white."

> Earlier in my career, I was regularly accused of "trying to be white." It got to the point where I would not talk to my family or friends about work, how I visited executives' homes for get-togethers, or how I went golfing with them. I felt like it was taboo to talk about these things and that I would be judged. I was raised in inner-city Chicago and was also enjoying a life in the suburbs—it was two worlds. It was very difficult during that time as I would have to suppress that part of my life in front of loved ones. However, regardless of how family and friends felt, I never stopped. I was committed to my development and blasted through and kept driving forward. Now I am here today sharing those same leadership lessons learned that are now more widely accepted as requirements if we want progress in our careers. The world has definitely changed and I feel happy to be able to share my experiences, while also showing how to layer in our Latinidad as a superpower!

As we end this section, it is critical that we commit to our united development in this space. We must be strategic, we must be bold, and we must be impactful on how we go about obtaining and leveraging those coveted sponsors! With the topics covered in this book, I am very confident you now know the importance of, as well as the capability to begin thinking about, how to build your sponsor network.

MENTORS VS. SPONSORS

Although we have focused primarily on sponsors in this chapter, mentors can also play an important role in your development. These relationships are particularly effective for skill development and situational analysis feedback. Mentors offer advice, guidance, and can be a sounding board for mentees; they can help you navigate career decisions, work though challenges, and be a role model (Reeves, 2023). According to an article by JP Morgan Chase, "Mentors provide advice, feedback, and coaching through formal or informal relationships" (JP Morgan, 2020).

As you can see, both the mentor and sponsor relationships are very important and serve two different purposes. As you plan and navigate your career journey, you must strategically and thoughtfully determine how you can leverage each type of relationship. This due diligence will put you in an advantageous position to develop into that workplace impact player you desire to be.

To also further help differentiate between the two types of relationships, here is a nice summary of the differences/benefits of mentorship and sponsorship:

Mentors	vs	Sponsors
Mentors have mentees	→	Sponsors have protégés.
A mentor could be anyone in a position with experience desired by a mentee who can offer advice and support.	→	A sponsor is a senior level staff member invested in a protégé's career success.
Mentors support mentees through formal or informal discussions about how to build skills, qualities and confidence for career advancement	→	Sponsors promote protégés directly, using their influence and networks to connect them to high-profile assignments, people, pay increases and promotions.
Mentors help mentee craft a career vision	→	Sponsors help drive their protégé's career vision
Mentors give mentees suggestions on how to expand their network	→	Sponsors give protégés their active network connections and make new connections for them
Mentors provide feedback to aid a mentee's personal and professional development	→	Sponsors are personally vested in the upward movement of their protégé
Mentors offer insight on how a mentee can increase visibility through finding key projects and people	→	Sponsors champion their protégés visibility, often using their own platforms and reputation as a medium for exposure.
Mentors passively share the "unwritten" rules" for advancement in their organization with mentees	→	Sponsors actively model behavior and involve protégés in experiences that enable advancement

Source: Inclusion.slac.stanford.edu—The Key Role of a Sponsorship for Diverse Talent

Now that we have covered the importance of obtaining and leveraging mentors and sponsors and how to incorporate it into your leadership capabilities, here are some additional insights and stories to show how they have impacted my career and those of other business leaders.

Personal Insight 1: Refugio A. Atilano, Business Leader at a Top-10 Pharma Company, ERG/DEI Leader, Author, *The Latino Leadership Playbook*

LEVERAGING NON-LATINO SPONSOR RELATIONSHIPS TO DEVELOP

When I started my journey to develop a network of trusted advisors a few years ago, admittedly I didn't know what a sponsor was, nor the importance of having one. I was lucky enough to fall into them because of my ability to naturally develop relationships at all levels. Given my growth in this area, I am now very intentional on how I go about attracting and engaging mentors and potential sponsors. It's something I take very seriously and handle with extraordinary care. These relationships are gold and I protect them at all costs.

Throughout my career, I have had several senior-level influential leaders who have taken me under their wing—and the way it worked out is that they were all white leaders. Although I didn't plan it out that way, it worked out to my benefit and overall understanding of the business world. I saw the way these leaders operated, the way they focused on business, what they did outside of work (which was different than my culture). To be honest, it's because of these experiences that I learned to do things like lead projects with a business lens, actively develop strategic relationships across the organizations where I worked, as well as find opportunities to play golf with other leaders. I know that not everyone plays golf; for me, it was a differentiator that helped me establish connections that I might have not otherwise achieved.

PART 3: HOW TO IDENTIFY AND LEVERAGE MENTORS AND SPONSORS

> I am now very intentional on how I go about attracting and engaging mentors and potential sponsors. It's something I take very seriously and handle with extraordinary care.

There is plenty of research that shows that we have a bias to be attracted to sponsors that look like us. In the CNBC.com article referenced earlier in this chapter, it was reported that there were a couple of key problems with sponsor relationships. For example, white executive males tend to support each other or people that look like them; they also found that women of color were also partnering up for sponsor-sponsoree relationships, which was leading to lesser pay.

Given this knowledge, my recommendation when finding a sponsor is to find ways to diversify your perspective and help break those unconscious biases. When I look back, my sponsors were white males—they showed me a world that I would have never seen without that experience. Now, I am focused on adding female sponsors to my network as it will provide additional perspective, insights, and exposure that I would otherwise not get. My sponsorship network is always a work in progress and am very thoughtful and careful where and how I engage.

Personal Insight 2: Refugio A. Atilano, Business Leader at a Top-10 Pharma Company, ERG/DEI Leader, Author, *The Latino Leadership Playbook*

LEARNING TO ADD VALUE TO YOUR MENTORS AND SPONSORS—IT'S A TWO-WAY STREET!

What I learned quickly is that if you want to land those coveted sponsors or high-profile mentors who can potentially become sponsors, you will have to find a way to add value for them. This shows that you are all-in and are serious about the relationship; this approach will also provide more ways to showcase your skills, your value, and your impact for the sponsor and organization.

If you want to land those coveted sponsors or high-profile mentors who can potentially become sponsors, you will have to find a way to add value for them.

As an example, for one of my mentors I shared my passion for developing leadership capabilities in others and she had an immediate opportunity for me to partner with one of her key members on her team. I took this assignment (opportunity) very seriously; I developed a plan, engaged the new team members, worked to develop a strong bond, and worked closely with her over several weeks to refine various leadership skills. In addition, I regularly reported back to the mentor on how well things were coming along and I made sure the team member and I were always in sync on our messaging.

Although this was a short example of how to add value, it was an impactful example on how to listen for and take care of the needs of your mentor's or sponsor's business, team, or organizational needs. Make sure to listen carefully and determine where your prospective mentor or sponsor has a need and how you can help address it. This will show you are a good listener, problem solver, go-getter, and impact player that they will be happy to champion!

Personal Insight 3: Alina Moran, FACHE, FABC, Hospital President and CEO, Dignity Health, California Hospital Medical Center

HOW TO IDENTIFY AND LEVERAGE MENTORS AND SPONSORS

Sponsorship is one of the best methods of accelerating your career. However, many young professionals believe that mentorship and sponsorship are synonymous. In terms of career development, a mentor is a person who gives you advice, answers questions, and provides professional development. A sponsor is someone who actively promotes or advocates for you to other people to help advance your career.

PART 3: HOW TO IDENTIFY AND LEVERAGE MENTORS AND SPONSORS

Data provided by a Coqual Study, The Sponsor Dividend, states that employees of color receive a particularly large boost from sponsorship. In fact, they are 65% more likely than those without a sponsor to be satisfied with their rate of advancement and 60% less likely than those without sponsors to plan to quit within a year. However, the most remarkable aspect of sponsorship is that the benefits that are felt by the sponsored employee are also felt by the sponsor.

Early in my career, I was very fortunate to have participated in leadership development programs like the Pew Civic Entrepreneurship Program, the National Urban Fellows Program, and the National Hispana Leadership Institute. Through these types of programs, I was exposed to the importance of mentors and provided with three key strategies to identify and leverage mentors.

First, you must have a clear understanding of your career goals. This will help you to identify the type of mentor that you need and can help you to succeed. This understanding is also critical in helping to identify industry-specific associations and events where you meet or identify a potential mentor. Secondly, you must learn to leverage your existing network, such as professors, classmates, colleagues, friends, or family members, who have expertise or experience in your desired career. These individuals may also be willing to mentor you or may know someone who could be a good fit. They could be used to serve as an advisory council that can help provide support or guidance with critical decisions. Lastly, understand that mentors are busy individuals, so you should be respectful of their time. It is important to clearly communicate your expectations, establish a schedule that works for both of you, actively listen to their advice, and be open and receptive to feedback. But remember that finding the right mentor or sponsor takes time and effort. Be patient and persistent in your search, and don't be afraid to reach out to multiple people until you find the right fit.

As I progressed in my career, I began to understand the importance of sponsorship and how it was very different from mentorship. As Latinos/Hispanics, the concept of sponsorship is not one that we learned about or had exposure to. Therefore, when we arrive at the workplace, it is a difficult process for us to navigate. For example, I had been working for a healthcare organization in New York and, while I had continued to receive additional responsibilities and participate in high-level assignments, I was seeing other colleagues with less education and experience being promoted to executive level positions. As a result, I began to question whether or not I had the skills and expertise to be successful in the organization.

Thankfully, I had a supervisor who asked me one simple question, "Where do you see yourself in five years?" This question changed my life, since I was able to clearly communicate and affirm my desire to become a Chief Financial Officer (CFO). She guided me in creating a professional development plan to build my skills and financial acumen. She exposed me to different projects and helped to amplify my visibility in the organization. She became my first sponsor and created opportunities for growth and development. A year later when there was a CFO opening at one of our hospitals; she reached out to the CEO and asked him to interview me for the position. While he initially hesitated, she advocated for me and shared with him the impact that I had in my current role. During my series of interviews, I was able to provide clear and concrete examples of the financial impact that I was able to achieve, and the rest is herstory!

In my new CFO role, I learned to be proactive about sponsorship and began to build key relationships with the board of directors, our executive team, and our corporate colleagues. I learned the importance of volunteering for system-wide initiatives that will help to enhance my resume and provide positive exposure in the organization. This led to additional responsibilities and stretch assignments that would build my clinical and operational skills. Through these opportunities, I was able to significantly impact the financial health and operations of the hospital.

These key strategies continue to be relevant in my current position, as I navigate the process in a new health system. As a CEO, I have the opportunity to pay it forward and create a culture of sponsorship. There are three strategies that you can deploy as a leader to ensure that this is intentional and integrated into your organization. First, you should ensure that there is a clear mandate that supports sponsorship. This is accomplished through clear communication of policies and expectations and then modeled by senior leadership. Secondly, sponsorship should be reinforced through evaluations and performance metrics. You should take opportunities to amplify and advocate for your leaders that are natural sponsors and are building this culture within their teams. Lastly, take every opportunity to educate others about the importance of sponsorship, including your board of directors. As the leader, you have the most responsibility to serve as the spokesperson for creating this type of culture in your organization.

KEY TAKEAWAYS:

- Sponsorship is one of the best methods of accelerating your career, but remember that finding the right mentor or sponsor takes time and effort, patience and persistence.

- Remember to leverage your existing network, such as professors, classmates, colleagues, friends, or family members, who have expertise or experience in your desired career to connect you or serve as your mentors, advisory board, or sponsor.

- As a leader, it is your responsibility to create a culture of sponsorship by modeling behavior, communicating expectations, and rewarding employees for positive contributions.

Personal Insight 4: Alexandra Turcios, Senior Solution Consultant, Adobe

HOW TO IDENTIFY AND LEVERAGE MENTORS AND SPONSORS

I still remember the first day of my "big girl" corporate job in downtown Chicago. Bright and early, I joined the droves of people making their daily commute downtown. It felt like joining a new club, with its own language I was eager to learn about.

As I entered the glass building of the prestigious management consulting firm, I recall nearly pinching myself. On the 47th floor I soaked in the immaculate office: floor-to-ceiling windows, a fully stocked kitchen, and marble decor. My gratitude was through the roof. I imagine many first-generation professionals, like myself, feel the same way on the first day, but this facade and disillusionment was the beginning of many lessons I would learn as I navigated corporate America.

I made a lot of mistakes early in my career, but that doesn't mean you have to make the same ones. In this chapter, I'm going to share what I wish I knew sooner about people and relationships.

Lesson 1: Peers as a Benchmark

In my first corporate job, I wanted to prove myself. I thought that figuring everything out on my own was demonstrating I was capable—but I was wrong. One day, a manager pulled me aside and shared feedback that would completely change my mindset. I was told that I wasn't performing at the level of my peers and that I could benefit from more training.

This was soul-crushing. I was under the impression I was excelling, but I didn't have an accurate gauge on my performance because I relied solely on myself and operated in a silo. My idea of being self-sufficient had a counterintuitive effect. I realized that by working in a bubble, it stifled my competency and I lost the competitive edge gained by learning from others.

In that moment, I decided to make a shift. The first step I took after receiving the feedback was to look around the office and identify the "rockstars." I needed a role model to learn from and the best bet was to reach out to my peers at my level or one level above. From there, I set up weekly meetings with my peers to learn tips and tricks, to build my tactical knowledge and to share what we were each working on. Asking for help felt unnatural for me. I needed to step up and do it anyway. Unfortunately, I eventually got laid off from this first "big-girl" corporate job, but the ripple effects and hard lessons learned were profound and taught me to lean into peer mentorship as much as I can.

Lesson 2: Formal Mentoring and Feedback Should Be Asked for Directly

After recovering from the whiplash of being laid off and transitioning to tech consulting, I took the blinders off to focus on my growth. This started with being vocal and explicitly asking for help, and it was not easy.

I still live by the mantra "feel the fear and do it anyway." The reality is there are unspoken and often ambiguous rules in the office and it differs by employer. The best way of acclimating to a new environment is to seek out formal mentorship from someone who has been there a while and can pull back the curtain. As a consultant for several years, I had to be a chameleon to different environments, learn the unspoken culture and dynamics of each respective company, and it was my responsibility to adapt. With intentional practice and repetition, I am now very confident in asking higher-ups for guidance and formal mentoring.

Formal mentors are typically those in a position you aspire to be in and who can act as a coach, provide structure to your professional development, and give you feedback from the lens that a manager would. My argument here is that you need both informal and formal mentoring arrangements to maximize career outcomes. Often, you will need to seek these out and explicitly ask someone, "Will you be my mentor?" In my experience, I've had people outright say, "No," and they don't have the bandwidth to take on another mentee. In those situations, it's important not to take it personal. I still like to keep in touch with those individuals and follow their journey on LinkedIn or other platforms where I can indirectly learn from them.

The maintenance of a formal mentoring arrangement is part two of the formula. It's important to respect each other's time and to come with an agenda to each meeting. I like the "rose, thorn, bud" approach to a check-in which allows you to share a positive update, a growing opportunity, and any roadblocks or challenges. Part of building formal mentorship is putting a spotlight on what you're working on and accentuating your skills. After all, you never know who can recommend you for the next role or opportunity.

Lesson 3: Embrace the Spotlight and Be Visible to Attract Sponsors

Informal and formal mentors are critical components of someone's personal "Board of Directors" or champion network. However, it's also important to consider the political clout and influence someone has within an organization. This is where sponsors come into the equation. I remember when I first joined the Accenture office as an analyst, I networked and learned from my peers, signed up for the formal networking program, and my manager on the project quickly became my formal mentor with weekly or bi-weekly check-ins on the calendar. However, I came to realize that business unit decisions, promotions, and other opportunities were left in the hands of the executives such as Managing Directors.

I started to build my circle of sponsors in the way I did my peers and even formal mentors: through a lens of curiosity. I wanted to learn about what books and podcasts they were reading, what they like to do in their free time, and what kept them up at night. By organically developing relationships, I felt comfortable offering help to alleviate their workload and comfortable asking for advice and support in professional discussions. It was a win-win. Over time, I was asked to take on more visible roles within the office.

Now that these lessons are crystallized—what's next?

Ultimately, the glittering building and floor-to-ceiling windows on that first day taught me many valuable core lessons but the most important was to embrace confident humility. I had my foot in the door, but that wasn't enough. I had to intentionally foster my growth and lean on others. I had to be willing to admit that I didn't know it all and to accept that relationships mean everything.

PART 3: HOW TO IDENTIFY AND LEVERAGE MENTORS AND SPONSORS

KEY TAKEAWAYS:

- Informal peer-to-peer relationships are great for building your brand, advocating for your needs, and having a risk-free environment to learn new skills from others.
- Formal mentorship with a manager+ is important to peel back the layers of an organization and understand the political considerations and soft skills needed to advance. Come prepared with an agenda and treat it with respect.
- Sponsors have the political clout and influence to connect you to leadership opportunities and to amplify your current work. Share your achievements and offer to help where you can.

Personal Insight 5: Yared Oliveros, Staff Diversity, Equity, and Inclusion Partner, Tesla

HOW TO IDENTIFY AND LEVERAGE MENTORS AND SPONSORS

I learned about the art of networking at the age of 22 when I was working for a company that sold life insurance. While I was part of this community, I learned from the best, Patrick Bet-David, currently one of the most influential entrepreneurs and investors today. We would practice and role play on networking in every single meeting with the objective to close a deal or ask for one. Little did I know that this skillset was going to open many doors, including choosing and identifying mentors in my career path.

As I started my career in University Recruiting, I realized that one of my strengths was a people connector. I had the ability to connect and build strong foundational relationships which allowed me to form genuine relationships where I was able to leverage a HR leader in the company to be my mentor. Don't get me wrong, I was still intimidated by people in higher positions and the thought of asking any one of them to be my mentor was terrifying. Nevertheless, we already had established a great relationship before my formal ask—the mentorships that come organically tend to be the most successful.

I have participated in both formal and informal mentorship programs either as a mentor or a mentee and both have been rewarding. However, I did learn along my career that internal mentors only lasted during my tenure inside the company. I was blessed to find an external mentor through my Master's Program. She was an executive at Boeing, currently retired, but to this day, she has been a strong sounding board—challenges me, allows me to be vulnerable, and always has my best interest.

Identifying a sponsor is another level of the playing field in your career. This is where you are making internal connections inside your company or business for an advocate who can vouch for you. Your credibility, work ethic, value add contributions, and impact to the business plays a big role. I had the pleasure of meeting Ref Atilano, who helped guide me in how to seek a sponsor. He was able to demystify all my myths on this topic. His guidance on what questions I should ask, such as, "How I can contribute to this individual's business?" were great starting points to motivate me to set up a coffee chat meeting and begin an organic conversation. I did just that, the executive leader accepted the invite, and I was so excited! Unfortunately, a personal matter came up that I was unable to move and I needed to reschedule my coffee chat. Needless to say, I was unable to get that coffee chat time again after proposing new times for us to connect.

I look back at this experience and part of me wishes to have put my personal matter aside and just kept the invite. Who knows where this conversation would have taken me? Would this person actually be an advocate for me? There is always a time for everything to happen. I have learned that when that moment happens everything else falls into place. I now have the right tools to leverage in order to feel confident in seeking a sponsor that would truly and genuinely vouch for me—thanks to Ref!

KEY TAKEAWAYS:

- Seize the moment! I know it sounds cliché but take advantage of the opportunity that is at your doorstep—it may not come again. You can see from my coffee chat experience this didn't quite turn out how I planned.

PART 3: HOW TO IDENTIFY AND LEVERAGE MENTORS AND SPONSORS

- Have a "put me in coach" mentality and showcase your excitement and enthusiasm for new opportunities, such as mentorship programs and/or development programs that will allow you to network with new individuals internally and externally. This can open a door filled with opportunities.
- Take the initiative to identify someone who could potentially be your mentor or sponsor; have a plan of action on what you hope to get out of your conversations with this individual(s).

All of what you do in your personal and professional life will take courage. Nothing will come easy but it will be worth it at the end when you see all you have been able to accomplish. Como dicen mis padres, "Adelante mija," and that is what I keep doing.

AUTHOR'S GUIDANCE: HOW TO ASK FOR A SPONSOR

Given the importance of identifying and obtaining sponsors to help drive your career forward, the following section will be strictly focused on sponsorship insights. This section has been peer-reviewed by Jeff Martinez, Executive Vice President, PNC Bank. There is conflicting guidance on this topic as some say a sponsor has to select you; whereas others advocate that you can ask someone to be your sponsor. I'm not sure there is one rule as I have done both.

Before getting into how to obtain a sponsor, I wanted to share what sponsors look for based on research with current VPs who serve as sponsors: someone they have great chemistry with, high performers, confident, ambitious, enthusiastic, proven winners, goes above and beyond, has imagination, helps them meet their goals, offers new ideas, trustworthy, politically savvy, has seen them in action, sits in the front row, asks great questions, committed to making an impact, and brings something to the table.

Now here is some guidance that I can provide as a baseline to ask for a sponsor:

- It is critical that you have a great relationship with the potential sponsor and one who has seen your work—this is a non-negotiable.
- Make sure the person you select has a seat at the decision-making table, typically VP or higher.
- Strategically scan your corporate culture to determine who are the key influencers; if you don't work with them, find ways to get assignments to get you in front of them so you can begin to build that relationship and showcase your leadership ability.
- Work with your mentor and manager to get their thoughts on your sponsorship attraction strategy—they might have additional ideas that can accelerate your sponsorship.
- Only ask someone to be your sponsor once you are both extremely comfortable with each other—chemistry, trust, relationship, and more all play a role.
- Landing a sponsor takes time; it can take several months or several years, depending on how much you interact with them. Let the relationship develop organically; there is no fast-tracking a sponsor relationship.
- When asking someone to be your sponsor, do so thoughtfully. Lay out your case, what you are trying to achieve professionally, how you feel about the potential sponsor, and how you can see them helping you get to the next level. *Note: Always be ready for a sponsor to decline as they might not accept the opportunity for reasons they might be ready to share with you. Do not take it personally and understand there might be other factors at play in their decision.*

DOS AND DON'TS

Now that we have covered the background, stories, and insights around how to identify and leverage mentors and sponsors, here are some additional Dos and Don'ts to further support your development in this area.

PART 3: HOW TO IDENTIFY AND LEVERAGE MENTORS AND SPONSORS

Dos	Don'ts
Do: Be Enthusiastic and Passionate After talking to several executives who sponsor others, they like to see the passion, the fire, and enthusiasm for the relationship, the business, and their future. Sponsors want to be excited and would love to champion someone with great energy and drive to excel!	**Don't: Forget Sponsors are Vouching for You!** Your sponsors are putting their credibility and reputation on the line for you—it is critical that you stay aligned with them and deliver. Before they agree to be your sponsor, they will thoroughly vet you. Many times, sponsor relationships are organically developed from working closely together—this is very helpful to achieve sponsorship.
Do: Know Your Sponsor The personal relationship and trust you have with your sponsor must be air-tight; you each should have each other's back and you should always be transparent. Also, take the time to get personal—know your sponsor personally and professionally. This will further develop the relationship and ensure you are in a position to add value in ways you would not have otherwise.	**Don't: Forget to Have Your Career Map Ready** Make sure you can demonstrate to your sponsor that you know where you are going and it's a plan that is well-vetted and in alignment with your manager. Your sponsor is there to support and help drive your opportunities within the company—having your plan mapped out will help them know how to help you!

Do: Drive the Relationship; Gain Trust	Don't: Forget to Add Value for Them
Take ownership of the relationship. Your sponsor is extremely busy and your job is to make the relationship as easy as possible. Make all interactions as concise and impactful as possible. If you are able to show that you are optimizing their time, their value, as well as providing value to them, that's the place where you want to be—and where magic will occur with your career! They will be happy to advocate for you!!!	Constantly scan the environment for their needs—listen carefully to them and learn to read the rest of the organization for opportunities that might impact your sponsor. If you can identify and bring new opportunities to add value on your own, this is also a magical place to be. This would be another example of making the relationship easy while adding new value.

RECAP

As covered in this section, mentors are great for topics like skill development and being a sounding board for specific situations; sponsors are key for accelerating your career by providing opportunities, assignments, and exposure. Sponsors will advocate for you behind closed doors, they will put their name and reputation on the line for you to make sure you get the attention and consideration you deserve from other senior leaders. As discussed, to land this relationship gold, you will have to put in the work, showcase your talent in front of the right people, and work hard to develop and optimize the relationship. You will have to pay close attention to your sponsor's needs and find ways to add value, both professionally and personally. The relationship you have with your sponsor is second to none and I am confident that the insights and stories shared up to this point of the book will put you on a path toward landing that sponsor who will help you be a confident, informed, impact player in the workplace!

PART 3: HOW TO IDENTIFY AND LEVERAGE MENTORS AND SPONSORS

PLANNING AND ACTIVATING YOUR DEVELOPMENT

To support your development and to help you organize and activate the concepts in this chapter, please go to my website (www.refugioatilano.com) and download the free templates for **The Latino Leadership Workbook**—this is a great set of tools to help organize your target areas and map a plan on where to focus your growth. It also includes a notes page and a development roadmap template so you can begin to think through and draft your personalized improvement plan that will set you up for maximum growth and success.

HOW TO BUILD A NETWORK TO ADVANCE YOUR CAREER

> *"Networking is not about just connecting people. It's about connecting people with people, people with ideas, and people with opportunities."*
>
> **- Michele Jennae**

One of the most effective ways to create opportunities for yourself and to make yourself noticeable is through strategic, targeted networking—it's creating and taking advantage of opportunities to meet with other professionals that will put you in the best position to advance your career, your skillset, your thinking, or your impact. Per an article in Forbes.com, "no man is an island" has been proved to be the key to professional success—many individuals have reaped the rewards due to the strong networking channels built through their career journey (Cole, 2019). Similarly, Erin Eatough in Betterup.com shares that, "Building connections with the right people at the right time could be the key to taking your career to the next level" (Eatough, 2023).

> *Strategic networking has been and continues to be one of the most important aspects of my career. One of my mentors taught me early in my career that a great network can get you inside doors and introduced me to people that would have not otherwise have been possible. He taught me particularly the importance of and how to network "internally" with senior level leaders—have strong business acumen, learn their business, perfect my elevator pitch, be concise, and take time to understand their background and personal passions. Also, I know golfing is not everyone's*

PART 3: HOW TO BUILD NETWORK TO ADVANCE YOUR CAREER

sport, but I took up golfing as a result of these interactions—a lot of the relationships I built were on the course with both male and female leaders. I can't stress enough the opportunities that golfing creates; you get 5-6 hours of uninterrupted time with at least three others. If you strategically create your golf outings with those you are trying to build relationships, you will create great opportunities for yourself—and potentially others somewhere down the line! I will have more about the impact of golfing later in this chapter by the great Paola Meizner.

One of the most effective ways to create opportunities for yourself and others is through strategic networking—it's creating and taking advantage of opportunities to meet with other professionals that will put you in the best position to advance your career, your skillset, your thinking, or your impact.

NETWORKING 101

As Theresa Reaume discussed in her "Networking for Success" TEDx talk, "Networking is an opportunity for people to get to know your brand; it's about marketing yourself, your uniqueness, and what you stand for." She also went on to say that, "Your goal is to be memorable—for the right reasons. Make sure to always have mints on hand!" I couldn't agree more with Theresa's thoughts. In fact, I use networking as an opportunity to advocate for myself and always lead with an impeccable image and with my leadership brand. I prepare hard for every networking interaction—I take no days off and leave no doubt about the impression I want to leave whenever I engage with others. Networking is serious business and I always bring my A-game to the table!

BENEFITS OF STRATEGIC NETWORKING

In an article by Novoresume.com, "What sets networking apart from simply meeting new people is the intent to build a meaningful connection that will help both parties to speed up their career development" (Kurtuy, 2023). The same report shared the following data:

1. Networking is responsible for filling in 85% of job vacancies. (Source: HubSpot)
2. 70% of people report that networking helped them to find their current job. (Source: PayScale)
3. 95% of professionals think that in-person networking is crucial to maintaining long-lasting business relationships. (Source: *Harvard Business Review*)

As you can see, strategic networking is critical for your development and opportunity. Regardless of whether you are at a networking event and/or taking a more targeted 1:1 networking approach, I want to ensure you tee yourself up for opportunities that are going to move your career needle. If done effectively, thoughtfully, and strategically, networking is going to get you noticed, will provide opportunities to showcase your brand to influential leaders, it will lead to new ideas, can make you more confident, and will lead to connections that can accelerate your career in the short, medium, and long-term!

HOW TO NETWORK STRATEGICALLY

For the purpose of creating impact, I am going to focus on strategic, or targeted, networking. I want to position you to establish meaningful, mutually beneficial, long-term connections with influential leaders that are going to help you drive your career.

Your first order of business is to determine what you are trying to achieve. Are you looking to create career opportunities (internal/external to your organization)? Looking to upskill? Create a network of champions/potential sponsors? Build your skillset, or all the above? This will be key in understanding who you want to engage and how you want to engage them.

As an example, if you are looking to develop your leadership skills/brand, then I would start scanning your organization for the leaders that resonate with your target skills. If you see a leader who is an amazing speaker and you want to develop your communication skills, schedule time to meet with that person. You will find that almost everyone wants to genuinely help, especially those within the same company. Here are some tips when networking with senior level colleagues:

- **Do your homework -** Always prepare. Know your elevator pitch, have a plan and know what you are trying to achieve in the discussion, think through questions, develop an agenda and structure the meeting to make sure you cover key points and reach your goals. Study the leaders' background, LinkedIn, volunteer passions, and ask those in your network about their style. The more information you have, the better you can find ways to connect, and the more impactful your discussion will be.
- **Send an introductory email -** Explain who you are, why you are reaching out, and how you think their insights can facilitate your development. Ask if they would be open to a discussion, and, if so, who you can work with to get the meeting booked. They will often times direct you to their admin.
  - Note: If you have someone in your network that can make a soft introduction over email, that would be even better. Take advantage of the relationships you have in place!
  - Always send the agenda and discussion topics in advance; this will demonstrate that you are organized and begin to instill confidence in your leadership ability.

- **Show up with you're A-game -** Whether you are meeting in-person or virtually, always be prepared, make sure your image in pristine, use open body language—including great eye contact, and always make sure to conduct yourself in a professional manner. Show your passion and your focus on developing yourself! This goes a long way!

- **Think in terms of long-term relationships and adding value -** Just as in personal life, business relationships also take time to develop. It's good that you will be able to get some great insights in the first meeting, but also think how you can support the leader in return; find ways to collaborate and begin to develop an even deeper relationship. These are the kind of relationships that can turn senior leaders into mentors, champions, and even sponsors!

- **Always follow-up -** Keep those coveted strategic relationships active. First, thank them for their time and insights. Share the details of what you learned and how you plan on applying them to your role. Also, let them know that you will be checking back in after a few months to catch up and share your progress—remember to get the meeting on the calendar asap. If you are providing support to the leader in any way, be sure to also cover your game plan on the actions you committed to—and then execute and communicate periodic updates. This is how you build strong rapport, trust, and great relationships!

*Note: You could use this same approach for every strategic, targeted networking interaction, whether it's internal or external to your organization. Your goal is to establish meaningful, mutually beneficial, long-term connections that are going to help you drive your career.

> Your goal is to establish meaningful, mutually beneficial, long-term connections that are going to help you drive your career.

PART 3: HOW TO BUILD NETWORK TO ADVANCE YOUR CAREER

Personal Insight 1: Refugio A. Atilano, Business Leader at a Top-10 Pharma Company, ERG/DEI Leader, Author, The Latino Leadership Playbook

USING MY NETWORKING SKILLS TO BRING THE LATINO LEADERSHIP PLAYBOOK TO LIFE!

As an aspiring first-time author, I learned quickly that credibility is king. To make the kind of impact I wanted, I knew that I had to add some serious firepower to this book—I had to get the "Best of the Best" Latino/a and other influential business leaders at the table and agree to share their stories and insights. In short, this was no small task and it put my strategic networking skills to the test!

If you think about it, I had to engage these great leaders (over 50!) who knew nothing about me, get them aligned and excited about what I am trying to do with this book, and then have them trust me enough to agree for them to put their reputation on the line and take time out of their very busy schedules to contribute. Had I not been able to do this, this book would not be the product it is today.

So, how did I go about getting all these leaders at the table? It's simple, I followed the same principles shared earlier in this chapter. I knew in order to have maximum impact, I would need to identify the most influential leaders today: I did my homework and attended conferences to meet potential contributors in person, had those in my network make soft introductions, collaborated with several potential contributors so they could see me in action, showcased my brand and achievements on LinkedIn, etc. In each interaction, I made sure my brand, my image, my story was always razor sharp. I also ensured that I made my ask clearly and at the right time—I wanted to make sure there was comfort and trust before anything else. In the end, I am happy say that I engaged almost everyone I wanted to be part of this book and I am extremely excited for you—for us—and for the future of all Latinos!!!

Networking is a skill, and it should be used to its full advantage—

it should be a big part of your leadership brand. Once you get to a certain level, you will also find that you will become a "connector" in that you can help so many others by driving the warm introductions and making recommendations for others to drive their careers. You can also use your network to advocate for others, when needed. In short, having a strong, active network can be a game-changer for you and your leadership brand. When used effectively, it will be a key enabler for your impact in the workplace!

Personal Insight 2: Dr. Jairo Borja, President of Borja Consulting Group, LLC and Real Estate Investor

VOLUNTEERISM TO NETWORK

Volunteerism, what do I mean by that? Volunteerism means being able to join a board of directors and making an impact. Understanding that you may not get monetary compensation, but you are building your network while at the same time helping with the cause of the organization. Some benefits of volunteerism include building your skills that you normally would not build at your business or place of employment, building your resume to give you a competitive edge in the job market, building your profile on social media sites, such as LinkedIn, where recruiters can see what you do outside of work, giving back to the community and assisting with the nonprofits' cause, and, lastly, building your network—especially, if the board of directors is connected to a national organization. These things are a great advantage to the volunteers because now you have access and can connect with fellow members regionally, nationally, and internationally.

For example, I volunteered for a security organization that assists with certifications, monthly networking events, webinars, and expos throughout the world—as well as an international show nationally every year. I volunteered as a co-Young Professional Liaison for the NYC Chapter. I was able to connect with the NYC board. I was also able to do educational programming and networking events for young professionals. It went so well, I volunteered for the Young Professionals Council for the security organization nationally.

Now, why would a business major join a security organization? At the time, at the alma mater where I worked needed more opportunities in Criminal Justice. I was given a task to find jobs and build relationships for Criminal Justice majors. I discovered this organization which emphasized in security—so many opportunities working for guard service, IT, physical, and cybersecurity.

I met so many people that I now can call my dear friends throughout the world. Your network is your net worth. Now, why did I mention all of this? I wanted to show you how volunteering and giving back to the community can assist you with your career goals. Lastly, my volunteering for this security organization has assisted building my network internationally. Whenever I need to ask anything, I have an international organization at my fingertips. I will discuss in my next section some techniques that also share in my best-selling book, *Networking Your Way to Success*.

TECHNIQUES FOR NETWORKING TO GROW YOUR BOOK OF BUSINESS

First, I highly advise you to do research on the type of events you would want to attend. Once you determine what type of event, do some research on the panelists and guest speakers, try to see what articles or products they have. This way, once you see them at the event, you can connect with them.

Also, what is dress attire for the event? Business casual, black tie affair, etc. Next, make sure your LinkedIn profile is up to date. Make sure you have a professional headshot, decent headline, and your summary is up to date. Also, making sure all your experience, volunteer opportunities, and certifications are up to date. Lastly, capture any recommendations that you have from other professionals on your profile. If not, I highly recommend asking for them. The better the recommendations, the more recruiters or your ideal customer will want to work with you.

Next, make sure you have your elevator pitch. I will not spend much time on the elevator pitch. However, I would say your name, where you work, title, what problem you are trying to solve, why you, and some type of next steps.

Once both parties exchange their respective elevator pitches, now what? I discuss with the FORMEA method to strike some type of conversation with professionals at networking events— Family, Occupation, Recreation, Motivation Education, and Achievement. Establishing that common ground can help make connections. (i.e., Both married, have children—that's family. Both in security? That's occupation. Both like to play basketball or softball, that's recreation. Both are motivated by passive income in real estate, that's motivation. Both have an MBA, that's education. Both have run the NYC marathon, that's an achievement.) After a few minutes of speaking to the individual, I would write a few facts about the person on the back of their business card. The Call to Action should be that you reach out to set up some time to connect either in-person or over a zoom call.

KEY TAKEAWAYS:

- You are in business to solve a problem; money will come after that.
- Understand the process of how you are acquiring customers.
- Be intentional with your networking to build your brand, network where your ideal customer is.
- Have your elevator pitch ready to go; Use the FORM or FORMEA (mentioned in my book) to build rapport with someone.
- Have a follow up system and leverage your customer relationship management (CRM) software to do so.
- Give back, join a board, assist with the cause, build your network, connect with other thought leaders, build leadership skills, give back and the universe will reward you back one way or another.

PART 3: HOW TO BUILD NETWORK TO ADVANCE YOUR CAREER

Personal Insight 3: Ingrid Harb, CEO of Nota Inclusion

HOW TO BUILD A NETWORK TO ADVANCE YOUR CAREER

I grew up in the north of Mexico, where culture is rich in community, family, and traditions.

You see, in Mexico everything revolves around community, who you know and, to be frank, on what your family's last name is. On the other hand, what I love about the United States (if you're not near a border city) is that nobody cares what your last name is. That really set me free—giving me a blank page to make a name for myself—to dream big, to "pursue my Mexican-American dream" like we say it here in the States. And I did, but I knew that I had to start by building my network.

Now, I grew up in an educational system that rewarded discipline over creativity and curiosity. Curiosity is what I would say is key to building a network. Being genuinely curious will take you far, at least for me, it has helped. Curiosity in college drove me to starting an organization called, Women Ambassadors Forum—a week-long forum where our main goal was to build a community for women across the world. The first year we received applications from two countries, and quickly grew to getting applications from over 150+ countries. If I would've sat in class and waited until I had the skills to run this movement, I never would've started. I knew that my curiosity would lead me to meeting the right people that would help me make it happen.

To build your network, you have to be persistent, disciplined, very intense, and fully committed to what you are doing. What helped me was that everywhere I went I was present to those who surrounded me. I was in the moment, and this led me to meeting executives, leaders, sponsors, and women who could join my network.

The second thing you have to be is open and clear on exactly what it is that you need. Back then, I needed sponsors to make the forum happen. I remember being so clear that I would write down exactly how much money I needed to fundraise. Year after year, I would match that amount. Later I started adding a few zeros at the end—just in case I could meet them.

The most important key that helped me continue to build the network year after year, and then founding my own consulting firm, is because I deeply cared about what I did; when I would meet people, I would share that exact passion. That helped me build a deeper connection with my sponsors, mentors, and the women who attended my forums. The connection was never about the transaction; I cared and they cared too. People will always be able to tell if your essence and intentions are pure or not. My advice as you build your network and you leave your legacy is to get to know yourself first. Get very clear on what you need, and what you care about.

Throughout my journey of building and working with women from across the world, and now working with 70% of fortune 1000 companies in the space of diversity, equity, and inclusion through Nota Inclusion of which I am CEO, what I realized is that the more I reconnected with the core of who I am, the more my network grew. Now, I'm not talking about the size of my network, because it's never about the size. It's about the quality of one's network. The more you elevate who you are, the more you're likely to attract people who operate in the spaces that you want a seat in.

I'm going to give you an inquiry that I use, as I embarked on a journey of self-love, of really doing what I was meant to do on this earth—when you're walking that path, the people will appear. Of course, you want to look for them too, but being present, open, and ready makes all the difference.

KEY TAKEAWAYS:

- Sit with this: what are you curious about learning, doing, becoming?
- Let your curiosity guide you and take you to places you never thought were possible. Ask your curiosity, what's next?

Once you do, you'll be surprised at how you'll start to notice the people that you need to get you there.

Personal Insight 4: Paola Meinzer, Founder, LEXGOLF

USING GOLF TO BUILD MY NETWORK AS A LATINA

If you ask me, I will say that "I'm just a girl from Colombia," but if you want to connect the dots, here is my story and journey to golf.

I am an immigrant who moved to the United States as a young adult and had to start my entire life anew. Just like many others, I tried my hand in various industries before finding my calling. Having traveled the world, I have always recognized the significance of networking and building connections. Therefore, when I began working, I joined a local chamber of commerce and have since become a member and even a board member of many reputable organizations in my area for many years. I believe that being a part of these groups has been instrumental in my career growth and gaining recognition in my business community.

Being a member of various organizations has allowed me to access numerous beneficial programs. However, after spending years attending events and supporting these organizations, I noticed some gaps in certain activities and areas. This led me to conceptualize a new organization that would fill these gaps and provide opportunities for Latina professionals, like myself, who aspire to excel in their careers.

Latina Executive Golf Organization (LEXGOLF)

I recognized a lack of Latino, particularly Latina, participation in golf activities. This realization came to me when I reflected on my experience as a high-level executive at a Fortune 500 company. While I had sponsored numerous events, including golf outings, I often found myself as "the designated driver." It made me feel uneasy and out of place, preventing me from building meaningful connections with my male counterparts. This was part of my motivation to found the Latina Executive Golf Organization (LEXGOLF).

Golf has become my passion and purpose. Through it, I have learned to respect the game and all that it represents. Unfortunately, many Latinos, including myself, were not introduced to the sport during our younger years due to various social and cultural reasons. This inspired me to take action and change the narrative. My organization's goal is to engage more Latinas in golf, as we have been underrepresented in this space. By doing so, we hope to provide more opportunities for business, career advancement, and networking.

About Golf and its Benefits

Golf is a sport that has historically been dominated by white men, but there is a growing recognition of the importance of encouraging minorities, especially Latinos, to engage in golf. Beyond the health and recreational benefits it offers, golf provides unique opportunities for personal and professional growth, empowerment, and social inclusion.

Promoting Physical and Mental Well-being

Engaging in golf promotes physical fitness by providing a low-impact form of exercise that improves cardiovascular health, flexibility, and muscle strength. Additionally, golf is known for its mental health benefits, as the sport requires focus, concentration, and strategizing, all of which contribute to stress reduction, improved cognitive function, and increased self-confidence.

Networking and Career Opportunities

Golf provides an excellent platform for networking and creating professional connections. By participating in golf, women, including Latinas, can expand their social circles, build relationships with influential individuals, and increase their chances of accessing career opportunities. Golfing events, such as corporate tournaments and charity fundraisers, offer unique spaces where women can interact with business professionals, potential employers, and mentors, ultimately empowering them to advance their careers. Let's not leave money on the green!

Overcoming Gender Stereotypes

By engaging in golf, Latinos, especially Latinas, can challenge and break down gender stereotypes prevalent in society. Historically, golf has been seen as a male-dominated sport, but increasing female participation demonstrates that women are equally capable and passionate about excelling in this discipline. Encouraging women, regardless of their background, to embrace golf encourages a shift in perceptions and promotes equality, diversity, and inclusion.

Empowerment and Self-Confidence

Participation in golf can have a transformative impact on women, especially those of color by fostering empowerment and boosting self-confidence. Mastering the skills required in golf, such as hitting precise shots, overcoming challenging obstacles, and maintaining composure under pressure, instills a sense of achievement and belief in one's abilities. The confidence gained through golf can extend beyond the sport, empowering women to tackle challenges in various aspects of their lives.

Cultural Integration and Business Community Building

For Latinos, engaging in golf can serve as a means of cultural integration and community building. Golf clubs and courses often serve as community hubs, where people from diverse backgrounds come together. By actively participating in golf, Latinos can bridge cultural gaps, foster understanding, and build connections with individuals from different ethnicities, backgrounds, and generations. This integration can lead to enriched social experiences, increased cross-cultural awareness, and a stronger sense of belonging.

Mentorship and Role Modeling

Encouraging Latinos to engage in golf allows for the establishment of mentorship opportunities and positive role models. By providing guidance, support, and inspiration to aspiring golfers, successful Latinos in business and business organizations can empower younger generations and encourage them to utilize golf benefits to pursue their career dreams and other areas of life. These mentorship relationships play a vital role in building self-esteem, setting goals, and fostering a sense of belonging within the golfing community.

Legacy and Cultural Heritage

Latinos engaging in golf help preserve and celebrate their cultural heritage. By participating in a sport that is not traditionally associated with their backgrounds, Latinos can demonstrate the richness and diversity of their cultural traditions. Their involvement in golf showcases their determination to excel in unconventional fields and serves as a source of pride for their communities.

KEY TAKEAWAYS:

- Through participation in golf, Latinos can improve their physical and mental well-being, access networking and career opportunities, challenge gender stereotypes, foster empowerment, and self-confidence, integrate into diverse communities, establish mentorship relationships, and celebrate our cultural heritage.

- By encouraging each other to embrace golf, we can create a more inclusive and equitable society while reaping the numerous personal and societal benefits that the sport offers.

LEXGOLF! My friends!

PART 3: HOW TO BUILD NETWORK TO ADVANCE YOUR CAREER

Special Note from Refugio about Golf: This is one of my favorite topics as I love to golf and understand the impact it can have on one's career. This section is critical for your development and can help provide access to senior leaders who can be a major influence on your career. Simply put, golf provides 5-6 hours of uninterrupted time and creates a great opportunity to advocate for yourself and develop strong relationships with those in your golf group—this is relationship development gold! My recommendation is to get lessons and learn the game, be strategic on who you invite to golf with you, and you will find yourself in the driver's seat to have quality interactions with influential leaders! Also, if you are ever in Chicago, I am available anytime to golf with you—just ping me on LinkedIn!

DOS AND DON'TS

Now that we have covered the background, stories, and insights around how to build a network to advance your career, here are some additional Dos and Don'ts to further support your development in this area.

Dos	Don'ts
Do: Do Your Homework Never show up cold. Before engaging with any prospective strategic networking contact, do your homework. Look up their social media profile, understand how they fit into the organization, ask colleagues about their style, and find common interests. Find out what's important to them and deliver a message and use an approach that will resonate—this is especially important as you can network with senior leaders.	**Don't: Forget that Networking is Constant** Networking is always happening and it's up to you to keep developing it. As you get more skilled at it you will find that your network will grow quickly. Not only in quantity but with quality. You will start getting calls for information, opportunities, collaborations, etc. Keep pushing yourself to build your network, even when you have a strong one in place—play in different areas and find ways to bring value from them!

Do: Find A Way to Add Value

Adding value to the strategic networking interaction is critical if you want to develop it into a long-term relationship that can even grow into a sponsorship. Find ways to plug into their business, to volunteer for short-term assignments, to be a connector with others in your network.

The more value and collaboration opportunities you can bring to the table, the more likely your chances are to develop strong relationships with influential professionals.

Don't: Forget to Be a Connector

As you develop your network, you will find more often that you are in a position to turn into a connector, someone who can create strategic connections to elevate the careers of others. This is so critical for your leadership brand and impact. This will show the organization, your peers, and your community that you are leading and elevating the success of everyone, and not just yourself.

Do: Keep Relationships Active

For the relationships that are strategically important, work to keep them active—it doesn't take much. You can connect as little as a couple of times per year or several times a year, depending on the nature of the relationship and what you are trying to accomplish.

Also, make sure to follow-up on agreed to actions, make sure to send thoughtful thank you notes, as well as periodic updates. This shows that you are engaged and serious about the relationship!

The bottom line is to make the time to keep it warm or warm enough. Remember, these relationships are key for our success—nurture them and treat them like gold, your career depends on it.

Don't: Forget to Keep Building Your Network

Networking is a constant—it is your job to develop it, nurture it, and keep it growing. Make network development part of your personal goals—integrate your strategic network development with your professional development goals.

If you are focused on a certain skill, align with leaders who are great at that skill. If you are looking to learn more about a business unit, find a way to connect with a leader in that business so you can engage. Make your network development intentional—be thoughtful, well-prepared, and execute. This will facilitate your overall development and impact.

Do: Keep Your Network Broad

I would highly recommend to broaden your perspective and create networks across your organization, as well as outside of your organization. Strategically chart a plan to meet as many people as possible that can influence your development, growth, and/or opportunities.

Don't: Forget to Use the Resources in this Book

I have intentionally provided some great resources for you in this book. Be sure to connect with all of them and use them personally or for your company, organization, or school.

PART 3: HOW TO BUILD NETWORK TO ADVANCE YOUR CAREER

For example, you can approach a leader from a different company to get their perspectives in a safe environment. You can also get involved with professional organizations (i.e., HACE, HACR, etc.) to build your network and expand your reach. Remember, the more senior the connection is, the more influence. However, be sure to connect with professionals at all levels as anyone can have a key relationship.	You literally have some of the best in the business at your fingertips, and they all have incredibly vast and powerful networks. Use them! They will all be super.

RECAP

Strategic networking can be a game-changer for your career, as well as for the careers of everyone you touch. I always tell my connections, "My network is your network." I am serious about that! I built my network to help others just as much as I built it to help myself. If we are going to attack the 4% senior level representation gap discussed earlier, then we must unite and operate as one. A big part of that approach includes sharing our networks to elevate the careers of all Latinos!

As you continue your journey to becoming that confident, informed, impact player, remember to take full advantage of the network in this book. You have immediate access to some of today's most influential business leaders who can open doors for you and offer great career advice. Remember, follow the same principles when reaching out. Use thoughtful, strategic, and organized communications to show who you are, what you are trying to achieve, and how we can best support you in reaching your goals! I hope you enjoyed this chapter and good luck in your journey to add impact to your career in new ways.

PLANNING AND ACTIVATING YOUR DEVELOPMENT

To support your development and to help you organize and activate the concepts in this chapter, please go to my website (www.refugioatilano.com) and download the free templates for **The Latino Leadership Workbook**—this is a great set of tools to help organize your target areas and map a plan on where to focus your growth. It also includes a notes page and a development roadmap template so you can begin to think through and draft your personalized improvement plan that will set you up for maximum growth and success.

How to Create and Leverage Your Unique Brand

> "Your brand is what people say about you when you're not in the room."
> — Jeff Bezos

Personal branding is one of my favorite topics because it's one that has had the biggest impact on my leadership development. I still remember earlier in my career how I didn't care about how others perceived me. My thinking was as long as I did my job, and did it well, great things would come. Yeah, not the case! As stated earlier in this book, it wasn't until one of my senior level mentors called out my lack of focus in this area that initiated real change for how I approached this topic.

> *Once I realized the importance and impact of my personal branding, I reflected deeply on how I was coming across to others, particularly to senior leaders who seemed to never call upon me at the time. I quickly realized the elements in my game that needed immediate work: my image was not as professional as it could be, my communication skills needed serious sharpening, I was not effective in managing up and understanding the political landscape, I needed to find ways to add value and impact above and beyond my core job responsibilities. After this self-reflection and conferring with my mentor, I developed a game plan and made a commitment to work on these gaps. I felt like I was given a super-power to see the unseen and was excited to immediately take my leadership game to the next level! I spent the next few years developing and refining my brand.*

> Today, my professional brand includes being a strong communicator, a connector, having great presence, and being the ultimate team player. And it's still a work in progress!

I felt like I was given a super-power to see the unseen and was excited to immediately take my leadership game to the next level! I spent the next few years working on and refining my brand.

WHAT IS PERSONAL BRANDING

Simply put, your brand is how someone feels about you—it's what they say about you when you are not in the room. As Jennie Flinders states in her TEDx talk, "Own Your Personal Brand," "People are always assessing you; it's human nature. They are looking at things like your body language, tone of voice, your image, eye contact, what you represent, and how well you listen." This is so true, as I am always assessing others with whom I come into contact with.

> When I mentor Latinos, the first thing I look for is their brand and try to piece together the makeup of the person—I observe their image, confidence, communication style, preparation, ideas, poise, eye contact, etc. I quickly try to assess what makes them tick; what they are passionate about; what makes them unique; are they focused on making an impact; are they prepared for the discussion; have they done their homework on me; what do they need from me? I also like to showcase my own brand. I make sure to prepare for the meeting; I lead with my elevator pitch, my passions, make sure my image is always on point, and ensure I communicate effectively and confidently. I want them to know that when they deal with me that I am ready for a great discussion every time without exception!

PART 3: HOW TO CREATE AND LEVERAGE YOUR UNIQUE BRAND

As you can see, I put a lot of thought and effort into how I operate and how I want to be perceived. My brand is always on point, but also always a work in progress. It's critical for me to periodically check in with others to ensure my brand is radiating the desired intent. If it is, great; if not, then time to reflect and determine how to get it back in balance. I think Jennie Flinders in the TEDx talk referenced above said it best—your brand is your trademark, so make sure it's what you want it to be. This is such a great perspective as you are your own walking billboard. The question is what do you want your billboard to say and represent about you? To be an impact player in the workplace, your brand must exhibit impact behaviors, an impact image, and impactful performance. My intent with this section is to bring awareness to your brand and ensure you have a game plan to put it into practice so you can achieve your desired impact in the workplace.

WHY PERSONAL BRANDING IS IMPORTANT

A strong personal brand can be a great asset to your career if developed and used effectively. Per an article by Thebrandingjournal.com, "Branding strategy can help increase visibility, credibility, and opportunities when done correctly" (Julian, 2022). During my development journey, I quickly discovered that it could help create opportunities for special assignments, provide access to senior leaders, ERG leadership assignments, new roles and promotions, as well as help you land influential sponsors within your organization.

As an example, a few years ago when I started working on it, I was hand selected by our VP to represent our team in a town hall; it was because of my new brand/image that I was noticed by our leadership team. I quickly realized that the executives appreciated my professional look, confident approach, and my willingness to tackle big things, as well as my online presence! For example, in that same town hall meeting, the executives put my LinkedIn posts for a new product launch on the large screen to show how to generate excitement for our employees and customers. I remember being caught by surprise by all the attention from that post and I knew that the hard work I put into my own brand was starting to pay off and put me on track for continued leadership development. It was at this moment that I began to understand the importance and impact of a strong brand.

Since then, I have put maximum effort into refining a brand that meets the needs of my career and business for that moment in time. Like I said earlier, it's very intentional and always a work in progress. Furthermore, if leveraged correctly, a strong brand can differentiate you from the pack and give you a distinct advantage over other candidates for those highly coveted senior level roles.

> Your brand is always radiating—it's not something you can fake. I know we hear a lot about how first impressions matter; in my opinion, every impression matters!

Taking control of and driving the brand you want will be critical if you want to be an impact player in the workplace; it will require careful thought, strategy, and planning to develop and execute upon the impression you want to convey. Your brand is always radiating—it's not something you can fake. I know we hear a lot about how first impressions matter; in my opinion, every impression matters! Every time you are interacting with others (formally or informally), you are showcasing yourself. So, take the time to know your brand and make sure it's always on point, especially if you want to be top of mind and considered for those great, high-profile opportunities!

HOW TO CREATE A PERSONAL BRAND

There are many personal branding frameworks you can reference online or through formal training. I will introduce a basic method to initiate your personal brand development so that you can begin to leverage it in the workplace and accelerate your career and workplace impact.

PART 3: HOW TO CREATE AND LEVERAGE YOUR UNIQUE BRAND

- **Figure Out What Drives You** - Take time to document these key foundational elements of your brand:
  - What are your passions?
  - What skills are you most proud of?
  - What type of work excites you?
  - What are your superpowers?

- **Think Through How You Want to Be Known** - Start to build out what unique elements you can bring to the table that will drive your business and career forward:
  - Align your drivers (above) with the organizational goals.
  - Identify the key elements in your drivers that help you stand out in your organization.
  - What are differentiators you would like to build into your brand that you currently don't possess?
  - Incorporate current skills/experiences gaps into your future-state brand.

- **Develop a Branding Strategy** - Determine how you are going to connect with your target audience:
  - Identify those who need to experience your brand in action.
    - Organizational leaders, manager, mentor/sponsor, peers, advisors, etc.
  - Determine how you are going to communicate your brand.
    - Determine where you plan to make your brand visible: Online, project/work performance, meet and greets, informal meetings, volunteer opportunities, ERGs, etc.
  - Develop and exhibit consistent brand messaging.

- Take time to develop your desired personal brand messaging (i.e., elevator pitch) and target where you are going to reinforce that messaging.
- Make your brand messaging and performance part of your DNA; commit to sharing it and living it every day. This is how your desired brand will be established.

- **Define Your Brand** - Bringing it all together:
    - Take time to develop your desired personal brand messaging (i.e., elevator pitch) and target how and where you are going to reinforce that messaging.
    - Pressure-test your brand with others to ensure it's accurate; use colleagues, friends, family members to validate your brand and make updates, as needed. You always want your brand to be accurate and authentic so it can be trusted.
    - Note: A great way to determine your current brand is to ask 5-7 people in your network to provide your five strengths, as well as two words that describe you. Once you get the feedback, you will see themes develop. That is your current brand. The question is, is that what you want it to be? If not, make the updates to get you to the desired state.

- **Execute On Your Brand** - Share it with the world!
    - Make sure your messaging, performance, and behaviors always represent your desired personal brand—no exceptions.
        - Personal branding is not just about being able to talk about your brand; it's about showing what your brand is day in and day out. Your brand must be consistent and will be built over time.

- Consistency is king; ensure your branding is the same across all platforms and interactions. This will show people your true brand and that it can be trusted.

Now that you have the foundation and understand the importance of personal branding, here are some stories and insights that will facilitate your development as you begin to refine your brand and leverage it in your career.

Personal Insight 1: Refugio A. Atilano, Business Leader at a Top-10 Pharma Company, ERG/DEI Leader, Author, *The Latino Leadership Playbook*

YOUR BRAND IS ALWAYS BEING REFINED

As covered earlier in this chapter, my personal brand has evolved over time and with new experiences. For example, before deciding to write this book, my brand was focused primarily on my core job responsibilities and my development areas. That has now changed, and I have pivoted based on current events. Instead of just focusing on core job and organizational responsibilities, my brand has been updated and now includes being at the forefront of Latino leadership for our community.

Before going down this road, I took a step back to determine what I needed to do to be an impact player in the Latino/a leadership arena, which already has so many great and well-established leaders. I knew that if I wanted to be recognized by my peers as a credible Latino leader, it had to be developed and executed with flawless messaging, execution, and consistency. Therefore, I established a group of trusted and influential Latino/a advisors, developed an elevator pitch on who I am, communicated what I was targeting to accomplish and why I was trying to accomplish it. In addition, I wanted to show that I was a person of my word—I always met my commitments and communicated what I set out to do. I also leveraged LinkedIn to drive my brand and used consistent and targeted messaging to keep the audience engaged and laser-focused on the goal and progress of this book.

> My Latino leadership brand development was the product of careful thought, targeted and consistent messaging, and flawless execution against my goals.

In short, my Latino leadership brand development was the product of careful thought, targeted and consistent messaging, and flawless execution against my goals. The other thing I would like to call out is that *it takes time to develop a brand*. For example, when I first started this journey without any credibility or supporting network, it was very tough to get meetings with any influential Latinos/as to talk about this book and potential collaborations. I had to prove myself and build this initiative brick-by-brick. Fast-forward 10 months to today, my new network is solid and growing and now is much easier to engage with other influential Latino/a leaders to bring great insights to all of you!

Personal Insight 2: Sergey Gorbatov, Managing Partner, InTalentSight, Professor, IE Business School, Madrid, Spain

HOW TO CREATE AND LEVERAGE YOUR UNIQUE BRAND

Understanding of my signature strengths led me to realize the true value of my personal brand. This perspective has led me to explore various career pathways, including making the pivotal decision to start my own business, leveraging my signature strengths to achieve success.

When I was in high school, one of my teachers used to say that success in life comes to those who are the best, the first, or different. Over the years, I've carefully considered this advice. Joining a team where a crucial skill was missing, striving to be

PART 3: HOW TO CREATE AND LEVERAGE YOUR UNIQUE BRAND

the best became my strategy. I also embraced the opportunity to learn new things easily. Capitalizing on an easily fillable gap gives you a competitive advantage, making you a pioneer. Although I wasn't the first researcher on personal branding, I was the first to produce scientific literature on the subject and create a validated scale to measure personal branding and personal brand equity. Finally, being different has always come naturally to me: always a foreigner, always with a unique perspective...

This formula—best, first, different—worked for me, but I wasn't entirely sure why. More importantly, it didn't provide me with a clear sense of direction. I knew something was missing.

Linda Rodman, from Rodman Resources LLC, helped me make sense of my unique advantages and their implications for my personal brand and career. As an executive coach with over 30,000 hours of experience, she firmly believes in the power of embracing your true self. "You want to be fiercely who you are," she says.

When Linda began coaching me, she first interviewed my key stakeholders. From their feedback, she distilled my signature strengths, which are largely true, aspirational, universally agreed upon, and quintessentially me. These are the 4-5 things that define who I am, and when you ask someone for examples, they will just go on and on. Even those who may not be fond of me would acknowledge these qualities.

Here are my signature strengths:

- Deep Talent Expertise (including being a good judge of talent)
- Prolific Thought Leadership (with a focus on how it benefits the company)
- Entrepreneurial Spirit (finding creative solutions to make things happen)
- Astute Problem Solver (brilliance in tackling strategic and operational challenges)
- Curiosity (and continuous learning)

Having gained a clear understanding of my strengths, I finally acquired the sense of direction I had been searching for. Essentially, it became evident that my colleagues highly value my expertise in talent and thought leadership, which not only benefits the organization internally but also brings external recognition. Moreover, my entrepreneurial mindset, astute problem-solving abilities, and innate curiosity empower me to tackle challenges with a creative, strategic, and growth-oriented approach.

This newfound perspective opened my eyes to the various career pathways available to me, both within established companies and as an independent consultant. Recognizing this, I made a difficult but pivotal career decision to embark on the entrepreneurial journey and start my own business.

The signature strengths are not just a part of your brand; they are your brand. Understanding who you are and who you are not helps you make informed career decisions, develop intentionally, articulate your value to others, and position yourself for success. While striving to be the best, the first, or different is valuable advice, it can lead you astray without a clear direction. However, when combined with a robust personal brand anchored in your signature strengths, it makes you career-ready.

KEY TAKEAWAYS:

- **Embrace your unique advantages** - Success in life can come from being the best, the first, or different. Identify the skills and perspectives that set you apart and capitalize on them to gain a competitive advantage.

- **Discover your signature strengths** - Working with a coach or seeking feedback from key stakeholders can help you identify your signature strengths. These strengths, which are true to your character and universally acknowledged, define your personal brand and provide a clear sense of direction in your career.

- **Anchor your personal brand in your signature strengths** - Your signature strengths are not just components of your

PART 3: HOW TO CREATE AND LEVERAGE YOUR UNIQUE BRAND

brand; they are your brand. Developing a strong personal brand based on your unique strengths empowers you to navigate your career path with confidence and readiness.

Personal Insight 3: Cylia Troche Quiñonez, Marketing and Finance Strategist, Top-10 Global Pharma Company

HOW TO BUILD YOUR BRAND

Brands are all around you, whether you're driving down the highway passing billboards, shopping down the grocery aisle, watching your favorite Netflix show, or browsing throughout your house. Brands create recognition and the more you recognize the brand the more likely you are to engage. Brands are used as a way to connect with their audience and build trust. One of the many reasons brands are successful is because they have a message that is clear and consistent with who they are. But it goes beyond that—they understand the needs of their customers, reflect those needs in their purpose, are authentic to the problem they want to solve, and, most importantly, have a compelling story to share.

Think about your favorite brand, what makes them special to you and what about them do you connect with? As Latinos, brands are just as important and brand loyalty is high in our community. Do you remember a product from your childhood? Do you still buy it today? I bet just thinking about it brings a smile to your face or the smell evokes a memory.

Just as companies have brands for their products, so should we. Having a personal brand is becoming increasingly more important. So, what is a personal brand and why do you need it? A personal brand is an intentional and conscious effort to control the narrative of who you are, what value you offer, and why they should engage with you. Initially, I thought, well, we all have a brand whether we realize it or not, but actually that's not true—we have reputations. So, what's the difference? Reputations are all about credibility and often not something you can control.

They are based on others' opinions of you and their experiences to your actions. Whereas a personal brand is an intentional and conscious effort. Personal brands can be used to help control the narrative around your reputation. Consider the quote by famous footballer, Steve Young, "Perception is reality. If you are perceived to be something, you might as well be it because that's the truth in people's minds." Reputations can be powerful, but so can your personal brand.

In an increasingly competitive environment, having a personal brand can help set you apart from the crowd. People may know you and your work ethic, but your personal brand can help break through all the noise and set the stage for what YOU want to be known for. Now, let's be real, words are words, but if your actions don't back up what you're saying your story falls flat. As they say, actions speak louder than words.

Here enters the Latino Cultural script—where we were taught not to brag about ourselves. I can hear my dad's voice now, "Work hard, mama, it will happen." Well, that's not always true if you just work hard but no one knows about it, you won't get the recognition and credit you deserve. It can be challenging speaking about yourself and even overwhelming to identify your strengths and share that with someone. We were raised to always work hard, do what you have to do, so for us this is all normal. But it's not, we are that special sauce. We are worth bragging about, even if it's just a little, but you have to do it not just to keep up but to get ahead.

Personal branding is the process you go about in creating your personal brand. There is no one right way to go about this process. In fact, if you google how to create your personal brand, you'll be quite overwhelmed. I, myself, have gone through quite a few of these exercises. They each contributed to my understanding of how I'm perceived and the value that I bring to the table.

It can be overwhelming so let's break it down.

1. Start the process of exploring yourself from your own perspective. Write down what you feel are your strengths, even if you're not sure just write it down.

PART 3: HOW TO CREATE AND LEVERAGE YOUR UNIQUE BRAND

2. Then think about what you've heard from your peers about you. What compliments or awards have you received? What was stated in your performance reviews? Why do people like working with you?
3. This is my favorite part and something I highly recommend: Identify at least five individuals who have worked with you directly and/or know you well to provide you feedback. Ask identified individuals to provide you a list of your five top strengths and if they had to describe you in two words what would those words be.
4. Once you collect back their inputs, you will want to review and see if there are any patterns and/or themes that are consistent amongst their responses. If you're a data driven person, like me, you can take this information and drop it into a spreadsheet to identify and highlight themes.
5. Once the themes are identified and you start to review the words that are showing up, are the themes aligned to your perception of yourself? If so, great—you have done a great job in living up to your reputation that aligns with your personal brand. If not, then we have some work to do.
6. Now that you know how you are perceived, think about how you want to be perceived or, better, what you want to represent. You have your starting point with your initial assessment, now it's time to identify your goal—your personal brand.
7. The next step will be to identify what changes you need to make to achieve your personal brand.
8. Lastly, share with others. Speak about yourself using your personal brand. When someone leaves you, what is it that you want them to remember about you?
9. After implementing those changes, you could always reassess in 6-12 months to see if you have changed their perception. Remember perception is reality.

KEY TAKEAWAYS:

- Other ways to go about this exercise could be to leverage self-assessment tools, such as Insights Discovery and/or Strength Finders. Both of these assessments will help you to better understand yourself as well as others. These resources can be found online.
- Personal brands are not static, they are dynamic and ever changing. This is not a one and done exercise.
- Be prepared to revisit your personal brand message as you grow and learn more about yourself and how YOU want to show up.

Personal Insight 4: Louis Sandoval, CEO/Managing Partner, Halo Advisory Group, Inc.

THE ESSENCE OF PERSONAL BRANDING

My career has taken a non-linear path. During the first third, I held operating positions in sales, marketing, and operations management within the biotech/pharma sectors. In the middle third, I ventured into entrepreneurialism by purchasing an established marine dealership with a business partner. We modernized the business, putting the customer experience at the forefront. Applying what I learned in corporate and business studies, I put theory into practice. The final third was in corporate innovation and technology. Here, I have led the development of technical products and software companies. I have also consulted with early/growth stage companies and Fortune 500 corporations, leveraging technology to improve their efficiency and growth trajectory.

People often ask how I pivoted from industry to industry while maintaining a high level of expertise and credibility. The answer is simple: the agile development of my brand. In simpler terms, a personal brand is what you are known for and the experience that companies have with your leadership or management style.

PART 3: HOW TO CREATE AND LEVERAGE YOUR UNIQUE BRAND

When people think of brands, they often think of iconic logos of global brands such as Apple or Nike. These logos have become synonymous with innovative products, sleek and disruptive design, high sports performance, and the achievement of excellence. BMW's bi-colored roundel signifies high performance and an experience with their products that creates exhilaration for the driver. Meanwhile, Starbucks Coffee provides a consistent experience and quality of coffee across its over 16,000 stores in North America. Disney's brand offers a top-notch experience in their theme parks that spans generations and movies that connect viewers to the wonderment of their youth. These iconic brands focus on the feeling and experience that one engages in, and that's where I'd like to begin my connection with your brand.

When someone encounters you and your brand, what experience should they come away with? Execution and top-level results are some features that come to mind. Our careers are seldom static, and we often find ourselves having several inflection points. According to the Society for Human Resource Management, the average time in a position for most employees is 2.5 years. This can mean 8-12 jobs in a 20 or 30-year career, and many pivots if you stay in one specific industry. Therefore, it's important to have a brand with core components, which I refer to as operating principles and critical value points, to develop a career that is consistent with who you are as a professional.

My operating principles as a team member or leader are to foster teamwork, collaborate, create camaraderie, provide transparency, operate with integrity, and celebrate victories. High levels of transparency, integrity, and collaboration are critical components of my persona. I will not compromise these because they are essential to who I am as a person.

The outcome of all of this is that I am a builder and operator of high-performing brands, teams, and companies. I leverage technology and innovative approaches to deliver transformational growth and results. Despite the various pivots in my career, this has been the central theme in all that I do. It's the experience you can expect with my brand, much like the exhilaration and performance you get behind the wheel of a BMW or the quality coffee and ambiance in one of the over 16,000 Starbucks stores.

I have arranged all of these in a framework that you can apply called the True North Value Pyramid ®.

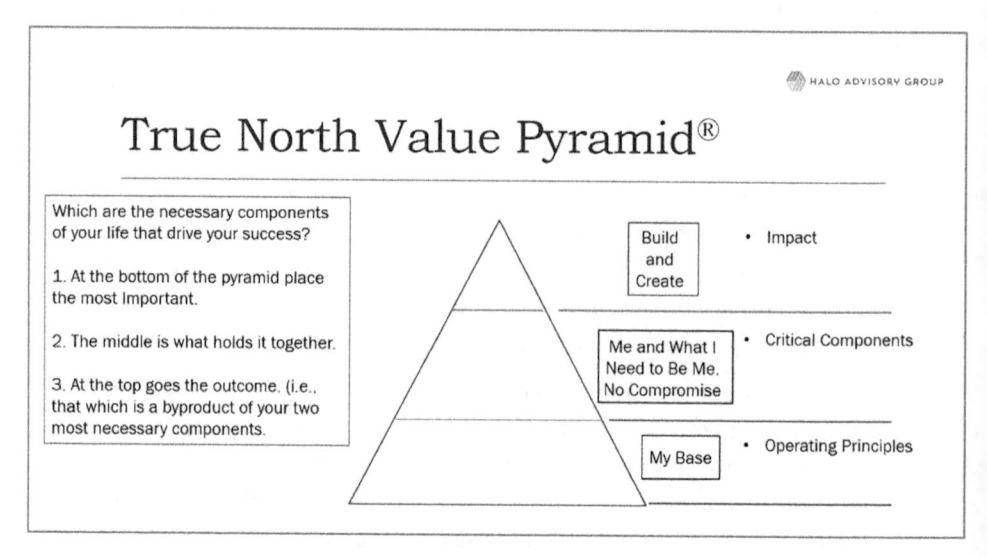

True North Value Pyramid®

HALO ADVISORY GROUP

Which are the necessary components of your life that drive your success?

1. At the bottom of the pyramid place the most Important.

2. The middle is what holds it together.

3. At the top goes the outcome. (i.e., that which is a byproduct of your two most necessary components.

- Build and Create — Impact
- Me and What I Need to Be Me. No Compromise — Critical Components
- My Base — Operating Principles

True North Value Pyramid ® is a trademark of Halo Advisory Group Used with Permission_ All Rights Reserved

KEY TAKEAWAYS:

Your personal brand is unique to who you are as a professional. It defines the 'experience' that an organization can expect from you and identifies the unique qualities that you consistently bring to your various roles. It should identify the following qualities about you:

1. What are your operating principles as a professional?
2. What are your critical values (i.e., those values that define you without compromise)?
3. Your personal brand is the outcome of the operating principles and your critical values, it is what you ultimately deliver, consistently and without restriction of industry and market.

PART 3: HOW TO CREATE AND LEVERAGE YOUR UNIQUE BRAND

Personal Insight 5: Jacqueline Ruiz, CEO of JJR Marketing Inc. and Fig Factor Media Publishing

HOW TO CREATE AND LEVERAGE YOUR UNIQUE PERSONAL BRAND

Your personal brand is your legacy.

It was the fall of 2022 and I had just graduated from an entrepreneurial program at Stanford University. This program was designed to help us scale our business exponentially. In my cohort, there were another 76 amazing entrepreneurs who were either the recipients of over $500,000 USD in funding or had annual revenues of over 1 million USD. My situation was the latter. I was so proud of reaching such an important milestone in my business the year before in order to qualify for this program, but my biggest surprise did not come from the business being accepted—it came from the incredible feedback that I received from many of the participants about my personal brand. One of them told me, "I want to be like you when I grow up." Another one said, "How did you build your personal brand? It's amazing. You are everywhere."

It was this last inquiry that got me thinking... what did I actually do over the last decade to build and share my personal brand in four continents?

I was honest and asked the inquirer to give me a couple of days to think about it. You see, I am a marketer. I have been doing marketing for 20 years of my 40 years in this planet. I have invested over 10,000 hours in the field in order to become an expert. However, I was too close to my personal brand to know what I was actually doing. I wanted to take a moment to reflect, to review, to assess how I actually got here.

- Was it the creation of my website because someone requested it?

- Was it the creation of an image for my logo because they wanted to feature it at an event?
- Was it fact that I had defined the topics that defined my purpose to share with audiences around the world in four continents?
- Was it the fact that I was featured in hundreds of media interviews through radio, tv, print, magazines, and social media?
- Was it the fact that I had gotten dozens of awards?
- Was it the fact that I created the world "pilotina" which means pilot+Latina when I got my pilot's license?
- Was it the 33 books that I have published under my name?

The answer is... all of the above.

Building my personal brand has been like weaving the most beautiful fabric with the most exquisite threads and ribbons. Each of them adding a new tone, color, and brightness. It was like listening to the most beautiful song with all kinds of instruments, all coming together to form a melody—but I did not know that at the time of bringing them together. It wasn't until someone asked me reflect on my journey that I discovered all the gems along the way that helped me develop, unbeknownst to me, the brand that I am known for globally today.

I do not expect everyone to stumble upon the creation of their brand into a global brand. Knowing what I know now helps me create a sense of urgency to tell all the leaders looking to build a legacy to start building their personal brand today. No time to waste.

In the reflection of my journey, I clearly identified the following three steps to capture their legacy starting as soon as possible:

1. DOCUMENT your journey

Your personal brand is the common denominator, the non-negotiable in all of your accomplishments. People get to know part of who you are, but not ALL of who you are depending on the ecosystem you are in. In your personal environment, they might not know all of your amazing professional accomplishments and in your professional career, they might not be aware of all the extracurricular activities you get involved in that make you the extraordinary leader that you are. Sitting down to document your journey through lessons, connections, accomplishments, certificates, experiences, etc., allows you to truly see your whole self in a different, more complete light. You must take the time to review and capture all of it.

2. ENCAPSULATE your experiences

Once you have documented all of your journey, it is time to start thinking strategically and positioning into segments or buckets to serve different audiences. In other words, how does a certain experience or expertise you have serve a specific audience? How can you turn that experience and segment into different products and services? How can you turn your journey into an integrated offering that benefits others and you get compensated for?

3. PACKAGE your legacy

The final step in the process is to package all of that experience and expertise into actual products or services. Every topic that you have to share with the world can be turned into at least 3-5 offerings. Take for example, the topic of "resilience." You can do a keynote presentation on "5 Steps to Becoming the Most Resilient Person You Know," followed by a workshop on same topic, followed by a series of downloadable free tools to identify your points of resilience, followed by a deck of cards on the 50 ways to be resilient, followed by the ultimate, a book about resilience! The possibilities are endless. Content is king when it comes to building your legacy. The more content you create, the more that your legacy expands.

The time to start thinking about your personal brand is today.

The moment you make the intentional decision to start with the steps above is the moment that you will start building your personal brand equity and grow your impact and bottom line!

Personal Insight 6: Veronica Torres Hazley, Founder, Hey Chica!, CEO, Torres Hazley Enterprise, LLC

HOW TO CREATE AND LEVERAGE YOUR UNIQUE BRAND

I have always been a competitive sports type, even as a little girl. My drive to compete remained in my spirit through college and even more when I entered corporate America. In my early 20's I would challenge myself to remain resilient and nibble. It wasn't until I turned 30 that I realized that my body was not built to burn and go. I remember the moment that changed my career trajectory like it was yesterday. I was sitting at a lunch meeting with a friend and the entire left side of my body began to go numb. I was rushed to the hospital to find out I had a stroke. It was at this very moment that I had my first awakening in my career. I was forced to face the reality that being "busy" didn't mean I was successful or even fit to lead.

I was forced to reevaluate my career and my approach to climbing the corporate ladder. I was afraid I would be overlooked for the next promotion because of my incident. I knew that I had to take my personal brand on a deconstructed strategy session to include a new lifestyle and a serious commitment to my health. When I reflected on my Mexican roots and upbringing, I began to see the gaps in health and mental disparities that often cripple our success in leadership. Connecting work to the body is an afterthought. I was shown to work hard, don't put myself first, and never speak up or become a burden to anyone. We were never taught to build capacity.

I wanted to change this mindset and approach for myself and for my family. I decided to take a holistic approach to my health and search for my own healing and advancement. I began to develop my NEW BRAND with conviction and integrity. I chose to start with my mindset and internal state of awareness. The change in my habits included meditation, yoga, mindfulness, and community. I launched my Hey Chica Movement and began curating conversations, conventions, and communities that aligned with feeling better, leading better, and defining our legacies that we want to leave behind. The Movement became a mindset and lifestyle that advanced conversations, opportunities, and ecosystems that move life.

When we are in corporate settings, we are holding space for ourselves and others in the room. Our personal brands are assumed and evaluated by how we look and feel. Our careers can also be restricted and judged based on our physical appearance, beliefs, and attitudes around our emotions and moods. Acknowledging the human biases and the power to take control of our personal brand and awareness will be the difference between making a true IMPACT and living in our fullest potential. It's our time as leaders to become aware and ask ourselves: Who Am I? Where am I in my life? Where do I want to go?

This self-reflection will open our curious and often anxious minds to explore the possibilities of living strong and healthy to progress and compete to our highest potential. The confidence that it takes to own our space and command a room without holding back or playing safe is our opportunity to own our own brand and become liberated from judgment.

This is the power of the Movement. In my business I work with c-suite executives to define what their best self looks like and how they can get on a path that allows them to be fit to lead and to be led.

The power of self-care starts with you and your intention to WIN the day, the job, and the journey. After the COVID pandemic, now more than ever our personal brand alignment to our self in health is crucial. How will you choose to lead? Strong, resilient, and healthy? I hope so.

The keys to success follow a simple format. How will you make an impact? What is the actual impact you will have on other people? I encourage you to design your brand with your health in mind. Explore your past experiences and learnings, old habits, and cultural beliefs. Are they still working for you and your brand? Can you choose wellbeing at every opportunity and design a brand that brings your community and wellbeing back to life?

KEY TAKEAWAYS:

Use journal entries to help you along the way and answer the following questions:

- What is my purpose?
- What energy do I need to create and sustain my brand?
- What will make me resilient in wellbeing?
- How will I curate a life with movement?

DOS AND DON'TS

Now that we have covered the background, stories, and insights around how to create and leverage your unique brand, here are some additional Dos and Don'ts to further support your development in this area.

Dos	Don'ts
Do: Drive Your Brand Your brand is your trademark—own it, breathe it, use it to your full advantage. This means staying on top of it and where it needs to be. Be sure to revisit your brand at least twice a year and make adjustments as needed. Engage your manager and trusted advisors on what you are trying to do with your brand and get their input on how to maximize its impact!	**Don't: Forget to Engage with Audience** Branding is not just about pushing out what you want the world to know—it's about actively engaging with your target audience. This can be a discussion, an email, a thought-provoking LinkedIn post, etc. The bottom line is that you want to form a connection with your target audience so that they can "feel" what you are trying to do, rather than just seeing what you are doing.

Do: Be Intentional with Your Brand

When developing your brand, use the framework provided in this section or others; the key is to land on a brand that you can leverage to add impact in the workplace.

Be certain to focus on those elements above and beyond core job responsibilities. Showcase your unique strengths and experiences that are going to help you stand out to your target audience and get you to the next level.

Don't: Forget to Use Your Latino Superpowers

This is low-hanging fruit for all of us! Use your respective Latino superpowers as part of your brand at all times! Remember, we are natural problem-solvers, innovators, collaborators, team players, global thinkers, and very passionate about what we do.

When used correctly, they will propel your impact in the workplace!

Do: Be Consistent; Show Up on Point!

Having a consistent brand is king. Make sure all brand messaging, work performance, and interactions are aligned with your desired brand in all settings. If you want to be known for something, you have to behave/perform your way into it; words alone will not do it.

Tip: Intentionally focus each week on 1-2 elements of your brand based on what's going on in your world. Keep working on different elements of your brand; people will see your intentionality and results of your focus and hard work.

Don't: Forget to Respect Your Personal Space

Remember, you don't have to make your brand about everything in your life. Some things, especially personal things, can be off limits.

You are the best judge of what to share and not share. If there is ever a question, discuss it with your manager or trusted advisors. They will always provide a perspective to help.

Do: Create the Narrative You Want

Use your brand to create the narrative you want. If you are working on being a strong communicator as part of your brand, then find opportunities to showcase your communication skills, especially those in high-visibility situations.

The key is to create opportunities to shine and an environment where you can show your brand. Don't forget to use your manager and trusted advisors to help create these situations—not only will they help create them, they will also often advocate for you in doing so!

Don't: Forget to Be Ready to Articulate Your Brand

After all the homework you did on your branding, be ready at any time to share your elevator pitch with your brand messaging. You never know when the situation will present itself. If you find yourself in a situation with a senior leader and they ask about what you do, this is an excellent opportunity to incorporate your brand.

These are the type of interactions that get you noticed and show that you are always ready, have a strong message, and on point! This is a great place to be!

RECAP

In closing, I want to call upon all of you to take ownership and drive your personal brand. All too often, I have seen professionals treat this as a check-box activity when they go to a workshop and never to be visited again. If you want to be a confident, promotion-ready, impact player in the workplace, you will need to be fully aware of your brand and demonstrate what you are doing to elevate it. Your manager, senior leaders, peers, and other influential decision-makers must experience your brand and how it's going to help drive the organization forward. As Gaby Natale said in an interview with me, "Use your brand to build influence; the survival of your business (your career) MAY VERY WELL depend on it!"

> "Use your brand to build influence; the survival of your business (your career) MAY VERY WELL depend on it!"
> – Gaby Natale

The great part is that you are in full control to shape the perception others have of you. With self-reflection, thoughtfulness, consistent and targeted messaging, and work performance, you will be positioned to create the narrative you are trying to achieve. Take the time to practice with formal personal branding workshops and tools. When done effectively, you will find that you will begin to stand out from the crowd and start to be considered for those new high-profile roles, opportunities, and even potential sponsors!

PLANNING AND ACTIVATING YOUR DEVELOPMENT

To support your development and to help you organize and activate the concepts in this chapter, please go to my website (www.refugioatilano.com) and download the free templates for **The Latino Leadership Workbook—**this is a great set of tools to help organize your target areas and map a plan on where to focus your growth. It also includes a notes page and a development roadmap template so you can begin to think through and draft your personalized improvement plan that will set you up for maximum growth and success.

How to Build Your Executive Presence

> "It is executive presence—and no man or woman attains a top job, lands an extraordinary deal, or develops a significant following without this heady combination of confidence, poise, and authenticity that convinces the rest of us we're in the presence of someone who is the real deal."
>
> - Sylvia Ann Hewlett

Since I was a teen working with my uncle doing electrical work in factories, I was always fascinated with leaders who walked through the plant and operated with that great confidence and swagger where you knew that those were the people in charge. Similarly, once I started my professional career, I continued to be wowed by the leaders who just seemed to always be in command—their image, their confidence, their positivity, their vision, their warmth, how intently they listened, and how others followed them. As a younger and even mid-career professional, I didn't really know what "it" was they had and definitely never thought it was something that I could ever achieve. I thought this was a special skill only taught to executives and all I could do was sit back and admire it, which I did! After researching this experience over the past few years, I came to realize what I witnessed was Executive Presence.

> I spoke about the story earlier in this book when a senior executive provided me with the insight that to be seriously considered for senior level roles I needed to start acting the part and looking the part—what she was referring to was executive presence. Since that moment six years ago, I became a fierce student of the game. I studied every video and article, I began working

on different elements of my presence in the workplace, and I refined and pivoted as needed. From then to now, I have been able to master key elements of my presence like my image, confidence, body language, and communication. My presence is now one of my superpowers and it's consistently recognized as part of my brand by my peers and management team. One of the big reasons I am writing this book today is because a few years ago my manager asked me to mentor others on this topic. Once I started doing that, I thought to myself, why not coach on all the topics I have mastered? And the rest is history... The Latino Leadership Playbook is a true story of a spark igniting a fire!

I became a fierce student of the game. I studied every video and article, I began working on different elements of my presence in the workplace, and I refined and pivoted as needed. From then to now, I have been able to master key elements of my presence like my image, confidence, body language, and communication.

WHAT IS EXECUTIVE PRESENCE

There are many definitions of executive presence because it's such an elusive concept—it's like chasing a shadow because it's so multi-faceted. Many have described presence as having that "wow" factor or the "it" factor; it's that special something that helps you stand out, get noticed, and be memorable. Of all the definitions that I have come across, I think the following one from an article in Forbes resonates best with me: "Executive presence is about your ability to inspire confidence—inspiring confidence to your subordinates that you are the leader they want to follow, inspiring confidence amongst peers that you're capable and reliable, inspiring confidence among senior leaders that you have the potential for great achievements" (Valentine, 2018).

PART 3: HOW TO BUILD YOUR EXECUTIVE PRESENCE

After studying and applying this capability over the years, presence is about interacting in a way that draws people to you and the experience and impression you create for those around you. I learned that presence is really the output of a culmination of mastered leadership capabilities, and they boil down to the following three elements:

Communication: There is no substitute for being able to effectively and efficiently communicate your message with any audience at any time. This includes:

- Being able to influence others and create buy-in on ideas is critical to your executive presence. Your delivery must be thoughtful, concise, and compelling.
- Being decisive and using good judgement based on analysis of the facts. You want to provide an informed point of view so that you can have a central role in key business decisions.

Operating with poise and composure; prepare hard and be ready for any situation, question, style. Show that you have strong command over yourself, your emotions, and thoughts.

Key Insight: When delivering your message, a kiss of death is too much info. Be mindful of the number of slides, the amount of information on slides, and put your notes aside when presenting—know your content well when you deliver your message.

Image: People are always placing a value on you, so always be prepared for how you present yourself in the best light. This includes:

- Making sure to present an image that exudes confidence. You should be well-versed in your domain and be ready to go five questions deep at any time.

- Having a polished presentation of yourself and aligning it with your business setting. For example, my signature attire always includes a sportscoat; however, your attire can be very different in a tech company setting or a manufacturing setting. Regardless of your environment, always be presentable and ensure it reflects your personal brand (see the previous chapter for personal branding).

Key Insight: When in meetings, eliminate device use at all costs. Leaders find this profoundly discourteous and gives the impression that you are not fully paying attention.

Body Language: Your body language says everything. Per Albert Mehrabian, 55% of communication is nonverbal (Masterclass, 2021). This includes:

- Posture: As my mentor told me, if you want to be a leader then use confident body language; work on your posture and build it into your image. You will see yourself feel differently and project differently. This is low-hanging fruit, so please make this adjustment.
- Eye Contact: In Western cultures, eye contact is a great tool to establish a connection, show you are listening, and exude confidence. There are many online videos and books on this topic—please study and practice in the workplace. This can be a game-changer towards establishing your desired confidence.

Key Insight: Make sure to read the chapter on "How to be a Strong Communicator" in this book; it covers additional body language elements that can facilitate your impact.

To achieve exceptional executive presence, it will require time, commitment, practice, successes and failures, and refinement—this is all part of your development journey. Find out what works best for you and your style—keep trying new pieces. I still do this today! All elements must come together and be in sync for others to trust your presence. You will know you have reached your goal once others start to comment on your presence or ask for advice on how you got there. This is a great place to be and adds to your impact in the workplace.

WHY EXECUTIVE PRESENCE IS IMPORTANT

Per an article by Erin Owen on LinkedIn.com, executive presence is a foundational quality needed if you want to move to the next level. Mastering this concept provides access and opportunity—for growth, stretch assignments, high-visibility projects, and promotions (Owens, 2022).

This statement could not be truer. Once I started mastering my executive presence, I have leveraged it for many types of opportunities to drive my development, my brand, and career. For example, I have been able to quickly work my way toward leading a global Latino ERG; it has landed me opportunities across the organization to develop and drive strategic, high-impact initiatives; it has positioned me to grow my executive level network exponentially (obtained additional executive mentors and sponsors); and, finally, it has provided with me the great opportunity to mentor others across our company! As you can see, my fingerprints are all over the organization and in ways that will impact or advance our business! This is an example of the importance of and how you leverage executive presence to be an impact player for your organization.

Personal Insight 1: Refugio A. Atilano, Business Leader at a Top-10 Pharma Company, ERG/DEI Leader, Author, *The Latino Leadership Playbook*

LEVERAGING EXECUTIVE PRESENCE TO LEAD GLOBAL PROGRAMS AND TEAMS

My professional background is in complex, strategic project, program, and portfolio management. What that means is I run point in organizing large, cross-functional global teams to bring new solutions to market. When getting engaged to lead new initiatives, I have to quickly pick up the business subject, understand the problem/opportunity, and all the key players involved. To obtain the confidence of new project team members at the operational, management, and senior executive levels, I must effectively use my executive presence to demonstrate that I can lead the team to success.

When I start a project, I study the business, the proposed solution, and the people. I do my homework so I can have a game plan for each interaction and position myself for a great start and strong working relationships. To make sure it's as impactful as possible, I make sure I am well-organized and that my image and my messaging are all in rhythm. I make sure that I have an agenda, that I am concise and compelling with where I am going, why I am going there, and how I see us collaborating on driving toward our goals. I rehearse my delivery (i.e., message, body language, pace, tone) before each meeting and take a very professional approach toward running my projects. For me, this is my business and I make sure there is no doubt that I am in charge; I know exactly where I am going and how I want to get there.

I share this story because much of what I described are easy wins for you to begin making an impact in your current role. My challenge to you is to begin showing up differently for all meetings and use some (or all) of the behaviors described above and in this chapter. Once your peers and leaders see you well-prepared, super-organized, and taking the lead to drive the business forward, it's game on for your career! This is needle-moving leadership behavior that will turn heads!

I will leave you with this last and very important insight, always show up to a meeting with ideas that are well-thought through and documented in a way that can facilitate discussion. One of the pet peeves of many senior leaders (including myself) is not showing up to a meeting prepared or with something to react to. I see many early and mid-career professionals not show up with anything and want to develop solutions in the meeting real-time. DO NOT DO THIS. Perform your due diligence in advance and come ready with something that's already framed out. This will automatically set you apart from everyone else! If you want even greater impact, send your framework/ideas ahead of the meeting (24 hours in advance with an agenda), so the leader can prepare. This sounds so simple, but it's almost never done.

One of the pet peeves of many senior leaders (including myself) is not showing up to a meeting prepared or with something to react to. I see many early and mid-career professionals not show up with anything and want to develop solutions in the meeting real-time.
DO NOT DO THIS.

INTERVIEW WITH AN EXECUTIVE LEADER: Marisa Solis
Senior Vice President at the National Football League

Favorite Quote: "I am the master of my fate: I am the captain of my soul." - William Ernest Henley, Invictus

I had the privilege of meeting Marissa at the 2022 We Are All Human Hispanic Leadership Summit. She's one of today's most prominent leaders in our Latino community and is passionate about developing the current and next generation of Latino leaders. I had the honor of interviewing Marissa for this book, and she shared the following insights around executive presence and leading with impact.

Executive Presence is About Inspiring Confidence and Action

The concept of executive presence can mean so many things. For Marissa, it's being able to inspire confidence and action in others at all levels of the organization. It's the "X Factor" that gets you to the top and is required for you to have a voice in decision-making rooms. The trust and confidence that you obtain from senior leaders is what is going to get you in the door.

Executive presence is the ability to lead, develop, and articulate a vision; having gravitas; being able to add value in different ways, build trust, and change others to do big things. It's bringing others along to achieve goals and being focused on impact rather than just visibility. Success will be based on your influence; the focus and effectiveness of your executive presence is critical toward your development and opportunity for senior level roles.

Know and Impact Your Business

Marissa stated often to "know your business cold." This is a requirement if you want to be a recognized leader and in a position to add strategic value to the organization. Take time and do your research on the data that drives your area of the business—learn what drives growth and identify and articulate how you can directly impact that growth. The holy grail of impact is being able to "Create something from nothing!"

> "Know your business cold." This is a requirement if you want to be a recognized leader and in a position to add strategic value to the organization.
> –Marissa Solis

She also strongly recommends to "not be defined by your job." If you do, you will risk being stuck in the same position for much longer than necessary. Learn to take on responsibilities and opportunities nobody else wants; use your business knowledge (as described above) to see opportunities nobody else does and have the conviction to see them through. Make taking risks part of your DNA; work beyond your bubble and always seek unique ways to impact the business. For example, she discussed taking a risk through pitching, creating, and leading a new business arm for one of her previous companies. Initially, she did not have the support of leadership; however, through data collection, business case development, compelling story-telling, and pure grit to see it through, it turned out to be a top money-maker for the organization and she was recognized for this achievement in many ways—including it being a stepping stone for her current role!

Latinos Must Unite in Order to Achieve Our Desired Impact

Marissa shared that, as a community, we need to work towards changing the narrative on how we support each other. We have a tremendous opportunity to unleash and realize our full Latino potential if we are able to commit to elevating and supporting each other consistently and meaningfully. Instead of getting in each other's way, we need to move to a world where we are facilitators, connectors, cheer leaders, mentors, sponsors, champions, etc. In addition, we can't do this alone; we must invite and engage allies to accelerate our development and impact as a community. Allyship and will be a critical component towards our collective professional success and overall impact in the workplace.

We Need to Build a Culture of Accountability

Marissa discussed how some of her most impactful growth was facilitated by feedback from others; she called it "tough feedback with the spirit of love." In order to develop collectively as Latinos, we need to begin holding each other accountable for our joint progression. This can be something as simple as pointing out something in real-time after a meeting or can also take the form of something more formal. The point is that we need to start helping and pushing each other develop our leadership capabilities and call each other out when we see something our Latino colleagues might not. As long as it's done with the "spirit of love," this single act can start to move the Latino leadership landscape in a positive direction.

Once Inside—Insights on How to Operate

Once you have successfully made it to senior leadership, you will have a new set of leadership capabilities to bring forward. Once you gain the trust of those around you, you can use your Latinidad to your advantage. Specifically, lead with humility, empathy, and a keen insight of our Latino community. Be ready to work in ambiguity and solve new business challenges, while being the bridge that brings people together. In senior leadership, you will have to navigate the political environment as well as many egos. This is where some of your natural Latino superpowers can help you provide unique value and bring a different perspective than non-Latinos.

Personal Insight 2: Kshitij Sharma, Executive Coach and Founder of Coach Kshitij Executive Coaching LLP

HOW TO BUILD YOUR EXECUTIVE PRESENCE

In a curious twist of fate, despite consistently being rated as a top performer and receiving the highest accolades within my organization, I was repeatedly overlooked for senior roles in my corporate career. When seeking an explanation from my superiors, I was met with the statement that while I excelled in my performance, I lacked the essential quality of "Executive Presence" required for higher positions. This left me frustrated and perplexed by the vague and elusive nature of this concept.

Executive presence is undoubtedly one of the most misinterpreted terms in the corporate world. This realization compelled me to delve deeper into the subject, becoming a dedicated student who learned the intricacies through grueling trial and error. Eventually, I embarked on a mission to support numerous leaders in their journey toward cultivating and boosting their own executive presence. These individuals possessed exceptional competence in their respective domains. Yet, their progress up the corporate ladder or expansion of their business ventures was hindered due to their perceived lack of this elusive quality.

For context, allow me to shed some light on the symptoms and undesired outcomes of a mild presence:

- In team meetings, you go unnoticed, and your contributions are overlooked.

- Despite your efforts, promotions seem to elude you.
- High-profile projects are consistently out of your reach.
- A sense of tension and unspoken conflicts permeate your team dynamics.
- Demanding stakeholders often push you aside or disregard your input.
- You're frequently labelled as either excessively aggressive or overly submissive in your communication style.
- Speaking opportunities are consistently relinquished without a second thought.

Take a moment to reflect on the symptoms mentioned above. If even one or more of these resonates with your experience, addressing and enhancing your executive presence becomes imperative.

My journey toward understanding and honing my executive presence has led me to write a book titled *Demystifying Executive Presence*. Within its pages, I provide a comprehensive framework that elucidates what executive presence truly entails and offers practical guidance on its development. This invaluable resource has the potential to assist individuals who encounter similar challenges, providing them with a roadmap to improve their professional presence.

THE STORY OF THE TRANSFORMATION OF SAMUEL

Among the countless corporate clients who have ascended to senior and c-suite positions and numerous entrepreneurial clients who have achieved remarkable business expansion, I would like to highlight the inspiring journey of one specific individual. This client, driven by an unwavering passion for enhancing his executive presence, embarked on a transformative path that yielded remarkable results, thanks to his genuine and diligent endeavors.

Let's call this person Samuel. Samuel was a Vice President—of

IT at a Global Bank in Seattle. (Name, role, and industry changed due to confidentiality). Samuel was a super knowledgeable person who was highly respected in his organization, but despite that, he could not grow vertically for nearly eight years. He had an intense desire to reach the c-suite roles. The problem with Samuel was that he was uncomfortable talking about his accomplishments. His mindset was that his work should do that talking. He always expected others to know about his work and give him due credit, and he believed that if he was talking about his work, it was equivalent to boasting, which is wrong.

Samuel's transformation journey began with his realization that he needed to overcome his discomfort in talking about his accomplishments. He understood that in a busy and self-absorbed world, a constant showcase of his good work was necessary to be recognized and remembered by those who mattered. He realized that his reluctance to talk about his work stemmed from a childhood belief that showcasing one's work is equivalent to boasting.

Another challenge Samuel faced was his mild demeanor, which prevented him from effectively communicating his points in meetings. To address this, he focused on three modes of expression: tone, body language, and word choice. Through deliberate practice, he learned to modulate his tone to be polite yet firm, improved his body language to appear confident and approachable, and selected words that created a positive and poised impact. These conscious changes in his external expression resulted in a significant shift in his presence.

During subsequent conversations, Samuel realized that he lacked a clear sense of purpose despite his high performance. With guidance, he engaged in an exercise to articulate his life purpose and discovered his key drivers and "why." This newfound clarity energized him and allowed him to become laser-focused in his approach to work, ultimately changing stakeholders' perceptions of him.

Samuel's journey exemplifies the importance of working not only on skill set and mindset, but also on the level of being.

PART 3: HOW TO BUILD YOUR EXECUTIVE PRESENCE

By addressing his discomfort with self-promotion, improving his external expression, and finding his sense of purpose, he experienced a definitive shift in his career trajectory.

The impact was visible in his overall presence. He started receiving positive feedback from his stakeholders, his voice was heard and acknowledged in the board room, and he was able to influence people across the spectrum. After consistent effort over one and a half years, he finally achieved a well-deserved promotion to the next level.

Three Key Insights to Cultivate an Influential Executive Presence:

- **In terms of mindset** - Embrace the confidence to proudly present your work whenever and wherever it is deemed essential.
- **In relation to skill set** - The internal perceptions of self hold minimal significance compared to the three critical components of effective communication: tone, word selection, and body language.
- **Regarding the aspect of being** - Foster clarity regarding your "why/purpose," identify your strengths, and construct your entire foundation based on these elements.

Personal Insight 3: Anthony López, Founder L&L Advisors, Senior Executive, CEO, Board Director, Leadership Expert and Author, Leadership & Management Consultant and Executive Coach.

EXECUTIVE PRESENCE: A GREAT LEADERSHIP ACCELERATOR

Ask three people to define executive presence (EP), and you will likely get three uniquely different responses. The reason for this is because it's a rather subjective concept. What one person may perceive as critical elements for someone to demonstrate good executive presence will vary depending on their own style, communication preference, cultural background, and many other factors. As hard as it may be to precisely define executive presence, one thing may be universally true and that is: we know it when we see it.

Possibly another universal truth about EP may be this: while it may be tough to define what it is or how you "develop it," we can say that properly leveraged, good EP will enable you to inspire confidence among the people you lead and influence. It will give your followers and colleagues the motivation to follow and model after you—and in the end, that is the purpose of leadership! Thus, there is a direct correlation between a leader's executive presence and their effectiveness as leaders.

Some years back, when I was in a director level position at Johnson and Johnson (J&J), I also served as the Chairman of the Board for HOLA (The Hispanic Organization for Leadership and Achievement is the Latino Employee Resource Group at J&J). I, along with the leaders of the other J&J Employee Resource Groups, had the opportunity to meet with Bill Weldon, our CEO, two or three times a year. It was a terrific chance to brief him on the state of the diversity initiatives in J&J and speak about progress that each of the groups were making.

I recall one specific meeting when we were all sitting in the boardroom at J&J Headquarters in New Brunswick, New Jersey. We were all taking turns briefing Bill on the latest happenings within each of our groups. I had the unique opportunity to be sitting right next to him, and what I observed from the moment he walked into the room to the moment the meeting was over was a wonderful example of a leader with good executive presence. I remember feeling quite impressed with the questions he asked. They had a subtle brilliance to them. They were simple but profound, provocative but not intimidating, and they always elevated and guided the discussion in a particular direction. On several occasions during the brief one-hour meeting, when he would ask a question, I recall thinking, "Man, that is a great question, why didn't I think of that?" Bill was leading simply with the questions he was asking, more so than the statements he was making.

PART 3: HOW TO BUILD YOUR EXECUTIVE PRESENCE

A few years later, when I was serving as President of Ansell Healthcare and as Chairman of the Board for PROSPANICA, a professional Latino non-profit organization, I had the unique opportunity to share the stage with Alex Gorsky, the J&J's CEO who had replaced Bill Weldon. I facilitated a "fire-side chat" with Alex during PROSPANICA's Annual Conference. After the event, I remember thinking, "Wow, I thought I was polished and elegant in my delivery and presentation, but Alex is smooth as silk." He was extremely confident yet humble, intelligent but not overbearing, friendly but with a touch of formality. Alex oozed executive presence; it seemed to come naturally to him.

Both examples that I have listed here, and many more that I have personally experienced, certainly have shaped my thinking on executive presence. Although, I still believe it is hard to precisely define what it is, I do know it when I see it. Moreover, I think there are some characteristics and behaviors that leaders must demonstrate to be perceived as having a high level of executive presence. Importantly, I am certain that demonstrating these has enabled me to enjoy a healthy amount of executive presence. Finally, and this is good news, I do believe one can develop a higher level of EP.

Traits to Demonstrate a High Level of Executive Presence:

1. **Being authentic and demonstrating high character and integrity:** In leadership there are only two non-negotiables as far as I am concerned, and they are character and integrity. When you violate these, you create an immediate handicap to your effectiveness as a leader. Being our authentic self and remaining steadfast in our values is a way we demonstrate that high level of character and integrity that is vital to being perceived as a leader with a great executive presence.

2. **Composure and personal style:** Demonstrate a calm and cool demeanor. Not too many people are going to want to follow a leader that does not demonstrate an ability to remain calm even in the most intense situations and

strategically work through whatever the issues are to reach a resolution.

3. **Intellectual curiosity:** Asking the right questions is a powerful way to lead a discussion and move the agenda forward. Leaders must be strategic in the questions they ask and ensure that they are always elevating the conversation to the next level.

4. **Communicating for impact:** The best leaders are excellent communicators. They also can be brief, bright, and gone! Meaning, they communicate for impact rather than to impress. How a leader communicates clearly impacts how they are perceived.

5. **Confident but humble:** People want to follow confident leaders, but they are not too keen on getting behind arrogant or narcissistic individuals who focus more on themselves than those they are privileged to lead. Simple rule, always put your team and their needs first!

6. **Effective use of body language and bearing:** No doubt we can all agree that what we say with our body language is more important than what we say with our words. Thus, good executive presence includes using our body language to send the right signals and having the best approach that suits our personal style.

7. **Demonstrating a high level of emotional intelligence (EQ) and cultural intelligence (CQ):** Most of us are familiar with IQ (our intelligence quotient), and EQ (our emotional intelligence quotient). Fewer have learned about perhaps the most important form of intelligence relative to the effectiveness of a leader—cultural intelligence (CQ). The great news is that unlike IQ, which can't fundamentally be altered (i.e., if you were not born to be Einstein, you will likely never be able to develop a genius level IQ), we can dramatically increase our EQ and CQ levels by learning and modifying our behaviors over time. Higher levels of EQ and CQ enables leaders to exhibit the qualities most people associate with a high executive presence individual.

PART 3: HOW TO BUILD YOUR EXECUTIVE PRESENCE

Developing as a leader requires a constant "view in the mirror" to evaluate ourselves, learn from our experience, our mistakes, and from others around us, to evolve to become an increasingly better leader. The journey to having a high and healthy level of executive presence is directly proportional to our ability to increase our EQ and CQ, while remaining true to our authentic self, firm on our values, and never violating our character and integrity. We should walk confidently but humbly, remain intellectually curious, and learn to communicate effectively in order to always aim to inspire and motivate others to achieve their greatness.

Personal Insight 4: Arabel Alva Rosales, President & CEO, AAR Tech, Founder and Producer of Runway Latinx RLx (your fashion week), Founder and Chairman of Pivoting in Heels (PIH), NFP all RLx profits benefit PIH

HOW TO BUILD YOUR EXECUTIVE PRESENCE

I am considered an active business leader and am civically involved. I serve on several boards and in many cases find myself to be the first or the only woman and, therefore, the only Latina. When I chaired the Illinois Hispanic Chambers of Commerce (IHCC), I was the only woman on the board, but worked diligently to bring on more women.

My focus as a leader is to have the best outcome, and in doing so, I must be the best I can be. I am clear on the fact that I must be fully prepared and use my creativity to provide solutions. However, the fact is that being "well put together," especially for a woman, means being and looking your best. Being a leader in the fashion industry, I do not mind striving to look my best. I understand the look of "power" well, and feel that it is part of my brand, as well as a way to share my art (fashion). So, I don't mind planning my wardrobe in advance. When I am doing this, I use it as a sort of ritual. I actually visualize myself going through the meetings, being successful during them, or if there is a fun moment to be had; I allow myself to visualize it all. It's my Fashion Ritual.

When I was appointed to be a board member on the Chicago Transit Authority (CTA), the second largest transit system in the country, I was once again the only woman serving on the board. The CTA has approximately 11,000 employees and at the time a budget of approximately $1.25 billion. I always take every role I am involved in very seriously. I study, come prepared, but also enjoy putting my #VidaArabel look together—feminine, stylish, powerful, yet very comfortable. I truly believe it's hard to make great decisions if you are uncomfortable, so why do that to yourself? Our meetings at the time were all open to the public and shown live on a Chicago cable station.

When I first became part of a group, I tended to initially listen and observe. I do that at all my introductory meetings. I wore a well-tailored red suit. At my second meeting, I noticed all my colleagues were looking quite a bit more dapper! When the meeting was over, a few of the female staff members whispered to me that my fellow board members were looking so well put together—suit, tie, pocket square, etc. They asked if I noticed. One of the staffers said, "They know about you, about your fashion background." Another shared, "We love the effect you're having," and she winked. I liked it too. To me it also meant a sign of respect.

As time went by, I made sure to always be prepared with good questions and have a clear understanding of the facts. I was vocal with disagreements, but always respectful. I eventually became Vice Chair of the board, then acting Chair for almost a year during one of the most difficult times our history has faced, Covid. I am very proud that our CTA team not only made it through that extremely tough period, but we achieved national accolades for the work done during that time!

All these elements are critical for success: Feeling confident, being prepared, and looking the part. However, none of this, including having a successful looking style, come by chance. I believe that if you practice using these elements, success and respect will become a habit. I consider being a woman, especially a Latina, an asset that attracts respect. Taking everything into account, being successful is not just dressing the part, but also

PART 3: HOW TO BUILD YOUR EXECUTIVE PRESENCE

planning and executing success daily. I have led and continue to lead by example in every aspect of my life. When you respect yourself, others in turn will respect you. This is my ritual and key to success.

DOS AND DON'TS

Now that we have covered the background, stories, and insights around how to build your executive presence, here are some additional Dos and Don'ts to further support your development in this area.

Dos	Don'ts
Do: Lead with Confidence Executive presence is all about confidence—to inspire confidence in others, you must master self-confidence. The leadership concepts outlined in this book, along with your commitment and practice to develop, will carve out the powerful, confident leader within you. Keep pushing yourself and put yourself out front using the tools, techniques, and insights covered in this book. Use your trusted advisory network for guidance and practice with peers. In the end, you will be the confident leader you aspire to be!	**Don't: Forget to Be an Expert** One of the best things you can do to increase your presence is to know your industry, your company, and your business unit, in addition to your team's goals. Become an expert—by doing the above, you will be able to position yourself to add value and contribute to key business decisions in new ways. You will move from doer to strategic thinker and a leader who drives priorities forward. This takes time, homework, and checking in with SMEs across the organization. This is a critical investment.
Do: Always Be Poised and Composed One of the easiest ways to achieve this capability is to over-prepare. Before going to meetings, especially senior level meetings, game plan for how you will approach it: body language, messaging, answers to potential questions, where you sit in the room, etc. The more prepared you are, the more you can stay in control and deliver your messaging with confidence and authority.	**Don't: Forget to Deliver Results** All this being said, strong performance and achieving results are expected and a requirement just to get in the game of advancing your career. It's no different with executive presence; in fact, this capability is a tool that will help you achieve those desired results and impact. Use it to your advantage and always position yourself to be a strong performer.

Do: Show Flexibility; Pivot Effectively Be a great active listener. Part of being an effective leader is knowing how to read the room (your audience) and pivot if you see something is not hitting the mark. A leader who can quickly identify concerns and unwanted body language (i.e., people looking at their phones) will be able to make real-time adjustments to messaging and approach. Doing so will help get the discussion back on track and in a good position to move the ball forward.	**Don't: Forget to Understand People, Political Landscape** Executive presence is about inspiring and connecting with people. You want to leave a great impression with everyone you touch, and especially with the senior leaders who make decisions for promotions and special assignments. We will cover political savviness in an upcoming chapter—this is a teaser and want you to start thinking in terms of effectively navigating within your organization.
Do: Be Consistent Your executive presence will be a journey and will take time (often years) to build. For example, I have been working on my presence over the past six years tirelessly and it was about year three or four where everything clicked. Make a plan to work on all elements and commit to it, but one at a time. Master one thing and then keep moving on to the next. Your peers and your leaders will notice your development and you will see your career shift in great ways before you know it!	**Don't: Forget to Deliver Results** One of our natural Latino superpowers is our passion. Find ways to strategically use your passion when connecting with others. I am not asking you to be Mr./Ms. Latina all the time in your company; instead, use your passion when talking about a new idea you are presenting and why you are excited about it. If leading an ERG, talk about your passion to elevate Latinos; if you are leading a volunteer initiative, show your passion on why it's important to you. People will remember this great energy—being memorable for your passion is always a great place to be!

PART 3: HOW TO BUILD YOUR EXECUTIVE PRESENCE

RECAP

Executive presence has always been a fascinating topic to me—when you see it, it's magnetic and provides that "wow" factor. In this chapter, you have been provided with some of the most tangible and actionable insights to improve your executive presence game. My goal is to position you to leave the best possible impression and experience for those around you. When you leave the room, I want them to say, "Who was that!" I want you to have a central role in shaping business decisions because of your compelling communication style. I want you to show up strong, professional, and with ultimate poise, warmth, and composure. Finally, I want you to be that confident, informed, high-impact, and promotion ready Latino leader that sets the tone for the organization. Now we are talking! Good luck and I look forward to your development in this area until it's mastered!

PLANNING AND ACTIVATING YOUR DEVELOPMENT

To support your development and to help you organize and activate the concepts in this chapter, please go to my website (www.refugioatilano.com) and download the free templates for **The Latino Leadership Workbook**—this is a great set of tools to help organize your target areas and map a plan on where to focus your growth. It also includes a notes page and a development roadmap template so you can begin to think through and draft your personalized improvement plan that will set you up for maximum growth and success.

How to Lead with Impact and an Extreme Ownership Mindset

> "If you think you are too small to have an IMPACT, try going to bed with a mosquito."
> – Anita Roddick

Hands-down, this is my favorite chapter. This chapter is key towards taking your leadership game to the next level, to be noticed by senior leaders, and to drive immense value for your organization. Having an impact and ownership mindset will immediately put you in the driver's seat of your career and creating new, exciting opportunities for your future.

OPERATING WITH AN IMPACT MINDSET FOR YOUR ORGANIZATION

Operating with impact means delivering and being able to articulate your or your team's value against your organization, business unit, and immediate team priorities and goals. You should be very thoughtful and intentional in how you support the goals of your company at each level. All the work you do should directly align with supporting your company's objectives. There are different ways to begin operating with an impact mindset and one method is to find ways to get involved in high-visibility strategic initiatives—these are the projects that senior leaders have on their direct radar. If you are not engaged in work activities and projects that support those critical company goals, then have a discussion and work with your manager, mentors, and sponsors on a game play to land assignments that will provide those opportunities and great exposure. (Note: This assumes that you are already meeting your performance goals.) Once you are able to be involved with and/or lead strategic initiatives, it will automatically put you in a high-visibility position and allow you to collaborate with other visible team members, showcase your brand, and drive results in front of senior leaders.

PART 3: HOW TO LEAD WITH IMPACT AND AN EXTREME OWNERSHIP MINDSET

Regardless of if you are on a high-visibility strategic project or not, it's important that you always lead with an impact and value mindset—think through, understand, and be able to articulate "why" you are doing the work. You must determine the desired end goal of what your work is meant to achieve, and then be able to communicate how you are adding to that goal/value. When you communicate in terms of the value you are bringing, business leaders will automatically be intrigued. This shows that you have done your homework and thought through understanding the business and who you are helping to advance the company goals. This is leadership!

As you know, there is a huge representation gap for Latinos in senior level roles, leading with an impact mindset and approach is an area where a mindset shift can begin to make a big difference. Rather than sitting back and/or focusing on "working hard" or doing work that you can't articulate as adding significant value for your organization's goals, I challenge you to think differently and show up differently. For example, if you are in an ERG leadership position, then identify, lead, and execute upon new ideas that will bring new value for your organization, community, or members; identify and deliver new impactful solutions that will turn peoples' heads. Use these opportunities to be bold and showcase your ideas to your ERG sponsors and leadership team (reminder: use good preparation, idea vetting, and storytelling) and establish the momentum, support, and excitement that will put you out-front and in a position to make an impact for the organization! Remember to always tie your initiatives to corporate goals; this will get you automatic visibility and the support you need to drive it forward.

The more you operate and communicate with a business-impact mindset, the better you will position yourself to deliver new, unique value for your organization—this is the type of capability that can accelerate your career!

As captured in an article by Indeed, demonstrating your impact in the workplace can help you make a good impression. "It enables the organization to recognize your ability and value, resulting in increased pay and other benefits" (Tips for Adding, 2022). You will be better positioned as a leader and find yourself getting tapped on the shoulder for special assignments, access to senior leaders who want to learn how they can help you, as well as potential promotions. In short, the more you operate and communicate with a business-impact mindset, the better you will position yourself to deliver new, unique value for your organization—this is the type of capability that can accelerate your career!

OPERATING WITH AN OWNERSHIP MINDSET FOR YOUR ORGANIZATION

Now that we covered the importance of operating with an impact mindset, it's time to go deeper and talk about how to operate with an ownership mindset. In fact, I will take this a step further, I am going to talk in terms of operating with an "extreme ownership" mindset. As Latinos, we need to attack and master this concept if we want to be known as strong leaders in the workplace. As discussed in the Navigating Our Cultural Scripts part of this book, putting ourselves out-front and in the spotlight is not natural for us. However, you are now armed with an awareness of the importance of breaking through that barrier as well as tactics for doing so. Let's now focus on activating this capability!

Operating with an ownership mindset is taking the initiative and being the lead on developing and bringing new ideas to life. It's owning the vision, the strategy, the plan, the problem-solving, while effectively leading a team (at all levels) to realize that vision. When you are taking an extreme ownership approach, there should be no doubt who the leaders is—your command of the initiative, management style, and team effectiveness will be evident! "Ownership means more than being responsible and accountable. Ownership means being resolute, solving problems, assuming liability, and owning the consequences of actions.

PART 3: HOW TO LEAD WITH IMPACT AND AN EXTREME OWNERSHIP MINDSET

Ownership can be the cornerstone of one's sense of leadership. It is a strong sense of responsibility, unafraid to be accountable and brave enough to say, 'I take ownership of this'" (VXI Marketing, 2021).

When you are taking an extreme ownership approach, there should be no doubt who the leaders is—your command of the initiative, management style, and team effectiveness will be evident!

Personal Insight 1: Refugio A. Atilano, Business Leader at a Top-10 Pharma Company, ERG/DEI Leader, Author, *The Latino Leadership Playbook*

THE LATINO LEADERSHIP PLAYBOOK: ELEVATING ALL LATINOS

I often get asked, "Refugio, why did you write this book?" or, "Why did you get so many contributors?" The answer is simple—it's because I feel a deep sense of responsibility to add maximum impact to our Latino professional community for now and generations to come. I know and have lived through the painful frustration of seeing others around me get noticed, promoted, and recognized when I knew I was ready for those same positions. Once I figured out the secrets to leadership success and specifically Latino leadership success, it was game on for me to share those insights asap! (Note: I was originally going to wait five years to write this book!) As for the number of contributors, I carefully vetted each one and every single person brought a unique and passionate perspective; these perspectives will stand the test of time and are all critical towards adding maximum impact for you and all Latinos!

Being a professional project manager, a strong communicator, and a relationship builder has put me in a unique position to bring this playbook to life. From the beginning I took ownership of this vision. I put in careful thought, pressure tested my ideas with leading Latino/a industry experts, and refined my vision along the way. I knew that if I wanted to be regarded as top-tier Latino leader, then I better know my stuff inside and out, while getting the input, perspectives, and blessings of all those who came before me. I wanted to make sure to build something special on top of the great work that was already in place.

Once I had a strategy and other Latino leaders and contributors aligned, I mapped out a plan to write the book. I laid out the chapters, ran focus groups, and assigned contributors to certain sections based on their area of expertise. I laid out a writing framework, examples, and tweaked along the way. The bottom line is that I had a strong strategy and game plan, and I knew exactly where I wanted to go and how I wanted to get there. I also consistently communicated updates, checked-in personally, and continuously solicited ideas for improvement. I ensured to attend conferences to make those ever-important personal connections with my contributors and network; I made sure to take the time to understand their respective worlds better and incorporate any additional key nuggets into the book.

What I just described is what it means to lead with impact and an extreme ownership mindset. I challenge you to identify how you are driving impact for your organization, business unit, your community, or team, and then take an extreme ownership approach and drive it hard! Leave no doubt about who is in charge and who is leading the way. Once you start taking this approach and delivering tangible results, you will begin to stand out as a highly regarded impact player in the workplace. This is where you want to be!

Personal Insight 2: Refugio A. Atilano, Business Leader at a Top-10 Pharma Company, ERG/DEI Leader, Author, *The Latino Leadership Playbook*

BE COMFORTABLE WITH BEING UNCOMFORTABLE:

Many companies are focused on recruiting unrepresented talent into their respective organizations and I think this is a great thing—a much-needed thing. The question is how does this work get done, who owns it, and who's in the best position to drive it? In my opinion, our Latino ERGs are in a great position to support our company goals in this space for Latino talent. We have connections with professional organizations, we have capable and passionate ERG members who want to help with the recruitment and interview process, and we know the Latino professional culture better than anyone.

Although recruitment is a Talent Acquisition function, we are in a unique position to partner with them and help bridge the gap with the Latino community. As an ERG leader, one of my responsibilities is to help my company reach its goals, and if hiring underrepresented populations (such as Latinos) is one of those goals, then I am all in! This is taking an impact-focused approach.

Now you may say, well I know nothing about recruitment. I say to you, that's okay. You are Latino, which means you are a natural problem solver, innovator, and relationship builder who leads with passion and a deep understanding of our community. Use those natural superpowers and talk to experts in your organization, do your offline homework, use your Latino network to get insights and use your grit to build and pressure-test a strategy, and to finally develop a game plan for how you are going to attack the opportunity.

INTERVIEW WITH AN EXECUTIVE LEADER: Andrea Best

Vice President at Top-10 Global Pharma Company

Note from Refugio: I have had the privilege of getting to know Andrea over the past few years. She is passionate about leadership development and empowering others to reach their maximum potential and has been a great mentor to me. I was able to sit down with her and glean some amazing insights that she would love to share with all of you when it comes to operating with an impact and ownership mindset!

Passion to Learn and Understand the Business: Lead with an Inquisitive Mindset

If you want to be regarded as a leader who can add strategic value, you need to know the business. You must understand the company goals, the data, and how the different parts of your respective business connect. Doing so takes curiosity and determination—once you have a grasp of the business, you will be able to add value in unique ways and gain the trust of your leadership and teams.

Get Others Excited About Jumping on Your Bus

A leader is not considered a leader simply because of a title. A true leader is one that can influence without power, and this can be done from anywhere, and at any level, within the organization. Some key leadership elements are as follows:

1. Do not blindly follow other people's routes; know the business well enough to question and/or create a new vision for the direction or help course correct as needed.
2. Be able to craft and articulate a concise, relatable, and well-vetted vision that connects the business; help your business see the unseen. This is the type of leadership that will add most impact for your organization and your career.
3. Know what you don't know and ask for help. Keep inquiring about areas of the business you don't understand and fill those gaps quickly so you can increase your potential impact for the organization.

"Be able to craft and articulate a concise, relatable, and well-vetted vision that connects the business; help your business see the unseen. This is the type of leadership that will add most impact for your organization and your career."

- Andrea Best

Understand Your Value and Operate Beyond Your Immediate Remit

It's critical that you find ways to add value where you can across teams and the organization—performing your core role is expected. One of Andrea's pet peeves is when people say, "That's not my responsibility." She has grown her career exponentially by taking on new responsibilities with open arms. She views them as opportunities to develop her career, skillset, and organizational influence. I once asked her how she has accumulated so many different business functions under her organization; she reported that it's because she's always willing to take on new challenges and then becomes the resident executive expert in that area.

Empower Others

Andrea reported that one of the best things you can do to add impact as a leader is to elevate and empower your teams. Let them drive their own bus and define their own routes. Of course, this should come with your oversight and advice on any bumpy roads they may encounter. You don't need to tell them what to do as the assumption is that you have very talented people on your team that are looking to grow and add unique impact for the organization and their careers.

Personal Insight 3: Pedro Lerma, Founder & Chief Executive Officer, LERMA/ Advertising

EMBRACE THE JOURNEY OF LIFELONG LEADERSHIP LEARNING

During the early stages of my career, my fascination with self-help audio books flourished. A significant portion of my time was spent driving, affording me ample opportunities to immerse myself in these valuable resources. The subject that captivated me the most was human-centered leadership. I swiftly discovered that this style of leadership resonated perfectly with my personality and values. As I interacted with colleagues, supervisors, and clients, I endeavored to apply the knowledge I had gained. These experiences not only refined my ability to establish positive connections with people but also honed my efficacy in accomplishing tasks. Among the profound lessons I gleaned from those encounters was the crucial distinction between managing and leading.

Handling to-do lists, calendars, resources, and budgets equips individuals with the capacity to manage people and projects. The realm of management is akin to a mathematical puzzle, focused on propelling tasks towards completion.

In stark contrast, leadership revolves around the art of forging a compelling vision that captures hearts and minds, allowing individuals to believe in and contribute to that vision. It entails involving people in a manner that unveils their integral role and highlights the personal benefits of bringing that vision to life. When executed masterfully, people are naturally drawn to you as a leader and to the work itself.

Moreover, I discovered that the ability to communicate with clarity and persuasion serves as the cornerstone of success in nearly every endeavor. Throughout my journey, I have witnessed brilliant and talented individuals struggle to convey their knowledge and ideas effectively. As a result, they often fail to achieve the success their intellect would suggest. Conversely, I've seen individuals with more modest talents thrive immensely simply due to their exceptional communication skills.

As the owner of an advertising agency, I frequently have the privilege of hosting college students on tours of our offices. Without fail, during our interactive Q&A sessions, a student inevitably poses the question, "What would you recommend I focus on in my education?" My response remains unwavering: Become a lifelong student of leadership and devote attention to the study and practice of effective communication.

Furthermore, I wholeheartedly endorse two indispensable books to anyone seeking guidance. The first is Dale Carnegie's timeless classic, *How to Win Friends and Influence People*. This remarkable work delves into the realms of human relations, communication, and leadership. The second recommendation is *Primal Leadership* by Daniel Goleman, an illuminating book that explores the realms of emotional intelligence and its role in leadership.

Rest assured; I am a firm believer in practicing what I preach. To this day, I wholeheartedly consider myself a student, embracing the philosophy of lifelong learning. Wisdom permeates from various sources: the people around me, the pages of books, my MasterClass subscription, and countless other outlets that offer opportunities for growth and enlightenment.

KEY TAKEAWAYS:

- Distinguish between managing and leading: Managing is about tasks, while leading is about vision and inspiring others.
- Effective communication is key: Clear and persuasive communication is vital for success in leadership.
- Embrace lifelong learning: Adopt a student mindset, seeking wisdom from various sources to continuously develop as a leader.

Personal Insight 4: Lucy Sorrentini, MBA, CPC, Founder and CEO, Impact Consulting, Changing the World through Inclusive Leadership, Board Director, Columbia Bank and Board Advisor, Girls Incorporated

HOW AN OWNERSHIP MINDSET CHANGED MY LIFE TRAJECTORY

My Early Years

It is often said, no two journeys are alike. My personal story and how it helped shape my perspective and career trajectory is on the surface not too dissimilar to many other Latinos, but it is in the details and the journey where the differentiation lies. Many Latinos come to the United States in search of better economic opportunities and a chance for a brighter future. In my case, as a second-generation Latina with Puerto Rican heritage, I was born here, but as a family we too were in search of opportunities and a brighter future. While my parents did leave their families to come to New York City from Puerto Rico, I was fortunate enough to have my very large family (I was the youngest of seven) close by despite having lost my father to a heart condition when I was just a baby.

Upon arrival, we faced language barriers, cultural differences, and the need to adapt to a new way of life. Since English was my first language, this was not an issue for me. In fact, growing up bilingual had and continues to have its many benefits, although I did not recognize it at the time. Many Latinos had low-wage jobs, often in industries such as agriculture, construction, or as was the case with my family, the service sector. I am the proud daughter of a Bodega owner. Here is where I learned the true meaning of what it means to have "grit."

My experience is a tale of two stories since, as a light-skinned Latina with an Italian last name, I likely benefited from many privileges my darker complexion family members and friends did not. Yet, coming from a low-income household, I was economically disadvantaged. However, I didn't realize the magnitude of this because we always had food on the table, a warm bed to sleep in and clothing on our backs.

Latinos are known for their resilience, strong family values, and determination to succeed. I learned all about the importance of family, faith, and grace from my most favorite role model, my mom. In our neighborhood, we looked out for one another—not because we were asked to, but because that's what real "community" is all about. Over time, many Latinos contribute significantly to their adapted country, enriching its cultural fabric and making valuable contributions to its economy. Such was the case for us. I am confident that as a family, we have contributed in meaningful and impactful ways to the cultural fabric of our amazing country.

PART 3: HOW TO LEAD WITH IMPACT AND AN EXTREME OWNERSHIP MINDSET

Leading with an Ownership Mindset

So here is where and how having an "ownership mindset" changed my life trajectory. My path to leadership started when I was a young girl, and it has been shaped ever since by my diverse experiences, unique circumstances, and broad perspectives. As the youngest of seven children, I spent much of my early years learning how to fend for myself and thrive in an environment focused on survival of the fittest.

I grew up believing that with God all things are possible. With this deep faith, I honed my skill at "perspective taking" and relied largely on my imagination to reimagine a better world and life for myself and my family. I knew both by example and intuitively that this better life would require me to be in the driver's seat of my life and my career, and so I set on a learning path that would be filled with new experiences—some familiar and some not—that have shaped who I am today.

The one common theme across these experiences is that each time they taught me valuable life lessons about who I am and what I really care about, and those directly aligned with my Latina heritage. In their simplest form they included family first, faith always, a strong work ethic, making the world better for others, being proud of who I am and where I came from, being able to take care of myself and those I love, living life with passion, always respecting and valuing others, being open to new things (even if at first glance they presented themselves as fear), and never giving up on what was put in my heart by a higher source. And trust me, these are not just words on a page. They are real beliefs and values that have been foundational to my personal and business life.

KEY TAKEAWAYS:

As I reflect on what made the real difference then and what makes the real impact now, I believe it has a lot to do with the following:

- Growth mindset is about believing that my basic abilities can be developed through dedication and hard work and recognizing that brains and talent are just the starting point. This view creates a love of learning and a resilience that is essential for us to get ahead.

- Values and vision are foundational to who we are as people. Our values are part nature and part nurture. They get formed in early childhood and continue to develop and strengthen over time. Whereas vision takes a bit more work. It's an idealistic view of a future state that inspires and excites us, and not something many people are comfortable exploring. In part, because it takes coming out of our comfort zone and taking risks to realize our why. Much of what inspires us in life is directly linked to our personal "why."

- Strategic focus, roadmap and accountability are where our mindset, values, and vision come to life. For many, this proves to be a difficult task, but it is so essential to growing and sustaining positive change and success in life, no matter what life stage we are in. We can't do all the things, or be all the things, to all people without suffering burnout or creating diminishing returns. However, with a clear strategy, plan of action and accountability, we can deliver improved and sustained results and impact over time.

Now, it's your turn to challenge yourself to be the CEO of your life and career. Never forget who you are and where you came from. Dare to live your purpose and define your why. Put a plan in place to help you achieve your goals in alignment with your values. Hold yourself accountable to achieve amazing results. Identify and rely on your tribe to support you along the way. There's nothing more inspiring than leaders who are on a mission to be the best version of themselves, and who are also making the world a better place one person and one action at a time. The time has come for Latino leaders to rise up. We owe it to ourselves and future generations of Latinos to create the change we want to see in the world one person and action at a time.

PART 3: HOW TO LEAD WITH IMPACT AND AN EXTREME OWNERSHIP MINDSET

A CALL TO ACTION: GET COMFORTABLE BEING UNCOMFORTABLE

It's interesting that, in general, Latinos are averse to taking risks and putting themselves out there; however, what's more interesting is that we are built to problem solve and to take on those risks head-on! So, my call to action for all of you is to get comfortable being uncomfortable. See each problem as an opportunity to come up with a new, innovative solution that will add maximum impact and experience. These are the moments that present themselves when you least expect it; make sure to seize them and use it as an opportunity to showcase your leadership brand and ability to deliver impactful results for the organization.

Note: This example applies to any part of your business—continue to scan the environment for unique, impactful ways to drive your business forward and be sure to always communicate (i.e., advocating for yourself) your ideas, strategies, and plan to your direct manager and other key stakeholders. As Cid Wilson, CEO of the Hispanic Association for Corporate Responsibility, stated, "Speak for your work; don't let your work speak for you!"

"Speak for your work; don't let your work speak for you!"
- Cid Wilson

DOS AND DON'TS

Now that we have covered the background, stories, and insights around how to lead with impact and an extreme ownership mindset, here are some additional Dos and Don'ts to further support your development in this area.

Dos	Don'ts
Do: Always Operate with an Impact Mindset Be very thoughtful on how you are adding value to your organization. Make the time to understand your company goals and be able to articulate what you are doing to advance them. The way I look at it is you only have so many hours in the day; make sure that you are optimizing your time and effort to add maximum impact. Once you get a reputation as an impact player, doors will open up for you.	**Don't: Get Lost in the Details** It's super-easy to fall back on what's comfortable and to be busy with non-business critical work. Remember, you have to add value—you must be impacting your company, business unit, or team objectives if you want to stand out as a strong leader. The more mindful you are of how you spend your time, the better positioned you will be to be on strategic, high-visibility projects and delivering value on projects that don't have high visibility.
Do: Work Closely with Your Manager You need your manager on board with your plan of action to get involved with high-visibility work and projects. Make sure to prioritize this relationship and take care of her/his needs. This is another great way to add impact! If you can help your manager reach their goals, then you will more than likely have a strong advocate for you to senior leaders.	**Don't: Communicate with Impact with Senior Leaders** When operating with impact, you need to communicate with an impact focus. Senior leaders will not be as interested in the process and detailed planning. They are there to help make decisions and clear the road in order to drive the business forward. Be sure to refine your story-telling and focus on the impact of your idea/work/progress to the organization and what you need from them (awareness, decision, help).
Do: Study and Know Your Business Area One of the most important attributes you will need as a leader is credibility. In order to add value to a given business area, you must know your business well. Study your area, do industry research, bring in new ideas based on that research, talk to experts in your area, etc. The more you know about your business, the easier it is to add value, connect the dots, and share new, impactful ideas.	**Don't: Forget to Use Extreme Ownershipr** When you see an opportunity to add value, embrace that moment (raise your hand), own it, drive it. Leave no doubt about your leadership approach, capability, and who's in charge. If you see an opportunity to lead a pet project for a VP, take it. If you see a high-impact opportunity that nobody else sees, then educate them—own it. Note: Always align with your manager on why you want to take on something and share your plan on who it will/will not impact core responsibilities. Once you have them on board, it's game on!

PART 3: HOW TO LEAD WITH IMPACT AND AN EXTREME
OWNERSHIP MINDSET

RECAP

Now you know the importance of operating with an impact and extreme-ownership mindset. When doing so, it automatically positions you as a leader and can make you very visible in your organization, especially if you begin to add significant value in different parts of your organization (i.e., core job, ERGs, special assignments, volunteer events, etc.). You now have the insights and guidance to begin developing your impact in the workplace and I trust that you will be proactive in limiting your "busy work." Keep pushing yourself to drive value in uncomfortable areas, keep pushing past the imposter syndrome barriers, and keep pushing others to do the same. Being a strong Latino leader who is fearless and takes ownership and accountability to drive their business forward is the type of leader who gets promoted and lands the most influential sponsors. Let's roll!

PLANNING AND ACTIVATING YOUR DEVELOPMENT

To support your development and to help you organize and activate the concepts in this chapter, please go to my website (www.refugioatilano.com) and download the free templates for **The Latino Leadership Workbook**—this is a great set of tools to help organize your target areas and map a plan on where to focus your growth. It also includes a notes page and a development roadmap template so you can begin to think through and draft your personalized improvement plan that will set you up for maximum growth and success.

How to Be a Change Leader

> "The people who are crazy enough to think they can change the world are the ones who actually do it."
>
> **- Steve Jobs**

Change leadership is one of my favorite topics because it's all about connecting with people, understanding their needs/reservations, and guiding them through what's possible—like I am doing with this book! This capability has helped me tremendously as a leader given the constant change in today's business environment. Having this skill in your toolbox sets you up to lead organizations through new projects, transformations, and strategic priorities—things you will need to stand out to be an impact player in the workplace. If you think about it, business is always changing, and any improvement or new strategies will require some degree of change for the people in the organization. This is a great time for Latinos to be leaders of change and seize this opportunity to take their leadership to the next level!

> Change leadership is one of my favorite topics because it's all about connecting with people, understanding their needs/reservations, and guiding them through what's possible.

> As Latinos, we are built for change and making critical adjustments when needed. For example, we are phenomenal at pivoting in our family environment. I still remember times when we had to take in family members into our home. It seemed that we were always ready for what life gave us and we embraced those moments—for us,

it was just part of the deal and we automatically went into problem solving mode. When my cousin moved in with us when I was a kid, I remember it temporarily disrupted our lives, but we adapted quickly and made the most of it. Looking back, it was natural for us to welcome someone into our home, and it doesn't surprise me how easy we were able to do it. We are natural change adapters and are ready for whatever life throws at us. This still holds true today as we have pivoted as a family after the loss of my father two months ago.

WHAT IS CHANGE LEADERSHIP?

Change in business is inevitable. It can't be stopped and we must be ready to embrace, adapt to, and drive it at all times. Change can impact all levels your organization and it's critical that we are strong, thoughtful, and positive leaders that can help the organization navigate through it effectively in order to reach the desired outcomes. As captured by Indeed.com, "Change leadership is a style of management that emphasizes the importance of improvement and adaptability in an organization. Change leaders excite interested parties about the benefits of changes in a business" (Leadership During, 2023). Moreover, it is "the practice of approaching changes across an organization with positivity, enthusiasm, and a growth mindset. By practicing change leadership, you can adapt your business practices to market changes and prepare for unexpected scenarios and learn about exciting new technologies" (Leadership During, 2023).

> Change in business is inevitable—it can't be stopped and we must be ready to embrace, adapt to, and drive it at all times.

In a business setting, there is always an opportunity to be a change leader. It's taking a confident leadership position through utilizing an approach that focuses on the big picture, a thoughtful change management strategy, and providing the support and conviction to see it through to the end. It's setting the tone by developing clear messaging, removing roadblocks, and being front-and-center spearheading the change. If there is a strong change leader, there is greater potential for successful desired outcomes. As Latinos, we have a great opportunity in front of us to leverage our natural strength to adapt to change and become change leaders in the business world.

> *As an example of being change-ready and pivoting to unexpected scenarios (from a personal perspective), up to the start of the 2020 pandemic I worked for a phenomenal global airline company. I had very strong performance and had planned on being there for a long time, with the plan to potentially close out my career at the company. Needless to say, the pandemic threw a monkey wrench into my plans. Because there were no customers flying at that time, the airline industry was decimated—there was no revenue and employees were asked to voluntarily look for other external opportunities. I was one of the few employees who took a leap of faith and found another opportunity—even though I was very comfortable in my current job, I embraced the opportunity for change and went all in. I knew there was more I wanted to accomplish with my career and saw the change as an opportunity to further develop my leadership capabilities at a world-class pharma company. Over the last three years, this was easily one of the best moves I have made. I have grown exponentially as a leader, have had tremendous support from my company on my passions, and am now here writing this book as a result. The lesson learned here is to always be change-ready—embrace, adapt, and drive it with an all-in approach and you can position yourself for great things to happen.*

STRATEGIES FOR CHANGE LEADERSHIP

As discussed, being a strong change leader is critical to the success of your organization. It will support the desired implementation of new initiatives, organizational structure changes, merges and acquisitions, inclusivity priorities, new technologies, new processes, etc. The idea here is that change is everywhere in your business; the opportunity to lead and impact your organization (and your career) is limitless! It is critical that you scan the environment to find opportunities to be a change leader (small or big change is okay) and begin to establish a reputation as someone who can help be a catalyst and inspiration to take the organization to the next level. Be sure to talk to your manager, mentors, and sponsors about your interest and personal game plan in this area so that they can help tee you up for the best possible opportunities for experience and exposure.

Here are some basic strategies for developing your change leadership capability—and some of them are ones that we have previously captured in this book:

- **Lead with an Impact Mindset:** You want to get people excited about the proposed change and one of the easiest ways to do this is to show how the change helps to advance business priorities and goals.
- **Use an Innovative and Growth Mindset:** Based on your understanding of the business and your cultural experience, develop new solutions that will help drive the business forward. People will become excited about supporting an initiative that propels them into the future.
- **Be a Change Champion:** Actively show and talk about the importance of being change-ready. See every change as an opportunity to showcase your change leadership—embrace and adapt to change in meaningful ways that set an example for the rest of the organization.
- **Be a Strong Communicator:** Being able to articulate changes with concise and compelling storytelling will

be critical for your success as a change leader. Using the strategies outlined in the "How to Be a Strong Communicator" chapter, will position yourself to be an effective leader who can inspire others to initiate and execute upon needed change.

- **Understand the Needs of Those Impacted by the Change:** Take extra time to understand who the change will impact and how those users feel about it. Make them part of the process to develop and execute on the change. Lead with empathy and make sure to walk through the change in their shoes—this will tee you and the organization for the desired outcomes.

- **Lead with Conviction/Passion:** Being a change leader is having the ability to inspire others. Once you do everything above, use your natural passion and align teams and drive the change forward. Make sure you are visibly leading the way and see things through until the end. The team and your organization will remember you for your leadership!

Now that we have covered the basics of change leadership, let's cover some stories with insights from influential industry leaders who can help accelerate your development in this space!

Personal Insight 1: Refugio A. Atilano, Business Leader at a Top-10 Pharma Company, ERG/DEI Leader, Author, *The Latino Leadership Playbook*

THE LATINO LEADERSHIP PLAYBOOK: CHANGING LATINO LEADERSHIP

Targeting to increase Latino representation in corporate senior level roles to mirror our population representation numbers (20% and growing) is a significant undertaking and requires major changes on different fronts. For example, 1) Latinos (starting with this book) need to develop our leadership capability so that we are promotion- and senior leadership-ready; 2) companies must recognize the new generation of Latino leadership and do their part to recruit, develop, and advance our capable leaders; 3) the overall Latino community must unite and collectively advance and promote the next generation of strong leaders in our community.

For the purposes of this book, I am currently focused on #1 above (note: I will be tackling #2 and #3 next). Focusing on #1 is an incredibly major change leadership effort in that I needed to first create a vision and framework to advance our community of new Latino leaders. I still remember talking to Latino leaders early-on about my vision when it was only an idea. Some of the feedback I received was that, "We already tried that," or, "There are already Latino leadership books out there," or, "Who are you to drive this forward?" I knew at that time that I needed to document my vision to show my concept and how it was different than anything else. Also, I had to demonstrate that I had done my research (reading Latino books) and spoke to the most influential Latino/a experts to gain perspective, insights, and alignment. The bottom line is that I needed to prove that my vision was thoughtful and well-vetted before I could put it out there for people to support.

Since those early days last year, I have refined my vision and the Latino Leadership Success Model so that they are airtight. I worked hard to ensure my materials tell a compelling story and to show the pathway to success for our professional community. In addition, I have taken time to understand the needs of our community through focus groups, through book contributor insights, and perspectives of the most influential Latinos and non-Latinos in my network. And finally, I have absolutely no quit in me—I am extremely passionate about doing my part to carry our professional community forward and to lead with strong conviction until we change the game. I left no stone unturned as I wanted to make sure I provided the best possible product for you and all Latinos.

> I have absolutely no quit in me—I am extremely passionate about doing my part to carry our professional community forward and to lead with strong conviction until we change the game.

I hope this story demonstrates the power of change leadership as there are so many elements to it. You need a strong, thoughtful, well-vetted vision that others can easily understand and get excited about supporting. It's just as important that you are visible, active, and leading the charge to see the results come to life. These are the behaviors that any of you can apply to your current role, and when done effectively, will help you stand out as an impact player in the workplace that is on their way to becoming a promotion-ready leader!

Personal Insight 2: Dr. Maria Espinola, CEO, Institute for Health Equity and Innovation

HOW TO BE AN EFFECTIVE CHANGE LEADER

From a very young age, I always sought to promote change. I believe our lives gain meaning when we become able to change society for the better. When I was 11 years old living in Argentina, I became a human rights advocate. I was born during the last dictatorship in Argentina, and I felt driven by the idea of promoting democracy and justice for all. As an adult living in the United States, I have advocated for public policy changes to help vulnerable populations, particularly child victims of different types of traumas. In organizations, I have promoted a wide range of changes to increase opportunities for underrepresented minorities, improve healthcare services for underserved groups, and foster more equitable systems.

During speaking engagements, I see many people get excited to hear about the idea of becoming a change leader, but I also see them get scared and overwhelmed. They share they don't know where to start. To help them, I'll share a four-step process here that has been useful to me and that I believe can be useful to others:

In terms of the very first step, my recommendation is to always start with you—recognizing what matters to you, and getting in touch with what drives you. Since this is a book about Latinos, my hope is that those who are reading it care about lifting other Latinos up. Personally, I do feel driven by a desire to increase Latinos' representation and success and I have promoted institutional changes to make that happen. There are many examples that I can share but I will choose one that I think can help illustrate the points I am trying to make.

After I received a faculty appointment at University of Cincinnati College of Medicine, I had a very difficult time finding other faculty members from Latino backgrounds. Every time I asked, people would mention the same two individuals, so I naturally reached out to them, and we began meeting. They knew two other Latino faculty members, so we became a group of five. All five of us felt that it should be easier for people, (other faculty members, students, community members) to identify Latino faculty members at the University.

As a psychologist who specializes in multicultural issues, I know how important it can be for people to connect with others with similar life experiences and interests. I also know how fundamental it can be for students to see faculty members who look and sound like them. Not only do I know this through the research that has been conducted on these topics, but from my own personal experiences. I know how life changing it was for me when as a student, I had the opportunity to meet someone with a similar background who had been able to achieve what I wanted to achieve. Dreams that at the time seemed impossible became possible in my mind after I met her (a Latina psychologist who had immigrated here as an adult, had an accent, and had trained at my two dream schools: Boston University and Harvard Medical School). She did not give me guidance on how to get accepted, but the fact that she existed was sufficient for me. She helped me by simply existing. A few years after meeting her, the dream of getting trained at those schools became a reality for me. That is the power of role models and why representation matters.

My colleagues had other stories that motivated them, but we all agree that lack of representation was a problem. And that is the second step in this process. Once you identify what drives you, you have to identify a problem that you would be driven to solve. The problem can be something that affects you personally, your organization, and/or a group of people you particularly care about.

Third, you have to develop a solution for it, which will promote a specific change. The solution can be something that you designed alone or with a group of people. Either way, it's very important to do research on the topic. Investigate if anyone had tried the same solution or a similar solution before you. Research what worked, what didn't, and why.

For the problem we had identified, we felt that a potential solution was to create an affinity group, specifically for Latino faculty members and call it Latino Faculty Association (LFA). During our research phase, we reached out to the Black Faculty Association and to Latino faculty affinity groups at other universities, and we learned a lot from them. After reviewing what we had learned, we decided that the mission of the LFA was going to be to promote the well-being and advancement of Latino faculty, students, and the larger Latino community at the University. We planned on accomplishing this mission by building connections and providing a network of support, facilitating and advocating for opportunities to celebrate Latino identities, and building powerful coalitions to advance the Latino community.

Fourth, you have to identify the barriers to implementing this change (financial issues, low number of members) and again developing solutions to overcome those barriers. Regarding the financial issues, we identified sources of funding, applied for grants, and obtained the money we needed to start the affinity group. Regarding the lack of members, we were able to advertise the group and identify about 85 full-time Latino faculty members. This discovery surprised everyone, even people who had been at the University for over 20 years. It turned out that lack of visibility was a bigger problem than lack of representation.

Co-founding the Latino Faculty Association was very rewarding. In the process, I met many faculty members who shared how important it was for them to have a group that supported them. The support came in different forms, for some it was the ability to come to a meeting and feel welcomed, connect with others with similar experiences. For others, it was the opportunity to have access to subject matter experts or to a group that can actively advocate for them.

One of the most rewarding aspects of co-founding the LFA, was to meet students and community members who shared how excited they felt to discover new role models and sources of inspiration. For some, the inspiration came from directly connecting to Latino faculty members and getting advice or mentoring from them. For others, it was the simple existence of the group that made all the difference. Something that did not exist before now did and it had opened new possibilities for them and others. Something that needed to be changed, had effectively been changed.

KEY TAKEAWAY:

- To become an effective change leader, you have to recognize what matters to you, and get in touch with what drives you.

Personal Insight 3: Jeffrey Mohr, Senior Leader with management experience in many Fortune 500 companies

HOW TO BECOME A CHANGE LEADER

Change leadership is a learned skill that requires conscious effort, practice, and is increasingly important as one advances in their career. A well-rounded change leader utilizes a growth mindset to look beyond how one operates today, to identify opportunities for improvement. And can turn that vision to reality through an understanding of the business and the needs of the people. Over the past 17 years I have developed that skillset through a practical application, apprenticeship, and conscious learning.

What is change leadership and why is it important?

Change leadership is often considered the ability to lead oneself, or others, through change that happens "to" them. This is incomplete. An equally, or perhaps more, important aspect of being a change leader is the growth mindset to seek out change. To understand that what works today may not work tomorrow, or to identify a better way of business. Then to build the excitement and to have the courage to lead that change in a way helps others to see and realize that same vision.

In today's dynamic and ever-changing business environment, it is difficult to name a successful business leader who is not an effective change leader. Change leadership is a necessary capability for broader business leadership. It is also one of the most easily recognized capabilities by one's leaders, peers, and junior team members. Leaders see the curiosity in identifying needed change and the business results once that change is delivered. Peers are often partners in crafting solutions and will see the initiative and drive in developing a brighter future. Junior team members will experience the leadership from a standpoint of being engaged and brought along in the journey.

These are key inputs to career development and advancement. Job descriptions do not always spell out change leadership, particularly early in one's career. But as one advances, solely delivering on the responsibilities laid out in one's job description will not lead to reaching that next level, that requires moving beyond stated responsibilities with an eye toward the horizon. Broadening one's business acumen and perspective and identifying and implementing opportunities for improvement (i.e., being a change leader).

What does it mean to be a change leader?

The first step in being an effective change leader is to be proactive in identifying "why." This is driven by awareness of one's environment. Professionally, this means understanding one's business and being aware of the internal and external drivers of change. These could be macro-economic forces, such as regulatory changes in one's industry, natural disasters impacting supply chains, or the entry of a new competitor. Alternatively, change could be internally driven, such as the need to develop a new capability, the acquisition of new a business, or turnover in leadership. Change leaders with a growth mindset are continuously looking at the environment to proactively understand if, when, and what change is needed. And they are thoughtful, but not fearful, of instituting the change to address a dynamic environment.

Regardless of the source, if caught off-guard, or unaware, one will be starting the change journey from a disadvantaged, reactionary, position. Awareness of the change drivers allows one to answer the "why" behind change, which is critical to contextualizing the "what" is changing.

The next step in being a change leader, is understanding the "how." How will the change impact, or be perceived by, one's stakeholders. In most cases there is not a single answer to this question. Each stakeholder group, or even individual, may be impacted differently. Considering each point of view allows the change leader to be able to have an authentic conversation on the concerns or excitement the change may elicit. Additionally, it allows change leaders to formulate a strategy for any actions to lead stakeholders through the change.

Finally, change leaders are able to combine the "why," "what," and "how," to direct the narrative of the change in a way that speaks to the individual and promotes understanding and confidence. In many cases this results in excitement about the future vision or what's to come. But it should not be confused with spinning a conversation to a false reality. In some instances, it may include delivering a hard message. If that is the case, change leaders will address it head on with the same authentic leadership and acknowledge that difficult changes are necessary, with a clear articulation of why, and what will ultimately be achieved.

How has being a change leader influenced my career?

Being a change leader is a learned skill that requires time, conscious effort, and practice. Professionally, I have spent my career developing this skill from Day 1. Beginning my career as a management consultant, I was introduced to the concepts of change leadership from my very first client engagement where I was asked to lead a team of client staff (from multiple competitive organizations) through the change of collaborating together in a joint venture. It was a learning experience, to say the least. While I could execute tactical elements of the project, I had not yet developed the business acumen or relationship management skills to be an effective a change leader. Fortunately, I had a strong senior team around me whom I could learn from.

This pattern continued, with each engagement showing advances and contributing to promotions in the firm. Eventually I was a Director, leading complex engagements as a change leader. However, that was the job description—and successful client engagements were the expectation. To achieve the next level, Senior Director and on the path to Partner, demonstrating even more advanced change leader competencies were required. I had to look beyond my client engagements to identify broader impact and understand what change I could lead for the business. Identifying gaps in services or methodology where I could build a business and bringing others along in that vision. Successfully partnering with senior team, peers, and junior team members to bring that vision to life was incredibly rewarding and only possible because of an advanced change leader skillset.

That formula carried with me beyond consulting where I have led global, cross-functional transformations focused on product portfolio transformation, customer strategy, digital transformation, organizational redesign, and more. Most rewarding of all, leading teams of transformation experts rooted in the same principles of change leadership. Today, working alongside my team as a change leadership collective, we identify and execute programs that will set up our function for long-term success. Sharing our learnings, our successes, and supporting one another on our professional journeys.

PART 3: HOW TO BE A CHANGE LEADER

How does one become a change leader?

Becoming a change leader takes time, practice, and is never complete. It's a continuous learning journey with new situations, challenges, and opportunities presented. Three simple strategies to keep in mind:

1. Be curious and proactive - Take the time to learn the business and its influencers. Take time to have conversations with those who know more, or at least different, than you and don't be afraid to ask "why?"

2. Vocalize your ideas - If you spot an opportunity, discuss it. Bring it to your leaders, your peers, or whomever may have a perspective. The best-case scenario is that you gain traction and can move ahead. Worst case scenario is you learn why your idea can't proceed—which is valuable knowledge and you are better for it. Either way you will be thought of as someone who looks for ideas and brings them forward.

3. Understand your stakeholders - Simply having an idea, or being in position to be a change leader from the business side is not enough. One must be able to execute the change, which requires understanding the perspectives, motivators, and needs of those impacted by the change.

KEY TAKEAWAYS:

- Change occurs in every facet of life—personal and professional. There are anticipated or foreseen drivers of change, and others that catch us by surprise (anyone remember Spring 2020?). Regardless, being a change leader means recognizing, planning, and directing the impact of that change—for yourself and others.

- Change is in the eye of the impacted. The same driver of change will look and feel different. One cannot be a change leader without being willing and able to understand how that change is being felt by those impacted.

- Takes conscious effort and practice - take steps to develop a well-vetted vision and then execute with agility to reach your desired outcome.

DOS AND DON'TS

Now that we have covered the background, stories, and insights around how to become a change leader, here are some additional Dos and Don'ts to further support your development in this area.

Dos	Don'ts
Do: Lead with Passion and Conviction As you become a change leader, lead with your natural Latino passion and make sure you see the solution through to the end. Your team and organization want to see you front center in leading change. This type of leadership will enhance your brand and provide additional opportunities to lead impactful changes for your company. Your conviction in leading change will inspire others to get excited about and support the change you are targeting. This leadership style will increase your chances of realizing the desired outcomes and career benefits.	**Don't: Forget to Celebrate Wins** Keep a pulse on your team and organization around the amount of change being processed and be sure to celebrate wins along the way. Change is not easy and requires a lot of thought and care as it's being managed for those involved and impacted. Continuously scan the environment for change fatigue and ensure you are introducing consumable change; this is especially important if there are multiple change-impacting initiatives across the organization. With effective planning, you can navigate these waters with success and help you stand out as an impactful change leader.
Do: Be a Change Champion Lead by example and set the tone for your organization to be change-ready from both a mindset and skillset perspective. Provide a positive and enthusiastic attitude towards change and use it as an opportunity to show how it will position the organization for long-term success. Every organization needs great change champions. Change is a constant, and it will be critical for you to show your leadership in this area if you want to elevate your career.	**Don't: Forget to Lead with Curiosity** When introducing change, continuously scan the environment and ask questions to keep refining your approach as needed. Keep tabs on what is working and where you can improve so you can ensure you hit the desired mark for a quality change. Change leadership is continuous, especially for larger, complex efforts. Being able to demonstrate you are thoughtful, engaged, and in touch with those impacted will continue to add to your leadership brand.

Do: Be an Innovator

Always scan the business environment and develop new ways to add value to the organization. Just as importantly, once the idea is proposed and approved, be the change leaders that will help shape the solution and inspire/lead the organization to bring it to life!

Show that you are an idea and execution machine—a catalyst that knows the business, understands the solutions that can advance its priorities, and can lead with the conviction to bring it all to life!

Don't: Forget to Use your Latinidad

When it comes to change leadership, make sure to fully leverage your natural Latino superpowers: ability to connect with others, passion, ability to quickly adapt, problem-solving, innovative, empathy.

These capabilities are already in your toolbox (as covered in the culture part of this book) and it will be important that you use them to add value in ways that will help you stand out in the workplace!
nd out as an impactful change leader.

RECAP

As demonstrated in this chapter, being a strong and effective change leader will be critical for your leadership development, promotion-readiness, and overall career success. You must be able to inspire and lead teams through key organizational changes and strategic initiatives to meet company goals and objectives. It will be important to be able to develop a culture of change readiness and be a champion of change that leads with conviction, passion, and enthusiasm. Your ability to create vision, concise messaging and frameworks, as well as inspire others to act to do big things are what will set you apart. At the same time, you have many natural Latino superpowers in your toolbox that can be leveraged to accelerate your development in this area. For example, we can tap into our natural ability to connect with others, our passion, ability to quickly adapt, problem solve, innovate, and lead with empathy. As Latinos, we are built to be change leaders and now that you have the background, framework, and insights, you are better positioned to add impact in this space! This is the type of leadership capability that will help you stand out as an impact player and add to your leadership brand as a strong change leader in the workplace! I look forward to your development in this area!

PLANNING AND ACTIVATING YOUR DEVELOPMENT

To support your development and to help you organize and activate the concepts in this chapter, please go to my website (www.refugioatilano.com) and download the free templates for **The Latino Leadership Workbook**—this is a great set of tools to help organize your target areas and map a plan on where to focus your growth. It also includes a notes page and a development roadmap template so you can begin to think through and draft your personalized improvement plan that will set you up for maximum growth and success.

PART 3: HOW TO BE POLITICALLY SAVVY

How to Be Politically Savvy

> "An executive without political savvy is like a smartphone without a wireless carrier; you will have something to do, but you won't be connected to who and what you want."
>
> **- Dr. Rob Fazio**

I always found political savviness such an interesting concept. When I was first introduced to it, I definitely had a negative perception towards it. This topic was something that seemed like a game of chess at the senior levels and I thought it came along with a zero-sum approach, where someone had to win and someone had to lose—and at a cost. To me, it just didn't sound like this was a space where I wanted to play (or was capable of playing well) as my thinking was that I didn't want to get caught up in any political games and impact my career or reputation negatively. That was until one of my mentors talked about what it actually was, and how this capability was important to develop for my career.

> To help provide a relatable story on this topic, it reminds me of when I wanted to have a family reunion many years ago. I have a large extended family and most of us are in the Chicagoland area. I knew it would require a lot of buy-in, engagement, and scheduling to get something like this done—and, as with any family, there was always family drama to manage. I knew that in order to get everyone on board for this type of event that I had to go to the most influential people in the family—my four aunts, my father's sisters. They were the ones who everyone listened to, and I knew that having them on board and

actively engaged would help get everyone else to fall in line—and quickly. So, I took the time to call a meeting with my aunts to understand their point of view of what it would take to pull off this event; they had a unique family-wide vantage point that could inform me on what we needed to tackle. After identifying and addressing all key points, we were able to align and develop a game plan to move forward. From there, they each went to their families and others to spread the word to get people engaged and onboard. This was critical towards having everyone attend and have a beautiful successful event. This is an example of being politically savvy to achieve a desired goal. Trying to do this event without their input, engagement, and buy-in would have led to a very daunting effort with an unknown outcome, for sure.

WHAT IS POLITICAL SAVVINESS

In doing research on this topic, I think the Center for Creative Leadership captured it best, "Being politically savvy in the workplace isn't about playing games or taking advantage — it's about maximizing and leveraging relationships to achieve shared goals" (6 Aspects, 2020). As you can see from the example above, this is what the power of good political savviness can help achieve. As you begin to think more about this topic, my goal is to help reframe your mindset and approach towards becoming politically savvy so that you can begin to drive impact for your organization as well as build your brand as a leader who know how to leverage relationships get big things done.

> "Being politically savvy in the workplace isn't about playing games or taking advantage — it's about maximizing and leveraging relationships to achieve shared goals."

PART 3: HOW TO BE POLITICALLY SAVVY

When it comes to reframing your mindset, it is important to understand that having political skill and being able to navigate and leverage relationships effectively to drive decisions and results is just part of the deal. It's not good or bad, it's something that is there that you need to be aware of and know how to lean into. There are many elements of this skill that we will cover in this chapter and I'm excited to share key insights and experiences that can help accelerate your impact in the workplace!

THE IMPORTANCE OF POLITICAL SAVVYNESS

Now that we have reset on what this topic means, let's cover the benefits of this capability so that you have line of sight to what this skill can do for your development, organization, and overall career:

- Build your brand as someone who can work with other leaders to drive key decisions and results for the organization.
- Show that you are politically astute and understand the inner workings (from a people perspective) of the organization.
- Makes you promotable—this is the gold that comes along with mastering this capability!

The Latino Leadership Playbook *development process is a great case study on this topic. As covered earlier in this book, I knew that if I wanted to tee up the book to make a great impact and have the entire Latino community behind it, I had to align, engage, and account for the input of some of the most influential Latino/a leaders in the country—this was required for establishing credibility. As I identified and engaged those great leaders, I had to ensure that I led with a strong brand, excellent communication, executive* presence, and a well-vetted vision and game plan that people can easily understand and support; these are all concepts covered in this book. It was also just as critical that I listened to and incorporated their needs and concerns. They all brought invaluable perspectives and key insights that made the overall solution better for all of you! This is the essence of political savviness. We have to ensure we create those networks/relationships and partner closely to identify and address key needs, while developing solutions that move the needle for the great cause. This is also known as collaboration, which we will cover in detail in the next chapter.

STRATEGIES FOR POLITICAL SAVVYNESS

As Kate Keddell writes, "If you are politically savvy you are likely to have better career and sales prospects. If you avoid or ignore the political realities [...], you are probably missing out on opportunities and connections" (2022) that will drive your career forward. I love this statement because it clearly articulates that there is tremendous opportunity for us, if we want to take it to accelerate our impact in the workplace. It's no longer good enough to say that you are not going to play the political game. It's a non-negotiable if you want to be successful, build your brand as a strong collaborator, build your network, and be considered promotable.

> If you are politically savvy you are likely to have better career choices; if you avoid the political realities, you are probably going to miss out on opportunities and key connections that will drive your career forward.

Now that we have the foundation around political savviness, I would like to get into some of the tactics. The following model and insights were shared by William (Bill) Gentry, best-selling author and leadership development researcher and practitioner. To help baseline us on the topic, Bill states that political savviness should be viewed as a neutral concept—it's not good or bad. It's simply part of what's all around us; it's like the air we breathe. Given this approach, let's begin to focus on how we operate within this space.

POLITICAL SKILL DEVELOPMENT MODEL

Interpersonal Influence: As covered throughout this book, understanding how to influence others is critical for your success. You have to provide well-vetted visions, game plans, and compelling stories (backed up with facts) to influence others in your organization. It's critical that you understand the various communication styles of senior leaders—some might like data-packed slides, some might prefer a discussion, some might prefer more storytelling. The point is to always do your homework and be prepared for your target audience; your ability to influence depends on it! As Bill states, "To help others understand your message, it will be important to dial-up or dial-down depending on the style of your target audience." This approach will also be key towards developing advocates—the more advocates you create, the more your influence will grow throughout the organization.

Social Astuteness: Bill spoke about the importance of knowing yourself before anything—know your strengths, weaknesses, and needs. This will be your starting point as you begin to network and collaborate with others to help move the business forward. The next step is to do your homework to understand other's goals, values, purpose, and needs. Doing so will help you begin to find common ground and develop solution options that you can confidently bring to the table. Finally, it's critical to understand and be in touch with environmental factors. What is going on with the macro and micro business environments? These are key elements to account for as you develop solutions so that you can demonstrate you have the pulse of what's going on around you. Showing your maturity in these three areas is key for your development and leadership brand; mastering them helps you make better solution recommendations, business decisions, as well as develop stronger networks.

Insight: Account for different cultures when studying environments. For example, the Latino culture is very open and inviting, whereas Asian cultures might be more closed. It will be important to be aware of these differences and to navigate them effectively.

Develop Great Networks: One of my favorite quotes that Bill used is to "know people who know people." As covered in some of the personal stories earlier in the chapter, identify and engage the influential leaders in your organization and on your teams. These are the ones who can provide invaluable insights, recommendations, and the muscle to move ideas, decisions, and solutions forward. When you strategically and effectively collaborate with these influencers, you will see how effectively and efficiently business gets done. In addition, when these leaders see you in action, it's a great way to advocate for yourself and build your brand which can lead to career opportunities!

Lead with Authenticity, Sincerity, and Integrity: As Latinos this comes naturally for us and is a big part of our culture of giving respect to everyone we meet. As a leader who is political savvy, it is critical that you lead with these traits without exception. You want to clearly and consistently demonstrate that you are the ultimate team player, a transparent and honest business partner, and want to be a part of advancing the company goals. You should never lead with hidden or self-serving agendas; these will be quickly sniffed out and will stifle any desired leadership positions in the future.

Now that you have the background, benefits, key insights, and framework on what it means to be politically savvy, let's cover some additional stories that can accelerate your workplace and career impact.

Personal Insight 1: Refugio A. Atilano, Business Leader at a Top-10 Pharma Company, ERG/DEI Leader, Author, *The Latino Leadership Playbook*

UNDERSTAND THE ENVIRONMENT AND PIVOTING

I have always been good at developing relationships inside and outside the organization and it's something I take pride in doing. It has been an asset for me at the various companies I have worked at with the exception of one—it was associated with only one team within the company. Instead of focusing on the organization, I will zoom in on the experience so that you can learn from it.

When I joined the group and the new organization, I knew how important it was for me to establish relationships and trust with those on my immediate and project teams. As usual, I did meet and greets, found common passions, business needs, talked about families and personal preferences—all standard items when building professional relationships. In this situation, and like many others, I was able to quickly build rapport with the senior executives that were on my project teams. I thought that this was great and it represents not only me, but my broader project management team on how we integrate with and support our business teams.

I still remember that it was within my first three weeks of being on the job that the leader of the group called me into the office and as we were speaking, he mentioned how he noticed I had a good relationship with a senior executive. I thought it was amazing to be recognized for what I thought was my ability to put us in a good light. That was until I heard what came out of his mouth next, "That wasn't a compliment." I was in shock and didn't know how to respond to his statement. I remember feeling dumbfounded and misaligned with the expectations of the team leader. As we went further into the discussion, I realized that this was a different team culture and I would have to pivot.

After taking time to learn more about the new group, I came to find that the team leader had a military background and was very chain-of-command-centric. It was very important that the key relationships were with him before anyone else. As a result, I was very mindful of my interactions and made sure I followed the rules of the team leader. Whether I agreed with it or not, that was the culture of the team and I had to pivot if I wanted to remain on the team.

Through sharing this story, my recommendation is to always be on the lookout and scan the environment for the dynamics of your team, your boss, and your company so that you can quickly identify any potential potholes in the road. Doing so requires active listening, anticipation, agility, and a big picture perspective so that you can effectively assess and navigate any cultural and environmental situations you need to navigate.

Personal Insight 2: Carlos F. Orta, Founder & CEO, LATINOS In Procurement. Former CEO, Hispanic Association on Corporate Responsibility (HACR), and Co-Founder of the Latino Corporate Directors Association (LCDA) and its Foundation.

HOW TO BE POLITICALLY SAVVY

Regardless of your profession, you will probably deal with "office politics" throughout your career. The higher you go up the ladder, the more intense it can be. Let us first define what it means to be politically savvy. One definition I like used by the National Institutes of Health: Office of Management is: "The ability to exhibit confidence and professional diplomacy, while effectively relating to people at all levels internally and externally. Demonstrates an understanding of the interrelationships, roles, and responsibilities of your organization."

I credit my success in corporate America, going from manager to director to VP level roles at five global Fortune 500 companies to working in politics, first in campaigns and then working for elected officials. That's how I got my "savvy on." But you don't need to work in politics to get yours. You can certainly learn on your own. Below I outline the five most important things you should do to help you become politically savvy or improve that savviness:

1. **Emotional Intelligence (EQ)** - This is a must have. EQ is your ability to manage your "emotions, behaviors, navigate social complexities, and make personal decisions that achieve positive results," according to Dr. Travis Bradberry, co-author of Emotional Intelligence 2.0. Ever been in a room when someone says something, and you think to yourself, *What were they thinking?* That's EQ.

2. **Managing Down** - Everyone can figure out how to "suck up" to their boss and/or people in positions of power. The more difficult task is learning how to manage down. By that I mean, getting people that report to you or who you are responsible for to do their job, not because they have to, but because they want to. Because you've inspired them to be their best, and they are eager to show you what that looks like. When managing teams, I spend most of my time managing down, not up.

3. **Sponsors and Mentors** - In Kenneth Wyche's book, *Good Is Not Good Enough*, Wyche writes about "Who's wearing your t-shirt?" at work. This is a concept I experienced first-hand when I worked at Ford Motor Company. I was part of the corporate affairs department, and when it came to staff promotions, 4-5 director level executives would meet annually and collectively decide promotions. In other words, your boss had one vote, so they would need to convince the other members to vote for their candidate. As soon as I realized this unwritten rule existed, I made sure to get to know and work with the other members, so that when the time came for my promotion, everyone was "wearing my t-shirt," thus making my bosses' job much easier.

4. **Differentiation** - Early in your career, it is important to get noticed by corporate executives at your bosses' level and above. This is usually accomplished by either volunteering for or being assigned to a special assignment. However it

comes, take it! In doing so, you have separated yourself from the crowd. Next step is to be good—really, great—at something. For me, it was that I was always willing to help, even if it wasn't my job any longer. Even if I thought the challenge could not be solved; I always got credit for helping and for trying. Over the course of my career, what I've found is that for me, I am at my best, learning the most and leading most effectively, when I am challenged, and not when things are going well.

5. **Invest In YOU!** - We tend to spend money on all kinds of things, yet very little on ourselves. To be the best, you must be mentally and physically healthy. Spend money on a personal trainer. Spend money on a resume writer, on a professional coach, and/or on a psychologist if you need to.

Invest in leadership development programs like Aspen Institute, Gallup, the Center for Creative Leadership, and other regional and local mainstream ones. Invest in Hispanic ones too! Take executive education certificate programs at prestigious schools on topics that will make you a better, well-rounded leader and manager.

While at Ford Motor Company, Anheuser-Busch, and as CEO of the Hispanic Association on Corporate Responsibility (HACR), I hired coaches a few times to confirm I was on the right track, that I was managing the team well, and that I was managing up appropriately.

Final Words

My experience has taught me that the higher you go up the ladder, the less individuals you can depend on and there are fewer people you can completely trust. You need someone on your side 100% of the time. It takes a lot to be 100% at your best, and you really cannot do it alone.

If in the end, being politically savvy isn't your thing—and I get that—make sure you surround yourself with people who are. It will be hugely beneficial to your career and peace of mind at work.

Personal Insight 3: Dave Tang, PharmD, Recently Retired and Former Vice President, Global Medical Operations, Global Medical Office, and U.S. Medical Affairs for 3 Top Global Pharma Companies

FOCUS ON HOW TO BE POLITICALLY SAVVY

I would like to highlight the importance of taking the time to listen, observe, and assess as one takes on new roles, especially when one is joining a new organization or team. While one typically expects a new culture when joining a new company, cultures can also differ significantly across teams within an organization.

As each of us progresses through our lives, we are fortunately able to utilize our past experiences and learnings to help us address new challenges and opportunities. When I started my Medical Affairs career in the pharmaceutical industry, I found that my interest in all aspects of the business encouraged me to partner with cross-functional colleagues to create solutions that benefited our broader organization. I was fortunate to join an organization where cross-functional collaboration and open dialogue amongst colleagues regarding issues beyond their individual areas of responsibility were key aspects of the workplace environment. There were many opportunities to contribute to projects across the business functions because the ultimate focus for all of us was to benefit patients and healthcare professionals. Over the years this has allowed me to share many medical insights with partners, as well as learn about new approaches to communications, strategy, and tactics from them. These cultural norms were key to my early career successes, and I integrated these practices into my method of partnering with colleagues. This worked well for me as I progressed into roles of increasing responsibility within the same company.

After spending almost a decade on the East Coast, I needed to relocate my family back to California for personal reasons. This resulted in my first change of company since joining the pharmaceutical industry. As I interviewed for a promising new position based in California, I spoke with senior executives about the organizational culture and their expectations of leaders within the organization. I was very encouraged to hear them describe many of the same cultural norms that I also believed in—strong cross-functional collaboration and willingness to contribute beyond our individual areas of responsibility. I was fortunate to join the new organization's Global Medical Affairs leadership team and was excited to work with my new colleagues. Based on my learnings from the interviews and conversations I had with cross-functional colleagues while onboarding, I felt confident that I could leverage my approach to collaboration and make an impact for the new organization!

As I was completing my onboarding, I was invited to participate in a potentially contentious meeting with my Medical Affairs colleagues and cross-functional partners within R&D. At the meeting, I learned that some of the more sensitive topics did not impact all of our Medical Functions equally. However, I followed my typical approach and offered my thoughts regarding each topic, regardless of whether they fell within my team's area of responsibility. As the meeting progressed, I could sense there was tension rising with my Medical Affairs colleagues after I made my comments.

After the meeting, I had a quick scrum with my colleagues to follow up on the discussion. There I learned that they were quite upset that I had commented on topics that fell within their team's remit. They shared that they interpreted my approach as trying to assert dominance over their groups and potentially commit them to obligations without their agreement. Although that was certainly not my intent (and fortunately it was not how our R&D colleagues interpreted the discussion), it created an unnecessary challenge in the early days of joining a new company.

This served as an important reminder that I should not make assumptions about cultural norms across all teams so early in my tenure with the organization, despite my impressions from prior conversations. In retrospect, I would have focused on listening and observing team dynamics and communication styles in a few early meetings, while taking a more measured approach with my early contributions. As I observed the dynamics of this new Medical

Affairs leadership team, I better understood the cultural norms of the team. As a result, I was still able to share my insights but learned that it would be more effective and impactful when delivered in a preparatory meeting with the individual leaders so that they would be able to candidly share their thoughts on the ideas.

KEY TAKEAWAYS:

- Take time to learn about the cultural norms when joining a new company or team.
- Don't assume that what has worked well in the past will be successful in a new environment.
- Even if the desired culture has been described through the interview process or by senior leaders, verifying the true culture through your own observations can help you be more effective and avoid frustration.

DOS AND DON'TS

Now that we have covered the background, stories, and insights around how to be politically savvy, here are some additional Dos and Don'ts to further support your development in this area.

Dos	Don'ts
Do: Focus on Self-Awareness	**Don't: Forget to Be Innovative**
Understanding yourself is not something that should be taken for granted. Invest the time in understanding your style, biases, and perspectives so that you are informed and armed with the information needed as you work with others. The more self-aware you are, the better positioned you are to have rich collaborations and discussions to drive the business forward.	Use political savviness as a way to bring new ideas to the table that can work for everyone. As stated earlier, you will often have to work with others to get things done, while accounting for multiple agendas/needs. The more you can do your homework and understand how to connect the dots across the business, the better positioned you are to identify and present new solutions for the business.
Being in tune with yourself will also help you to make better decisions and drive solutions that will meet the needs of the business.	This is a great way to stand out and be a recognized business leader who can work with other leaders to get big things done!

Do: Build a Strong Network You will find that your network of influential leaders will grow as you develop this capability. You will be identifying, partnering, and collaborating with key decision makers in your organization to move business forward. In addition, these leaders will get a first-hand look at your brand, your ideas, and performance. This is a tremendous way to advocate for yourself and get other leaders excited about supporting your development and career.	**Don't: Optimize Each Collaboration Opportunity** Developing yourself as a politically savvy leader will take time and consistency. Use every collaboration opportunity to develop this capability and add to your brand. Work towards establishing a reputation as someone who can navigate the environment and leverage different relationships in different situations to drive the business forward.
Do: Think Before You Speak Before engaging in critical business matters, take the time to be thoughtful in your approach and ensure you always lead with poise and confidence. As you interact with other business leaders, you want to ensure you are putting your best foot forward so that you add to your leadership brand, rather than risk any negative impacts. As you prepare, follow the same steps outlined throughout this book—have a well-vetted vision/idea, use concise, compelling storytelling, use data and facts to support your position, and go in with a confident mindset and approach.	**Don't: Forget to Use Your Latinidad** As always, don't forget to use your natural cultural superpowers for this capability. You are a natural problem solver, relationship builder, and team player. Use these key traits when collaborating to achieve business results. Finally, keep character and integrity at the forefront of everything you do. This is non-negotiable; you should always operate from a place of sincerity and operate in good faith. This will be critical towards your leadership brand and promotion potential.

PART 3: HOW TO BE POLITICALLY SAVVY

RECAP

Political savviness is essential for your leadership journey and promotability. As discussed in this chapter, being effective in this space will show the organization you can work well with other leaders to make key decisions and drive the business forward. One of the goals of this chapter was to educate and level set you on what political savviness means and the power of it once done successfully. My expectation and hope is that you will be able to take the information, stories, and insights provided to begin developing your political savviness capability and making impact in new ways for your business and career. Additionally, this can a great opportunity to start leaning into collaboration opportunities with a different mindset. One where you see them as an opportunity to work with other leaders to find common ground to deliver results in new ways, while also improving upon your leadership brand as someone who can navigate the organization to get things done!

PLANNING AND ACTIVATING YOUR DEVELOPMENT

To support your development and to help you organize and activate the concepts in this chapter, please go to my website (www.refugioatilano.com) and download the free templates for **The Latino Leadership Workbook**—this is a great set of tools to help organize your target areas and map a plan on where to focus your growth. It also includes a notes page and a development roadmap template so you can begin to think through and draft your personalized improvement plan that will set you up for maximum growth and success.

How to Be a Strong Collaborator

> *"I bring ideas and put my hand up to pitch in on deliverables; you just can't be talk in collaboration."*
>
> **- Jamie Walters**

Collaboration—now you are talking my language! As Latinos, we are natural team players and collaborators. I can't tell you how many times this superpower positively impacted my career. It helped me find new job opportunities, broaden my strategic network, landed ERG leadership assignments, and even positioned me to write this book with some of the most amazing leaders in the world today!

Being a collaborator is in our blood and it's how we were raised. I just think about the numerous big family parties and celebrations in our Latino culture. We all come together to play a role and to bring the event to life; everyone has a part to play and the family counts on each and every one of us to carry our weight. As Jamie states in the opening quote above, "you just can't be talk in collaboration." This is so true—just like when we help to prepare for key celebrations, you must roll up your sleeves and do what it takes to make sure the family event is highly successful. Whether it's setting up tables, grilling the food, picking up the food, getting the ice, etc., our family counts on us to lean in, take care of our responsibility, and make sure we work with others to do what's needed. This is just one example of many of how we collaborate with others to bring things to life... and business is no different.

Being a collaborator is in our blood and it's how we were raised. I just think about the numerous big family parties and celebrations in our Latino culture. We all come together to play a role and to bring the event to life.

PART 3: HOW TO BE A STRONG COLLABORATOR

COLLABORATION AND ITS BENEFITS

So, what is collaboration? As shown above, it is people working together towards achieving a common goal. It's as simple as that. You can collaborate with others from wherever you are: whether you are leading project teams, are a people leader, or working on a task with someone else, you are in a position to collaborate. So, why is being a good collaborator important? As covered in the previous chapter ("How to Be Politically Savvy"), in order to make big things happen for your organization, you will most likely have to collaborate with others in doing so. Therefore, it is critical that you develop this skill and make it part of your leadership brand; it is vital for your promotability. Your organization will want to know they can trust you to drive business forward through working effectively with others, no matter where they sit in the business. In addition, being an effective collaborator can open doors for you across the organization for opportunities, such as being an ERG leader, being tapped on the shoulder for special assignments in other business units, as well as exposure and access to senior leaders. This is always a great place to be!

There are also several benefits of successful collaboration for your organization. As captured by an article by Kissflow.com, they report that a strong collaborative culture puts your organization at the head of the pack and miles ahead of the competition (2022). To build on that, in a report by Slack.com, they suggest that a strong collaborative environment "energizes teams, releases creativity, and cultivates a work culture that is both productive and joyful" (Samur, 2022). I have tried to capture the essence of these points in the following personal example:

> As you already know from reading this book, I love using The Latino Leadership Playbook development experience as a test case for these topics. To reach the desired goal of elevating the leadership capability of all Latinos, I knew that it would require strong collaboration to generate excitement and to release the creativity and great

insights from everyone involved. For this project, I had to literally engage, develop relationships, and collaborate with hundreds of people. Whether they were a contributor, peer reviewer, strategic network member, influencer, industry leader, mentor, or sponsor, there was some element of collaboration with them all. Depending on the nature of our collaboration, I had to be clear on the goal (reminder: fill the talent pipeline with confident, informed, high-impact, and promotion-ready Latino leaders for the current and future generations), define the role each of us played, and how we would execute and check-in on our collaboration. In addition, I knew that every collaboration and relationship was critical and was aware that my brand/reputation depended on it. Therefore, I handled every relationship and every interaction with careful thought, consideration, and execution. I knew that to make this project a wild success that I would have to get everyone on board and in lockstep. This was a test of extreme collaboration for me and everyone else involved; I am proud that we were able to use this natural Latino superpower to bring this to life for all of you!

I knew that to make this project a wild success that I would have to get everyone on board and in lockstep. This was a test of extreme collaboration for me and everyone else involved; I am proud that we were able to use this natural Latino superpower to bring this to life for all of you!

PART 3: HOW TO BE A STRONG COLLABORATOR

STRATEGIES FOR COLLABORATION

For you to develop your collaboration capability, it will be important to you to have a framework from which to start. I have been fortunate to make this natural Latino superpower into one of my strengths in the workplace. As covered earlier, my background is in leading large, complex, global initiatives and being a strong collaboration is critical for my role. I have created the following framework to support your development in this space so that you can begin to develop, and soon master, your collaboration effectiveness for your organization.

- **Step 1:** Take time to develop relationships. My guiding principle is to always take time to get to know your colleague on a personal level before business. Find a way to connect and find out what are things they like to do outside of work, find out their passions, understand what makes them tick—and share your story as well. Once you know the person and develop rapport, business and collaboration becomes easy!

- **Step 2:** Determine fellow collaborator business needs and challenges. Take time to understand what's going on in their world; find out if they are up against any pressing deadlines, other high-priority business commitments, etc. The more you know about their world, it will position to you effectively navigate around it and have an impactful collaboration that people will appreciate and remember.

- **Step 3:** Once you agree to collaborate, set the goals and roles. Remember to align on how your collaboration is tied to adding impact for the organization. It will be important to prepare extensively for this engagement; put in the thought and consideration on how you envision the collaboration working so that you achieve the desired result. Going back to Jamie's quote: be sure to show what you will own and drive. As discussed earlier in this book, take an extreme ownership approach to drive impact. TIP: Never show up to a meeting without having thought this through. Always come prepared with a vision and plan, even if just in draft form.

- **Step 4:** Execute your game plan. Whether you have agreed to jointly develop deliverables and/or just perform regular check-ins, stay committed to the process and your schedule. Make it clear that you are serious about the collaboration and the progress you agreed to make. At the same time, be supportive and flexible when needed. Life happens, business priorities change and it's important that you quickly identify these moments and pivot as needed. Being an effective supporter is one of the things people will remember most when working with you and will also add to your leadership brand.

- **Step 5:** Complete the work; share/give credit for the results of your collaboration outcome. When the collaboration is complete and the desired results are achieved, giving credit and showing appreciation is extremely important for your relationships as well as your leadership brand. It will demonstrate that you understand the importance of building up teams to achieve results and to drive the business priorities forward. Again, people will remember how they felt when working with you; it will be important to stay on point and finish the job all the way through recognition for outcomes. TIP: There might also be times you don't reach the desired outcome. In these cases, take ownership of the short-fall and perform lessons learned exercise. Once complete, craft and share a readout of your findings (key themes) and develop a game plan for how to do things differently in the future that will lead to better outcomes. This will show that you take ownership as a leader and have the maturity to commit to the continuous improvement of the organization.

Now that you have the background, benefits, key insights, and framework on what it means to be strong collaborator, let's cover some additional stories that can accelerate your workplace and career impact.

PART 3: HOW TO BE A STRONG COLLABORATOR

Personal Insight 1: Refugio A. Atilano, Business Leader at a Top-10 Pharma Company, ERG/DEI Leader, Author, *The Latino Leadership Playbook*

SHARING AND GIVING CREDIT FOR COLLABORATION OUTCOMES

As a leader, you have many responsibilities to your organization and one of them is to show that you can develop other leaders. Throughout my career, I did not always take this approach as I thought my success was based on my performance only. As I learned later in my career, how you develop and elevate others is just as important as your individual performance. Once I was aware of this responsibility, I made the adjustment to go all-in on developing others whenever I had the opportunity.

I have had the pleasure and honor of collaborating and delivering results with many professional colleagues in various workplace settings—I have collaborated with others on project teams, organizational teams, mentoring programs, ERG leadership committees, and various other opportunities across the company. I go into each collaboration with the mindset of elevating the collaboration experience while jointly delivering high-impact results for the organization. For me, one of the most important and powerful elements of collaboration experiences is to use the opportunities to elevate the development of others. I do this because I am passionate about developing other leaders, and just as equally, I am passionate about showcasing the value and impact of their contributions. There is no greater satisfaction than to see others shine and know that I had a role in helping them do so!

In helping others shine and sharing their contributions with the organization, I use the following strategies:

1. I always send a thoughtful and thankful note of the person's contributions, approach, and collaboration effectiveness to their direct manager and, often times, copy the senior leaders of that person.

2. I make sure to tell the person directly (in-person, if possible) about my pleasant experiences and thank them for their efforts and the great relationship we developed.
3. Make plans to keep our relationship active after the collaboration. I see collaborations as the start of a life-long relationship opportunity.

Using collaborations to elevate others and help them shine remains a passion and is now second-nature for me—I have impacted so many people and have developed many meaningful, quality relationships as a result of my collaborations. I am a true believer in servant leadership and will always go above and beyond to help others. This is part of my leadership brand and hoping you can take these lessons to add to your development and improve your workplace and relationship impact.

Personal Insight 2: Jamie Walters, Senior Director, Top 10 Global Pharma Company

I am a leader that is known for turning around teams by providing an environment where people thrive and an expectation and skill to create operational excellence where the business thrives.

HOW TO BE A STRONG COLLABORATOR

Several years back I was asked to participate in a cross functional project that was meant to focus on people development, specifically how to get people to take the lead on their own development. I have a passion for this topic, but beyond being a leader of people I don't have a specific responsibility regarding how people are developed. I came to the project as I typically do, all in to support the team and ultimately the staff that would stand to benefit from this project. I came to the project team in advocate mode. When statements were made about how we develop staff in a way that were not accurate regarding the "real life" practices, I would check the group. I would say things like, we can't really fix this if we are not honest with ourselves. To me collaboration starts with authenticity, not only in being yourself but also being honest about the situation at hand. We cannot work together to solve a problem if we are sugar coating the problem and using corporate speak. That being said, we must stay professional and respectful while calling it as you see it. I challenge people to get real, but in a positive way to push for excellence.

During this project there were times that I thought maybe the HR person on the team was getting irritated with me. She was the one, more often than not, that I was challenging. I brought ideas and put my hand up to pitch in on the deliverables. You can't just be talk in a collaboration. As the project went on, I went from being just one of the team to being a thought leader. Other team members would reach out to me while working on their deliverables to check in and get my thoughts amplifying my impact on the work. The team was a buzz with energy and passion and I like to think I was a key part of that passion. It was my first experience with a high performing team. When the project launched it was a great success. We heard from colleagues and leaders across our function about the impact we had on how people saw their role in their own development including their empowerment to take action. For me though, I created bonds with team members that we have leveraged for the benefit of our careers and the business over the following years.

Months later I was invited to a meeting by a VP in HR that I had never met. I was unsure why. During that meeting she explained that she was seeking a leader from the "business" to come and lead the Diversity and Inclusion team for an 18-month development opportunity. She wanted to try something new as there had been difficulties in getting engagement and she thought that a business leader would be able to engage more with the other business leaders on the topic. She said she had heard that I was an "all in team member" and "a tireless advocate." I was a little surprised and was not sure where this was coming from and then I learned that the HR person that I had thought I had irritated in the development team meeting had instead seen these qualities in me. So much so, she had advocated for me to get a development rotation role in HR. I took that opportunity and continued to show up in the same way, authentic and real, but all in to get the work done together. Now I get to make an impact across the business and beyond my original function. This was an amazing opportunity that allowed me to add new tools to my toolbox when I rotated back to my function.

KEY TAKEAWAYS:

1. Show up as the real you. People want to engage more with someone who is authentic.
2. Try not to come with an ask, but instead come asking how you can help them. It is disarming and shows you are willing to support the collaboration and the collaborators. This builds a quick rapport and will carry on once the specific collaboration is done.
3. Be direct, yet always respectful, and in a way that provides positive momentum even when what you are saying may be negative.
4. Know your strengths and gaps. Be honest and lean in to where you can be most helpful and ask for others' help and support where you are less strong. It is a collaboration, not a platform for only you to shine.
5. Give credit to others and when you see a spark, sponsor them when future opportunities are available. When you learn someone excels at something, be like my HR colleague and tell people about it. Connecting people to others or opportunities creates strong bonds for the future.

This one collaboration made a big impact on my career and on the way I think about collaborating. Not only did I come to understand that I showed up in a way that I want to continue on throughout my career, but I also learned from my peers additional ways of operating that I have now incorporated in my collaborative behaviors.

Personal Insight 3: Enrique Acosta Gonzalez, CEO, Triad Leadership Solutions, LLC

HOW TO BE A STRONG COLLABORATOR

In leadership there is no clear way to win. A leader wins personally, as a team, as an organization, and in the eyes of the world. Therefore, it's so important to understand that working smart includes others. It requires you to collaborate individually and as a team to have the best chance at a win. Early in my career I believed that all my wins had to be done singularly and only I could stand on the top tier of the stand. As years went by and my experience with the benefits of collaboration expanded, I realized that a true win benefit all and not just me.

I started adding smart win goals to my strategy. This required input of the goals and desires of my team and considered what I could do to help their efforts. When I started to help the team win, I won the more. Not long after this strategic approach was implemented, I started getting the attention of the organizational leadership and was lauded for the way my team was shining and the example they set for other departments to follow.

The biggest lesson I learned here is that I could have invested all my energy into my own wins and negated all others. It would have been easier to do so but then that would have meant that I was no leader at all. When I chose to strategically plan out my wins and the team's version of winning, we all won. Be a strategic thinker in all you do and see that working hard can get you to the next step, but working smart gets everyone to the next step and beyond. This type of approach will not only prove you are a great leader, but also allow your team to become great future leaders.

Personal Insight 3: Maryanne Pina Frodsham, CEO, Career Management Partners

HOW TO BECOME A STRONG COLLABORATOR

We all need to strike a balance between individual and team

contributions. In our Latino culture, we're more inclined to emphasize the group's needs before the individual. This is also known as collectivism. For some people, it comes more naturally. In fact, if you value collaborating, you're not alone, 52% of employees in the U.S. rate teamwork as being very important.

For me personally, it's been an educational journey learning how, when, and when not to collaborate. As a young professional, I had my first lesson in collaboration during a leadership meeting. I was usually quiet, taking notes, and only talked when asked a question. However, there came a point where our director was making an executive decision that would affect hundreds of people, and I disagreed. I vividly remember standing up and speaking up with research-driven data and metrics to oppose his logic. I shocked everyone in the meeting, but, most importantly, I protected the stakeholders.

It takes both personal accountability and collaboration to achieve great things. Despite our collectivist tendencies, taking initiative and speaking up is important when it adds value.

Now, the how and when to collaborate is clear.

Collaborate when:

- There is a need for making major decisions affecting many people.
- Dealing with complexity.
- Leveraging diversity.
- Don't collaborate when:
- It's not a priority—people will appreciate when you collaborate and focus on high-priority goals and activities.
- Alignment isn't needed—there are some activities you can get done without the input of others. This will also save you and others needless time.
- Values collide—this is true for optional collaborations. If you find that there is a strong mismatch in values, take a step back and rethink the collaboration you are seeking.

As you develop your collaboration skills, remember to approach every situation with an open mind and a willingness to learn from others. Don't be afraid to share your ideas and contribute your unique perspective. We can achieve more when working together while still honoring our individual strengths and contributions.

DOS AND DON'TS

Now that we have covered the background, stories, and insights around how to be to be a strong collaborator, here are some additional Dos and Don'ts to support your development in this area.

Dos	Don'ts
Do: Seek Opportunities to Collaborate Developing your capability and your brand to show that you can effectively collaborate with others across the organization, regardless of where they sit is critical for your development and promotability. To develop this capability, continue to identify ways to collaborate and try to find different areas of the business to do it. This is a great opportunity to showcase your agility and ability to develop impactful relationships across the enterprise to get big things done!	**Don't: Forget to Be Flexible and Supportive** The one thing about business, and life, is that change is a certainty. Be ready to identify it and pivot as needed. Use change as an opportunity to demonstrate your ability to be in tune with the environment, as well as how it impacts your collaborations. Be thoughtful and develop workarounds and alternate solutions to get work done, or suspend work if absolutely needed (of course with business team sign-off). When needed, be able to demonstrate that you are a strong leader who can quickly identify issues and implement alternate approaches that work for everyone.

Do: Give/Share Credit

One of your responsibilities as a leader is to create more leaders. As you have successful collaborations and achieve results, it will be important for you to demonstrate the maturity to share/give the credit where it's due.

Remember, leadership is not about your sole performance; how you are able to influence and elevate other leaders will show the organization your leadership brand as you get ready for your next role!

Don't: Forget to Operate with Impact

Throughout the collaboration process, remember to keep your eye on the "impact" ball. As discussed earlier in this book, it will be critical that you show the value and impact you bring to the organization.

This remains the same for your collaborations. Also, make sure it's tied to company, business unit, or team goals and priorities. This will keep your impact brand at the forefront and ensure you are viewed as an impact player in the workplace.

Do: Establish Strong Relationships

There is no substitute for great relationships and a strong strategic network. Even if the person you are collaborating with is not a senior leader, often times, a great collaboration experience will make them an advocate for you.

With advocates, they will provide rave reviews, be more than happy to make introductions to their senior leadership teams for you and support you on future initiatives. Leverage collaboration opportunities to develop powerful networks that can pay dividends now or in the future.

TIP: You must also do the same for them—this is a two-way street!

Don't: Forget to Use Your Latinidad

As always, don't forget to use your natural cultural superpowers for this capability. Because of our family-oriented approach, you are a natural team player and relationship developer. You will always lean in to support the team and will do so with fierceness until the desired outcome is realized!

At the same time, remember that this is an opportunity for you to take a bold stance and leadership position. Make sure you are out-front and leading the way. Being a strong collaborator requires thoughtfulness, preparation, and a plan to take lead and help elevate others.

PART 3: HOW TO BE A STRONG COLLABORATOR

RECAP

Being a strong collaborator is critical for your development, brand, and promotability. As covered in this chapter, this skill is a natural Latino capability. Our family-oriented approach positions us nicely to be great team players and collaborators. Whether we are on projects, teams, ERGs, or volunteer events, Latinos are always at the ready to go all-in to contribute to the overall goal. At the same time, we need to realize that it's important to develop this capability and use it to add impact across the organization. We should be out-front seeking impactful collaboration opportunities so that we can continue to develop this capability and show that we can work with others to get big things done. Being a strong collaborator has facilitated my growth, development opportunities, as well as provided access and exposure to other senior leaders. My goal in sharing the insights and stories in this chapter is to create those same experiences and opportunities for you as you improve your leadership brand and impact in the workplace!

PLANNING AND ACTIVATING YOUR DEVELOPMENT

To support your development and to help you organize and activate the concepts in this chapter, please go to my website (www.refugioatilano.com) and download the free templates for **The Latino Leadership Workbook**—this is a great set of tools to help organize your target areas and map a plan on where to focus your growth. It also includes a notes page and a development roadmap template so you can begin to think through and draft your personalized improvement plan that will set you up for maximum growth and success.

HOW TO ASK FOR A PROMOTION

> *"People don't get promoted for doing their jobs really well. They get promoted by demonstrating their potential to do more."*
>
> **- Tara Jaye Frank**

The next two chapters have been included as a direct result of focus groups I performed earlier this year. In the session, the group asked a great question, "When I develop myself and do all these cool things to make an impact, how do I ask to get promoted?" This question led to an ah-ha moment for me as I was not going to originally include this topic in the book. However, this is a real unknown and pain point for our community and it's something I knew I had to address head-on for all Latinos.

There are at least two ways to getting promoted:

1. Being given a promotion by your leadership. This is a great position to be in and I hope you fall into this bucket with all the insights provided in this book!

2. Asking for a promotion/larger role within or outside of your own company. This is the scenario that causes the most discomfort and will be the primary focus of this chapter. Because so many of us struggle/have struggled with how to ask for a promotion, I wanted to make sure to give you the best possible advice so that you have the right mindset and the right skillset when seeking a promotion. As such, I have asked some of the best Human Resources (HR) industry experts (Latino and non-Latinos) to weigh in and provide their experiential stories and insights.

Unlike previous chapters, this chapter will be short and very tactical with guidance from experts in this space. It will cut right to what you need to know as you prepare to ask for a promotion in the workplace and will focus on both skillset and mindset.

THE LATINO MINDSET AROUND ASKING FOR PROMOTIONS

As covered earlier, we Latinos (generally speaking) don't like calling attention to ourselves. Because of our family-oriented mindset, we are always looking out for the needs of the group first, rather than our own needs. Doing otherwise is unnatural and can often lead to feelings of guilt. However, as evidenced in the data in leadership roles, we are not getting promoted, and as Claudia Romo Edelman says, "We need to flip the script!" This is exactly right; we need to change the way we look at driving our career forward. This includes setting up ourselves as strong, confident, high-impact, and promotion-ready leaders who understand and execute flawlessly on what it takes to getting promoted.

As reported in an by Best Colleges, "Sometimes, as a child of immigrants – being Latino in particular – you'll always feel like you need to take care of your family," Maria Gironas, senior media partnership manager at Reddit said. "[But] If you don't take care of yourself first and foremost, you won't be able to properly take care of your family" (Schneider, 2022). This is exactly right. The days of only focusing on your role, working hard, and "hoping to get promoted" are over. It's now time to show up big and to swing big! It's time to take bold action and for the new Latino/a leader to step up and show the real impact our community is ready to make!

> The days of only focusing on your role, working hard, and "hoping to get promoted" are over. It's now time to show up big and to swing big! It's time to take bold action and for the new Latino/a leader to step up and show the real impact our community is ready to make!

> *I have had three promotions during my career—two were given to me and I had to work hard for one of them. Like most of us, I didn't have guidance on how to go about seeking promotions and I figured things out as I went along. In fact, I didn't know that I should even be thinking about them as a strategic part of my career development. My focus was on doing my job and doing it well—that's all I knew about how to operate. When I look back at the two promotions that were offered to me, it was strictly because I had great relationships with my sponsors who set them up for me (and I didn't even realize it at the time!). How crazy and fortunate is that? Although this example reinforces the tremendous impact of sponsors, I want to continue to push you to take a more comprehensive approach; focus on developing your leadership capabilities (sponsor network being part of that) and to be thoughtful, ambitious, and effective in driving our career development. This approach will cover all the bases and will greatly increase your chances for maximum effectiveness and promotability.*

Another insight around promotions that I want to share is that when applying for a new role that you don't need to meet all the requirements of the job description (JD). According to Harvard Business Review, "If you meet about 60% of the criteria, apply!" (Phan, 2022). This is especially important for Latinas as not all requirements need to be met to apply for a role. Similarly, "If you're five years into your career, and the criteria asks for eight years, apply. This goes for all roles — there's typically two to three years of wiggle room when it comes to work experience." Also, "If you're a college graduate, count internships relevant to the role in your 'years of experience'" (Phan, 2022).

PART 3: HOW TO ASK FOR A PROMOTION

> "If you meet about 60% of the job criteria, apply!"
> – Harvard Business Review

I hope this first part of this chapter has begun to shift your mindset around the importance of and how to ask for a promotion. Now it's time to get to the meat of this topic and let our experts further set you up for long-terms career success! Let's roll!

Personal Insight 1: Dana Santos, Director, Organizational Excellence, Talent Leader and Human Resources Professional, Top 10 Global Pharma Company

HOW TO ASK FOR A PROMOTION

I was on a team where I, along with my peers, were each dedicated to supporting a different business unit at our company. Some of my peers led large teams, some small, and some, including me, did not have any teams underneath them at all. When I started on the team, I assumed that the number of team members dedicated to support each business unit was proportionate to the size of the business unit. I supported one of the smallest business units, so that's why I didn't have a team.

As I became more familiar with the data across our organization, I started doing the math in my head, and it didn't seem to add up. The ratio of team members to business unit size varied significantly across our team. I had enough experience with the organization and the line of work to know that while the ratios should probably not be exactly equal, they should be more similar. I scheduled a meeting with my manager, compiled my data, and prepared my proposal for my promotion and the addition of two team members who would report to me. I was nervous! I knew this was a big ask. I had a good relationship with my manager and if she said no, I was worried this would somehow damage our relationship. Letting fear dictate your actions (or inaction) is never a good strategy, so I delivered my proposal.

Here are some of the steps I took to prepare:

Know Your "Why"

What is the motivation behind your desire for a promotion? It's critical to do some self-reflection and ask yourself, "Why do I want this promotion? What is my current situation, and why is a promotion the right action to address my situation?" Know what you're asking for. In many cases, asking for a promotion means you're asking for a bigger title and higher compensation. These things often come with an expanded scope of work, more complex work, having direct reports for the first time or leading a bigger team than what you have today. If it's simply more money you seek, consider asking for a raise instead of a promotion.

Here are some examples of strong "whys":

You're ready to take on more:

- Strong performance – If you've sustained higher than average performance over an extended period of time, you've gone above and beyond your responsibilities and your results have had a strong impact, there's a good chance you have the ability to take on more (more scope, more complex work, a bigger team, etc.).

You've already taken on more:

- Scope change – The scope or complexity of your work has increased; the work you're doing has materially changed.
- Seeking equity – Perhaps others are doing comparable work to you, but they have a more elevated title and/or higher compensation. You're already doing the work and want to be recognized through a promotion.

Build Your Case

After you determine your "why," it's time to build your case. This step involves compiling examples, or evidence, that support your request for a promotion. The less subjectivity in your evidence, the stronger it will be. Here are some examples:

PART 3: HOW TO ASK FOR A PROMOTION

Less Subjectivity = Stronger Evidence	More Subjectivity = Weaker Evidence
I earned superior performance ratings for three consecutive years. Because of my work on the Sample Project, our team has increased our client base by 20%.	The quality of my work has improved lately.
The scope of my work went from contributing to this project to leading this project.	I worked harder this year than previous years
I'm currently a manager, but my responsibilities and scope of work are comparable to the senior managers on the team.	I do more work than my co-worker who is higher in the organization than me.

If your "why" is that you're ready to take on more work, the goal is to highlight examples of times when you demonstrated the capabilities needed for the promoted role you want. If you seek a promoted role where you'll lead people for the first time, think of projects or initiatives you led where you gave guidance and direction to team members and held them accountable for a deliverable. How did you motivate them toward a shared goal? How did you ensure the success of that project? Maybe you've never led people before, but providing examples of answers to these questions shows that you've built foundational skills for that promoted role.

If your "why" is more aligned with how you've already taken on more, like the previous "why," identify examples of how your work has changed or how your work compares to those at more elevated levels. Focus more on the type, scope, and level of complexity of work and less on specific people. This will help you maintain a more objective approach and make your case stronger.

Prepare Your Delivery

You know your "why" and you've gathered your evidence, now

it's time for the delivery. Schedule a one-to-one meeting with your manager for the discussion in a private meeting space like an office or meeting room. I recommend 30-60 minutes. If possible, allow yourself time before and after the meeting to get in the right mindset and decompress after the meeting if needed. Give your leader a heads up on the meeting topic. It can be as simple as, "I'd like to have a career discussion with you at our next meeting."

Don't let the first time you ask for a promotion be the moment you're actually asking for a promotion from your manager. The first ask is usually not the best. Practicing will help you be more comfortable, reduce your anxiety, boost your confidence, and position you for a more effective delivery. Write down your list of points you want to make (your "why" and your evidence) and practice on a trusted colleague, mentor, or partner. Ask them for feedback. Incorporate the feedback and practice again.

In addition to practicing your delivery, plan your responses to a few different possible reactions from your leader:

1. **"Yes, I think a promotion is right for you."** - Congratulations! You obviously had a strong "why" and evidence. Bask in your success after work. In the moment, gratitude is best. Thank your leader for their openness and for their support for your career advancement.

2. **"I'll need to think about it and get back to you."** - Know that your manager may not be able to make the decision in the moment or have the final decision rights at all. In large organizations, many times the manager will need to get alignment from his or her leader and/or Human Resources. Your manager may genuinely need some time to reflect. Be gracious and allow for time needed. Ask when would be an appropriate time to follow up.

3. **"No, a promotion is not right for you."** - Obviously, this is not the response you were hoping for, but it's important to manage your disappointment in the moment. Take this as an opportunity to ask for feedback and find out what you can do differently to position yourself for a promotion in the future.

PART 3: HOW TO ASK FOR A PROMOTION

To my surprise, my manager had already been contemplating the ratio issue on our team, as well as a promotion for me. She thanked me for the data I compiled. She was clear though, she could not give me a decision in that moment. She didn't have the decision rights for what I asked. My promotion and the addition of one team member came four months later. While I was thrilled for this new step in my career, what I'm most proud of is that I saw an issue that needed to be fixed, I took the time to reflect and build a strong case, and I had the courage to voice what I thought was best for me and our broader team.

Personal Insight 2: Brenda Pineda, Director Human Resources, Latinas Rising Up in HR Co-author, 2022

HOW TO ASK FOR A PROMOTION

You will find throughout your career and life that there are many different ways to ask for a promotion. First of all, it can be nerve wracking to the point where you will just decide to let it be. Especially for Latinos. For so long we are taught to be quiet, polite, and grateful for what we have, and that means accepting what you are given and not complaining or asking for more—would be considered rude, entitled, or disrespectful. This is a struggle for many of us. A struggle that we begin to overcome much later in our career. We look back and say to ourselves, "Wow, I should've done this years ago."

This was the case for me. I have been in Human Resources most of my career, with a brief stint in Sales and Operations. As long as I can remember I often looked outside of work for my next career move. There was never a time when I thought to myself, "I am going to ask for a promotion." I just never thought I could make anyone believe that I deserved more. Honestly, I believed that I was lucky to just be where I was (at that time). Of course, as you get older, you look back on your life and realize that you have experienced many wonderful successes, which you quickly recognize as your accomplishments.

Every time you do this, you gain more and more confidence in yourself and believe that you can do anything. I encourage you to do this exercise every year. Make it an annual trip you take on your own, for new year's or your birthday—sit quietly, surrounded by tranquility, and take it all in. Have a notebook and pen and start writing. You will find out quickly how much you have done and how many goals you can now check off. Life goes by so quickly, unless you take the time to really sit with your thoughts and put them in writing, you will never realize how far you have come.

USING PERFORMANCE REVIEWS AND ANNUAL GOALS TO YOUR ADVANTAGE

And now for performance reviews. Although they get a bad rap, your annual performance review is one of the tools you can use to help you in getting promoted. Performance reviews (when done correctly) should include the quality of your work, accomplishments, as well as the timeliness in meeting your goals. This is very important to showcase because it demonstrates progress, it means you get things done. Make sure to include the responsibilities your manager does not see or know that you do well in your day-to-day actions.

When finalizing your annual reviews never miss an opportunity to add how you collaborate and support others outside of your role and outside of your department. If you can get reviews from partners outside of your role, do it and add them to your final assessment. Another great addition to your annual assessment would be your personal/development goals. These goals are primarily created by you. If you have an external project outside of work that will help you in strengthening your presentation skills, or building your leadership capabilities, or in any way contributes to your development at work, add it as your development goals.

Several years ago, while working as a Human Resources Senior Manager, the VP of HR that I reported to sat with me to discuss a promotion to the Director level. I had already built my goals around elevating me to the next level. I made sure while discussing them with my VP, that they were SMART goals and challenged me to come out of my "comfort zone." I worked on taking more of an initiative to be part of projects outside of HR, but with HR as a critical member. I met with each of my client groups to gain a deep understanding of what they need to get to the next level and how I could help them make that happen. I was careful in getting the details and being aligned with what success looked like for each of these objectives.

Throughout the year, I began revising my performance review with updates for each of my goals. I knew this would help me present all the milestones with specific details of what I was directly responsible for. I was on my way. One month prior to the end of the year, my VP shared that she had accepted another offer (closer to home) and would be leaving the company in two weeks. I was shocked. While I was very happy for her, I could not help but think, "What about my promotion?"

The next couple of days, it was all I could think of. What will I do now? She was my greatest supporter, and we had a plan. I thought to myself, "If I wait for the next VP to come, it will be another year or so before I can be promoted." Because of course he/she will need to get to know me and see how well I work. It will take time to start from scratch again. I could not believe this was happening. I had my own personal goal and timeline and being promoted was quickly approaching. I could not afford to wait another year.

Preparing to Ask for My Promotion

Over the Christmas holiday, I began to gather my performance reviews for the last two years and collect feedback from the heads of my client groups. I met with each of them to evaluate how my partnership has supported the team in achieving their overall objectives. I kept a log of all my meetings and added the document to my folder. That was the easy part. How in the world would I convince the CEO to promote me to Director? I took a hard look in the mirror and made a commitment to myself that I would be my biggest supporter and champion. I promised not to let my career fall into the hands of another. I took the time to revisit the conversations with my previous VP who always empowered me and presented me with opportunities that I needed to stretch out of my comfort zone.

I remember one time a staff member came to me looking for guidance and when I asked him, "Did you ask the VP?" He said, "She told me to ask you." That was the moment I took as the "green light" to unleash my capabilities and prove what I can do. I was over the moon. Taking the time to reflect on my previous experiences gave me the confidence I needed to meet with the CEO.

The day arrived, and an overwhelming mix of nerves and anxiety came over me. Though I attempted to dissuade myself from taking the leap, deep down, I knew that if I didn't summon the courage to do it now, I might never muster it again. Determined to give it my all, I prioritized a restful night's sleep and rose early, preparing myself for the pivotal moment ahead. Donning my finest suit, I made my way to work, ensuring I arrived well in advance to gather my thoughts and rehearse my words one final time.

As I glanced out my office window, I could see the CEO pulling into his designated parking spot. A cascade of perspiration formed, and my heart thudded rapidly in my chest. Resolute, I refused to let these physical signs hinder my plan. Instead, I recognized them as indicators that I was about to embark on a journey beyond the confines of my comfort zone. Granting him a few moments to settle in, I mustered the courage to reach out with a message requesting a meeting. His response, a simple, "Come on over," sent a jolt of nerves through my system.

"Yikes!" I thought, knowing that this was the moment of truth, the make-or-break instant where I had to give it my all. With determination and resolve, I braced myself, reminding myself that this was the opportune time—now or never—to seize the moment and put my confidence to the test.

Entering his office, I took a seat while his curious gaze was fixated on the folder clutched in my hand. Despite feeling a surge of nerves threatening to overwhelm me, I made a conscious choice to dismiss them and I proceeded to plunge into the conversation. With unwavering determination, I reassured him of my capability to handle the day-to-day operations of HR during the search for a new VP. I elaborated on the extensive work and projects I had undertaken, all in pursuit of my promotion to Director of HR. Passing the folder over to him, I maintained composure as he delved into its contents. Steadying myself, I silently reaffirmed my confidence. To my astonishment, he looked up and uttered a simple, "Okay." The disbelief was palpable, making me instinctively glance over my shoulder, ensuring that he was indeed addressing me.

Before making my exit, I turned back one final time, seeking confirmation, "Director, right?" With a smile and nod, he affirmed my promotion, leaving me with an indescribable sense of achievement.

Bring it All Home for You

Reflecting on the entire experience, I find myself contemplating various scenarios. Did I really need my past performance reviews? Did I need feedback from those I had worked with? Could I have just asked for the promotion without any of that documentation? Maybe. Would he have said yes? Maybe. What I know for sure is, without a doubt, I approached the situation fully prepared. Armed with every possible resource at my disposal, most notably, unwavering confidence. Even if the outcome were to be a, "No," I had the assurance that it wouldn't be attributed to any overlooked or forgotten details. I had meticulously covered all the facts, leaving no stone unturned.

Since that momentous occasion, a profound transformation has taken hold within me, instilling an unwavering confidence, and igniting an insatiable desire to strive for greater heights in my career. Such experiences serve as powerful catalysts, revealing the immeasurable value we possess and the contributions we bring to the table.

KEY TAKEAWAYS:

1. Begin by collating all your performance reviews, spanning both past and present. Thoroughly examine and highlight the numerous accomplishments you have achieved throughout your journey.

2. Seek feedback from those individuals with whom you closely collaborate. Their perspectives and insights can shed light on your strengths and areas for growth.

3. Consider creating a comprehensive feedback form that showcases your versatile skill set and ability to collaborate across functions. This document will serve as a compelling testament to your cross-functional capabilities.

4. Outline precisely how each of your achievements has significantly contributed to the organization's overarching business objectives. Demonstrating this correlation emphasizes the value you have brought to the company.

5. Articulate how your elevated performance and results have effectively prepared you to shoulder increased responsibilities. Emphasize your readiness to take on new challenges and lead with confidence.

6. Lastly, always incorporate your carefully crafted goals and objectives for the desired role. This demonstrates foresight, ambition, and your commitment to further advancing the organization's mission.

By incorporating these key insights into your approach, you will undoubtedly present a compelling case for your promotion, highlighting your exceptional contributions and illustrating your potential to excel in the next phase of your career.

Personal Insight 3: Luz H. Perez, HRBP Director, CDW

HOW TO ASK FOR A PROMOTION

Hard work, loyalty, dedication: three words often used when Latino parents describe skills needed to get a job. Surprisingly,

PART 3: HOW TO ASK FOR A PROMOTION

there are few discussions about career progression. I was often told, "Once you get the job, work hard and do as you are told, be grateful you have one." As you get older, you hope your dedication speaks for itself, wait to be recognized, but instead of a promotion, you get an 8x11 thanks, and because you are grateful, you move on without asking, yet expecting to be noticed.

Throughout my professional journey, I have learned not asking for promotions or negotiating is a challenge Latinos face. Lack of resources and development opportunities are common barriers that amplify the gap of Latino representation in leadership positions, which then impacts the desire for growth. This chapter will help you explore strategies you can leverage to successfully ask for a promotion and elevate your brand.

When I entered corporate America in 2012, I was thrilled to have been offered a job; I accepted the first offer. With no hesitation eagerly said yes; I was an HR Manager and took an HR Generalist role. I was grateful to have a corporate job. I remember calling my now husband and sharing the offer details. He asked if I had negotiated. I said, "No, why would I?"

He said, "Luz, with six years of HR experience and a master's degree, you are worth more." I did not understand his reaction and tried to justify my actions because I believed I had to prove myself worthy, so I ignored him and moved on.

After a few short months in the role, I was excelling and happy. Then my boss left, and I felt overlooked for a promotion. Though qualified, I didn't enquire about the position. I thought if management felt I was ready, they would ask, right? Before leaving, my boss shared that she thought I was ready, yet I felt I was still too new. My boss's replacement was hired, agreeably I coached and trained the new leader; it was then when I realized why my husband's advice was so critical. I failed to recognize that I had enough experience to be considered, and that based on my performance, I was capable.

Having learned this valuable lesson, I spent the last few years working hard, but also engaging in advancement opportunities. Turns out hard work, loyalty and dedication are Latino superpowers, ones you can leverage to create a strong brand, and establish value.

There are a few other misperceptions I learned along the way:

- Asking questions makes you seem incompetent: *Quite the contrary; asking questions gives you clarity and leads to meaningful conversations.*
- Long tenure and loyalty to a company will lead to a promotion: *Loyalty and longevity hardly has a bearing on a promotion decision.*
- Self-perception that you do not "deserve" a promotion: *Promotions are earned, which makes you deserving of it. Do not indulge in self-doubt, especially when everyone agrees you are ready for the promotion.*
- If you ask for help it will make you seem incompetent: *Being vulnerable and authentic are critical leadership traits that demonstrate professional maturity.*
- My boss knows I want to get promoted; I will wait for them to tap me: *You and only you own your career. It is not your boss's responsibility to get you promoted, you are the driver of your own career.*

Misconceptions often lead to assumptions and over time these assumptions can quickly become reality. Self-awareness of your performance, your value, and your readiness level are table stakes when asking for a promotion. Always be mindful of the impact you've made and be ready for the conversation.

Before asking for a promotion, empower and prepare yourself:

1. Consistent performance is key. Strive to be the best at your job. Don't assume long tenure will result in a promotion. This mindset often disappoints, especially when performance isn't strong.

PART 3: HOW TO ASK FOR A PROMOTION

2. Practice self-awareness and solicit frequent feedback, especially constructive feedback. It is important to understand your brand and others' perception of you. Feedback is essential to closing potential gaps and work towards evolving perception that may be not true to who you are.
3. Self-assessment: Take some time to assess your own performance. Reflect on your achievements, responsibilities, and contributions to the company. Consider how your current role aligns with the requirements of a desired or elevated position.
4. Be visible. Promotion decisions often require more than one voice, so it's critical to network and find opportunities for self-advocacy by sharing successes, best practices, and collaborating on new ideas with coworkers outside of your core team. This can sometimes open doors to participate in new projects and tasks which can further create opportunities for visibility.
5. Create a personal Board of Directors that includes three key roles: Advocate, Mentor, and Influencer—Take your time getting to know people in the organization and understand who has a seat at the table and can contribute to your career journey. Choose someone who will advocate and/or cheer for you even when you are not in the room. Seek a mentor who will not only coach you, but also help you navigate the inner workings of the organization. Finally, know who has a critical voice when opportunities come up and can influence decisions.
6. Request and schedule 1-2 career conversations a year with your leader. Express regular interest in career advancement and skillset development. Ensure you have your manager's support for upward mobility.

How and when to ask for a promotion

Asking can be rather simple; knowing what to say and how to

say it requires effort. Research and business acumen are impactful to having informed conversations with your manager. Timing is also important.

In-place promotion or non-competitive opportunities, can be requested when you have:

- ✓ Mastered your current role/level
- ✓ Assumed greater responsibility
- ✓ Elevated the role's performance
- ✓ Acted as a peer leader (where applicable)
- ✓ Identified the need to oversee a team, strategy, or program

When a competitive promotion comes up, request an exploratory conversation. Ask questions about how the job, role expectations, and how it aligns to the corporate strategy. Evaluate how this role aligns with your interests, and if you are interested, express you want to be considered. Discuss the opportunity with your manager, ask for advice on how to prepare, if there are any gaps or areas of concern, and request to work together to build a development plan regardless of outcome. Check in with your Board ask for feedback that helps strengthen your candidacy and can bring awareness to any potential gaps.

Once you've scheduled the promotion conversation, or interview:

1. Leverage self-assessment and feedback received to discuss your personal and professional growth and why you are ready for the next level. Share examples of accomplishments and skill development, and successes you've had.
2. Showcase your business acumen, ideas you've developed to support the company's strategy; articulate how the expanded scope can address company needs. Share projected outcomes.
3. Request feedback and be prepared to discuss any

concerns or areas for improvement. This is equally a learning opportunity, acknowledge the learning curve and your commitment to ensuring success and continued development.

4. Lastly, establish next steps: Inquire about the timeline, and any additional steps you need to take. Ask for feedback on how to enhance your chances for promotion in the future; share appreciation for the time spent.

Closing out

Be clear about what you want and don't be afraid to ask for it. If an offer will be made, be prepared to negotiate. Yes, Latinos we are grateful, but we now also know our value!

RECAP

First and foremost, I want to give a special thanks to Dana, Brenda, and Luz for their amazing contribution! They are all extremely committed to your development. This is the type of guidance and insights that will impact the promotion effectiveness of all Latinos for the current and future generations!

With the information provided in this chapter, you can go into any promotion situation informed, confident, and with a game plan to execute towards getting the role you want and deserve. Also, remember that you are not alone on this journey. As covered earlier in this book, continue to use your trusted advisors, mentors, and sponsors to help you prepare and practice your promotion-asking approach. You have not come this far just to come this far; so make driving forward hard and ensure you continue to prep well, practice hard, and execute your plan flawlessly. With this mindset, approach, and skillset, your future will be one of great options! I look forward to hearing about your next promotion(s)! Remember, show up big and swing big—that's now how we roll!

HOW TO PREPARE FOR AND NEGOTIATE SALARY

> *"In business as in life, you don't get what you deserve; you get what you negotiate."*
>
> **- Chester L. Karrass**

One of the biggest issues for Latinos in the workplace today is pay equality and it's more pronounced for Latinas. As covered in the "Latino Data" chapter, there is a significant pay gap between Latino/a

41% of Latinos are more likely to **earn lower wages** than non-Latinos

Median household **income for Latinos is $60.5K** vs. $75.5K for white Americans

Latinas get paid 54 cents for every dollar a white male makes

Source: WeAreAllHuman.org

It's clear that the Latino pay gap is a serious issue that needs to be addressed immediately. We are at the point where we must take decisive and collective action to achieve pay equality in the workplace for all Latinos. Although there is no silver bullet to tackle this issue, one significant way that we can jointly begin to shift the narrative (within our immediate control) is to become strong, tough negotiators when it comes to our pay and compensation packages.

> It's clear that the Latino pay gap is a serious issue that needs to be addressed immediately. We are at the point where we must take decisive and collective action to achieve pay equality in the workplace for all Latinos.

PART 3: HOW TO PREPARE FOR AND NEGOTIATE SALARY

Like the previous chapter ("How to Ask for a Promotion"), this chapter is the result of focus groups performed earlier this year. The team thought (and I agree!) it was critical to provide guidance to Latino readers on how to optimize our pay/compensation potential, particularly if we are going to be showing up differently as impact players in the workplace. As a result, I have engaged and brought in guidance from some of the most influential experts in this area who can also talk to the Latino cultural mindset around how we prepare for and negotiate pay.

THE LATINO MINDSET AND NEGOTIATING PAY

Early on in our lives we are taught to be modest, to think of the family/group first, and not to be greedy. While these values are supremely important and effective in our personal setting, they can hinder us when we are fighting for what we are worth in the workplace. I have heard of, seen, and personally experienced the struggles of our approach when it comes to negotiating our pay.

> As covered earlier in this book, my mindset for compensation success was to make more than my parents—reminder, my father was a truck driver and my mother was a secretary when she wasn't taking care of our family. Early in my career, when I was offered and accepted a $65K salary, I was on top of the world! I jumped at the opportunity to take that pay because it was more than anyone in my family ever made. I was very excited and happy about my position, until I discovered what my non-Latino peers were making, doing "the exact same thing" I was doing. I overheard one of my white male counterparts say (and complain about!) only making $95K. This unsettled me and I knew something was off. Even knowing that fact, I still continued to accept the inequality at the time. I didn't know any better and thought that's just the way things were. Fast forward to today, I do not think that way any longer and neither should you!

The purpose of the chapter is to provide awareness on the importance of and the need to negotiate your pay/compensation for any job you get. I want to ensure you are set up to get the maximum pay for what you are worth. You must prepare hard and fight hard for what you want, no exceptions. It's time we take ownership of our side of this issue and begin to show up differently at the negotiation table.

> The purpose is to provide awareness on the importance of and the need to negotiate your pay for any job you get. I want to ensure you are set up to get the maximum pay for what you are worth. You must prepare hard and fight hard for what you want, no exceptions.

Like the previous chapter, this one will also be very tactical. I will get right to what you need to know on how to improve your negotiating mindset and skillset. Let's get started.

Personal Insight 1: Beatriz Albini-Ruiz PCC, CPC, ELI- MP, PHR, Executive Leadership and Career Success Coach, CEO of Prime YOU Coaching LLC

HOW TO PREPARE FOR AND NEGOTIATE YOUR SALARY
The Importance of Salary Negotiation

Mastering salary negotiation can be daunting for everyone, but even more of us Latinos are due to generation conditioning and generational trauma. However, as with any skill, it can be mastered by embracing a combination of mechanics and mindset. My experience from being a junior employee now to a seasoned professional has taught me that it doesn't hurt to ask. If you want to be successful in negotiation, we have to reframe our mindset so we can enter the discussion with confidence to get what we really deserve.

PART 3: HOW TO PREPARE FOR AND NEGOTIATE SALARY

How to Prepare for and Negotiate Your Salary

Nothing taught me the value of mastering the skill of salary negotiation, like failing to negotiate my first corporate offer.

Having grown up in Colombia and migrating to the U.S. as a young adult, I had no clue that salary negotiation was standard practice and expected as part of the recruiting process in corporate America. I was raised to believe I needed to be grateful and humble for any opportunity. Getting a foot in the door and working hard would eventually lead to success—and a fair salary. Therefore, unsurprisingly, when that offer came in, I did not hesitate to accept it immediately.

Later I learned, to my frustration and disappointment, I was the lowest-paid employee amongst my peers with the same title and similar years of experience. After that, I decided to take action and become a student of negotiation. Moreover, I asked to work with the talent acquisition partners to get a first-hand view of the process. It was an eye-opener and one of the best learning experiences. I saw how candidates and recruiters would negotiate offers and how this was absolutely normal. It struck me that I had sabotaged myself by not even considering the possibility of negotiation. So, when the time came for me to negotiate my next job offer, I did it successfully. In hindsight, two things worked against me: having the wrong mindset towards negotiating my salary and my ignorance about the mechanics of negotiation (how to). Today, if I have to advise anyone on salary negotiation quickly, below are the three main focus points.

Takeaway 1: Preparation is the Cornerstone of Salary Negotiation

Preparation is 90% of salary negotiation. It helps assess if we are getting the short end of the stick, anticipate challenges, and, more importantly, it's a proven way to build confidence (more on that shortly).

When preparing for a salary negotiation, several areas are advised to prep for. However, two are a must, and those are preparing your salary targets and preparing for curve balls.

To prepare the salary targets, conducting good market rate research is crucial. Knowledge is power and doing your homework can make or break your salary negotiation. Many online tools can help you understand the typical pay for a role. I recommend sites like Salary.com, Glassdoor salary calculator, Levels.fyi, and Payscale to research the average salary for your geographical location and industry.

What you should come away with are three numbers:

1. **Your Maximum.** This would be a perfect case scenario (moonshot) in setting your salary for an ideal financial goal.
2. **Your Absolute Minimum.** Anything below this should be your walkaway point unless there is another benefit or perk that is of high value (i.e., education assistance, 401k match, remote/hybrid).
3. **Your Midpoint.** This is usually a more realistic number, and it should be the sweet spot both based on your research as well as your personal finances.

These three numbers should be internal information that helps you gauge the salary numbers' fairness. Do not disclose any numbers up front, but instead have a range to provide if asked. See the example below:

> "Based on my experience, skills, and the market rate for this position, I am looking for a salary range between [top number - min number]."

When it comes to preparing for curveballs or potential derailing scenarios, what I learned is to anticipate and practice. Prepare your responses for difficult questions, especially objections around salary expectations and experience, and practice as much as possible. The more you practice, the higher your success rate will be.

PART 3: HOW TO PREPARE FOR AND NEGOTIATE SALARY

Takeaway 2: Own Your Worth

When entering any compensation negotiations, confidence is extremely important. Often, when it comes to negotiation, we Latinos tend to be our worst saboteurs and let our self-doubt, fears, and limiting beliefs in the driver's seat. Entering any negotiation with fear and hesitation will only lead to poor results.

Some common thoughts that get in the way can be exemplified by the following:

- Am I good enough?
- Am I experienced enough?
- Am I leadership material?
- Am I going to lose this opportunity? (Aka fear of rocking the boat.)
- I should be grateful for this opportunity.

To be fair, it's understandable that we experience any or all of these sabotaging thoughts. After all, many of us are the first in our families to go to school, get a higher education degree, or work in corporate America. Moreover, our cultural conditioning and generational trauma often play in the background. Therefore, we tend to doubt our value, play it safe, and lowball ourselves and thus lose even before entering a negotiation.

Instead, we must reframe how we see ourselves and the value we bring to organizations. In other words, we need to start believing and owning our worth before negotiating. One powerful way to build confidence is by doing self-reflection and taking stock of all the strengths, experiences, and unique talents one brings to the table.

Make a list. Ask yourself, what is my special "sazon"? How does that add value or impact the organization? For example, speaking from my own personal experience, being a Latina who had to start from the bottom, navigate two cultures, build a network, and climb the corporate ladder with an accent, I can say with confidence that besides my experience, I bring a lot of natural people skills, resilience, adaptability, and grit. These are all highly prized leadership traits in today's business world. That's why I always advise not to discount anything. ALL our experiences, diverse perspective, and cultural richness are valuable—own it.

Takeaway 3: The Squeaky Wheel Gets the Grease

So far, everything that I shared with you has been around pre-negotiation. The last piece of insight is specifically one to deploy when an offer has been extended—that is, to get comfortable with asking for more. Either more salary, an education stipend, a flexible schedule, or time to think about that offer; whatever it is, don't be afraid of asking. This piece of advice also applies when negotiating at work for more resources or budget to be successful. The trick here is in the delivery. Try to bulk your requests so the recruiter or manager does not get annoyed and ask nicely—make sure your tone of voice is as calm and neutral as possible.

I know asking for more is uncomfortable. Many of us Latinos repeatedly heard that we need to be "humilde" (humble) and that working hard will yield recognition and fair compensation. For others, especially Latinas, we might internalize that in "boca cerrrada no entra mosco" and might be afraid, as I was, of coming across as difficult, but believe me when I say if you don't ask or raise your hand or put yourself forward, you will never get it. As the common phrase says, "The squeaky wheel gets the grease!"

Personal Insight 2: Yennie Rautenberg-Loya, Inclusive Leadership Coach & Trainer, Rautenberg Coaching

AMA: THE NEGOTIATION PROCESS

Awareness, Mindset, Action (AMA) is the framework I use often in my coaching practice. It is simple and straightforward: **Awareness** to identify narratives that determine how you view the negotiation process. Reframe these limiting narratives into inspiring **Mindsets** that empower you to move forward. Take

A- Awareness

Action. AMA is a great tool to use from the beginning of a job search all the way through the hiring process. Let me break it down for you.

A- Awareness

It is vital to bring awareness to the narratives that limit your viewpoint, such as your beliefs, thoughts, fears, and concerns. Without effort or intention, our minds tend to default to automatic and pervasive narratives that are limiting and disempowering. They are created and stored in our minds throughout our lives, based on upbringing, background, culture, experiences, and beliefs. While they are designed to keep us "safe" and to avoid among other things rejection and failure, they also limit our opportunities and options, and the actions we take.

To practice awareness, start by identifying the disempowering narratives that are already in your mind and have the power to get in the way. Answer these questions being brutally honest with yourself: What do think about your worth and your abilities? What do you think about the salary? What do you think about the potential outcome of your interaction with the employer?

The range of the immediate responses might go from "That's way too much money," "That's greedy!" "I'd feel bad earning that much!" to "I deserve more money, but what if my ask is too high and they hire somebody else?" "Someone else will be better," to "What if I can't deliver?" "They will find out I'm not that good." What are yours?

Take time to write down every thought, belief, fear, and concern that comes to mind. This will bring those unconscious narratives to the forefront, and make you realize that most of them are baseless, some even irrational, and a few others are actionable.

M-Mindset

Once you are aware of your disempowering narratives, you need to reframe them into powerful mindsets under two categories: Your anchors and the negotiation.

1 - Your Anchors

Start by identifying "anchors" to keep you grounded in who you are, your skills, talents, and your unique contributions to have a positive impact on the position.

Most people have a hard time speaking about, or even acknowledging, their own accomplishments, qualifications, strengths, and talents. This is especially true about Latinas/os, who, since childhood, have been bombarded with messages such as "sé humilde," "no presumas," "no pidas." These messages are so ingrained that they limit and skew how we see ourselves and also create disempowering narratives about money and prosperity.

"It's not bragging if it's based on facts," is probably my favorite quote from #IAmRemarkable, a workshop I have successfully facilitated for hundreds of people.

In this training, participants usually struggle listing their accomplishments. They tend to tell themselves: "That achievement wasn't a big deal," "I was just doing my job," "I did that, but my colleague did much more." The workshop helps to work through their initial barriers and to start recognizing their accomplishments and gaining confidence in themselves.

To identify your anchors, reflect on and inventory your achievements, skills, and strengths. Be proud of them, they are yours! Also embrace your shortcomings and reframe them as learning opportunities. Your anchors also include how your life experience translates into the impact you would have on the job. Use your anchors to create an inspiring mindset about yourself that fits the job description and your salary expectations.

2 - The Negotiation

Negotiating a salary tends to be an uncomfortable and stressful activity, perceived as one party winning and the other party losing, turning the employer into an opponent. For this reason, reframing your view about the negotiation into a powerful mindset is critical.

Think of it as an opportunity to partner with your future

employer. Consider that the employer is as interested in you as you are in them. Express your excitement and your commitment to the job and your willingness to negotiate a salary that works for both of you.

A- Action

Actively think about what is important to you in a job, what you are willing to let go of and what your non-negotiables are. For example, you might be willing to earn less if you have a short commute, or if you are able to work remotely. Research the compensation trends in the industry, in the specific company and for the type of job you are applying for. Talk to people in your network who work in Human Resources, other resources are Glassdoor.com and Indeed.com.

Find out how the company manages their compensations. Most employers have a salary range for each position and there may be significant variations between the lowest and highest ends. Get a sense of the salary range for the position you are applying for so that your expectations are realistic. If the salary you have in mind is higher than what they offer for the position, consider asking for a higher title! Based on your experience and qualifications, you may be able to negotiate a higher title and a corresponding higher salary range.

Take into account the entire compensation package the employer offers, including benefits and perks such as 401k, vacation time, bonuses, company stock, professional development, stipends, etc. Some companies also offer sign-on bonuses or may be willing to pay off student loans.

Armed with this information, provide the employer with a range of your salary expectations instead of a specific number. Make sure that the lowest number you present is still an amount that you would be okay with. I recommend you review the AMA process and constantly remind yourself of your anchors. Practice your new mindsets as many times as you need to feel comfortable with them. Also, anticipate difficult questions and be prepared to address them.

Final Thoughts

If the negotiation conversations do not meet your compensation expectations, do not be afraid to walk away. Be gracious and thank the employer for their time and interest.

It is common for people to accept subpar offers, even though they do not feel right, as a way to get their foot in the door. They expect that once inside they will demonstrate their value and have a chance to renegotiate their salary. While there are exceptions, negotiating a salary once you are on the job rarely works. It is also important to remember that the salary you accept becomes the baseline for future raises, bonuses, and another benefits.

Regardless of the outcome, make time to reflect on the process, on what worked, what didn't, and on what you can improve the next time.

Personal Insight 3: America Baez, Talent Acquisition and Diversity, Equity & Inclusion Leader

HOW TO PREPARE FOR AND NEGOTIATE YOUR SALARY

Years ago, I was looking for a job and after interviewing with many companies I finally got an offer. However, it was lower than what I was looking for. I talked to the recruiter about my expectations and what the market rate was for this type of position and level, not to mention my deep expertise in the area. I counteroffered and I got a slightly higher offer, but certainly not close to what I was looking for. They said it was the last offer and I had to decide whether to take it or not. After careful consideration, I decided to take the offer because I needed the job and I wanted to get the experience. However, in hindsight I wish I could have stayed firm on what my salary expectation was and I had pushed back more to the recruiter.

This happened at a time when candidates were required to disclose their salary history and that put me at a disadvantage. Luckily, now more states around the U.S. are banning employers from asking about the candidate's salary history. However, there is still a long way to go in terms of equal pay, especially for women and underrepresented groups.

Having endured pay inequality for many years, more people are openly speaking about salary nowadays. This is good because now people feel more comfortable talking about it and disclosing their salaries, which in turn helps candidates looking for jobs to be able to access that information online or by word of mouth. In addition, salary transparency has become more important now and some companies are voluntarily disclosing their salary ranges, which gives you an idea of what other companies are paying for those types of positions.

When negotiating salary, think of the overall compensation package and whether the perks and benefits might make up for the salary difference (if the offer is lower than expected) and if that is going to benefit you in your life and career (i.e., equity, flexible time, work from home, additional vacation time, paid trainings or certifications, or a salary review within the first six months of employment, etc.). It is up to you to decide what is best for you and whether you can flex on your target salary.

In your job search, when asked about your salary history turn it to the recruiter and ask what their salary range is for the position or what are they thinking about salary for the position. Some recruiters might open up more about the salary range when you ask those questions. Remember, recruiters should only ask you what your salary expectations are, instead of your salary history.

KEY TAKEAWAYS:

- Do not disclose your salary history and refer to salary transparency laws if pressed.
- Research the salary of the positions you are applying to. That includes salaries in the same industry, level, location, and competitor companies. Research salaries online in job boards or sites where company employees disclose information anonymously.
- Talk to someone who works in that company or similar

companies to get insight about their responsibilities and compensation.

- Know your worth and your salary target number. Although companies offer other perks and benefits, it is important to know your target number so that you can stay firm during the salary negotiation process.
- Be prepared to push back to the recruiter and walk away if they do not meet your salary expectations: stay firm in the salary negotiation process
- Continue interviewing with other companies so that you can choose the best offer.

Personal Insight 4: Jon Orozco, MBA, SHRM-SCP, Fractional Chief People Officer

HOW TO PREPARE FOR AND NEGOTIATE YOUR SALARY

During my teenage years, I landed my first job as a bank teller at Washington Mutual through the High School Intern Program. The pay was modest, starting at $7.50 per hour. Little did I know, on the first day of employee orientation, that the new employee orientation trainer imparted valuable career advice that would stay with me: "Keep your resume updated, as it will not only reflect your value, but also prepare you for future opportunities in life." Although I couldn't fully grasp its significance back then, I understood the importance of maintaining an updated resume to thrive in the corporate world.

Following my passion for business, I pursued a college education. My advisor, recognizing my strong interpersonal skills and problem-solving abilities, encouraged me to explore a human resources (HR) career. Taking her advice, I completed my master's degree in HR and obtained national certification as an HR professional. Starting as an HR business partner, I steadily climbed the corporate ladder, progressing to roles such as HR director, vice president, and ultimately, Chief HR Officer. Along this journey, I learned valuable lessons about negotiating compensation as we advance in our careers.

PART 3: HOW TO PREPARE FOR AND NEGOTIATE SALARY

It's common for many of us to feel discouraged right when a job posting goes live on the internet. We come across a "dream job" that ignites our passion, only to be plagued by imposter syndrome, doubting whether we meet every qualification listed. We often tell ourselves a story that we are not fully deserving of such opportunities.

Here's my recommendation for you, ignore those limiting beliefs and continue forward; put your hat in the ring and be counted. Here's a quick guide to help you navigate the salary negotiation process effectively:

Do Your Homework

Research market rates: Utilize neutral websites such as PayScale.com, GlassDoor.com, and Indeed.com to gather information on salary ranges for your position. Understanding the competitive offerings for top talent in your field will provide insight into your worth.

Ask About the Salary Range

Don't hesitate to inquire about the salary range when applying for jobs. Politely reach out to the hiring manager, expressing your interest in the position and kindly asking if they could share the salary range. This ensures alignment before proceeding further in the hiring process.

Prepare Thoroughly

Study the job description: Familiarize yourself with the job requirements, company details, products, and target audience. This knowledge will enable you to effectively align your skills and experiences with the organization's needs.

Practice interview questions: Research common interview questions and tailor them to the specific role you are applying for. Practice answering these questions in front of a mirror or with friends to enhance your confidence and delivery during the interview.

Excel in the Interview

Showcase your value: Utilize the interview to demonstrate your passion for continuous learning and dedication to the field. Share examples of your educational background, relevant certifications, and personal interests that align with the job. Showcasing your multifaceted abilities will leave a lasting impression on the interviewers.

Ask insightful questions: Ask questions about the company's culture, the team's perspective on working there, and their expectations for the role's success. This displays your genuine interest and helps you gather information to make an informed decision.

Engage in Salary Negotiations

Highlight your value: When discussing salary, express your enthusiasm for joining the team and ask if it's a suitable time to review the offer. State your desired salary and why it aligns with your qualifications, skill sets, and experience. Emphasize that it falls within the fair and equitable range based on your research.

Handling unexpected offers: If the offered salary is slightly below your expectations, express your appreciation for the confidence shown in you and politely inquire if the person you're speaking with is the right person to discuss the offer. Take the opportunity to showcase your worth by emphasizing your skills, achievements, and contributions.

Ongoing Negotiations

Explore internal opportunities: If you're considering a raise within your current company, bring up the topic during your annual review or regular check-ins. Share your exceptional performance rating and express your interest in discussing a market rate adjustment for your salary. Utilize the knowledge and strategies outlined above to drive the conversation forward; remember, you are worth hundreds of millions of dollars, but are meeting your employer at their budget, so get as much value as possible.

KEY TAKEAWAYS:

- Knowledge is power: Conduct thorough research on market rates to understand your worth and negotiate confidently.
- Preparation leads to success: Study job descriptions, practice interview questions, and gather company insights to present yourself as a well-informed and highly motivated candidate.
- Articulate your value: Clearly communicate your skills, experiences, and accomplishments to demonstrate your worth and justify your desired salary.
- Remember, salary negotiation is an opportunity to advocate for yourself and secure fair compensation. You can position yourself for success in the employee market with proper preparation and confident but friendly communication.

RECAP

First, I want to give a very special thanks to Beatriz, Yennie, America, and Jon for their contribution! The frameworks, insights, and guidance they shared will position you nicely for understanding and getting what you are worth in any pay/compensation package negotiation.

As covered earlier, the time to take ownership of the Latino/a pay gap issue starts now with us. It's time to change the game and begin to quickly close this gap. You are now armed with the intelligence needed to be a force at the negotiation table—our goal was to provide you with both the right mindset and right skillset to execute a great negotiation that will forever impact you and your family. Further, when you get what you are worth, you add to getting the worth of all Latinos—a win for you is a win for all of us! I am excited about your next negotiation as I know you will get what you deserve! Let's roll!

PART 4:

Bringing it All Together: Leveraging Our Natural Passion and Grit

---

"The new Latino leader needs to dream BIG, show up BIG, and swing BIG!"

- Refugio A. Atilano & Michael Atilano

I have waited an entire year to write this chapter and am so incredibly excited for all of us to be at this point! This journey started with a simple lunch conversation in August 2022 with my good friend, Greg Macias. I remember telling him, "I see so many common themes of frustration in the Latino professional community and I feel I need to do something about it." He said, "You should!" The rest is history, and I am here today to give you, and this chapter, everything I've got to make sure you and the generations of those behind us are set up for maximum leadership success. Let's roll!

TODAY IS WHEN OUR COLLECTIVE LEADERSHIP DEVELOPMENT BEGINS

The days of Latinos not being informed, confident, high-impact, and promotion-ready professionals are over. We now have the insights, framework, and expert guidance needed to drive our careers forward with maximum leadership impact and potential. **The Latino Leadership Playbook has set you up to deliver overwhelming and undeniable impact**—there is no turning back to operating the way you did before reading this book. You are now the new Latino leader as the greatness in you is ready to be carved out for the world to see!

As my friend Miguel A. de Jesús, business development consultant, said to me earlier this year, "Every 'T' (team) needs a 'L' (leader). It's time we make the shift to being strong Ls in everything we do. Being good is no longer good enough. We must commit to always striving for excellence and work hard to get better every day, every month, every year—this type of focus will be the catalyst to maximize your full potential.

You now understand what it means to be an impact player in the workplace and how to go about developing a strong leadership brand. As Yai Vargas stated in her Foreword at the beginning of this book, "This playbook is like having a number of different counselors, guides, and mentors in the palm of your hand—giving you diverse perspectives and expert advice that will get you at least where they have gotten and more importantly, further than you could ever imagine for yourself." Furthermore, you now understand the workplace game and, just as importantly, strategies on how to compete at a high level!

As you start your journey as an impact player in the workplace, remember that failure is also part of the growth process. In my opinion, if you are not failing, you are not stretching yourself. The key part with failures is to turn them into improvement opportunities. Stay committed to the growth process and keep your mindset positive: 1) learn quickly from mistakes, 2) reflect on what you will do differently in the future to avoid the same mistake, 3) apply those lessons and build that new leadership muscle. This growth mindset will facilitate your development and add to your strong leadership brand.

INTERVIEW WITH A LATINA EMMY WINNER, SPEAKER, AUTHOR, ENTREPRENEUR: Gaby Natale

Favorite quote: "Every time we choose to pioneer, we move the world forward." – Gaby Natale

I had the honor of interviewing Gaby for this book and she wanted to share the following powerful insights as you PIONEER and drive your career forward to reach your maximum potential:

- **Embrace Your Uniqueness** - Being a leader is multi-dimensional; there is no one way that everyone must follow. As Latinos, we are resourceful, have deep cultural roots, and great personal stories. In addition, we know how to lead with a big heart and communicate from a place of truth.
- **Be What You Can See** - You have inner work to do, know the value you bring into each room you enter. Focus on breaking barriers; be aware of your feelings and work towards eliminating self-sabotaging behaviors. Take advantage of your natural social mobility strength as a Latino and envision your success, and then execute toward achieving it!
- **Latinos Need to Unite** - There is not a tree that exists where branches fight each other for space. We must take the same approach and make space for and support each other. Lead by focusing on commonalities rather than differences; putting emphasis on the little things will be self-sabotaging, so let's collectively work to move away from doing so.

- Being Latino is so much bigger than any individual—it's critical that we provide that cultural support and build each other up. This means we need to buy from each other, empower each other, and provide economic opportunities to advance our community.
- **Know Yourself, Network, and Drive Your Brand** - Make sure to take the time needed to know your personal brand! Use it to create influential networks (align yourself with influencers, connectors, and decision-makers). This will help your access, exposure, and mobility in your organization. Remember, networking is a two-way street—you can't be a taker only.
  - The world has changed and most business is done online. Use platforms like LinkedIn to build your influence in your own space!
- **Final Leadership Thoughts** - Being an entrepreneur has been an absolute privilege. It has created freedom and the expressions of work were a getaway for my journey. Also, being financially responsible allowed me to take smart risks throughout my career, while I also focused on breaking barriers. My approach has been to believe in a vision before results are realized—part of my brand is taking that leap of faith and I hope you will too!

INTERVIEW WITH A SENIOR EXECUTIVE: Jeff Martinez
Executive Vice President, PNC Bank

Favorite quote 1: "No one cares what you know until they know that you care." - Benjamin Franklin

Favorite quote 2: "Well done will always be better than well said.". - Benjamin Franklin

I had the honor of interviewing Jeff, who I met at this year's HACR Executive Programs conference. He's a visionary and

PART 4: BRINGING IT ALL TOGETHER: LEVERAGING OUR NATURAL PASSION AND GRIT

dynamic leader who is passionate about doing his part to elevate the leadership capabilities of all Latinos. Here are some of the insights he shared:

- **You Can't Be What You Can't See** - It's critical that we are able to see leaders that look like us at the top of organizations. In doing so, we can lead the way towards becoming a destination for diverse talent. As Latinos, we come from different cultures and countries and can create a broader cultural understanding in our companies. This background and the insights we bring can help connect better with diverse consumers and employees, which can in turn, accelerate the speed of business.
- **When You Can't See It, Create It** - As an SVP, there are not Latinos above me that I can tap into to show me the way; therefore, when charting new territory, it's critical to create your path strategically using the resources and your trusted network. Sometimes you will have be out-front and set the path for yourself and all others that come behind you. This is a great example of leadership.
- **The Superpower of Diversity and Courage** - It's critical that you understand that your uniqueness is invaluable. You bring a natural strength of diversity and there is no need to totally assimilate to the traditional white corporate world. You also have natural built-in courage that came from those before us; our families left their home country to make a better life for us and they took high risks/made great sacrifices to make it happen. Take that legacy of boldness and bring it to work every day! The world needs it!
- **We Need to Shift to Being Leaders, Instead of Just Being Informed** - We are the sandwich generation in that we are trying to be true to our culture while, at the same time, trying to advance ourselves in the workplace. Latinos must keep pushing forward and make it easier for all those who come behind us (just as we are doing with this book!). It will be important to position ourselves as experts and

leaders in connecting with the Latino community and help drive business forward. We are in the driver's seat to do more things to connect with our community and now is the best time for us to lean in and take/demand that leadership role.

- **We Need to Unite and Support Each Other -** In order for Latinos to move the representation needle, we must come together. It will be critical that we shift our mindset to focus on 80-90% similarities vs. the 10-20% differences within our community. This is a self-limiting community behavior that we should focus on course correcting immediately. Once we get effective at showing up as One Latino community, our world will change. We will move from making requests to making demands—that's the true power of how we begin to effectively leverage our numbers.

- **Pay It Forward -** While it is important to develop ourselves, it is just as critical that we make things better for the next generation of leaders. We must lift as we climb and operate with a sense of responsibility to current and future Latino leaders. Take the time to mentor, share knowledge, sponsor, etc. If you don't do it, who will?

- **Final Leadership Thoughts -** Today's Latina is a special breed. They are ambitious, operate with a growth mindset, entrepreneurs, and overall powerhouses. Now more than ever, there are tools and resources to support their development and success in today's world. Let's keep supporting our Latinas to help them achieve their wildest goals and dreams!

COLLECTIVELY ACTIVATING LATINO LEADERSHIP DEVELOPMENT

It's now time to bring *The Latino Leadership Playbook* elements to life. It does us no good for only a few of us to benefit from the concepts in this book; **we need everyone to benefit if we are going to shift our collective leadership narrative and representation in senior level roles.** Moving the needle will

PART 4: BRINGING IT ALL TOGETHER: LEVERAGING OUR
NATURAL PASSION AND GRIT

require all of us to lean in, it will require commitment, it will require a plan, and it will require execution. To get us all going in the same direction, I created the following framework that will help us move together:

Latino Collective Leadership Activation Model

| UNITY | ACTION | ACCOUNTABILITY |

UNITY

If we want to make a collective impact as Latinos, then we must come together—this is a non-negotiable. According to a Hispanic Sentiment Study 2023, only 55% of Latinos think we are very or extremely unified as a community (We Are All Human Staff, 2023). Although it's up 7% from 2018, it's nowhere close to where it needs to be in order for us to operate as a united front. If you think about it, the most successful teams (business, sports, etc.) operate as a unit; if there are broken or weak links, then the chain is broken or weak.

> Until about seven years ago, I didn't realize the importance and power of the collective Latino support. As a Mexican raised on the south side of Chicago, I grew up with an ignorance toward my Puerto Rican brothers. Because of the way the neighborhoods were segregated, I didn't interact much with other Latino nationalities and didn't really understand or care to understand the importance of our commonalities. I was definitely more focused on the differences and thought of everyone else as an outsider.
>
> Seven years ago, while I was figuring out my way

in a new role at a new company, I still remember, my now Puerto Rican brother, Jimmy Lopez, pulling me aside and giving me the insights needed to effectively navigate the organization. There weren't many Latinos in the business, and he went above and beyond (and gave it to me straight) to protect me and to limit any negative exposure in a tough environment. He was my rock and we looked out for each other. As Latinos, we were family first above everything else and I trusted him completely. Jimmy set the standard of how Latinos need to take care of each other in the workplace and I continue to use his example today in supporting all Latinos—for me, the more nationalities, the better!

Going forward, I am calling on all Latinos to follow Jimmy's example. The mindset of pulling each other down and thinking there's not enough room for all of us is obsolete. If we are serious about significantly growing representation (and I know we are), then it is time to elevate, support, and collaborate with each other like never before. Set the tone and be a role model for our community. This is the type of leadership that will change the game and set the stage for the new Latino leader!

ACTION

Now that we have UNITY top of mind, it's time to spring into action individually and collectively. As stated earlier, now that you are aware of what is required to be an impact player in the workplace, there is no going back to how you previously operated or thought about your career.

Activation Strategies - Making Your Development and Impact Real

PART 4: BRINGING IT ALL TOGETHER: LEVERAGING OUR
NATURAL PASSION AND GRIT

- **Individual:** Identify 2-4 capabilities in this book that you plan on practicing and mastering every six months. Talk to your manager, your mentors, sponsors, and trusted advisors to help you prioritize your development areas and then make them a formal/informal part of your development plan. Always keep them top of mind and continuously work to improve upon them.
    - Note: Remember to use the Latino Leadership Workbook to help you organize and prioritize your development focus areas. This should be a living document that you continuously revisit throughout your career.

- **Individual:** Remember to sharpen the saw and re-read chapters to develop and master your leadership capabilities in certain areas. A best practice for me is to review and re-review areas that I am focused on for development. In order to master topics, you must know the subject matter well so that you can effectively practice and implement the teachings. Using this approach will accelerate your leadership development and leaders in your organization will notice!

- **Collective:** A best practice to jointly activate with a group is to establish a Latino Leadership Club (LLC) and set the goals the group wants to achieve. This can be done through your ERG or any other group that wants to jointly develop themselves. Formalize your goals and share them with your respective managers and leaders; this will bring your development to life and will be a great way to advocate for yourselves. My recommendation is for a group to discuss one topic per month and discuss examples of what you learned and how you practiced on a given area. You will find that others are going through the same struggles as you are, and they will be able to provide additional key insights that have worked for them at your company or school. Also, keep studying and practicing on your own time

as well—take complete ownership of your development as you are the driver of your career!
- **Collective:** Feel free to contact me via refugioatilano.com to book time to talk to your group. I can walk you through the insights, lessons, and story examples to facilitate your development.

ACCOUNTABILTY

As we activate our development toward being new Latino leaders who strive to be impact players in the workplace, it will be critical that we support, elevate, and keep each other focused on improving each day to reach our goals and full potential. We can no longer just sit back, hope for the best, and "wing it." We need to be thoughtful, create and share our plan, and implement a standard of accountability for each other. As we set the tone for how we will show up in the workplace, we need to also set the tone for how we show up to each other. Changing the game will require all of us to move together and jointly develop our leadership capabilities.

Note: For those of us who are comfortable with our current position and career, that is also okay. My guidance is to do what works best for you and your situation. Everyone's path is different and you must take care of yourself and your family first, as your family is where your accountability starts.

I will leave this section with a great quote I captured from Victor Carillo, SVP at Comerica Bank. When I asked him for his thoughts around how Latinos can hold each other accountable for our collective development, he said that he will simply ask, "Where are you at in the book?" For me that said it all—if I see you, I will be asking you the same thing!

THE NEW LATINO LEADER: AN UNSTOPPABLE FORCE!

It's time to add bite to our bark and we are ready to collectively take serious steps towards cutting into the Latino 4% representation gap. You are now informed on what it means to be an impact player and you are also set up to operate with the confidence needed to accelerate your career and realize your full leadership potential. The contributors of this book are all-in on your development; we are your biggest cheerleaders and got your back. We have worked extremely hard to pave the way so that your journey will be smoother and more accelerated. From this point forward, there are no excuses for you not to stand out and be a recognized leader in your organization. Everything you need is at your fingertips with *The Latino Leadership Playbook*, and I am excited to see how far you can go!

FINAL THOUGHTS

Thank you for taking the time to read this book and committing to becoming an informed, confident, high-impact, promotion-ready Latino leader. On behalf of myself and all those who contributed and make this playbook a reality, I sincerely hope for and wish great success for you and your families.

My final request is one I ask of everyone I mentor, our journey together is just the beginning. I want you to pay it forward to everyone you touch. Please mentor others, share these insights and concepts, direct them to get their own *Latino Leadership Playbook*, be a connector, and support all Latinos—as well as non-Latinos. The more you give of yourself, the more you get in return!

Refugio's Key Takeaways:

- **Master your bicultural mindset** - This will take commitment and great practice so you will know when and how to step on the gas or push on the brakes for our cultural scripts.
- **Always lead with a strong game plan** - Know your business area well, focus on being thoughtful, come well-prepared/organized, and always show up ready to contribute something that drives the business forward.
- **Deliver impact in everything you do** - This can be business impact, career impact, relationship impact,

mentorship impact, and overall leadership impact. Lead the way to making BIG things happen for yourself and all others you touch! We are all counting on it.

Now, let's roll!

BONUS CHAPTER:

A Practical Guide for Non-Latinos on How to Support Latinos

In talking to non-Latinos about this playbook, I was asked to create this chapter to provide non-Latinos with key insights and guidance on how to better understand our community, our cultural values, and how they can be leveraged in the workplace. In addition, I was asked to answer the question, what can I do to help advance the Latino community?

This is a great ask and one that needs to be addressed as we Latinos need opportunities, exposure, access, sponsorship, and guidance to accelerate our careers like never before. I will propose strategies that can be used to facilitate the development and partnership with our professional community.

WHY DO WE NEED THE SUPPORT OF ALLIES

Because the Latino representation is so small at senior level roles, in addition to our need to expand our strategic network beyond those who look like us, allies are in the perfect position to help us advance. Today's Latino professional is eager and ready to develop, we just need to right guidance and support to help elevate us to new heights.

THE LATINO ALLY SUPPORT FRAMEWORK

I have broken down what successful support looks like in the following framework. The goal is to provide a simple way for allies to quickly understand what it will require to help move the needle to help advance the development of Latino professionals.

Insight 1: Understand the Latino cultural scripts - These insights will automatically put you in an advantage position with our community.

- Here is a simple breakdown of our most common cultural scripts and will establish the foundation for how to connect with us:
    - **We are raised to be very respectful.** We are not naturally comfortable talking about ourselves, being in the spotlight, or challenging the ideas of senior leaders. At times, this leads to not speaking up or coming across as submissive.
    - **We are very family and group oriented.** We are naturally collaborative and thrive in group settings. We prioritize our relationships and often see work colleagues as family.
    - **We are known to keep our heads down and work hard.** This starts at an early age as our parents preached to us to work hard and we will be rewarded—in today's environment, however, we learned that this is not the case.

- We are raised and operate with strong faith. In general, our faith is a big part of our lives and we put tremendous trust in it. We believe that there is a plan for us and that it's part of our destiny. This can sometimes lead us to believe that it's out of our control and in God's hands.

Insight 2: Partner with us to develop our mindset as well as our skillset - Most times, people try to help us by diving right into the skillset; however, without the mindset shift, the skillset development can often be limited.

- First, take time to identify and mentor a Latino/a professional—we are ready to engage.
  - Plug into the Latino ERGs, Talent Acquisition, DEI team, or your business unit HR partner to identify Latinos that would be great mentee candidates.

- Given the cultural scripts covered above, we need your help in breaking barriers. For example, provide strategies and work with us on the importance of being bold, advocating for ourselves, coming to the table with well-prepared ideas and perspectives, and how to present them confidently and effectively. Additionally, talk to us about the importance of adding value outside of our standard role and how to do it; provide ideas about how to strategically engage in other parts of the organization to develop ourselves and share our brand outside of our core team.

Insight 3: Help provide opportunities for exposure, experience, and access - Because we naturally work hard and keep our head down (only focus on our core job), we need your help to raise our head (awareness) and get involved in other parts of the business to add value outside of our core responsibilities.

- Assuming that performance is good, you know their key development needs, and the direct manager is on board, look for ways to engage your mentee in other parts of the business. Whether it be providing warm introductions for meet and greets with other senior leaders, advocating for a short-term volunteer assignment in another area, a recommendation for a new role, an ERG leadership assignment recommendation, etc. The goal here is to find ways to support your mentee's development through providing opportunities and access to other leaders and business units throughout the organization.

Insight 4: Hold us accountable for our development and adding value for you - The Latino development is not all on you; we also have work to do as this is a two-way street. As my brother, Michael Atilano, HR professional at Google, states, "It's important that we have the same level of accountability as any other mentee, so please don't go easy on us or lower the standard." Ensure to work with us to have specific objectives and scheduled check-ins. Your mentee should drive these touch points. Also, be sure to request how your mentee can help you achieve your business and/or team goals.

- It will be critical that the partnership is mutually beneficial. Who knows, this relationship can potentially turn into sponsorship down the line if done effectively.
- Also, be sure your mentee has a development game plan based on the concepts of *The Latino Leadership Playbook*—it provides the perfect development framework for us.

*Note: If you want to impact the greater Latino community at your company, an effective way to do that is to place an order of Latino Leadership Playbooks from my website: refugioatilano.com. You can hand them out and immediately help accelerate their leadership development.

A PRACTICAL GUIDE FOR NON-LATINOS ON HOW TO SUPPORT LATINOS

I am hopeful that you found the insights and recommendations of this section helpful. My goal was to put you in an informed position to connect with and effectively elevate the Latino professional. As discussed, there is a mindset, skillset, and opportunity element that all need attention when it comes to our development—you are in a great position to help us in each of these areas. We are ready more than ever before to partner with you, as well as support you and your business needs in return!

LATINA AND LATINO SPOTLIGHTS
A Closing Note from Yai Vargas

As a young Latina immigrant growing up in the New York City area and more specifically having been raised in corporate America by various mentors, I always make it a point to share how financial wellness (not literacy) has been a cornerstone of my professional journey. The reason I say it's not financial literacy is because if you don't have the necessary tools and resources available to you (yet), I wouldn't necessarily consider you illiterate in this space. It's simply, and fortunately, something you can learn to get better at understanding. Financial wellness has provided me with the stability, peace of mind and options to excel in my career. Most importantly, it has allowed me to pivot from corporate professional to entrepreneur to now non-profit leader.

Financial wellness goes hand in hand with career development and growth because if your financial life isn't in order, nothing is in order. It impacts your feelings, emotions, relationships, and freedom. For anyone, and especially my Latino community, achieving financial wellness is imperative when planning to create generational wealth. At a very young age we are taught the value of a dollar and at some point down the line, specifically at age 16 for young Latinas, we are paid less than white boys the same age. And the pay gap for us only grows from there. I have carried the responsibility of sharing what Latina Equal Pay Day means for us and how to start demanding more for ourselves.

For me, it has always been critical to talk about the cultural challenges that have put us in this position and more importantly WHAT to do to get out of it. This book connects directly to those solutions: self-awareness, self-advocacy, sponsorship cultivation, community engagement and intentional and strategic professional development. As you grow in your career, I encourage you to also seek mentors to help you make informed choices in saving, investing, and managing debt. In conclusion, my own financial wellness experiences have been the driving force behind my success which has allowed me to weather storms and seize opportunities like entrepreneurship. I hope that you too can take control of your destiny, break barriers and foster a legacy of prosperity for generations to come.

	DRR ADVISORS
	Dr. Robert Rodriguez is the Founder and President of DRR Advisors LLC, a diversity consulting firm specializing in Latino talent management initiatives. Many consider Dr. Rodriguez to be the nation's leading expert in helping companies recruit, retain, and develop Latino professionals. He has worked with over 300 companies helping them with their Latino talent strategy.
Note for Reader	Dr. Rodriguez is the son of Mexican migrant workers. He was born in Texas but grew up in Minnesota. His personal journey regarding his sense of Latino identity is what helps him connect with Hispanic professionals in the workplace. His previous work experience at such companies as Target Corporation, 3M, British Petroleum and The Washington Post is what allows him to have unique insights into how to implement effective Latino talent management programs that produce results within an organization.
Accomplishments	<ul><li>Top 10 Líderes Award. *Hispanic Executive magazine* (2020)</li><li>Maestro Award. *Latino Leaders magazine* (2019)</li><li>Top 100 Most Influential Latinos in Corporate America. *Hispanic Business magazine* (2010)</li><li>Advisory Council Member for the Hispanic Scholarship Fund</li><li>Serves on the board of Trustees for the National Museum of Mexican Art in Chicago, IL</li></ul>
Programs	<ul><li>Co-creator of the 2-day Latino Leadership Intensive (LLI) program with Angel Gomez, President of Angel Gomez Consulting LLC</li><li>Founder of the Consortium of Latino Employee Organizations (CLEO). CLEO brings together Latino ERG leaders on a periodic basis to network, share best practices, benchmark, and participate in professional development.</li></ul>
Publications	<ul><li>*Employee Resource Group Excellence*, (2021, Wiley & Sons).</li><li>*Auténtico: The Definitive Guide to Latino Career Success, 2nd Edition*, co-written with Andrés Tapia, (2020, Berrett-Koehler).</li><li>*Latino Talent: Effective Strategies to Recruit, Retain and Develop Hispanic Professionals*, (2008, Wiley & Sons).</li></ul>
Contact Info	Robert@drradvisors.com; www.drradvisors.com

NATIONAL HISPANIC LEADERSHIP COUNCIL

	Eduardo Arabu is the CEO at NHCC and The Latino DEI Collective, and is responsible for day-to-day operations including design, implementation, and execution of organizational development strategies. He also serves as the principal consultant to Fortune 1000 corporations to elevate Hispanic talent, consumers, suppliers, community relations, and ERG strategies.
Note for Reader	Eduardo Arabu is the son of Venezuelan parents. He was born in Caracas and raised in Chicago, IL. His personal and career development stems from working in corporate, non-profits, government, and sport sectors. Given the growing demographics, it is time for Hispanics to rise to leadership position across corporate America and in other sectors. It is important for us to be competent, celebrate accomplishments, and drive the confidence needed to serve in executive leadership roles. Preparation and competency, accomplishments, confidence along with opportunities will lead to greater leadership roles for Latinos.
Accomplishments	• Diversity Executive Leadership Fellowship, American Society of Association Executives (ASAE) • Hispanic Executive of Influence, Hispanic Lifestyle • Latino Leaders Worth Watching, Profiles in Diversity Journal • 4x Forty Under 40 with Color Magazine, NegociosNow, Connect Magazine, and Association Forum • Master's of Science in Public Policy & Management, Carnegie Mellon University
NHCC and Eduardo Services	NHCC has convenes leaders to connect, learn, share, network around thought leadership, best practices, strategies, and resources to elevate their respective Hispanic enterprise strategies. • Hispanic Strategies Development (for talent, customers, suppliers, community relations) • Employee/Business Resource Group Development (governance, operations, programming, engagements) • Keynote presentations and speaking engagements (producer, facilitator, moderator, panelist)
Contact Info	earabu@nhcchq.org; www.nhcchq.org

Bibliography

- Benstead, Sarah. "Seven Soft Skills that are Crucial for Great Leadership." *Breathe*, 12 Apr. 2023, https://www.breathehr.com/en-gb/blog/topic/business-leadership/7-soft-skills-that-are-crucial-for-strong-leadership.

- Carbajal, Frank, and Jose Morey. *Latinx Business Success*. John Wiley & Sons. Inc, 2022.

- Carteret, Marcia. "Cultural Values of Latino Patients and Families." *Dimensions of Culture*, 15 Mar. 2011, https://www.dimensionsofculture.com/2011/03/cultural-values-of-latino-patients-and-families/.

- CFI Team. "Communication Skills." *Corporate Finance Institute*, 17 Apr. 2023, corporatefinanceinstitute.com/resources/management/communication/.

- Clark, Connie. "How to Challenge your Boss Respectfully." *nzherald.co.nz*, 3 Nov. 2017, https://www.nzherald.co.nz/business/how-to-challenge-your-boss-respectfully/ARLRNHCBKAGRFQSEWUYV33P57E/.

- Connley, Courtney. "Report: The Race and Gender of Your Office 'Sponsor' Can Affect Your Salary." *CNBC: Make It*, 9 Sept. 2019, https://www.cnbc.com/2019/09/09/the-race-and-gender-of-your-office-sponsor-can-affect-your-salary.html.

- Dabbah, Mariela. "How to Leverage your Latino Traits in the Workplace." *Mamiverse*, 28 July 2016, https://mamiverse.com/how-to-leverage-your-latino-traits-in-the-workplace-3871/7/.

- "DEI+ at SLAC: *Diversity, Equity and Inclusion*." DEI+ at SLAC | Diversity, Equity and Inclusion, 2023, inclusion.slac.stanford.edu/.

- Den Heijer, Alexander. *Leader Quote*. 8 Dec. 2014.

- Diversity Jobs Team. "Hispanic Culture at Work- Understanding and Managing Hispanic Employees." *Diversity Jobs*, 15 Apr. 2022, www.diversityjobs.com/

BIBLIOGRAPHY

career-advice/team-building/hispanic-culture-at-work-understanding-and-managing-hispanic-employees/.

- Eatough, Erin. "What Is Networking and Why Is It So Important?" *BetterUp*, 15 Mar. 2023, https://www.betterup.com/blog/networking#:~:text=Networking%20can%20open%20doors%20to,your%20dream%20job%20one%20day.

- Emeritus Staff. "Why Are Communication Skills Necessary for Good Leadership?" *Emeritus*, 22 May 2023, https://emeritus.org/in/learn/why-are-communication-skills-necessary-for-good-leadership/.

- Flinders, Jenni, director. *Own Your Personal Brand. TEDxBellevueCollege*, YouTube, 10 May 2017, https://www.youtube.com/watch?v=QAd54DkXCr4.

- Gibbs, Vanessa. "85% of Career Success Comes from Soft Skills — Need A Crash Course?" *Blinkist Magazine*, 14 Sept. 2022, https://www.blinkist.com/magazine/posts/career-success-comes-from-soft-skills.

- Guilani, Carolyne. "Self-Advocacy: What Is This & How to Develop This Skill?" *Everhour*, 24 Aug. 2022, https://everhour.com/blog/self-advocacy/.

- Hansen, Hans F. *How to Stand Out.*

- Hansen, Aimee. "Why Creating Inclusion at Senior Levels Requires Formal Sponsorship." *The Glasshammer*, 13 Oct. 2022, https://theglasshammer.com/2022/10/why-creating-inclusion-at-senior-levels-requires-formal-sponsorship/.

- Hewlett, Sylvia Ann, et al. "U.S. Latinos Feel They Can't Be Themselves at Work." *Harvard Business Review*, 11 Oct. 2016, https://hbr.org/2016/10/u-s-latinos-feel-they-cant-be-themselves-at-work.

- HopGroup Staff. "Three Key Characteristics of Hispanic Culture That Can Support Your Strategy." *HOPGROUP*, 2023, hopgr.com/2020/03/19/3-key-characteristics-of-hispanic-culture-that-can-support-your-strategy/.

- Indeed Staff. "How to Gain Respect at Work ." *Indeed*, 27 Oct. 2022, https://www.indeed.com/career-advice/career-development/how-to-gain-respect-at-workplace.
- Indeed Staff. "Tips for Adding Value at Work (Plus a How-to Guide)." *Indeed*, 30 Sept. 2022, https://ca.indeed.com/career-advice/career-development/adding-value.
- Indeed Staff. "21 Soft Skills for Leadership Success." *Indeed*, 3 Feb. 2023, https://www.indeed.com/career-advice/career-development/soft-skills-for-leadership.
- JPMorgan Chase & Co. Staff. "The Importance of Mentors and Sponsors in Career Development." *JPMorgan Chase & Co.*, 2020, www.jpmorganchase.com/news-stories/the-importance-of-mentors-and-sponsors-in-career-development.
- Julian. "Personal Branding: Why It Matters." *The Branding Journal*, 4 Aug. 2022, https://www.thebrandingjournal.com/2022/08/personal-branding/.
- Keddell, Kate. "The Power of Being 'Politically Savvy' in the Workplace." *Linkedin*, 8 Apr. 2022, https://www.linkedin.com/pulse/power-being-politically-savvy-workplace-kate-hesson/.
- Keller, Kim. "Speaking of Miley: Hey Kid, Learn from Latinos and Respect Your Elders." *Fox News*, 12 Sept. 2013, https://www.foxnews.com/opinion/speaking-of-miley-hey-kid-learn-from-latinos-and-respect-your-elders.
- Kissflow Staff. "What Is Collaboration? A Complete Guide to Collaboration in 2022." *Kissflow*, 16 Aug. 2022, https://kissflow.com/digital-workplace/collaboration/what-is-collaboration/.
- Komen, Susan. "Breast Cancer Education Toolkit for Hispanic/Latino Communities." *Susan G. Komen*, 2022, https://komentoolkits.org/wp-content/uploads/2013/11/Applying-Culturally-Responsive-Communication-in-Hispanic-Latino-Communities.pdf.
- Kurtuy, Andrei. "Why Is Networking Important | 5 Benefits and Tips for 2023." *Novoresume*, 4 Jan. 2023, https://novoresume.com/career-blog/why-is-networking-important.

- Landry, Lauren. "8 Essential Leadership Communication Skills." *Harvard Business School*, 14 Nov. 2019, https://online.hbs.edu/blog/post/leadership-communication.
- Leading Effectively Staff. "6 Aspects of Political Skill." *Center for Creative Leadership*, 27 Nov. 2020, https://www.ccl.org/articles/leading-effectively-articles/6-aspects-of-political-skill/.
- Mantas, Jesus, et al. "Untapped Potential: The Hispanic Talent Advantage." IBM, 2020, https://www.ibm.com/thought-leadership/institute-business-value/en-us/report/hispanic-talent-advantage.
- Marsh, Anna. "5 Reasons You Should Dream Big In Life!" *Thrive Global*, 3 July 2018, https://community.thriveglobal.com/5-reasons-you-should-dream-big-in-life/.
- MasterClass Staff. "How to Use the 7-38-55 Rule to Negotiate Effectively." *MasterClass*, 7 June 2021, https://www.masterclass.com/articles/how-to-use-the-7-38-55-rule-to-negotiate-effectively.
- Metcalf, Christina. "Leadership During Change: How To Be a Great Change Leader." *Indeed*, 16 Mar. 2023, https://www.indeed.com/career-advice/career-development/what-is-change-leadership.
- Cole, Bianca Miller. "10 Reasons Why Networking IS Essential for Your Career." *Forbes*, 20 Mar. 2019, https://www.forbes.com/sites/biancamillercole/2019/03/20/why-networking-should-be-at-the-core-of-your-career/?sh=6b651c3b1300.
- Mind Tools Content Team. "Active Listening: Hear What People Are Really Saying." *MindTools*, 2023, https://www.mindtools.com/az4wxv7/active-listening.
- Nicoletti, Kimber. "¿Habla Español?: Working with Spanish-Speaking Victims/Survivors in a Rural Setting | National Sexual Violence Resource Center (NSVRC) ¿Habla Español?: Working with Spanish-Speaking Victims/Survivors in a Rural Setting." Multicultural Efforts to end Sexual

Assault. Just Rural! Conference for OVW Rural grantees, June 2010, Denver. https://www.nsvrc.org/sites/default/files/Publications_Habla-Espanol-Working-with-Spanish-speaking-Victims.pdf.

- Southern, Molly. "Employee Voice in the Workplace [Ultimate Guide]." *Oak Engage*, 8 Mar. 2023, www.oak.com/blog/employee-voice-in-the-workplace/.

- Owen, Erin. "Executive Presence—What Is It and Why You Need It." *LinkedIn*, 5 Oct. 2022, https://www.linkedin.com/pulse/executive-presence-what-why-you-need-erin-owen-mba-pcc/.

- Phan, Janet T. "Apply to a Job, Even If You Don't Meet All Criteria." *Harvard Business Review*, 20 July 2022, https://hbr.org/2022/07/apply-to-a-job-even-if-you-dont-meet-all-criteria.

- Rangaiah, Babs. *Napkin Sketch on Success*. 2012.

- Reaume, Theresa, director. Networking for Success. TED, Mar. 2018, https://www.ted.com/talks/theresa_reaume_networking_for_success_jan_2018.

- Reeves, Matthew. *Mentorship vs Sponsorship: Why Both Are Important*, 5 July 2021, https://www.togetherplatform.com/blog/mentorship-sponsorship-differences.

- Reeves, Matthew. "What is the Purpose of Mentoring Programs," Together, 1 May 2023. https://www.togetherplatform.com/blog/what-is-the-purpose-of-mentoring

- Rice, Hugh. "Fatalism", *The Stanford Encyclopedia of Philosophy* (Spring 2023 Edition), Edward N. Zalta & Uri Nodelman (eds.), URL = <https://plato.stanford.edu/archives/spr2023/entries/fatalism/>.

- Rios-Vargas, Merarys. "Hispanic Origin Population in the United States: Highlights from the 2020 Census and American Community Survey." Used in 2022 Hispanic Leadership Summit.

BIBLIOGRAPHY

- Rodriguez, Dr. Robert, and Andres Tomas Tapia. Auténtico: The Definitive Guide to Latino Career Success. Latinx Institute Press, 2017.
- Ross Saperstein, Samantha. "How to Find a Sponsor to Boost Your Career." *Time*, 24 Jan. 2022, https://time.com/charter/6130567/sponsor-mentor-career/.
- Northwest Executive Education Staff. "10 Leadership Traits for Senior Management." *Northwest Executive Education*, 17 Aug. 2023, https://northwest.education/insights/careers/10-leadership-traits-for-senior-management/.
- Kennedy, Julia Taylor, and Pooja Jain-Link. "Unlocking the Power of Latino Employees in the Workplace." *The Glasshammer*, 4 Oct. 2018, https://theglasshammer.com/2018/10/unlocking-the-power-of-latino-employees-in-the-workplace/.
- Sadun, Raffaella, et al. "The C-Suite Skills That Matter Most." *Harvard Business Review*, 26 Sept. 2022, hbr.org/2022/07/the-c-suite-skills-that-matter-most.
- Samur, Alex. "Collaborative Leadership: An Inclusive Way to Manage Virtual Teams." *Slack Technologies*, 17 Mar. 2022, https://slack.com/blog/collaboration/collaborative-leadership-top-down-team-centric.
- Schneider, Meredith. "5 Strategies for Salary Negotiation as a Latina." *Best Colleges*, 3 Aug. 2022, https://www.bestcolleges.com/careers/salary-negotiation-strategies-for-latinas/.
- Siena Heights Staff. "10 Reasons Leadership Is Important in the Workplace." *Siena Heights University*, 8 Dec. 2022, www.sienaheights.edu/10-reasons-leadership-is-important-in-the-workplace/.
- Spence, Jacq. "Nonverbal Communication: How Body Language & Nonverbal Cues Are Key." *LifeSize*, 18 Feb. 2020, https://www.lifesize.com/blog/speaking-without-words/.
- Valentine, Gerry. "Executive Presence: What Is It, Why You Need It and How to Get It." *Forbes*, 31 July 2018, https://

- www.forbes.com/sites/forbescoachescouncil/2018/07/31/executive-presence-what-is-it-why-you-need-it-and-how-to-get-it/?sh=8c8e2786bc7f.
- Vemparala, Tejas. "Navigating Your Career Path: How to Map It Out." *Business News Daily*, 28 Feb. 2023, https://www.businessnewsdaily.com/8651-career-path-planning.html.
- VXI Marketing. "Taking Ownership: A Leader's Best Quality." *VXI*, 2 Dec. 2021, https://vxi.com/blog/taking-ownership-a-leaders-best-quality/.
- We Are All Human Staff. "Hispanic Sentiment Study 2023." *We Are All Human*, 2023, www.weareallhuman.org/research/hispanic-sentiment-study/.
- We Are All Human Staff. "The Hispanic Perception Study 2020." *We Are All Human*, 2020. https://www.weareallhuman.org/wp-content/uploads/2020/12/H-Code_WAAH_The-Hispanic-Perception-Study.pdf.
- Willman, Nubia. "Culture Conflict: Being Humble." *Latinas Uprising*, 19 Nov. 2014, latinasuprising.com/being-humble/.

ABOUT THE AUTHOR

"The days of only focusing on your role, working hard, and "hoping to get promoted" are over. It's now time to show up big and to swing big! It's time to take bold action and for the new Latino/a leader to step up and show the real impact our community is ready to make!"

— Refugio A. Atilano

Refugio is a second-generation Mexican-American Latino born and raised in Chicago, IL. He's a first-generation graduate and business leader with vast experience working in many corporate environments for Fortune 500 companies.

Refugio's passion is in developing Latino leaders for the current and future generations. He strongly believes in the importance and power of sharing knowledge to develop the collective leadership capabilities for all Latinos. Because Latinos are currently almost 20% of the population, but only represent 4% of the seats in senior management roles, he is extremely passionate about using his experience and strategic network to develop tangible solutions to begin to close that gap!

Refugio strongly believes in the power and influence of the Latino community and is a strong advocate for our leadership potential. He is hyper-focused on developing our community's leadership capabilities through The Latino Leadership Playbook, with more programming to come soon that will be targeting college and high school students so they can be set up for leadership success at an early age and are workplace-ready coming out of school.

Refugio's brand is one of professionalism, determination, vision and execution, and exceptional relationships. He strongly believes that our natural Latino superpowers (i.e., problem solvers, passionate, and team-players) will be a game-changer for the new Latino leader. He is committed to showing how to bring those elements to life so that we begin to add unique impact as a professional community and set us up to be the new Latino leaders of tomorrow!

ABOUT *THE LATINO LEADERSHIP PLAYBOOK* CONTRIBUTORS

Illiana Acosta, Leader at Major Tech Firm and Global Speaker

Illianna Acosta is no stranger to community-building. Her leadership with ERGs, with a focus on Diversity, Equity, and Inclusion, goes hand-in-hand to help people and organizations amplify their connection to community, leadership, and belonging. With an infectious positive perspective, confidence, compassion, and layered high-energy, Illianna draws inspiration from humble beginnings that taught her a great deal about choosing a future outside of what she saw in front her. She was born to Dominican parents and raised by her single mom in Queens, NY, so hustle and grit flow through her in every way.

Illianna has over 20 years of experience in Ad Sales, Partnerships, and Tech Industry. Today, she is a Leadership Architect and Senior Manager at LinkedIn, managing Global AdTech Partnerships that accelerate innovation, revenue, and customer growth and the former Global Co-Chair of LinkedIn's Hispanic Employee Resource Group. She is a sought-out Speaker on Leadership Development and DEI topics, and author of *Lost in Translation*, a newsletter focused on highlighting challenges and limitations under-represented groups experience that have shaped who we are and how we show up in our personal and professional lives. Illianna was named one of Cornell's Notable 10 Under 10 Alumni and is the Co-President of the Cornell Johnson School NY Alumni Organization.

Enrique Acosta Gonzalez, CEO, Triad Leadership Solutions, LLC

Enrique is the CEO of Triad Leadership Solutions LLC, and has served as an Executive, Veteran and Advocate, Board Member, Non-Profit Administrator, Speaker, Mentor, Coach, and Avid Volunteer. Over the past 30 years, Enrique has held numerous executive advisor and senior positions while serving in the United States Navy and civilian sector. Through education and training, he helped strengthen organizations, providing sound decision support and creating open communication at all levels. Enrique also helped formulate and implement policies concerning morale, welfare, job satisfaction, discipline, and training of personnel.

Enrique was a 2023 Top 200 Biggest Voices in Leadership and 2023 Global 100 Executive Coach of the Year, for his work in the leadership development arena. He is a sought-after John Maxwell certified coach, trainer, and speaker and is an avid mentor in three national and international organizations. His impactful delivery of leadership truths leaves the listener with renewed hope and energized to regain their position in leadership and make an impact in their sphere of influence.

He is an award-winning podcaster, with four shows focusing on leadership development and career success. He was named the 2021 Active Duty, Veteran and Military Spouse Entrepreneur Awards, Media Professional of the Year by The Rosie Network. His down-to-earth approach on leadership has gained him notoriety as one of the most sought out leadership trainers.

Beatriz Albini-Ruiz, PCC, CPC, ELI- MP, PHR, Executive Leadership and Career Success Coach, CEO of Prime YOU Coaching LLC

Beatriz is a certified Executive Leadership and Career Success Coach passionate about empowering diverse professionals to lead with balance and confidence. In 2020 she founded Prime YOU Coaching, a boutique coaching and HR consulting firm where she provides services such as Executive Leadership Development, Transformational Leadership, and DEI/ERG coaching. Whenever she is not coaching, blogging, or delivering workshops, you can find her in her garden with her husband and two boys.

Arabel Alva Rosales, President and CEO of AAR Tech, Founder and Producer of Runway Latinx (RLx), Founder and Chairman of Pivoting in Heels (PIH), NFP

Arabel is an entrepreneur that has been described in *Chicago*

Magazine as a "Renaissance Woman" because of her ability to discuss concerns on Wall Street, global issues, and what is happening in our communities. She is a lifestyle and career expert, who offers personal insights in tech, finance, government, the arts, and fashion.

Arabel is President and CEO of AAR Tech, a successful Management and Technology Firm with over 17 years of experience. She is the proud founder of Pivoting in Heels, NFP, a digital non-for-profit dedicated to empowering women. Founder and CEO of Runway Latinx, a globally recognized social enterprise that encompasses fashion, gastronomy, entertainment, and has impacted thousands of lives as a successful social enterprise.

Arabel has a juris doctor degree from Depaul College of Law and has been a part of multiple gubernatorial transition teams. She is a recipient of over thirty local and national recognitions and awards, including the Anti-Defamation League, Women Achievement award, a Business Leaders of Color Recognition, and, in 2020, was named one of the 50 Most Influential Latinos by Negocios Now. She is also featured and co-author of *Hispanic Stars Rising*.

Michael Atilano, HR Operational Excellence Lead, Google

Michael is a Human Resources Leader with 20 years of experience across several industries and areas of HR. He is currently leading global insights for frontline HR with the goal of bringing "small company" agility to a large global organization. Michael practices servant leadership to foster an environment that values different perspectives to solve complex problems. Through this strengths-based team approach and data-driven decisions, teams are empowered to challenge the HR status quo and find new ways to meet business needs.

Michael is passionate about being a part of the solution that progresses Latinos/Latinas into senior leadership. Equipped with years of HR experience on how career decisions are made by leaders, Michael believes that senior leadership is within the grasp of mid-level Latino/Latina professionals if they can find a way to bring their authentic leadership to the workplace. Michael states, "We have the talent, we see the door... now we just have to open it."

America Baez, Talent Acquisition and Diversity, Equity and Inclusion Leader

America Baez has an extensive career as a global thought leader in talent acquisition and diversity, equity, and inclusion (DEI). She has implemented transformational global DEI talent solutions for Fortune 100 companies and is a co-author of *Today's Inspired Leader Vol. 4*. Her chapter is titled: "Become the Leader You Are Meant to Be."

America grew up in Mexico in a family of teachers, politicians, artists, and poets who inspired her to follow her biggest dreams. She attended the Universidad Autónoma de Tamaulipas in Mexico and earned her MBA at Texas A&M International University. There she began a leadership journey that took her throughout corporate America while giving her a chance to uplift others, which is vital to her personally and professionally.

Andrea Best, Vice President at a Top-10 Global Pharma Company

Andrea Best serves as the Vice President of Medical Aesthetics and Device Safety, Clinical Trials Safety and Insights for a top-10 pharma company, bringing over 25 years of experience in academia and the pharmaceutical Industry. Andrea's broad experience spans numerous therapeutic areas including aesthetics, medical devices, oncology, immunology, anti-infectives, renal, anesthesia, and general medicine. She has led discussions with global regulatory authorities and serves as a consultant to the Bill & Melinda Gates Foundation helping strengthen pharmacovigilance safety systems in low-middle income countries.

Andrea has a personal passion for the growth and development of young professionals. She is an avid traveler and enjoys sharing adventures with her family, including skiing, scuba diving, and hiking.

About the Latino Leadership Playbook Contributors

Dr. Jairo Borja, Master Networker, Small Business Champion, and Real Estate Investor

Dr. Jairo Borja has over 20 years of experience in financial services, higher education, nonprofit, multifamily real estate, assisting small businesses with business planning and access to capital. He helps people make double-digit returns by investing in real estate. He is the bestselling author for his book, *Networking Your Way to Success, 10 Steps to Building Relationships & Expanding Your Business for Entrepreneurs & Working Professionals.*

Dr. Jairo grew up in Corona, Queens, NY. He was the first in the household to obtain a college degree, one of the first in his family to obtain a Master's, and the only one currently with a Doctorate. He attended Walden University for his Doctor of Business Administration, Long Island University for his MBA, and Berkeley College for his Bachelor of Business Administration Degree.

Xavier Cano, President of Xavier Cano Coaching

Xavier Cano is one of America's leading peak performance coaches. For the last 20 years, he has been coaching individuals and groups on both professional development and peak performance topics, sharing his own methodology and a range of techniques for optimizing performance, cultivating resilience, and increasing the bottom line. Xavier is a certified coach by the International Coaching Federation, a published author, and an international speaker. In 2023, he delivered a speech in India in front of 20,000 people.

Xavier graduated summa cum laude from the University of Houston with a degree in Industrial Engineering and received his MBA from the University of Texas at Austin. He is a certified Project Management Professional (PMP), certified Black Belt in Six Sigma/Lean Methodology, and a certified Change Management practitioner. Xavier has 16+ years working for multiple Fortune 500 companies, including Dell, Bank of America, and Cigna.

In his spare time, he enjoys traveling, exercising, and spending quality time with his wife and daughter.

Dr. Marisol Capellan, PCC, CEO at The Capellan Institute, LLC and Author of *Leadership is a Responsibility*

Dr. Marisol Capellán, Keynote Speaker, Award-Winning Educator, Management and Leadership Consultant and Executive Coach. Dr. Capellan is the Founder of The Capellan Institute, a leadership, coaching, and corporate training company specializing in workplace culture, diversity, equity and inclusion, and soft skills development. Dr. Capellan is a former lecturer at the University of Miami, Miami Herbert Business School lecturer where she taught management and organizational behavior classes and served as the associate director of their Masters in Leadership program. She holds a doctoral degree in Higher Education Leadership and a Masters of Management with specialization in Leadership from the University of Miami. Her dissertation focus was on the trajectory of women to leadership positions.

As an Afro-Latina, mother, and immigrant, she has faced and witnessed many of the institutional and systemic barriers and biases that Black women face in their career trajectory to leadership roles, which sparked her passion for women's empowerment and the need to increase the representation of women in positions of power. As a result, she published her award-winning book, *Leadership is a Responsibility*, which highlights her career journey experience as a Black Hispanic woman in Academia, the stories of Black women in the workplace, and the need for responsible leaders to create a more equitable society where minorities can belong and thrive.

In addition, her personal story of resilience has been featured on CNN and Telemundo as an unstoppable woman, where she discussed how her mindset helped her life and career trajectory as an immigrant in the United States.

Frank Carbajal, Founder of Silicon Valley Latino Leadership Summit and President of Es Tiempo

Frank is co-author of *Building the Latino Future: Success Stories for the Next Generation,* an inspiring collection of success stories from the country's most prominent Latinos. *Building the Latino Future* offers insight and advice for Latinos in any industry who want to succeed spectacularly. He is also co-author, best-seller *Latinx Business Success* (Wiley publisher).

Frank Carbajal provides small business owners, CEOs, executives, managers, and directors, with the framework and tools necessary to achieve their personal best. Formerly a part of the Ken Blanchard network of keynote speakers and a former member of the Silicon Valley Coaching Federation.

Frank holds an MA, with an emphasis in Human Resources Management. Currently, Frank sits on the Advocacy Board for the Silicon Valley Education Foundation Advisory Board Member of Angeles Investors.

Elisa Charters, Founder of Juego.Juegos AI & Mobile App, Principal of EAC Business International LLC, Co-founder and President of Latina Surge National Nonprofit

Elisa Charters is a seasoned executive strategist with 30+ years of public-sector finance and transactional experience. She specializes in CSR-ESG strategies and the negotiations of major economic development, infrastructure, and transportation initiatives to advance public-private goals.

As a Cornell-certified Industrial Labor and Relations Diversity, Equity, and Inclusion (DEI) professional and as Co-founder and President of Latina Surge National 501c3 nonprofit, Elisa has continued to provide guidance on multiple corporate, government, university, regional, and national platforms, advocating towards advancement of women, especially underrepresented multicultural women. In 2004-2006, she served as President of the Port Authority Hispanic Society Employee Resource Group (agency with 8K employees).

In the last two years, Elisa's interests in AI and innovation have grown, especially relating to addressing mental health and driving the happiness factor via social in-person connectivity. She is the new Founder of the Juego.Juegos AI & Mobile Application, which will be launching its commercial BETA by the close of 2023. This app offers solutions to create "more time for fun and games," and specifically addresses social issues of mental health, bullying, single motherhood/at-risk children, and food insecurity.

Kristin Coleman, DEI Director, Advancing Hispanics and Latinos with a Top 100 Financial Services Firm

Kristin Coleman is a DEI Director, Head of Employee Engagement for Advancing Hispanics and Latinos at JPMorgan Chase, JP Morgan Chase and Co's Global DEI Center of Excellence, established in 2021 to promote the growth and success of Hispanics and Latinos across the globe both inside and out of the firm. Her work focuses on extending opportunities for students, employees, business owners, and communities to help them build a stronger economic foundation. Kristin is responsible for the employee careers and skills strategy and development programming to support increasing representation for Hispanics/Latinos globally, at all levels of the firm and especially executive pipeline. She manages strategic external partnerships with Hispanic/Latino serving professional and talent organizations and delivery of workshops, programs and mentoring to employees. She is responsible for managing key partnerships with JPMC's ERG/BRG network Adelante and the firm's Hispanic Executive/Leadership Forums across the globe to operationalize the strategy. Kristin is responsible for consulting with internal stakeholders, leaders across all JPMC businesses, managing relationships with JPMC's global Adelante network of 27k+ members, Hispanic Executive Forum and related employee groups to align and execute the global DEI strategy, including the Hispanic Heritage month global programming.

Miguel de Jesus, CPC (Certified Professional Coach), Executive Coach, and Sales & Marketing Consultant

Miguel is a highly accomplished, results-oriented C-level leader with more than 35+ years of experience leading business management global sales/marketing with two Fortune 500 companies and a sales executive force of over 1500. A leader in running a $225+M sales organization as a VP, Sales, and most currently providing Leadership and Sales Training to professionals as a Transformational Leadership Consultant and Coach.

As a keynote speaker and transformational change agent, Miguel brings his insights and wisdom to public and corporate audiences. He is a Certified Trainer with the TalentSmart organization in La Jolla, CA, and trains on emotional intelligence and leadership. Miguel is also a Certified Kolbe and Gallup Strengths Coach, focusing on building upon personal and organizational strengths-based learning and development.

Dr. Maria Espinola, CEO, Institute for Health Equity and Innovation

Dr. Espinola is a Harvard-trained psychologist who provides vision, leadership, and strategic planning for the development and implementation of health equity and trauma-informed initiatives in multifaceted organizations. She has a record of successful collaboration with leaders across universities, Fortune 100 companies, non-profit organizations, and the three branches of government.

As a psychologist, Dr. Espinola has provided multilingual psychological services (therapeutic services and psychological evaluations) to thousands of victims of trauma from all over the world. Her work has been recognized with over 25 awards for leadership, health equity initiatives, innovation, and community impact. Dr. Espinola has reached more than 1 billion people via media outlets, including the U.S. News and World Report, The New York Times, CNN, and Forbes.

Dr. Espinola was born and raised in Patagonia, Argentina.

Carlos Garcia, Vice President of Finance for a Global Food Company

Carlos Garcia is a seasoned Finance Executive with over 20 years of experience in the Hospitality and F&B industries. Carlos is known for his community involvement through HACE, local activism, and Latino sponsorship.

Carlos is a proud first-generation Mexican American of Oaxacan descent.

Mimi Garcia, Senior Manager, Growth Strategy and Innovation, Accenture Song

Mimi Garcia is a strategy and innovation leader at Accenture, with cross-industry experience focusing on growth strategies, customer experience design, voice of customer, product innovation, and digital transformations. Mimi has worked with global clients to redefine the customer experience through artificial intelligence and increase customer retention through enhancements to current capabilities, new products/services, insights, and servicing channels.

Mimi is first-generation, Mexican American born in Dallas and raised in the Chicagoland area. She's passionate about mentoring and giving back to her community and currently serves as the National Hispanic American Employee Resource Group Lead supporting 4,500 members. She is a recognized leader in her community being honored as part of Negocios Now Latinos 40 under 40 and Association for Latino Professionals for America (ALPFA) Most Powerful Latinas: Rising Star Award.

Ruby Garcia, Founder of Ruby Garcia Coaching, LLC., Leadership Coach & Hypnotherapist

As a seasoned leader with over a decade of Executive Coaching and Leadership Development experience, coupled with 15 years of sales and training experience, Ruby has always believed in the transformative power of education.

Ruby's work has been centered on the advancement of the Latine community and passing along education that isn't found in any classroom or textbook but comes through shared and lived experiences. Ruby understands the significance for diversity in our educational institutions and workplaces as she was often the only disabled Latina in the room. Her commitment is deeply rooted in her passion for representation and equity. Ruby is on a mission to make Latinos feel heard, seen and valued so they can be a collective force towards positive change.

Angel Gomez, Leadership Expert and Executive Coach to the Fortune 500

Angel's unique and collaborative approach to leadership and executive development, shaped by more than 25 years of diverse professional experiences, has made him a trusted partner to some of the world's leading companies, who count on him to develop better employees, better leaders, and better organizations. Through his workshops, consulting, leadership coaching, speeches, and social media channels, he has helped thousands of people and global brands, like Facebook, Gruppo Campari, Unilever, and Kraft, to strategically approach key initiatives through accelerated performance in marketing, sales, operations, finance and human resources.

Born and raised in Chicago, Angel received his Juris Doctor and his Bachelor of Arts from the University of Illinois at Urbana-Champaign, graduating with honors and distinction for his academic, research, and speaking achievements. Angel has been recognized by several organizations, including the Coach Foundation as a Top 20 Coach, iConexión, which presented him with the Game Changer Award, the Hispanic Alliance for Career Enhancement with their Maestro Award, and Hispanic Business Magazine, who in 2002 named him one of the Most Influential Hispanics in the United States.

Marlene Gonzalez, President LCG Group, LLC, Doctor of Business Administration Candidate in Organizational Neuroscience

LCG Group LLC Founder and president, Marlene González, specializes in leadership development, team effectiveness, and executive coaching. Her primary goal is to advance, develop, and promote minority leaders. She is a renowned executive coach and facilitator, passionate about training and development.

Marlene is the author of the *Leadership Wizard* coaching series, the #1 New Release book in the Education and Leadership category. Her book series focuses on transformational leadership topics and offers easy-to-implement actions with a straight-to-the-point approach.

To share her insights and resources on transformational leadership, Marlene combines Insights Discovery, the psychology of C. G. Jung, neuroscience, and her corporate career experience and professional coaching expertise. She partners with organizations to inspire and transform individuals and teams. Through studying various psychological techniques and exercises, she aims to understand what makes a leader confident, assertive, and emotionally resilient to stress. Please visit her at: www.marlenegonzalez.com.

Sergey Gorbatov, Managing Partner, InTalentSight; Professor at IE Business School, Madrid, Spain

Sergey Gorbatov is a management consultant, educator, and executive coach in the disciplines of human resources and organizational behavior with a wealth of experience in leadership assessment and development.

His systemic approach ensures comprehensiveness and sustainability of organizational solutions. Keenly focused on personal and team growth, Sergey excels in coaching executives and facilitating impactful team sessions at all levels within organizations. His engaging style, deep curiosity, and strategic acumen, consistently drive leaders toward lasting success. As an educator, he brings his extensive executive education and corporate HR background to empower individuals and teams to reach their full potential. He writes, speaks, and teaches about the complex science of human performance, while making it simple.

Delia Gutierrez McLaughlin, President/CEO | AzTech Innovation

Delia is nothing short of a luminary in the technology sector—a Digital Transformation Leader with over two decades of unparalleled expertise, and a STEM and DEI steadfast advocate. A first-generation college graduate, Delia's journey is a tapestry of tenacity and triumph, punctuated by a constellation of accolades that bear witness to her indomitable spirit. It is her spirit and tenacity that is captured in the chapter she co-authored: "Embracing a New Mindset: Working Smarter not Harder throughout your Career".

As an entrepreneurial savant and a vanguard for diversity, her advocacy for diversity and inclusion has not only earned her a place on the illustrious HITEC 100 list but has also made her a beacon for Hispanic communities and aspiring leaders that is deepened by her commitment to "changing the face of the game." Whether it's her passion for sports, like bowling and golf, or her ceaseless advocacy for underrepresented communities, Delia is a force of nature, seamlessly weaving her multifaceted talents into a life that is as impactful as it is inspiring.

Monica Guzman, Executive Coach and Motivational Speaker, Excellence by Monica Guzman

Monica Guzman is a leadership speaker and personal branding coach. She is also the author of *Fearless by Choice and Stop Being a Lazy Leader*. Monica has coached professionals at all levels to raise performance and increase confidence.

Monica was born in Colombia and received her master's degree in counseling psychology from Temple University. From there, she found a passion for business and began her speaking journey on an international level.

Ingrid Harb, Entrepreneur, Diversity, Equity, and Inclusion Consultant and Speaker

Ingrid Harb is an international speaker and founder of two globally recognized organizations, The Women Ambassadors Forum and a DEI Consulting firm, NOTA Inclusion. She also identifies as a #MexicanAmerican. Throughout her upbringing, neither country accepted her wholeheartedly, deciding she was always "too much" of one culture and not enough of the other. This limiting belief didn't stop Ingrid, and she relays the message that it shouldn't stop you either.

At only 29, Ingrid has raised $700k to lead over 20+ global and local forums that have reached women from over 135 countries. Under NOTA Inclusion, Ingrid continues to work with over 50+ Fortune 500 companies' year-round to help produce intersectional experiences and training that promotes and cultivates inclusive workplaces. Over the years, she has also built a speakers bureau arm to her business, working closely with over 150+ leading authors, educators, PHD holders, and experts in the space of diversity, accessibility, leadership, inclusion and equity. Most recently, Ingrid took over the TEDx stage for her very first talk on "The Power of Unlearning."

Lorraine K. Lee, Top-Rated Virtual Speaker, Consultant, LinkedIn Learning Instructor, President of RISE Learning Solutions

Lorraine is a top-rated global keynote speaker, a consultant, and an instructor for Stanford Continuing Studies and LinkedIn Learning. She has 300,000+ LinkedIn followers and 10+ years of experience leading editorial teams at top tech firms.

Lorraine has worked with clients including Zoom, Cisco, Atlassian, and McKinsey and Company. She was named a Top Virtual Speaker by ReadWrite and was also named a finalist for "Global Conference Speaker of the Year" by WomenTech.

Before starting her own company, Lorraine worked at companies including Prezi, SlideShare, and LinkedIn.

She has been featured in publications including Inc., ReadWrite, and Entrepreneur.

ABOUT THE LATINO LEADERSHIP PLAYBOOK CONTRIBUTORS

Pedro Lerma, Founder and Chief Executive Officer, LERMA/ Advertising; Visit me: lermaagency.com

Pedro Lerma has a vision. He sees a world where all people and all cultures are valued and embraced, and he believes in the power of cross-cultural communications, marketing and branding to reshape it. But Pedro is more than a visionary; he's an architect and a builder.

He founded LERMA/, an advertising agency and has been recognized by Advertising Age as Small Agency of The Year for both 2022 and 2023. Brands like Avocados from Mexico, The Salvation Army, He Gets Us and The Home Depot rely on Pedro and his team at LERMA/ for leadership, perspective, and business results.

Pedro is deeply involved in the community serving on the boards of the Catholic Charities of Dallas, United Way of Metropolitan Dallas, Booker T. Washington High School for the Visual and Performing Arts, SMU Meadows School of the Arts, and the Hispanic Marketing Council.

Anthony Lopez, Founder, L&L Advisors; Senior Executive, CEO, Board Member, Leadership Expert and Author, Leadership & Management Consultant and Executive Coach

Tony is a seasoned and well-recognized, successful global business leader. He has held positions such as President, Ansell Healthcare; CEO, AZZUR GROUP; SVP & GM, CareFusion Respiratory Systems; VP, DePuy, Johnson & Johnson, and numerous other corporate leadership positions throughout his career. He also served as a Captain in the United States Air Force. He is the author of seven books in the Legacy Leader Series, including his most recent work entitled *CQ: The Legacy Leader's Superpower: Driving Cultural Intelligence from the Boardroom to the Mailroom, The Legacy Leader as a Superhero: LegacyWoman,* and *Breakthrough Thinking: The Legacy Leader's Role in Driving Innovation.*

Rafael Magaña, Founder and CEO of Latino Professionals, Latina Professionals, and Latinx Professionals

Rafael Magaña stands as the visionary founder of Latino Professionals, Latina Professionals, and Latinx Professionals, united under a grand mission to establish the largest organizations globally. In his pivotal role, he spearheads strategies that catalyze substantial growth and helps leaders expedite strategy implementation within their respective organizations.

An esteemed Veritus Scholar, Rafael specializes in donor-centered philanthropy, adeptly serving as a Major Gift & Planned Giving Officer, facilitating connections that fuel meaningful initiatives. He also lends his expertise as a vital member of the Board of Trustees at the Hollywood Schoolhouse, championing educational advancement.

Residing in Los Angeles, California, Rafael channels his passion for leadership and philanthropy into insightful writings on management, philanthropy, and career trajectories, adding a vital voice to the discourse in these fields. At the core of his journey lies a steadfast commitment to uplift the Latino community, a personal and professional philosophy that continually drives his progressive and impactful endeavors.

Gabino Martinez, Regional Operations Manager, World Electric, President & Founder, Hispanos Unidos ERG, Sonepar USA

Gabino Martinez is currently a Regional Operations Manager with World Electric. He was born and raised in Puerto Rico, and currently resides in Miami, FL. He has over 22 years of experience in the Operations, Distribution and Supply Chain fields in the electrical industry with a Six Sigma Greenbelt Certification, iLead Leadership Essentials Certification and USHCC DEI Training Certification, leading diverse and multicultural teams and supporting the sustainable growth and expansion of World Electric. He has a passion for helping others and elevating Hispanics and Latinos/Latinas in the workplace.

In 2022, he founded and is the current President of the first

Hispanic ERG at Sonepar USA named Hispanos Unidos. He won the 2023 Latino Leadership Award from the Profiles in Diversity Journal. He is also a member of the LatinX Executive Alliance and the Association of Latino Professionals for America (ALPFA). He's an advocate for Hispanic advancement through education and personally, he's helping 4 young adults in Nicaragua, where his wife is from, go through college to change the Hispanic narrative not only in the U.S. but wherever he finds he can help.

Gabino has a Bachelor's in Business Management with Minors in Economics and International Business from Purdue University, where he founded and was the President of the Hispanic Business Student Association, and Treasurer/Regional Representative for the Society of Hispanic Professional Engineers (SHPE) among others. He enjoys traveling and spending time with his family.

Jeffrey Martinez, Executive Vice President, PNC Bank

Jeffrey (Jeff) Martinez is Executive Vice President and Head of Branch Banking at PNC Bank. In his current role, Jeff is responsible for more than 2,400 branches and nearly 16,000 employees, through PNC's coast to coast footprint. He also serves as Executive Sponsor of PNC's Latino and Multicultural Employee Business Resource Group, as well as PNC Unidos.

Martinez joined PNC in 2014 and adds more than 20 years of retail banking experience to PNC's senior leadership team. Prior to PNC, he held various roles at JPMorgan Chase for more than 10 years, including responsibilities as a First Vice President, District Manager.

Martinez also served the country for nine years in the U.S. Army National Guard. He deployed twice in support of Operation Iraqi Freedom and has been awarded three Army Commendation Medals and New Jersey's Distinguished Service Medal.

Martinez is passionate about giving back to the communities where he lives and works and is involved with several non-profit organizations. He is the Treasurer of the Statewide Hispanic Chamber of Commerce of New Jersey, a LatinoJustice PRLDEF

Board Member, and a Member of the NJCU Foundation Board and the Hudson County Community College Employer Advisory Board. Martinez is also an executive advisor to CAALE, whose mission is centered on supporting education within our community and he works with the Association of Latino Professionals for America (ALPFA) to educate students and professionals across the US.

Paola Meinzer, Founder, LEXGOLF

Paola is a Columbian native who migrated to the United States over 20 years ago. She holds a bachelor of arts in psychology and is currently VP of Business Development for Manning Silverman's CPS's and T&B.

Paola's personal passion and mission are to empower women and serve her community. She is the founder of "LEEN" and the Latina Executive Golf Organization (LEXGOLF), which promotes and engages women, especially Latinas, in golf activities to change the status quo. Organizations, like hers, help to accelerate the exposure, opportunities, and access to senior leaders for Latinas through golf.

Jeffrey Mohr, Senior Leader with management experience in many Fortune 500 companies

Jeffrey has over 15 years of experience driving organizational and behavioral change as a management consultant and leader in the healthcare industry. He is an experienced transformation and strategy leader driving growth by developing essential capabilities and aligning operations to support organizational strategy.

Jeff specializes in counseling senior level executives to improve business performance through enterprise growth strategy, capability development, and improved cost position and operational performance. He possess deep healthcare industry expertise including health systems, pharmaceutical and medical device manufacturers, provider networks, and healthcare payers/

insurers. Additionally, Jeff has cross-industry experience in consumer/ retail health and automotive sectors.

He holds a Doctorate in Chemical and Biological Engineering and his dissertation focused on the growth and differentiation of human embryonic stem cells. He has successfully published multiple academic research papers and has various patents issued.

Alina Moran, FACHE, FABC, Hospital President and CEO, Dignity Health - California Hospital Medical Center

Alina Moran is a dynamic healthcare leader known for championing initiatives in health equity, patient safety, and employee engagement, while actively advocating for local and historically marginalized communities. As President of Dignity Health - California Hospital Medical Center (CHMC) in Los Angeles since March 2020, she's overseen development of a leading-edge, four-story patient tower set to open in early 2024, and prioritized integration of CHMC's community health and educational programs with its medical care to be a "hospital without walls" that addresses social determinants of health.

Moran previously served as the CEO of NYC Health + Hospitals/Metropolitan and as the CFO of NYC Health + Hospitals/Elmhurst. She holds a bachelor's degree in mechanical engineering from Brown University and a master's degree in public administration from Baruch College. Moran has garnered national recognition from renowned publications, such as Becker's Hospital Review and the Los Angeles Business Journal. Her community leadership includes serving on the boards of the Hospital Association of Southern California (HASC) and Coro Southern California, and as the National Board Chair of Hispanic Alliance for Career Enhancement (HACE). Originally from the Bronx, New York, Moran now resides in Chatsworth, California, with her husband and two children.

Gaby Natale, 3-Time Daytime Emmy winner, Speaker, Author and Entrepreneur

Gaby is among just a few women in the entertainment industry who not only owns the rights to her media content, but also a television studio. This unique situation has allowed her to combine her passion for media and her entrepreneurial spirit, which continues to help her break barriers. In 2021, Gaby became the first Latina author to be published by the leadership division of HarperCollins.

Gaby has been featured in Forbes, CNN, Buzzfeed, NBC News, Univision, and Latino Leaders magazine. In 2018, *People* magazine named her one of the "25 Most Powerful Latinas," highlighting the inspirational story of how she went from a local TV show that started out of a carpet warehouse to becoming the only Latina in US history to win triple back-to-back Daytime EMMYs. In the digital world, she has a thriving fan base with over 52 million views on YouTube and 250K+ followers on social media.

A consummate entrepreneur, Gaby is also the founder of AGANARmedia, a marketing company with a focus on Hispanic audiences that serves Fortune 500 companies such as Hilton Worldwide, Sprint, AT&T, eBay, and Amazon.

Yared Oliveros, Staff Diversity, Equity, and Inclusion Partner, Tesla

Yared Oliveros is a Diversity, Equity, and Inclusion Leader at Tesla and serves as the current Employee Resource Group Program Advisor for North America and EMEA. Prior to joining Tesla, she began her career in Recruiting and shortly after in HR at Nestlé USA supporting all of Retail Sales in N.A. and drove performance and development training in addition to talent development efforts. Yared earned a master's degree in organizational management from the University of Phoenix and Bachelor of Science degree from Mount St. Mary's University. She is a contributing author for Latinas Rising Up in HR, Vol. 2 and *The Latino Leadership Playbook*.

Yared grew up in Inglewood, CA, is an active leader in her neighborhood and parish, St. Anthony Catholic Church. In her spare time, she puts together networking and inspirational events for local and nearby community residents, called Because We Can, in hopes to drive, inspire, and foster positive change in individuals' personal and professional journey by inviting industry leaders and guest speakers from different industries to share their own personal journey. Sigamos Adelante, si se Puede!

Jon Orozco, MBA, SHRM-SCP, Fractional Chief People Officer

Hailing from Guadalajara, Jalisco, Jon has traveled the world. Jon grew up in Washington State, establishing his roots on a migrant farm when his grandfather brought his children from Mexico to work as farm laborers, including Jon as a baby.

He has served as COO and CPO for several companies, including start-ups and mature growth companies. He is a trusted project principal for effective HR strategy and development projects. He is dedicated to developing and advancing the profession of People Operations, with a focus on preparing companies for a 2030 workforce. Through his work as a fractional Chief People Officer and HR Business Partner, Jon has helped hundreds of companies worldwide make meaningful progress in their diversity, equity, and inclusion initiatives and has facilitated difficult conversations around these important issues.

Carlos F. Orta, Founder and CEO, LATINOS In Procurement; Former CEO, Hispanic Association on Corporate Responsibility (HACR), and Co-Founder of the Latino Corporate Directors Association (LCDA) and its Foundation.

With a wealth of experience garnered at five prestigious Fortune 500 companies—Anheuser-Busch, Carnival Corporation, Ford Motor Company, Tyson Foods, and Waste Management—Carlos' expertise spans across government relations, communications, philanthropy, and diversity, equity, and inclusion (DE&I). He also served as CEO of the Hispanic Association on Corporate Responsibility, from 2006-2014.

A graduate of Barry University (BA), Carlos is presently pursuing a master's degree from Georgetown University. Born in Havana, Cuba, his family left the communist country and settled in Miami, FL in the early 1970s.

Luz H. Perez, HRBP Director, CDW

Luz Perez was born in the Dominican Republic, raised in New York, and is now a proud mother to two beautiful daughters. She describes her experiences and life transitions as ever evolving. Starting at a very young age, Luz developed a passion and drive to make a difference in her community. Her need to evolve and continue to learn about her roots led her to join college organizations where she gained leadership skills and community involvement. Luz earned a sociology degree and a master's degree at Binghamton University.

Luz has spent the last eleven years at a Fortune 200 company specializing in IT services and solutions, most recently, as Director HRBP and Head of HR for Canada. As part of the Canadian executive team, her job consists of partnering with business leaders to oversee the implementation of strategic initiatives and corporate policy practices and assisting with implementing solutions to meet talent goals. Throughout the years, Luz has developed a deep passion for the human resources field, and especially enjoys coaching and developing people. Her business goal is to always accept new challenges in efforts to expand her business acumen and to attain well-rounded experiences to start a future consulting business in HR.

Maryanne Pina Frodsham, CEO, Career Management Partners

Maryanne is the CEO of CMP, a talent solutions firm providing executive search, coaching, and transition solutions globally. In addition, leveraging CMP's decades of research, Maryanne created the Latino Career Assessment™ (LCA™), which provides assessment and development solutions for Latino professionals. Visit at: www.careermp.com and www.latinocareerassessment.com.

Brenda Pineda, Director Human Resources, Robertet, Inc.; Co-author, *Latinas Rising Up in HR*, 2022

Brenda Sanchez-Pineda is Senior Director of Human Resources at Robertet, Inc., a fragrance and flavor manufacturer with offices in New York, New Jersey, and Canada. She leads the first-ever diversity, equity, and inclusion strategy at Robertet, Inc., where she has been for six years. Prior to Robertet, Brenda held HR positions at Scholastic and Avon Products in New York City.

Brenda is committed to mentoring young women in navigating life and career challenges and volunteers her time when she can. She has a bachelor's degree in psychology and a master's degree in human resources management from the Milano Graduate School of the New School University.

Brenda is bilingual, of Puerto Rican descent. She loves music and spending time with her family. Brenda is married and lives in Pennsylvania with her husband, mom, and two Shih Tzu's, Toby and Mia.

Yennie Rautenberg-Loya, Inclusive Leadership Coach and Trainer, Rautenberg Coaching

Yennie empowers and develops leaders to flourish and leave a positive mark in the world. Through her proprietary Authentic Inclusive Collaboration® framework, she enables teams and individuals to build inclusive, productive, and collaborative work environments where everyone experiences a sense of belonging, is empowered to participate, and has equal opportunity to thrive.

Originally from Mexico, she is a bilingual (Spanish/English) and multicultural ICF-certified leadership coach with 25+ years of global experience in corporate and executive communications, and 15+ years delivering life and executive coaching and training programs to thousands of people. She has championed, participated, and served as an ally of multiple inclusion and diversity initiatives, and collaborated with teams in 25+ countries.

Yennie designs customized programs in the areas of inclusion and belonging, employee resource groups (ERGs), emotional intelligence, leadership, resilience, communication, career advancement, and career/life transitions (relocation, job termination, and retirement).

Alejandra Rodriguez Mielke, PhD, Solopreneur, Executive Coach, Speaker, and Intercultural Expert, Founder of Interculturalyst and Co-Founder of El Puente Institute

Dr. Alejandra Rodríguez Mielke is a highly respected diversity, equity, and inclusion and intercultural consultant and coach, as well as a keynote speaker. With expertise in Latino/Hispanic leadership development and intercultural solutions for cross-cultural organizations, she has dedicated her career to empowering Latinx individuals and fostering inclusive environments.

Dr. Mielke is the founder of the forthcoming Interculturalyst.com, a platform offering intercultural services for global organizations. Additionally, she is one of three co-founders of El Puente Institute which is dedicated to promoting organizational excellence and inclusive work cultures by recruiting, retaining, and nurturing Latino leaders in ways that respects and leverages their unique cultural values.

Melanie Rodriguez, PhD PCC, Elevate Latinas, LLC. Talent Management, Leadership Coach, Inclusion Advocate

As a people development specialist of over 19 years, Melanie serves as an executive coach and consultant in the areas of inclusion, leadership development, employee resource group development, and organizational capability. Melanie brings a wealth of knowledge about multicultural and multi-generational differences and how to leverage and integrate them to create organizational cultures that value the individual while building a sense of belonging for all.

Melanie comes from a long line of strong Latinas who never let challenges hold them back. She graduated from the University of Houston with a B.A. in Public Relations/Advertising and a minor in Mexican American Studies. She subsequently earned an M.A. in Organizational Management from the University of Phoenix, and an M.A. in Human Development and a Ph.D. in Human and Organizational Systems from Fielding Graduate University.

Melanie is overwhelmingly blessed to be supported by her wife Cindy and their two children, Arianna and Isaias.

Claudia Romo Edelman, Latina social entrepreneur, activist, philanthropist, and investor with 30 years of global mobilization experience

Leading marketing, fundraising and advocacy, Claudia has experience in the United Nations, UNICEF, the Global Fund to Fight AIDS, TB and Malaria, the United Nations High Commissioner for Refugees (UNHCR), and the World Economic Forum. She was part of the conception and launch of global frameworks like Product (RED) and the Sustainable Development Goals (SDGs).

Ms. Romo Edelman holds a Master's degree in Political Communication from the London School of Economics and after some experience as a journalist, she served as a diplomat for the Mexican government, in Switzerland and England. She has a robust international trajectory, as a Mexican, Swiss, and American citizen, that speaks six languages. Claudia is a frequent columnist and has published nine books to date on Hispanic-related topics and is recipient of numerous awards, including People Magazine's 25 Most Influential Latinas, ALPFA's 50 Most Powerful Latinas 2019 and 2020, Ellis Island Medal of Honor 2019.

Since 2017, Ms. Romo Edelman has served as the Founder and CEO of the We Are All Human Foundation, a New York-based non-profit organization devoted to advancing the agenda of Diversity, Equity, and Inclusion focused on unifying the U.S. Hispanic community. Under her leadership, We Are All Human has launched a number of initiatives and frameworks to advance the progress of Latinos by mobilizing Corporate America and increasing Latino perception and representation. We Are All Human partners with more than 300 companies and 100 of the most important Hispanic organizations representing more than 10 million Latinos.

Ms. Romo Edelman is also co-founder of the Hispanic Star Accelerator, focused on Latino entrepreneurs with Founders Factory in the United Kingdom. Currently, she is a member of the Investor Advisory Team of Touch Capital, a women-led fund for consumer goods. Claudia is also a member of multiple boards, such as the Hispanic Society Museum and Library, Friends of the Latino Museum, National Museum of Mexican Art, KIND (Kids in Need of Defense), a public company Canoo, and a candidate board member for Chobani.

Jacqueline Ruiz, CEO of JJR Marketing Inc. and Fig Factor Media Publishing

Jacqueline Ruiz is a visionary social entrepreneur that has created an enterprise of inspiration. With more than 20 years of experience in the marketing and public relations industry, she has created two successful award-winning companies, established two nonprofit organizations, published 32 books, the largest collection of Latina stories in a book anthology series in the world, and held events in four continents. She has received over 30 awards for her contributions and business acumen. She represents the 1.6% of women entrepreneurs with over seven figures in the United States.

Being a two-time cancer survivor activated her sense of urgency to serve others and live life to the fullest. Jacqueline is one of the few Latina sports airplane pilots in the United States. Visit www.figfactormedia.com, www.jjrmarketing.com, and www.jackiecamacho.com for more information.

Melissa Sanchez, First Generation Latina College Graduate from University of Chicago

Melissa Sanchez is a first-generation Mexican American. She grew up in Milwaukee, Wisconsin, and is the oldest of four. Thanks to a full-ride scholarship, she was able to attend the University of Chicago and has recently graduated with a degree in Political Science. She is now looking for her first job to start her professional career. Meanwhile, she works at We Are All Human to continue to support the team with their mission of advancing the Latino narrative in the United States.

Louis Sandoval, CEO/Managing Partner, Halo Advisory Group, Inc.

Lou Sandoval is the President and Managing Partner of HALO Advisory Group, a management consulting firm serving clients from start-ups to Fortune 500 companies. HALO helps their Private Equity and Venture Capital owned clients drive business efficiency, apply digital transformation, and apply technology to improve operating efficiency at scale to grow their enterprises.

Lou has three decades of global experience in diverse operating leadership roles in management, technology/innovation, marketing, and sales with Fortune 500 companies. He brings diverse experience from within the technology, financial services, consumer goods, management consulting, and biotech fields in leading business expansion, brand development, and the development of high-performing teams and companies. He is a thought leader on digital transformation and leveraging technology to scale business. Please visit him: www.LouSandoval.com.

Dana Santos, Talent Leader and Human Resources Professional

Dana Santos is passionate about equipping individuals and teams to excel in performance. She fulfills this as a human resources professional with expertise in talent management and organizational effectiveness from Fortune 100 and Fortune 500 companies.

Dana's interest in multilingualism as a connector across cultures and business led her to study and teach in South America and Europe. She earned a bachelor's degree in Spanish from the University of Michigan and a master's degree in International Educational Development from the University of Pennsylvania.

Kshitij Sharma, Executive Coach and Founder of Coach Kshitij Executive Coaching LLP

With over three thousand hours of coaching senior leaders across the globe, Kshitij has developed a deep understanding of the challenges executives on the threshold of CXO positions face. His expertise lies in helping these leaders build a powerful executive presence that propels their careers to new heights. Kshitij's insights and techniques have garnered recognition and praise, and his TEDx talk on "Demystifying Executive Presence" is one of the most compelling talks on the subject. Through his coaching practice and speaking engagements, Kshitij has established himself as a trusted authority in the field.

To learn more about Kshitij Sharma and his work, visit his website at: www.coachkshitij.com. Kshitij's wealth of experience and passion for empowering leaders make him a valuable resource for anyone seeking to enhance their impact and influence in the corporate world.

Marissa Solis, SVP Global Brand and Consumer Marketing, National Football League

Marissa Solis is a magnetic business leader with over 25 years of expertise in business consulting, CPG, Retail, and Sports marketing. Currently, Marissa leads all global brand and consumer marketing initiatives for the NFL, including all national advertising, both traditional and digital media initiatives, in-stadium marketing, and new fan development.

Marissa was born in Mexico City and moved to the U.S. at age 10. Her dream to become an ambassador inspired her to pursue an International Economics degree from Georgetown University and an MA in Public Policy from the University of Texas at Austin. She is an ambassador to the Latino community through her work.

Lucy Sorrentini, MBA, CPC, Founder and CEO, Impact Consulting, Changing the World through Inclusive Leadership, Board Director, Columbia Bank and Board Advisor, Girls Incorporated

Lucy Sorrentini is a nationally recognized strategy consultant, executive coach, author, and speaker who has been advising organizations on how to reimagine their workforce and improve their workplace culture for more than two decades. As a Latina, Bronx, NYC, native, Lucy's passion for inclusion goes beyond business; it is at the heart of who she is and what she cares most about. Her own experiences have influenced her commitment to creating opportunities and access for underrepresented groups, especially women and communities of color.

Visit her at: www.impactconsultingus.com.

Dave Tang, PharmD, Recently Retired and Former Vice President, Global Medical Operations, Global Medical Office, and US Medical Affairs for Three Top Global Pharma Companies

Dave Tang recently retired as the Vice President of Global Medical Operations for AbbVie. He has over 25 years of healthcare experience and served in a number of senior leadership roles prior to joining AbbVie, including the Vice President of the Global Medical Office for Allergan and the Vice President of U.S. Medical Affairs for AstraZeneca.

Dave received his Pharm.D. from the Massachusetts College of Pharmacy and his bachelor's degree in biology from the University of California, Berkeley. He is currently serving on the Dean's Leadership Council for the University of California, Irvine School of Pharmacy and Pharmaceutical Sciences.

Veronica Torres Hazley, Founder, Hey Chica!; CEO, Torres Hazley Enterprise, LLC

Veronica Torres Hazley is the CEO of Torres Hazley Enterprise, a collective bringing community and well-being to life. Her portfolio includes V12 Yoga Studio, Workplace Fit Co, RedBird Rising, and self-care brand, Healthy Latina Lifestyle. Veronica has expanded her reach with her consultant practice that ties her last 25 years of experience in several capacities that include:

community development, customer service, event production, content curation, cause marketing, and wellness.

Veronica is also the founder of Hey Chica! by Healthy Latina Lifestyle, a Latina Leadership Collective. A movement for chicas looking to collaborate with their fellow community leaders, advocates, and influencers to curate their dream goals with passion and gusto!

Cylia Troche Quiñonez, Marketing and Finance Strategist, Top-10 Global Pharm Company

Cylia has leveraged her Global Latino ERG leadership experience, diverse experiences, and transferable skills to navigate her career from finance to marketing for a top-10 global pharm organization. It was through these experiences she learned the power of establishing and leveraging your personal brand.

Cylia has always had a deep-seated desire to make an impact on those around her especially the Latino community. It was the Latino community who has contributed to her success through her collegiate scholarship to her professional career. Her contribution to this book is her opportunity to continue to give back to future generations to advance in corporate America.

Alexandra Turcios, Senior Solution Consultant, Adobe

Alexandra Turcios is an award-winning professional who has achieved two 40 under 40 awards, is a published author, and serves on multiple Boards.

She presently works on large-scale digital transformation initiatives for Fortune 500 companies and Federal Government Agencies to increase workplace productivity and collaboration and reimagine operating models. Her aptitude in change management and strategic communications has helped drive significant results across multiple verticals.

As a first-generation Honduran American, she has navigated new spaces and paved a path for other aspiring Latinx professionals who want to go into tech through her volunteer work and leadership in Employee Resource Groups.

She is a former Fulbright Scholar and is currently pursuing an MBA.

In her free time, she enjoys reading, hiking, immersing herself in art galleries, and traveling (30+ countries stamped in her passport!).

Jamie Walters, Senior Director, Top 10 Global Pharma Company

Jamie Walters is a registered nurse who transitioned from the hospital to the pharmaceutical industry in 2003. In her time in pharma, she developed deep expertise in pharmacovigilance and drug safety, while also spending some time in human resources focused on diversity and inclusion. Jamie has led several teams through turnarounds focusing both on culture and operational excellence.

Jamie has a bachelor's degree in nursing and a master's in leadership development. She has a passion for servant leadership and creating workspaces that allow for others to maximize their potential.

Jamie spends her free time with her husband John and two dogs, Nelson and Rigby. Jamie's daughter, Lily, is a teacher at a Montessori school in Arizona. When not working, she loves to travel the world and has a long bucket list of locations she wants to visit.

Printed in the USA
CPSIA information can be obtained
at www.ICGtesting.com
LVHW051501291124
797957LV00004B/182